The State, Class and the Recession

Edited by

STEWART CLEGG, GEOFF DOW and PAUL BOREHAM

CROOM HELM
London & Canberra
ST. MARTIN'S PRESS
New York

© 1983 S. Clegg, G. Dow and P. Boreham
Croom Helm Ltd, Provident House, Burrell Row,
Beckenham, Kent BR3 1AT

British Library Cataloguing in Publication Data

The State, class and the recession
    1. Standard and cost of living   2. Inflation
(Finance)   3. Economic conditions—1945—
I. Clegg, Stewart   II. Dow, Geoff
III. Boreham, Paul
332   HC256.6
ISBN 0—7099—0743—5

Library in Congress Cataloging in Publication Data
Main entry under title:

The States, class, and the recession.

    Includes indexes.
    1. Economic policy——Addresses, essays, lectures.
2. Capitalism——Addresses, essays, lectures. 3. Socialism
——Addresses, essays, lectures. 4. Social classes——
Addresses, essays, lectures. I. Clegg, Stewart.
II. Dow, Goeff. III. Boreham, Paul.
HD74.5.S72 1983   338.9   82—25491
ISBN 0—312—75609—7

Printed and bound in Great Britain by
Biddles Ltd, Guildford and King's Lynn

THE STATE, CLASS AND THE RECESSION

932854a

CONTENTS

List of Abbreviations
Preface
1. Politics and Crisis: The State of the   1
   Recession
   Stewart Clegg, Paul Boreham
   and Geoff Dow
2. Competitive Party Democracy and the   51
   Keynesian Welfare State: Some
   Reflections Upon their Historical Limits
   Claus Offe
3. The Historical Foundations of Class   72
   Struggle in Late Capitalist Liberal
   Democracies
   Nixon Apple
4. The Institutional Transformations of   129
   the Post *Laissez-Faire* State:
   Reflections on the Italian Case
   Franco Ferraresi
5. Technocracy and Late Capitalist   152
   Society: Reflections on the Problem
   of Rationality and Social Organisation
   H.T. Wilson
6. The Crisis of Representation in   239
   Class-Oriented Unions: Some
   Reflections based on the Italian Case
   Marino Regini
7. An International Participation Cycle: 257
   Variations on a Recurring Theme
   Harvie Ramsay
Notes on Contributors   318
Name Index   320
Subject Index   323

LIST OF ABBREVIATIONS

ACTU	Australian Council of Trades Unions
AES	Alternative Economic Strategy
AFL	American Federation of Labour
AFL-CIO	American Federation of Labour - Congress of Industrial Organizations
ALP	Australian Labour Party
BDA	West German Employers' Federation
BIM	British Institute of Management
CBI	Confederation of British Industry
CCL	Canadian Council of Labor
CDU	Christian Democratic Union (West Germany)
CFDT	French Democratic Confederation of Labour
CGIL	General Italian Confederation of Labour
CGT	General Confederation of Labour (France)
CIO	Congress of Industrial Organizations (United States)
CSU	Christian Social Union (France)
DGB	West German Trades Union Confederation
EEC	European Economic Community
FIOM-CGIL	Federation of Metal Workers, affiliated to CGIL (Italy)
FNV	Confederation of the Dutch Trades Union Movement
IBM	International Business Machines Ltd.
ICFTU	International Confederation of Free Trades Unions
ICI	Imperial Chemical Industries Ltd.
IDE	Industrial Democracy Europe International Research Group
IG Chemie	Chemical, Paper and Ceramics Trade Union (West Germany)
IG Metall	Metalworkers Union (West Germany)
IILF	International Institute for Labour Studies

ILO	International Labour Organization
IMF	International Monetary Fund
LO	Trade Union Confederation (Denmark/Norway/Sweden)
LKAB	Luossavaara/kiirunvaara A.B. (a Swedish state owned mining company)
NATO	North Atlantic Treaty Organization
NKV	Federation of Dutch Catholic Trades Unions
NVV	Federation of Dutch Trades Unions
OECD	Organization for Economic Co-operation and Development
OEEC	Organization of the European Economic Community
OPEC	Organization of Petroleum Exporting Countries
PCF	French Communist Party
PCI	Italian Communist Party
QWL	Quality of Working Life
RPF	Right Wing French populist party
SAF	Central Employers Association
SAP	Social Democratic Party (Sweden)
SPD	Social Democratic Party (Germany)
TCO	White Collar Trade Union Confederation (Sweden)
TGWU	Transport and General Workers Union
TLC	Trades and Labor Council (Canada)
TUC	Trades Union Congress (UK)
UCS	Upper Clyde Shipbuilders
UK	United Kingdom
UN	United Nations
US/USA	United States of America

PREFACE

The contributions collected in this volume were originally presented at the Organisation, Economy and Society (OES) Conference held at Griffith University in July, 1981. Without the conference there would have been no volume, so it is particularly apt that we should preface this text with an expression of thanks for the financial and administrative support that the School of Humanities, Griffith University, afforded the conference. We would also like to express our appreciation of the support for the conference provided by the Division of External Studies at the University of Queensland. We wish to record our particular thanks to the following people: Leon Cantrell, David Saunders, Marion McKinnes, Lyn Shorter, Jill Webber, Pat Noad, Malcolm Alexander, Dini Beekhuizen. Additionally, we would like to express our thanks to the many people who participated in the OES conference, not least the many other contributors who could not be included here. The manuscript was produced with the help of Sandra Smith, Lorraine Wright and Madelene Wischer of Griffith University. We would also like to thank Lyn Finch for her assistance in preparing the index and proof reading. The responsibility for any errors that have eluded our combined gaze rests squarely with the editors.

Stewart Clegg
Paul Boreham
Geoff Dow

Chapter One

POLITICS AND CRISIS: THE STATE OF THE RECESSION

Stewart Clegg, Geoff Dow and Paul Boreham

VARIETIES OF ANALYSIS

Understanding of the current recession requires preliminary analysis at at least two levels: the 'new' international division of production, and changes within domestic economies. Both have implications for class analysis. Capitalism, whether conceived as a world economy or as separate, interacting national economies, involves relationships between class groupings. During the current crisis these class relationships are in the process of being re-constituted. In consequence, state responses, major transformations in the degree and content of political control of the economy and the often ambiguous relations between capital and the state, become critical issues for the agenda of theoretical and empirical investigation.

Since the early 1970s the experience of economic crisis, in the form of simultaneous unemployment and inflation, has not only renewed enquiry from within the broad corpus of marxist social science and political economy, but also has stimulated other significant contributions. Germane to the current crisis has been the renewed theoretical critique of orthodox economic analysis that can be labelled 'Post Keynesian' or 'Cambridge' economics. This analysis draws upon older writings of Keynes, Sraffa and Kalecki, which were formulated during the 'first crisis' of economic theory and policy in the 1920s and 1930s (1). The focus of this renewed enquiry has drawn attention to the relation between economic downturns and changes in the class distribution of income; as well as to the pace of capital accumulation, the organisational strength of the working class and the ideological role of certain institutions of policy advice (2).

1

From within more recent traditions, interpretations of the global and national realignments of industrial production, state responses, social dislocation and political confusion have also burgeoned. Wallerstein discusses the realignment of the relationships between market economies and national boundaries in terms of the changing structural roles of states in the world economy (3); Mandel relates associated changes in state 'management' of the economy to 'long wave' fluctuations in the processes of capital accumulation (4); Gamble and Walton isolate apparent contradictions and inflationary consequences of state intervention (5); Urry seeks an explanation in changing relations between the state , social classes and social identities, social democracy and political parties (6); Stephens insists that in the most advanced capitalist states at least, a fundamental transition is occurring which will permanently alter organisational relations between capital and labour (7); while Holland argues that the crisis and its monetarist forms may give to labour movements an opportunity to assert democratic control over capitalist investment decisions and hence over the future pattern of capital accumulation and the impediments to its continuation (8). In all cases, political repercussions are postulated, and some transitional phase for the world economies is supposed. The transition, nonetheless, is one whose projection and resolution remain uncertain. The trajectory appears to be from a state of US economic hegemony, manifested by the post-1945 'age of growth' and presumed political quiescence in the 'core' nations, to the current, concomitant decline into an 'age of uncertainty' (9).

This volume includes contributions to the emergent political and economic debates about the implications of this uncertainty for the social structure of the industrial capitalist part of the world economy. The contributions encompass an awareness of the diverse range of available analytical approaches. The issues involve two themes: firstly, the effects of the decline into capitalist recession on the structures of modern political and economic democracy; and secondly, the limits to the rationality of 'social democratic' or 'labourist' state interventions derived from Keynesian policies as strategies for maintaining these spheres of democracy in this 'age of uncertainty'.

RECESSION AND CONFLICT

A common focus of neo-conservative assault on the welfare-statist consensus politics of the post-1945 years has been the so-called inability of Keynesian policy prescriptions to anticipate or to account for the existence of contemporary inflation. However, taken together, the work of Keynes and Kalecki has provided a forceful insight into that condition which has allegedly made the current recession different from its counterpart in the 1930s. Simultaneous unemployment and inflation was for some time considered a surprising, inexplicable and even paradoxical coincidence because it had been assumed that there was necessarily a 'trade-off' between the two. (A little unemployment will keep inflation down; high levels of inflation are a consequence of low levels of unemployment.) The appearance of inflation during recession was regarded as a sign of the inappropriateness of Keynesian demand-stimulation expansionary policies, and monetarist 'explanations' centring on the role of the money supply and (especially) government expenditure proliferated. Keynes, in fact, had realised that a long period of full employment would set in motion irremediable tendencies to inflation as workers' bargaining power increased and as corporations, especially those unresponsive to competitive pressures, increased prices commensurately (10). Kalecki elaborated the argument by pointing out that in times of general economic downturn, large corporations, faced with declining turnovers may more than commensurately increase prices in response to cost (e.g. wage) increases so as to maintain overall cash flows and profitability. As the unit mark-up is increased in the noncompetitive sectors, an important stimulus to inflation is introduced, to which workers will, in subsequent rounds, respond in the form of further 'catch-up' wage claims. In this sense, inflation becomes the manifestation of a struggle between capital and labour to maintain their respective shares of the economic 'cake'. The non-wage elements will be determined by the ability of capital to pass on costs more than commensurately, to stay in business; that is, inflationary price increases will depend on 'the degree of monopoly'. In the competitive sector, declining turnover may well mean the demise of the enterprise; in the monopoly sector longevity is secured at the expense of inflation. In the contemporary era, organised labour is able to demand

3

and frequently receive money wage increases despite
the persistence of high levels of unemployment. In
the 1930s not only real wages but sometimes even
actual money wages were cut. Inflation is thus a
reflection of class struggle. In times of
recession, it is not a consequence of 'too much
money chasing too few goods'; it is a consequence of
struggle over distributive shares. In times of
boom, the underlying conflict was masked by
continuing and increasing flows of income in
absolute terms; once growth stopped the importance
of the relative shares became apparent. Underlying
conflicts have been sharpened by circumstance and
have been the occasion for dramatic transformations
in political conditions.

Both domestically and internationally, economic
recession is the occasion for massive re-structuring
of industrial production, and this has produced an
intensification of class struggle and a
transformation of class relationships. These are
ongoing processes which generate new tensions within
both parties and states. Early post-war commitments
to permanent full employment have everywhere been
abrogated as economic crisis has been used to
facilitate the relocation and reconstitution of
capitalist economic activity. The role of the state
has become especially problematic. Contending
forces attempt to use it to defend profits and
productive prerogatives while others encourage
state-sponsored constraints on the ongoing
accumulation of capital. While the balance of
forces lies with the abandonment of policies to
produce or maintain full employment of people and
industrial capacity, and the social consequences of
this play themselves out in terms of a long term
restructuring of national autonomies, the need for
sustained consideration of the diversity of
theoretical positions and political strategies
becomes even more urgent.

At the time of the Great Depression, orthodox
economic analysis held that long term unemployment
was theoretically impossible, that freely
competitive market economies tended towards full
employment equilibrium and social harmony and that
the self-regulatory nature of the system would
render minimalist government the most appropriate
form of economic and social administration. Keynes'
achievement was to show the internal inconsistencies
in the orthodox arguments. There were no internal
mechanisms guaranteeing that the decisions made by
private capitalists with respect to investment would

result in full employment of people and industrial capacity. What was privately profitable was not necessarily socially desirable or optimal; there could be stability with long term unemployment; there could be 'under employment equilibrium'. To remedy this situation, Keynes advocated a permanent role for quite substantial government intervention into economic activity within a national economy. He argued that the mechanisms for equating private investment with public demand would need to be created by institutional intervention: 'I conceive, therefore, that a somewhat comprehensive socialisation of investment will prove the only means of securing an approximation to full employment; though this need not exclude all manner of compromises and of devices by which public authority will co-operate with private initiative' (11). Clearly his intention was to save capitalism from radical attack by remedying some of its internal defects. However as Joan Robinson has repeatedly insisted since the 1930s, Keynes was himself to blame for the subsequent bastardisation of his ideas by failing to pursue the radical implications of his own observations (12).

Keynesian policies became the economics of 'fine-tuning' - regulation via fiscal policy and monetary policy. The call for a 'somewhat comprehensive socialisation of investment' was subordinated to the conception that intervention was unnecessary except in times of depression. Additionally, large scale deficit financing was shunned and a leading role for the public sector was confined to those aspects of corporate-government interlocking that eventually produced the 'military-industrial complex' and those cold and hot wars which from time to time justified it. Keynes was re-synthesised into the orthodoxy and the rise of 'bastard Keynesianism' in the 1950s and 1960s signalled a shift from the promise of post-war reconstruction to a more politically acceptable role for the state appropriate to the era of monopoly capitalism. 'True' Keynesianism was never applied and the threat it implicitly posed to vested interests, the potential it apparently had to permanently eliminate recessionary phases through political commitments to full employment, were never put to the test.

A formerly neglected aspect of the 'Keynesian revolution' was the contribution of the Polish economist Michal Kalecki (13). Kalecki's theoretical and empirical enquiries (14) have since

become a major focus of 'post-Keynesian' analysis.
They pose a serious challenge to subsequent marxist
accounts of the boom-recession cycle and of the role
of the capitalist state which postulate a simple
trade-off between wages and profits. Kalecki's
work, with Joan Robinson's enunciation of it, has
produced a fuller understanding of the business
cycle than Keynesian 'demand-management' policies
were able to contemplate. Five major conclusions
emerge from this work.

(a) Kalecki suggested that once the principles
of anti-cyclical economic policy were understood,
once the awareness of how to avoid recession and to
maintain full employment were accepted into the
corpus of policymakers' knowledge, a new, political,
trade cycle would emerge in place of the traditional
business cycle. Even though fluctuations in
capitalists' investment activities would produce
concomitant fluctuations in employment levels, in
patterns of economic activity, in incomes and in
profits; and even though government intervention
could theoretically alleviate these tendencies, this
rarely became the preferred option. Instead, the
western capitalist democracies entered the phase of
'the political trade cycle' whereby government
expenditures, employment levels and economic
activity generally were all increased prior to
elections, while stringent conditions tended to be
imposed and unemployment tended to rise immediately
thereafter. According to Kalecki's argument,
neither business nor government favour permanent
full employment. The threat of 'the sack' ceases to
be a disciplinary device and workers collectively
are able to assert a certain degree of militancy and
political power, whether in the form of demands for
increased wages or for more control over the
conditions or content of production. Clearly, the
implication is that if capital is faced with the
choice between retaining profitability and retaining
political control over the economy, it will opt for
the latter and sacrifice profits. This is what
happens whenever anti-recessionary strategies are
shunned by the state. Economic policy thereby
becomes a quite complex, even ambiguous arena of
struggle within the capitalist state.

It is important to note of course that no
degree of conscious agency is necessarily implied by
this analysis. In so far as the philosophy of
fiscal restraint, the doctrines of monetarism, and
policies which purport to 'fight inflation first'
exert a powerful, ideological influence within the

institutions of the state and policy-formulation,
they do so in a way which renders opaque, even to
specifically 'political' agents, the most
significant effects of their implementation. The
experience of Labour Party responses to crisis in
the past decade indicates that even formal opponents
of such deflationary strategies will follow policies
which appear to be a less than adequate
representation of their own constituencies.

The political trade cycle theory accounts quite
well for the post-war experience of western
capitalism regardless of the political complexion of
the parties in office. Clearly there are definite
conditions under which the capitalist state will
allow the rate of capital accumulation and
associated profit levels to be unnecessarily
constrained.

(b) Kalecki was also able to argue, on the
basis of both empirical and theoretical analysis,
that the share of total production accruing to
capital and labour respectively was not constant but
changed according to the stage of the trade cycle.
In the early stages of a general downturn, the share
accruing to labour can be shown to increase and the
profit share to decrease, due not to enhanced
bargaining strength of labour but to the external
factors giving rise to the recession itself. The
first indications of a recession are declines in
turnover and hence in profitability; and it is only
when capital begins to respond to these conditions
by reconstituting the labour process or by
suppressing real wages or through other retaliatory
manoeuvres that the profit share begins to increase
relative to wages. In the initial stages of an
upswing it is usual for the wages share to decline
and for capital's share to increase. It is for
these reasons that no simple wages-profits tradeoff
can be presumed to exist in a capitalist economy;
and no simple 'profits-squeeze' thesis can be
accepted either as an unambiguous explanation for
capitalist crisis (15), or as a description of what
is occurring during recession. None the less, this
account does refute some polemical claims by
conservative politicians and other industry
spokespeople that reductions in wages are essential
to economic 'recovery'. The determinants of
cyclical movements in capitalist economies are of
the external secular or structural kind and are not
given initially by changes in the political power or
bargaining successes of organised labour. Obviously
then, nothing is to be achieved by concessions, on

7

the part of labour, concerning 'wage constraint'.
High money-wages may have an effect on profit levels
because they are an element of the costs of
production; but high real wages also have a positive
effect on profits in so far as they permit higher
levels of consumer demand, aggregate spending,
economic activity, production and therefore
profitability. Which tendency is determinant will
depend on the stage of the cycle. Thus, the form
and effectivity of class struggle changes at
different stages of the cycle (16).

(c) A corollary of the preceding argument is
that the distribution of income is not independent
of the level of income. This observation has
important implications for macro-policy during
recession. The more unevenly skewed is the
distribution of income, the lower will be the
average level of income. Consequently, higher
levels of income, employment, economic activity and
profits will, in general, be the outcome of a
downwards redistribution of income. This is because
the higher propensity for immediate consumption of
lower-income segments of the population would
unleash previously 'ineffective' demand if only such
a redistribution were to be effected. During
recession, low overall levels of economic activity
and significant class inequality of incomes go hand
in hand. Higher levels of incomes, employment and
activity themselves indicate a decline in
inequalities, while policies which effect a more
egalitarian distribution will, of themselves, enable
some anti-recessionary growth processes to come into
operation. To the extent that macro policy promotes
either inequality or deflation, it automatically
achieves both. The policies of restraint have
effects far beyond those championed by anti-
inflationary rhetoric.

(d) In any capitalist economy, the key to
overall levels of performance, profits, incomes and
employment is investment. This is why capitalists'
control over investment assumes such significance in
political and industrial struggles. The prime role
of capitalists' investment decisions in determining
the pace, trajectory and content of capital
accumulation has been fully recognised in both post-
Keynesian and marxist traditions (17), as well as by
advocates of post-capitalist transitionary
strategies. These analyses are precisely those that
have also revealed the unlikelihood of long term
stable growth in an unregulated capitalist
economy. Investment performs a dual function in

private enterprise capitalism: not only does it create the potential for enhanced profitability, it also sets in place extra productive capacity for the output of which profitable outlets must be found. This ongoing requirement for more purchasing power to realise more profits is what makes a profit oriented investment process inherently unstable (18). Furthermore, high levels of re-investment from profits increase not only growth rates for the economy generally, but also the profit share of total output, to the detriment of wages. Again, the dynamic nature of capitalist expansion has implications for political strategies and struggles: labour movement programmes need to insist on high rates of growth to avoid slumps and unemployment, but need simultaneously to check the concentration of wealth and power that accrues to the owners of capital during an expansionary phase (19). For these reasons, economic democracy, especially radical proposals of the kind advanced by the Swedish labour movement, needs to be a key aspect of a reflationary policy package. Without control of investment, fluctuations in incomes, employment and living standards will all remain capricious. It is capitalists' investment decisions, especially those decisions made at times of uncertainty or reduced expectations concerning future profitability, that determine the behaviour of all other economic aggregates. It is recognition of this key role that has occasionally given rise to the (somewhat inaccurate) analogy of 'investment strike', and to criticisms of capitalists' withdrawal of capital at certain crucial moments as major causes of economic crisis.

(e) Kalecki's amalgamation of marxian and Keynesian crisis theories led him to conclude that permanent full employment in a capitalist economy would be impossible without the development of new institutions which would reflect an altered balance of class forces (towards labour). The balance would alter if controls over both the level and content of economic activity were to pass to a more democratic constituency than that represented by capital's quest for profits. State intervention in the abstract would be able to maintain full employment without inflation but only if the rationale for its involvements was changed. Permanently high levels of employment and income and non-cyclical re-investment (accumulation) strategies would be possible only in so far as planning (to avoid disproportionality problems) and economic democracy (to avoid disjunctions between the privately profitable and the socially desirable) were instituted on a widespread basis. The requisite 'new institutions' would need to be seen not as mere concessions nor as anti-crisis improvisations but as permanent and fundamental reforms to facilitate a complete transformation in the criteria by which decisions concerning economic activity and capital accumulation were made. The economic rationale for industrial democracy is thus inescapably established.

All these insights have since assumed a significance that for nearly three decades (of welfare state expansion and steady growth in the core economies) had been ignored. The ongoing role of fundamentally antagonistic class forces, the non-neutral role of economic policy and the state, and the extreme unlikelihood of balanced, crisis free growth for a capitalist system have all been reaffirmed.

Writings on the state have also been reoriented significantly as explanations for the phenomenon of inflation have been sought. The recent wave of radical theories of the state (20) has produced a variety of attempts to integrate inflation into an account of contradictions faced or posed by the economic management functions of the capitalist state. From the viewpoint of Keynesian-Kaleckian conceptions outlined here, it appears that many of these accounts may be flawed. The 'fiscal crisis of the state' argument (21), for example, suggests that large scale or prolonged deficit-financing by governments necessarily required 'inflationary means' partly because of its association with 'the underproduction of capital' and the imposition of increasing burdens on the state's budgetary resources (22). While this argument owes nothing to monetarism's correlations between state expenditures and inflation, it shares with the new right an unwillingness to concede that some social expenditures may be instrumental in enhancing productivity, production, employment, capital formation and accumulation. Under such conditions, state spending up to the point of full employment of people and industrial resources, cannot be inflationary. This condition becomes significant for 'alternative' reflationary strategies based on an expansion of state spending through increased public enterprise, nationalised industries and deployment of pension funds. An influential body of writing none the less continues to ascribe inflationary consequences to the contradictions of state intervention *per se* (23).

THE STATE AND CRISIS

It is, of course, necessary to view the relationship between economic recession and modern state intervention in a historically realistic perspective. The contradictions characteristic of present-day capitalism are rooted in the context of the immediately preceding era. What cannot now be achieved solely through the key mechanisms of representative democracy, those of political and economic integration, must instead be accomplished through state intervention at the levels of industrial autonomy, economic redistribution, social expenditure and what increasingly appears as legislative retribution. Yet the same ideological onslaught that has legitimated deflationary policies at the state level has been deployed also to discredit both traditional socialist and more innovative alternative economic strategies. With political protest diverted towards what have been readily caricatured either as anachronistic or sectarian issues (internal party democracy, nationalisation), serious theoretical discussion has often been inhibited. Consequently, the growing complexity of the relations between changes in the world economy, domestic class conflict, political response and labour movement organisation have been inadequately understood.

The political and economic conflicts that are associated with recession have been variously referred to as downturns in economic growth, impediments to capital accumulation and interruptions to the ongoing process of valorization of capital. Some fundamental developments which grew out of the preferred strategic options of the dominant classes during the post-war years of economic expansion now stand, ironically, as impediments to the requirements of continued accumulation. One such development was the expansion of state expenditure on social welfare and associated measures and the general development of social legislation which has been charted by writers such as Gough, Sleeman and Ginsburg (24). From one partial perspective these developments may be viewed as concessions allowed by the dominant class in order to contain and delimit the arena of struggle occupied by a more politically adventurous labour movement (25). A great deal of the literature on

the welfare state has incorrectly perceived this
tendency as evidence of a potential redistribution
of national wealth toward the working class. Some
marxist writings such as those of Mandel argue that
such assessments prove illusory when placed in the
context of the reaction by capital to any fall in
the average rate of profit which might initially
derive from any such redistribution (26).
Inevitably, it is argued, such programmes of income
support, social security, subsidies to consumption
etc., attempt little more than to secure economic
stabilisation, and have not averted periodic
constraints on working class incomes as the share of
total income accruing as profits is restored and as
extraction of surplus value to provide new capital
for re-investment is assured or re-assured. On the
other hand, it is argued that a concurrent function
of the expansion of public sector expenditures has
been to guarantee the 'physical reconstitution' of
the labour force which, as a result of increased
exploitation following the transition from
competitive to monopolistic capitalism, might
otherwise have been threatened. The material basis
for this 'enlarged scale' of the state was provided
by a 'significant redistribution' of the value of
social production to the public sphere of economic
activity (27).

In times of transition or crisis, the relative
importance of these divergent, sometimes
contradictory roles for the state, will itself
change. Whilst the two tendencies might adequately
complement each other in the framework of social
democratic politics in times of economic expansion,
the relationship appears to falter during recession
when emphasis shifts from the former to the latter
requirements. Diversion of capital and economic
activity to the public sector is acceptable to
dominant classes only to the extent that it provides
the framework of stabilisation and enhanced long
term control over the process of valorisation of
private capital. Many state activities, apparatuses
and responses are intended to secure this control
and redistributive social expenditures have always
operated within such constraints (28). These
outcomes are, however, shaped only in part by forces
which are under state control, and only in part by
forces deriving from the general crisis of
capitalism (29). The internationalisation of
economic action, the boundedness and muddling
through of much state rationality, will both serve
to restrict this control. Legitimate authority and

real power rarely, if ever, coincide with any symmetry. None the less, state power, however imperfect, remains the key architectonic of contemporary capitalism.

Co-existing with this state power, exercised by centralising and reallocating surplus value, are individual, differentiated corporate centres of calculation of this value. For these centres and for the state in contemporary liberal democracy the strategic space for negotiation occurs within the tolerances of the formal institutions of representative democracy. These institutions appear to be more attuned to a former era of economic growth and its mechanisms of political and economic integration (30). Institutionally, the trajectory of post-war liberal democracy, (with a number of significant exceptions) has seen the deepening of the mechanisms of formal representation at the political level in capitalist democracies. At the same time as the state apparatus has been involved in the implementation of social and economic policies which have structured this representation, these policies have themselves been the context of struggle between organised class interests. However, it can not be inferred that the struggle has been equal. The 'rules of the game', particularly in recession, have been such as to handicap reformist labour parties in office. The balance of forces operative during periods of economic decline tend to enhance or to reconstitute the conditions for concentration and centralisation of capital and thus coincide with a relocation of class domination from the political sphere to alternative areas. Of critical importance for this changing balance of class forces is the contemporary tendency for the state apparatuses to be strongly drawn into increasingly more intense economic struggles (31).

The upper levels of the state apparatus typically tend to have been socialised into a fair degree of commitment to the purposes that the capitalist state is 'presumed' to serve (32). On the other hand, the role of the state apparatus may be to some extent structurally determined but it is also institutionally cushioned from the direct exercise of working class political power through its adherence to notions of professional and technical bureaucratic expertise. The institutional structure of national politics ensures that real power resides in the hands of a permanent bureaucracy (33), even though it frequently has to be exercised through the temporary occupants of elected office, in their moments of glory.

The agenda which shapes the legitimacy of electoral action is constructed by the impersonal interests explicit in capitalism, for which the overall criterion of profit appears to be the sole determinant of the capacity of that society to improve the future conditions of material life (34). Framing this electoral action are a variety of participative and consultative arrangements, which both 'protect' profits and 'represent' the working class. Including, for instance, social contracts and types of corporatism which have developed in recent years. From the vantage point of certain elements of the ruling class, these may present a potential threat. Such interventions may educate key personnel, those representing the working class, in the mysteries, management and mechanisms of the state's imperfect control of the means of economic and social power. A given set of means need not necessarily entail orientation towards a recurrent end without some limits on orientation. The advanced capitalist democracies now face a situation in which the working class has the potential and, for some elements, the orientation not only to hold but also exercise its political power through representative means. Although translation of that potential faces barriers routinely set in place by the institutional organisation of production and reproduction, the machinations of the state in times of crisis continually expose new, potential avenues of working class mobilisation, particularly as recession exposes the bankruptcy of existing ones.

Working class political power has been represented in the context of parliamentary democracy. However, the present conditions of capital valorisation and accumulation have made parliamentary democracy seem both a more fragile and less encompassing shell for the political than more propitious economic circumstances might have suggested. A developing intolerance and open repression concerning the normal freedoms which have been won by the working class, such as the positive achievements of the welfare state consensus, seems to be producing an awareness that conventional 'solutions' to class antagonisms are becoming increasingly untenable.

STRUCTURAL CRISIS

Since the beginning of the 1970s, the conceptual frameworks considered appropriate for analysis of the state in times of crisis have themselves been the subject of intellectual contestation. In response to the obduracy of capitalist institutions and social relations, and to the altered contexts in which they have operated, theoretical views of the state have been substantially revised so that the positions outlined above now contain an amalgam of orthodox and heretical, familiar and reformist elements. The importation of a plethora of qualifications into the corpus of theory has been an indication of the need to respond positively to empirical conditions which themselves have undergone dramatic transformation in recent years.

Of crucial significance to current debate concerning the state in crisis has been the increasing redundancy of analysis pitched solely at the level of the nation state. Most intellectual examination of changes in the way the state mediates crisis has necessarily been in terms of domestic economic conditions and domestic class relations. However, it is apparent that a major contributor to the current crisis in the world economies has been the realignment of the location and conditions of production at the level of the global economy. The new international division of labour (35) and the explicit political decisions which seem to have legitimated it (36) are said to be responsible for a systematic 'de-industrialisation' of significant formerly industrial economies. Clearly this tendency, caused partly by the movement of domestic manufacturing activities to low-cost, 'off-shore' locations, raises political and analytical difficulties. In a detailed commentary on the problems with British Labour's 'Regeneration of Industry' proposals, one commentator has argued that '... in an open economy, the question whether de-industrialisation can be in any sense be regarded as implying 'structural maladjustment' cannot be properly considered in terms of the characteristics of the domestic economy alone' (37). Under conditions of declining national sovereignty, the alternative prescriptions implied by the Kaleckian and Keynesian diagnoses face considerable complication. The political challenge is not merely to force industrial regeneration and reflation on a reluctant capitalist class, but to intervene in a process of global restructuring of manufacturing and

15

financial activity whose decision-making locus is particularly elusive. The precedents for a radical confrontation with multi-national corporations and international capital are not encouraging. It might well be the case, of course, that in the current recession, domestic strategies aimed at securing national autonomy, import controls, protected manufacturing, high wages and bi-lateral trading agreements (as opposed to those implied by an open or de-regulated international economy) are the most progressive and viable for national working class mobilisation. In such conditions, the relations between class, state and party will still need to be re-thought.

Even without these massive international dimensions to the current crisis however, there remains the important and politically difficult issue of domestic industrial structure. The Keynesian-derived analyses are more appropriate to conditions of a general decline in purchasing power along 'underconsumptionist' lines. In serious structural crises however, general declines are caused by specific downturns in the fortunes of specific industries, perhaps for unavoidable, secular reasons. In such circumstances it is not altogether clear that general expansionary manoeuvres by the state would invoke the orderly restructure of industry that full employment requires. In fact, a much more conscious, deliberate and disaggregated set of interventions would be necessary. Industry-by-industry policies would probably be required as would explicit political, as opposed to market-economic, decisions concerning the preferred long term industrial structure for the domestic and regional economy. Once manipulation of the level of economic activity can be politically legitimated, the question needs to shift to the content of that activity; political decisions about the types of production deemed desirable need to be made (38).

It is because restructure of industry is from time to time necessary, in any economy, that economic crises periodically occur; and it is for these reasons that crises can be seen as ways of 'resolving' structural imbalances. Crises are the solutions to crises (39). The only way to facilitate a non-repressive restructuring of industry is to plan for economic change. Under such planning, industries would not be phased in and out solely in accordance with enterprise profitability. Production would not need to be

restricted to effective consumer demand of the
presently available choices of goods and services.
Instead planning would extend to the realisation of
what people democratically decree without the
tyranny of restriction to 'effective' demand and
corporate profitability. Under market capitalism
the imperatives of profitability do not allow this
to occur. When the necessary structural adjustments
are on a world scale, the complexities are
commensurately exacerbated.

DEMOCRATIC IMPERATIVES AND STATE INTERVENTION

These developments can be seen to highlight a
central political paradox. It is one which centres
on the co-existence of 'the crass materialism of the
market society' (40) with the principles of
'extended' democracy. Liberal democrats, from Mill
onwards, assumed that a *rapprochement* between the
potential mass power of the working class, and the
economic authoritarianism of capitalism, could be
achieved. They justified such a *rapprochement* by
maintaining that capitalism rewarded merit and
effort. Through this exercise one could achieve, in
the market, the real freedom of consumer
sovereignty, the existence of which was guaranteed
by political liberty and produced by functionally
efficient mass subordination to capitalist relations
of production. The 'promise' of escape through the
competitive zeal of individualism was maintained.
Marx regarded such 'promises' as illusory, and in
his contributions to the First International,
envisaged that extended democracy would lead to the
overthrow of economic exploitation and
subordination. More recently, both right wing
pluralist theorists such as Dahl and Lipset (41),
and left wing critics such as Marcuse (42), have
assumed, for different reasons, that the tension
between the two organising principles has been
resolved, through either mass consent, or mass
deception masked as mass consent. The latter view
has been widely accepted by western marxism (43) and
has come to be known, and criticised, as 'the
dominant ideology thesis' (44). Given these two
contrasting, but equally one-sided, functionalist
views, the question of the degree of fit between the
two principles has, with very few exceptions, rarely
been raised.
   Therborn, for example, has noted a number of
tendencies which have led to the development of
capitalist democracy. Among them are the formation,

through the processes of capitalist development, of a combative working class capable of gaining extended civil liberties (45). Sometimes these liberties were granted by a bourgeoisie as a means of mobilising nationalist movements or a conscript army, or they might have been imposed by a foreign army victorious in warfare. Of more general applicability, however, is the creation by capitalist relations of production of an internally competing ruling class which is peacefully disunited into distinct fractions. These become the basis for a polity organised into competitive parties, within which sphere the labour movement develops, under rules of functioning already established. A final democratic thrust was provided, argues Therborn, by the development of productive forces, the growth of per capita material prosperity and other elements in post-war material expansion which allowed considerable freedom of manoeuvre for the governing party/parties in dealing with the exploited majority of the working class. Higher levels of taxation, for instance, enabled the development of substantial institutional reforms without destroying the material basis of capital accumulation.

It is this conjuncture that Claus Offe's chapter "Competetive Party Democracy and the Development of the Keynesian Welfare State" explores. He sees these as the two major principles that have mediated capitalist democracy in the post-war era. Competitive party democracy, in the view of commentators as diverse as Weber, Luxemburg and Michels, led necessarily to the bureaucratic routinisation of radical principle into modest and negotiable pragmatics on the part of the working class party, headed increasingly by a professionally trained and recruited elite. Bureaucratisation, it has subsequently been argued, accompanies de-mobilisation of popular activism as a mass base and leads to an increasing dependence on mass opinion surveys as the source of policy options. Precisely because of the mass, aggregate nature of such options, policy loses its base in a collective solidarity in favour of the broad constituency of diverse subjectivities as they find expression in civil society. This, we might say leads to a weakening of economic determination and a strengthening of status as the principle of political identification, which in turn, suggests Offe, leads to a weakening of the 'party principle' itself.

Status formation in civil society is possible on a wide number of diffuse axes which have become politically more noticeable during the splintered seventies. One of the first writers to alert us to this was Tom Nairn in his analysis of 'the break up of Britain' (46). However, to the ranks of regionalist/nationalist movements, one must also add axes of ethnic, urban, ecological, feminist, peace and youth movements. These status group movements, to borrow a phrase of Weber's, are similar to the old style radical labour movement in respect of their collective identity, but differ enormously in their demand not for representation but autonomy. Hence their struggle occurs outside the arena of competitive party democracy on the territory of a physical or moral terrain rather than a plebiscitary one, thus serving to weaken the existing party system.

This weakening of the party system has been most explicitly addressed in debates in Britain about the relationship between the feminist and labour movements. As if to underscore Offe's point we note that arguments proposing a *rapprochement* between the diverse groups in each movement have been published as a plea and an argument for moving 'beyond the fragments' (47).

Representation has been further weakened on a plebiscitary basis by the development of corporatist strategies of interest representation on the basis of institutions which are, in the terms of a famous definition,

> singular, non-competitive, hierarchically ordered, sectorally compartmentalised, interest associations exercising representational monopolies and accepting (*de jure* or *de facto*) governmentally imposed or negotiated limitations on the types of leaders they elect and on the scope and intensity of demands they routinely make upon the state (48).

Of necessity, this tends also to undermine the 'party principle' of representation, as does the drift towards 'authoritarian populism' (49) which some writers have observed in the development of the contemporary 'strong state', under the rubric of organising in the interests of law and order, be it against terrorists, muggers, aliens or whatever enemies of the people may be conjured (50).

It is argued by Offe that the end of the post-war ideological consensus confronted two problems which, because of an inverse relationship between them, could not be simultaneously resolved. On the one hand there was what Offe terms the 'production/exploitation' problem and on the other hand the 'effective demand/realisation' problem. In the process of solving the latter through strategies of demand management intervention, social insurance, welfare and protection, the former problem has been exacerbated by de-commodifying and rigidifying the supply of labour. This 'choking-off' of supply is paralleled in the capital market, as deficit spending allegedly increases interest rates. The strategy of 'supply side' economics flows directly from a right-wing analysis of these phenomena.

The attack on the welfare state is now an established plank of 'new right' policy, which in some of its diagnoses, if not its analysis and prescriptions, Offe is prepared to accept. Once more, the uncoupling of 'capitalism' and 'democracy' is on the agenda.

FULL EMPLOYMENT CAPITALISM

As already outlined, some major aspects of the Keynesian welfare state compromise had been anticipated by Kalecki, in terms of the opposition between a reformed 'full employment capitalism', based on 'new social and political institutions which will reflect the increased power of the working class', and an 'outmoded system which must be scrapped' if the 'recurrence of fascism' is to be prevented. It is with this formulation of the implications of full employment capitalism that Nixon Apple commences his comparative analysis of the Keynesian compromise in the years 1945-51, tracing the development of its abandonment as a policy commitment everywhere in the major OECD nations, except Sweden. In Sweden throughout the 1970s and into the 1980s, the level of unemployment has rarely risen much above 2%; elsewhere it has escalated to national levels as high as 14% (UK, September 1982) with regional, sex and ethnic instances being far greater. The analysis of 'Swedish exceptionalism' has a specific bearing on the uncoupling of 'capitalism' and 'democracy', in as much as the Swedish strategy of economic democratisation represents a further extension of the democratic principle into the heartlands of capitalist relations of production: private ownership and control of the means of production is being challenged by what has been proposed as 'the rights of labour' (52).

Apple's chapter, 'The Historical Foundations of Class Struggle in Late Capitalist Liberal Democracies' surveys the historical, political and economic conflicts that preceded the post-war settlement. This, as we have noted, was firmly based on US hegemony, which was consolidated in the period of international monetary reconstruction from 1940 to 1951, centred on the Bretton Woods Agreements. It was at Bretton Woods that Keynes' view, that international deficit spending should be permitted through regulatory bodies whose key task would be to maintain exchange-rate stability, was defeated by US opposition. Had it been accepted it would not have been as easy for bodies such as the IMF to impose deflationary policies, hinder domestic expansion and prevent effective demand management. It is upon this failure that an American export surplus strategy was constructed around the Truman Doctrine, the Marshall Plan, and the forced devaluations of British sterling and other European currencies in 1949. As Apple explains, these political and economic debates, strategies and struggles for international monetary hegemony between Britain and the US, were closely connected with the respective domestic debates, strategies and struggles around the issue of full employment.

In Britain this was centred on the role and importance of William Beveridge's proposals for full employment ('more jobs than people') which would be maintained by trade unions, in a 'social contract', trading off wage-restraint for price stability. Much hung on the definition of 'full employment' which was progressively broadened to include an increasing amount of unemployment through the 1950s. What was at stake was precisely the relative freedom or relative restriction of the supply side of the labour market. Full employment, or a restricted and virtually non-existent supply of potentially mobile and willing labour could only weaken ruling class power. This was because that power was based in part on the ability to dictate the level of business activity and hence employment. Debates around the meaning of full employment were also waged in the Labour Party, in the context of its overall post-war strategy. The ground shifted to the right, the unions agreed to the trade-off, while the commitment to policies for full employment along with other socialist strategies was emasculated. Meanwhile, in the political class struggle, the Conservative Party had also adopted the weakened conception of full employment, and linked it to an abandonment of 'irresponsible' controls on enterprise and curtailment of deficit-spending, which ushered in the thirteen years of Tory rule from 1950 to 1963. A similar, but more broadly based and effective 'free-enterprise' lobby similarly deradicalised the 1945 Full Employment Bill in the United States, when ruling class elements coalesced around their opposition to the proposed interference with the 'normal' functioning of the market.

Some similarities can be perceived between on the one hand, the Canadian and American, and on the other hand, the British and Australian struggles for full employment. However, there is little in common between the Australian and Canadian experience, despite their common 'dominion' status as recently incorporated semi-peripheral states in the world economy. The national histories and trajectories of politics prove to be decisive in each case, with the Australian Labor Party moving to a more national-integrative position offering less of a threat to 'business confidence' (53). Ruling class interests in Australia pursued the classical liberal democratic strategy identified by Offe, defining democracy as the freedom of 'capital' and dramatised most clearly over responses to the Labor government's plan to nationalise banks, in 1949. The defeat of this measure led to the defeat of the Labor Party and to twenty-three years of uninterrupted conservative rule. In Canada the working class was more fragmented politically, ethnically and linguistically, had weaker and less developed traditions of political mobilisation and suffered from its formation in the largely US dominated economy, in which there still persisted a large petty bourgeois fraction of small rural proprietors and producers (54).

While Australia and Britain, and America and Canada represent two clear variants in the development of struggles around full employment, in Germany, Japan, Italy and France, this struggle took second place to the battle to re-couple democracy with capitalism, rather than to extend it as something already given. The common factor was the defeat of the working class (rather than a compromise with it) by fascism during and preceding the war.

In Germany and Japan the economy and polity were reconstructed under American occupation and 'market-economics' tutelage for the ruling class, while bans and proscriptions against any socialistically inclined elements of the working class were favoured. Monetary deflation was introduced allegedly to stabilise the economy and also to discourage working class militancy, which in both countries had been seriously destroyed by fascism. It was the continuation of this demobilisation, together with the 'market economics' and monetary deflation which laid the basis for the post-war economic miracles of Germany and Japan.

Although both France and Italy were scarred by fascism, they also had in the PCF and PCI, the nuclei of the resistance movement and also the two largest communist parties in Western Europe. This proved decisive in reintroducing democracy and establishing conditions for the reform of capitalism. However, a communist party was a legacy of mixed blessing. In France it definitely helped to defeat a possible resurgence of fascism but at the same time its close links with Moscow led to a less militant and combative stance than· would otherwise have been likely. In Italy the structural distortions of the Mussolini era had exacerbated what had always been the basic problem of the 'southern question'. This took on renewed significance in the context of the northern liberation being effected by the resistance under PCI leadership, while the south was under allied occupation. Old divisions between christian democracy and communism were re-activated, leading to the institutionalised exclusion of the PCI from government, despite the popularity of its socialist programme, 'the Labour Plan'. Here too, market economics triumphed and the working class, although not defeated, was not a decisive victor.

During the 'long boom' full employment capitalism flourished after the religious and political defeats of the working class, from 1955 to 1965. There was a general decline in trade union solidarity during the 1950s in many of the OECD countries and a decline in left voting. The reasons for this general tendency are to be sought not in working class victories, but in the conditions of their defeat: namely, the consolidation of an international, export oriented economy under US hegemony (55), and the allied investment boom which generated full employment, founded on an increasing volume of trade between the core OECD countries.

A number of conditions maintained this regime of full employment, but between 1966 and 1973 they broke down, leading to the demise of export led

23

growth and its allied full employment, and a
resynchronisation of different national production
cycles after the OPEC inflationary shock of 1973.
The consequences of this are only too evident today,
when over 32 million people are unemployed in the
OECD states. In Sweden, however, in marked contrast
to the other case studies considered by Apple, the
political initiative was firmly in working class
control during the almost unbroken forty-four years
of social democratic rule which lasted until 1976.
Under the leadership of the blue collar union
central organisation, LO, a unique strategy of
radical reforms centred on the commitment to, and
practice of, full employment has developed. This
has, at the time of this volume going to press, been
vindicated in the 1982 elections. Based on active,
interventionist labour market policy and a massive
expansion of the public sector, this strategy has
now led to policies for the extension of democratic
principles from the civil to the economic sphere, in
a radical and innovative programme of economic
democracy (56).

Apple's analysis concludes with the argument
that if full employment is ever to be on the agenda
again, and 'democracy' to remain coupled with
'capitalism', let alone extended, then there must be
a more widespread adoption of the Swedish
strategy. Whether this is possible or not, it is
clear that there are real limits to the
generalisability of the Swedish social democratic
strategy for economic control, organisational
democracy and full employment (57). Chief among
these is obviously the existence of the political
and ideological mobilisation among the working
class, and divisions within the ruling class, which
are capable of producing a social democratic
government with a strong and coherent policy.
However, a further factor is the extent to which a
governing party has the *de facto* as well as *de jure*
power to seriously effect economic management in a
socialist direction. Sweden is a small country,
outside NATO, with relatively little multinational
penetration, and a small and highly concentrated
ownership of capital, with a primarily export-
oriented, nationally-based coterie of multinational
corporations. Consequently, to put it bluntly, the
US is little concerned at what happens in this small
country in the Scandinavian periphery. However,
what would be the reaction if such a strategy were
to develop in a major NATO and European power, in an
economy marked by US multinational penetration, and

with a ruling class that overcame the divisions that had weakened it, or where, as in the British case, a great deal of national capital was internationally invested and hence capable of rapid international flight and destabilisation of the national government? When Fred Block (58) considered this question, he ended up with a scenario which saw either the dilution of the socialist aims in order to preserve office on a platform of rule responsible to the mechanisms of 'business confidence', or their bloody defeat at the hands of a right wing coup. On the one hand the former seems to have been the fate of various reform-minded socialist governments in the post-war era, particularly the 1974 British Labour Government. On the other hand a trajectory which can lead in the space of a few years from The Socialist Challenge (59), to a conjuncture marked by the authoritarian populism of Thatcherism (60) is not encouraging with respect to the latter. If the success of the socialist challenge is dependent in large part, as Stephens has concluded (61), on the hegemony gained by a war of position, in Gramsci's phrase (62), then indeed great effort will be required not simply to gain a few yards of social terrain, but to regain the ground lost in a context in which mass unemployment has become, seemingly, normalised.

THE STATE AS ORGANISATION

The question of the state's *de facto* ability to effect reform depends on an assumption of its functional rationality as an organisational apparatus. It is assumed that these apparatuses are capable of means-ends rationality, of formulating goals and achieving them in a technically legal-rational manner. As Franco Ferraresi observes in 'The Institutional Transformations of the Post *laissez-faire* State: Reflections on the Italian Case', the fact that the *de jure* increase in state interventions has occurred does not necessarily signal a *de facto* increase in state power. Much depends on one's theoretical perspectives on the state.

Ferraresi notes that recent contributions to the literature on the state may be distinguished, despite whatever other differences may be identified, on an axis drawn between those perspectives which link the growth of the state to an increase in state power, and those on the other side which hold that this growth of the state signals a withering of actual state authority. A conviction that the growth of the state leads to an increase in its force is shared by such diverse theorists as Poulantzas (63) on the one hand, and Offe (64) and O'Connor (65) on the other, although in their particulars several points of differentiation are noted. The contrary position, that the growth of the state leads to a decline in the power of the state, is held by both neo-corporatist and overloaded governance theorists, who again, and this time in more explicitly left-right political terms, disagree strongly within the basic parameters of consensus.

These divergent views of the state point to a number of unresolved dilemmas concerning the power of the state; the role of the state *vis-a-vis* accumulation and the growth of state agencies and their significance for liberal democratic views of political participation. While these issues are theoretical and relate directly to the issue of whether or not there can be a theory of the state, let alone its components, they can be formulated in empirical terms in such a way as to identify the particular aspects of such changes in a particular case, in this instance that of Italy.

The disagreements between the differing perspectives on the state can be formulated as questions capable of empirical resolution. There are four unresolved dilemmas: does the state 'steer' the economy and society as a whole or is it simply another partner in the bargaining circuit which characterises the economy and society; does the state lay down substantive material commands in law or merely formal-procedural ones; are the state apparatuses constructed on a unified, centralised strategy or in a disjointed, non-rationalised form; and finally, if the latter, does it constitute space for democratic participation or simply a random fragmentation which favours the non-mediated predominance of the strongest interest groups? One reason why it would seem apparent that there can be no general theory of the state is that such central questions as these can be answered only in empirically specific circumstances. Considering the Italian case, Ferraresi finds that none of the available models of the role of the state fit the empirical facts. Certainly the state has a relative autonomy, but this is not the autonomy of a steering capacity so much as the bargaining autonomy of resource holders prepared to trade at terms advantageous to their own interests. While this bargaining autonomy exists, it does not appear to have led to a strengthening of the Italian state, nor to a neocorporatist vertical integration of interests, in large part because of the inability of the state to guarantee and to be able to enforce any specific 'rules of the game' and because of the reluctance of the major interest groups to be intermediated. While the Italian state suffers from what appears to be 'overloaded governance', in terms of the thesis (66), one major difference obtains. This is that demands on the state represent not a crisis of the recent extension of welfare democracy but the traditional clamour of bourgeois, clientelist interests (67).

To overcome the political cleavages, embedded in this Italian history of uneven development, system-wide reforms would have been required. Given the political imbalances contingent on this uneveness, such changes have never been implemented, and bargaining has been *ad hoc* and particularistic. This in turn produces the very opposite of the technically rational bureaucrat at the centre of the state apparatuses. Instead of the Weberian specialist, the functional prototype for the Keynesian administrator, the bureaucratic vocation embraces irrationality, wheeling and dealing, and the negation of pretensions towards universalism. Hence the Italian state is relatively autonomous, but not in any way that is functional for capital so much as for the expanded agents and kin of the state apparatuses. The crisis of Italian capitalism appears as the crisis of the Italian state; this, however, in a form which no recent crisis theorists have succeeded in capturing.

The conclusions reached by Ferraresi serve as the premises for the chapter on 'Technocracy and Late Capitalist Society: Reflections on the Problem of Rationality and Social Organisation', by Tom Wilson. Beginning with a discussion of Weber's ideal type, Wilson notes that it has now to be conceptualised within a set of societal circumstances quite dissimilar to those of Weber's day and the classic age of bureaucracy. These include the extension of the state and the virtual collapse of the public-private distinction in the terms of legal rationality, the extension of the private organisation into a form encompassing many states and their national rational-legal processes (in the shape of the multinational corporation in the world economy), the extension of scientific-technical rationality throughout public and private

27

organisational life, the 'socialisation' or 'statisation' of functional and technical modes of rationality, and the extension and dominance of intellectual models derived from cybernetics and game-theory which function as formal analogues for the increasing dependence on automated, robotic technologies. One effect of these developments is the production of a relatively unified elite class fragment of technocrats spanning the public/private interface. It is these persons, located in the organisational leviathans of the state and economy, who, through the technocratic ideology of an 'objective knowledge' which is, in practice, somewhat less than disinterested, serve to maintain the rationality of society; a society which is increasingly one of organisations. That these organisations, almost as a whole, and irrespective of their public/private vocation, are variants of the formal bureaucratic model of organisation, says less about the 'technical efficiency' of this model than it does about the legitimacy attached to models flowing from the vanguard of capitalist innovation. It is as if, as Alvin Gouldner (68) once suggested, a myopic metaphysical pathos had engulfed the creativity of those intellectuals oriented to the construction of the societal-organisational world. That the knowledge entailed in this construction and maintenance of 'post-industrialism (69), aspires to an independent, objective and non-ideological status has been the chief claim of writers such as Daniel Bell and J.K. Galbraith (70), a claim argued by Wilson to be the highest expression of technocratic ideology, as well as a *sine qua non* of bureaucracy in its modern form.

Technocracy and bureaucracy are not formally co-terminous; however, much of the substantive loci of technocratic expression coincides with bureaucratic organisation. The latter may be said to exhibit three basic clusters: the scalar or structuring of activities cluster; the functional or technical cluster and the career cluster. Technology is systematically compared by Wilson to each of these clusters in order to point out specific continuities and discontinuities between bureaucracy as a structure and technocracy as an ideology embedded within it. In this way a number of unresolved organisational dilemmas are brought into focus. These include the process whereby technocracy colonises formal legal-rationality as the base for an exercise of rational domination, an effect of which is the contradiction between the bureaucratic norm of individual responsibility and the increasingly factual collective basis of technocratic decision-making. One consequence of this, allied to the career cluster, is the development of a tenure principle for the bureaucracy, together with a norm of 'responsibility' (i.e. the possibility of dismissal as a retribution) applied to those functional 'chiefs' responsible both for 'the bureaucracy' and to those at the bottom of the structure, who translate technocratic imperatives into organisational action. Technocracy increasingly pushes bureaucracy into a corporate form.

It is from an oppositional tradition of 'critical reflection' that Wilson mounts his wide-ranging and discursive formulation, simultaneously elaborating an argument and constructing a critique of it, in which technocracy appears as both mythical (i.e. unrealisable in its objectivist terms) and spectral (because its argument masks the reality of domination with the spectre of technical administration). It is precisely this which makes the critical task so difficult, because it depends upon concepts drawn from those discourses which it challenges. It is also what makes criticism so imperative. As Wilson concludes, technocratic rationalisation must not become so routinised in organisational practice that it becomes the basis for a new tradition of unreflection, in which the 'iron cage' is no longer exterior but internalised into the constitution of any possible rational action.

Wilson and Ferraresi provide an interesting contrast. For the former, bureaucracy has become subsumed to an ideological particularism posing as a universalistic value; for the latter, traditional particularisms have never achieved rationalisation by bureaucratic universalism. In a most interesting way one is forcibly reminded not only of Marcuse's charge (71) that bureaucratic rationality can function to protect rather than cancel the legitimacy of domination, but also that it can be protected not only through the totalitarianism of an irrational conception of rationality, but also through the failure of the rationality potentially inherent in bureaucracy to protect the victims of particularism with the cloak of universalism (72).

LABOUR AND CLASS STRUGGLE

A major feature of post-war political development
which has contributed to the technocratic
corporatisation of the bureaucracy (as the apparatus
of government), is taken up by Marino Regini in 'The
Crisis of Representation in Class-Oriented Unions:
Some Reflections based on the Italian Case'. This
is the importance that the organised labour movement
has attached to making its co-operation with the
state on wage bargaining conditional on a form of
'social contract' being offered in return by the
state. This 'corporatist' strategy has received
considerable attention in the literature in the last
decade (73) although some of the claims made for
'corporatism', have, with hindsight, proved to be
widely inflated and wrong (74). The question of the
representation of non-parliamentary and organised
interests, primarily those of labour and capital, in
decision-making agencies of the state is likely to
remain a central feature of reflection upon and
practice in the state. Clearly, the involvement of
trade unions in the political system is central to
any social democratic strategy and although the
'paradigmatic' cases of Sweden, Austria and West
Germany have occurred under labour parties, the
strategy can be and has been pursued in states
characterised by conservative rule (75). However,
corporatism may be approached not only by the
incorporation of union peak organisations by the
state, but also as a result of unions increasing
their demands on the political system when their
traditional wage-related demands become increasingly
restricted at the level of specific enterprises. It
is the latter conjuncture which describes the
Italian case. It is this case which provides a
further focus for Regini, precisely because of the
existence of a widely organised and left-oriented
labour movement 'blocked' at the formal level of
governmental representation, despite the high levels
of political mobilisation achieved by left parties
in general elections.

The specificities of the Italian political
scene, already sketched by Apple and Ferraresi,
relate to the wartime resistance to fascism fought
through the communist party, and to the failure of
this resistance to be translated into an effective
political mobilisation in the cold war era, a
setting characterised by considerable political,
religious and regional cleavages. Despite these
cleavages, the union movement has remained combative

and militant, in part due to the continuing strength
of the Factory Councils. However, incorporation and
national organisation raise the problem of
'representation': how are interests capable of
mobilising the movement to be formed in and through
the representational bodies in which political
demands are formulated and transmitted; and how do
these 'interests' relate to the disposition of the
masses' ostensibly being represented?

The issue of 'representation' is one which has
been discussed from two quite distinct perspectives
in recent years. On the one hand, it has been a
central issue in recent debates on the relationship
between the metaphors of 'base' and 'superstructure'
in marxian discussions of the 'mode of production'
concepts. Here the consensus appears to be that
economic determination, and hence the positing of
'interests' in the political sphere as being either
'real' or 'false' depending on their representation
of 'true interests' as defined by the economy, is a
discredited and exhausted approach to any meaningful
political analysis. Politics has an irreducible
autonomy and it is in the process of political
organisation and representation that interests are
formed (76). On the other hand, discussions of
corporatism indicate that corporatist institutions
may well pose a 'crisis of representation' in as
much as centralised, peak organisations formulate
interests and demands which are transmitted in terms
of the mechanisms of that level, yet may differ from
those formulated at lower levels of political
representation and organisation. It is to this
latter issue which Regini contributes.

His concern is to analyse the specific
conditions which are appropriate to representational
interest mediation without there being a 'crisis' of
representation. These are identified as one of the
following: representational formulation of demands
compatible with those of the majority mass
membership; effective control by the
representational peak organisation over the
membership; or satisfaction of other aspects of the
masses' objectives in some meaningful, although not
analogous way, to the explicit requests of the lower
level organisations.

Regini argues that class-oriented unions, those
which seek a wider representation than simply that
of their membership, always fail to meet the first
demand and always carry out a profound modification
of their membership's explicit demands. This is
clearly indicated by Apple's discussion of the Rehn-

Meidner strategy of the Swedish labour movement. However, if the first of these conditions is absent, then unless they meet the other two criteria, a crisis of representation will not be averted.

For a time, during the post-war boom, these other conditions could be generally met under the limiting conditions of full employment capitalism. Under these conditions, union members could be persuaded to modify wage claims in return for guarantees on real incomes and employment. What has precipitated the crisis of representation today is not the incorporation of the union elite into a relationship with the state which places it in a classic role conflict of having to satisfy contradictory demands from the membership and the state. It is because capitalism has not continued to function at a sufficiently high level of demand for the 'trade-offs' to have continued. The trade-offs were in effect not so much a result of the bargained relationship but one of the conditions in which it occurred. Once these had been exhausted by the 1970s, the crisis became apparent.

The conditions appropriate to the class oriented representational strategy were those of steady economic growth seemingly guaranteeing full employment, and a calculable long term absence of overt distributional conflicts. The absence of labour parties in government in Italy served only to make the crisis more intense there than in some other states where labour party governance had been achieved. With the onset of sustained recession those trade unions which had become involved in the political system faced a crisis of representation for which only two solutions seem appropriate, in the absence of a neo-corporatist strategy. These are either a return to a purely 'economistic' role in bargaining only over wages and conditions or a move to a radicalised corporatism such as that of the Meidner strategy, which involves obtaining effective control over capital's investment decisions. Control over these spheres of strategic decision-making by the political representation of a 'general interest' appears improbable in the absence of a labour movement government, or, indeed, in circumstances of continuing low growth and high inflation.

Finally, Harvie Ramsay considers the effects of the recession on one of the major expressions of technocratic rationality. This is an evolutinary faith in the potential to eradicate major class cleavages through techniques of 'participative management', a view he severely criticises in 'An International Participation Cycle: Variations on a Recurring Theme' (77).

Organisational democracy has been a major issue in the advanced industrial societies in the post-war era, particularly in the EEC. Ramsay challenges the broad liberal consensus within industrial relations theory which regards moves for increased employee participation as part of a general evolution towards a more democratic organisation of work. His comparative analysis, closely sharing the scope of Apple's contribution, argues that this analysis is founded on incorrect extrapolation from the available data. Rather than a smoothly unfolding 'evolution' the comparative data demonstrates that there have been 'cycles' of managerial interest in participation. These cycles of interest have been contingent upon the pressures of class struggle, conditioned by the state of the labour market, profit margins, and international competitiveness, through the overall level of unemployment. Interest in participation on the part of management has been a response to those periods of full employment in which its control is challenged.

Quite a different picture to this emerges from the dominant technocratic literature on 'participation'. In this literature, as reviewed by Ramsay, quite unproblematical teleologies of rational evolution towards greater enlightenment and consensus are constructed as part of the more general transition to a 'post-ideological', 'post-industrial' world. What Ramsay's chapter does is to demonstrate the central importance of a conception of organisational relations as constructed around the struggle between management and labour over the control of the labour process (78). In this context the decline of the post-war boom in the late 1960s led to a new interest in participation.

Why should the onset of recession have generated roughly similar expressions of interest in participation in a diverse range of OECD countries? One of the main indicators of the onset of recession is a crisis of valorisation expressed in declining productivity. In order to try to improve productivity, management attempted to incorporate the workforce through 'participation' schemes to obtain co-operation for 'restructuring' or 'rationalisation' of the labour process, as well as to pre-empt the more radical currents within the working class which emerged around issues of 'control' after 1968, and which found expression in a strike-wave that has occurred in OECD countries since the late 1960s (79). Both the strike wave and the management responsiveness to 'participation' have the same underlying cause. This is the regulation of world capitalism by recession.

Ramsay's historical perspective and Apple's partisanship for Swedish exceptionalism together pose a dilemma. Ramsay's view of the Swedish Co-determination Act suggests less optimism about a Swedish transitional strategy for socialism being developed than does the work of authors such as Apple, Higgins or Stephens. Nonetheless, on the possibilities for 'socialist transition' implicit in these different national experiences we would argue that the Swedish experience, rather than the Italian, as writers such as Giddens and Mann (80) have suggested, is a more probable model. This is despite the appearance of the latter as a state in which a 'revolutionary socialist' labour movement has been formed under conditions where 'post-feudal' elements resisted emergent capitalist industrial-isation. Here we agree with Ferraresi and Regini in identifying obstacles to reform, at the level of the state, and to political class struggle, at the level of the class oriented unions. Flawed though it may be, the 'Swedish strategy' combined with elements of an Alternative Economic Strategy derived from and suited to specific national conditions, seems the only practical programme for permanent full employment and socialist transition available.

THE NEW RIGHT AND THE NEW ALTERNATIVES

Not only analyses of the recession but also proposals for resolving it have become more sophisticated in recent years. Development of alternative economic strategies in the past decade (81) has both depended upon and contributed to the recent upsurge in theories of the state in contemporary capitalism. Sections of the political left have been seeking political strategies which could effect a transition beyond, and solution to, capitalism in crisis. Among these there has been a burgeoning recourse to theoretical developments concerning the form and functions of the state. At the same time, the theories have become less partial and more aware of the complex nature of, and limitations to, strategies for change centred on existing institutions of political representation and class organisation. These developments, in turn, can now be used to ensure that unrealistic or naive counter-recessionary strategies are not proffered. Alternate economic strategies, like political strategies of Eurocommunism with which they are sometimes associated (82), need to know as precisely as possible the structural nature of, pressures upon and limitations to, the political and institutional environment in which they will be required to operate. They can be successful only to the extent that the obstacles and frustrations that have confronted *ad hoc* and reformist growth strategies in the past can be pre-empted. Moreover, they can secure intellectual and political integrity only to the extent that the arguments and policies of 'the new right' can be effectively countered.

Accompanying the recession has been a cogent revival of neo-conservative analysis assigning responsibility for the crisis to 'overloaded' government and calling, in various ways, for 'de-regulation' of capitalism. This body of analysis often embraces arguments very similar to those of the marxist critiques of welfarism (83); and itself gives an indication of the institutional limitations to state intervention, especially its redistributive policies (84). The 'new conservative' onslaught however, is so explicitly interventionist in its Reaganite and Thatcherist forms (especially in so far as it is attempting to transform the industrial-relations legislative protections that have been achieved since 1945), that it is not difficult to surmise that the 'fight-inflation-first' rhetoric is really a guise for a more deliberate re-negotiation and re-direction of state intervention, rather than a call for minimalist government. The traditional philosophical distinction between paternalist government (pro-interventionist) as advocated historically by conservatives, and minimalist government (anti-interventionist) as advocated by liberals (85), is therefore becoming blurred. None the less, the alleged causes and consequences of inflation, continue to provide powerful polemical succour to monetarism-in-practice, and continue to expose significant confusions within left parties and policy strategies. Daniel Bell has deployed an argument which focuses on 'the revolution of rising expectations' (86) to legitimate fear of inflation and public sector cutbacks; Samuel Brittan writes of the 'economic costs of democracy' to criticise budget deficits and the weakness of a liberal democratic system which allows politicians to use them as an easy option (87); elsewhere, there are charges of 'administrative overload' (88);

'ungovernability' (89) and, more rhetorically, of crisis caused by 'the process of overcentralisation, over-government and excessive taxation' (90). All these arguments implicitly claim that the contemporary epoch has produced a contradiction between growth and inflation, reflecting governments' inability to exercise restraint (91). Bell claims that the expansion of 'the public household' (the state) occurred without explicit public discussion or approval; that state intervention takes place in spheres of (illegitimate) 'wants' rather than 'basic needs'; and that the result is not only an inflationary crisis but also a legitimation crisis as basic allocative mechanisms (markets) are usurped by overtly political decisions and the 'submission to a heavy-handed bureaucratic Moloch' (92).

These arguments demonstrate the pervasiveness of the sense of the failure of Keynesianism but they seriously misunderstand the causes of inflation in recession and therefore seriously misrepresent both the nature of the crisis and the orientations that alternative strategies must take.

The limits of Keynesianism derive from its 'bastardisation' during the years of post-war affluence and not from its inherent inability to deal with inflation. In so far as Keynesianism became the legitimator of fiscal and monetary policy rather than of fully fledged public intervention into decisions concerning the content of economic activity, it failed in practice to play any part in averting the current recession. And in so far as the end of growth has caused class conflict over distributive shares of income to assume inflationary forms, then it is clear that an anti-inflationary policy cannot be developed in isolation from an anti-recessionary strategy. Control of inflation demands a social consensus over the class distribution of income; cut-backs in social expenditures, social services and measures of income support can only encourage the downwards recessionary spiral in economic activity and therefore exacerbate the very conflicts which are firing inflation.

Alternative policies therefore demand stronger, not diminished, institutions of public intervention. This is a requirement that is both politically and analytically contentious. As most social contracts and incomes policies in the past (including those negotiated by labour parties) have been the occasion for reductions in real incomes of wage earners (93), any attempt to secure democratic and political control over the distribution of income in any future 'left-labour' strategy would need to ensure first, that real wage levels were maintained, and second, that non-wage incomes (i.e. profits, interest, dividends, rents) were also included in the ambit of incomes policy. Doubtless, there are substantial difficulties involved in such a policy, not the least of which is the apparent need to deal with wage relativities that may have been disrupted during the past period of inflation. It seems, however, that adequate public control over the class distribution of income is neither technically nor administratively impossible. The war time success of wage and price controls in the US suggests that despite the likelihood of corporate avoidance tactics, control over all incomes can, with political will, be secured (94). The real obstacle will be not in devising anti-inflationary policies, but in insisting on the increases in production and output that any associated anti-recessionary strategy demands.

We have already argued that the state has historically played a significant role in ensuring that political control over investment remains with capital even at the expense, if necessary, of profits. We have also argued that expansionary policies, aimed at the provision of permanent full employment will necessarily involve a change in the locus of this control. At the policy level, in countries where it is appropriate (such as the UK and Australia), this will involve abandonment of Treasury dominance and the 'contempt for production' which it has nurtured for the past thirty years (95). These transformations obviously demand a realignment in relations between the labour movement, state power and capital accumulation. Consequently, a detailed, formal knowledge of what the capitalist state is will be required before one can gauge the extent to which an Alternative Economic Strategy (AES) can constructively intervene in such relations.

In discussion of the capitalist state, there has been an ongoing rejection of theories which grasp only part of what the state does, or which utilise definitions that do not distinguish the functions of a specifically capitalist state, or which too easily assume an unmediated relationship between economic interests and political processes, or which omit discussions of the limitations of state intervention (96). These theoretical interventions serve as a warning to those who believe that a left-labour alternative can be forged by parliamentarist means alone; but they also provide to such strategies a clearer view than heretofore of the conditions for a viable (and successful) transitional strategy. The capitalist state represents a specific mode of political domination and intervention. As forms of capitalist development undergo transformation (signalled by crisis), so do forms of state intervention (signalled by crisis-management). If new bases for economic decision making are to be constructed, the balance of class forces and political power will need to change. This is what an AES seeks to do.

Jessop argues that 'the state' should be conceived as 'a complex institutional ensemble of forms of representation and intervention' and 'state power' as 'a form-determined reflection of the balance of political forces' (97). This is what the essays in this volume demonstrate. The success of an AES depends, then, on the extent to which popular support can be mobilised for a widespread expansion of production and democracy; and it will achieve its objectives only to the extent that the types of institutions envisaged by Kalecki (though only partially realised in present state apparatuses) can be developed in ways which permit sustained reflation.

Systematic consideration of the changes envisaged by the AES probably began with responses to a 1974 British White Paper titled *The Regeneration of British Industry*. This document, which was associated with Tony Benn's tenure as Secretary of State for Industry (98), called for 'Planning Agreements' (to ensure co-operation, information flows and co-ordination between the private sector and macro economic planning agencies) as well as for an expansion of the National Enterprise Board (to stimulate investment, to subject some major capitalist developments to some degree of public control and to arrest the decline in manufacturing industry's contribution to overall growth and output).

Since 1974, the specific proposals of the White Paper have been ignominiously ignored by Labour-in-office. However, much has since been learned about the preconditions for a similar package in the 1980s. Similar proposals have since become the occasion for a substantial and sustained debate in Britain and elsewhere, concerning the form, content, political pre-conditions, limitations, potential and detailed components of an Alternative Economic Strategy. Debate has come from within the Labour party, from parties and groups to the left of the official opposition, from policy research groups, from academic advisers and even from the institutions of orthodox policy themselves (in the form of denials of the possibility of an alternative, and assurances that there will be no 'U-turn') (99).

Consequently, the Alternative Economic Strategy is a dynamic set of policies, proposals, analyses, warnings, caveats, documents and ideas that now has no single institutional or factional locus. It has been amended, supplemented, criticised and welcomed by a variety of contributors, and as such has begun to form the basis of an intellectually respectable and democratically derived political, economic and societal response to the current recession.

As the AES is still in a state of flux no definitive evaluation is possible. However, the ongoing analysis of articulations between the state, crisis and the recession suggests some of the demands which such a reflationary, counter-recessionary strategy will need to meet if it is to be successful. First of all, such a set of proposals will need to be reflationary, expansionary, and to regenerate industrial and other forms of economic activity. It must do so in ways which recognise the altered balance of national and international forces that are likely to be influential in the medium and long term future. It will need to concentrate on fostering industries that will be able to operate efficiently, democratically and purposefully in the appropriate national contexts and to allow the controlled phasing out of those industries which, for whatever good or bad reasons will not be likely to prove vi e. Although state support for some technically inefficient industry may be sanctioned, this will not necessarily be the case; although some loss-making public enterpise may well be socially and politically desirable, some may not. Careful political decisions will need to be made. Abrogation of responsibility for the content, structure and future development of a national economy will not be reasonable, whether in the name of market mechanisms or cost-benefit analysis or minimalist government.

There remains, however, a second set of criteria which feature prominently in the

formulations of an AES. Various parts of the
strategy are consciously attempting to anticipate
and to plan for the significant consequences and
repercussions of the changes it hopes to produce.
Inflationary consequences, effects on balances of
payment, regional ramifications, cost
considerations, institutional disruptions, corporate
and extra-national retaliatory responses, and
legitimation difficulties must come neither as
unexpected contingencies, nor as a pretext for a
flight back into orthodoxy.

It is this non-recognition that has resulted in
the discrediting, not only of particular reformist
strategies in the past, but also of the role of
'left of centre' groups, of strong links between
unions and labour parties, and of the party-system
itself. In Britain and Australia at least, there
have been spectacular recent examples of such
retreats and of the repressive and authoritarian
consequences that can follow. Just as new forms of
state intervention (the strong state characterised
by a weak parliament (100)) are emerging as the
forms of capitalism change (the internationalisation
of monopoly capital), opportunities exist for left
responses to crisis to create new forms of state
power that can secure the conditions for further
development of productive forces under collective
control and according to criteria of public need.
This does not suggest that all contradictions in the
political preconditions for economic expansion can
be resolved but that the current crisis can and
should be used to ensure that the state we have
inherited becomes a facilitator of renewed capital
accumulation under public rather than private
ownership and control. Although a 'business as
usual' approach to renewed capital formation would
result eventually in an economic upturn (once the
labour process or other conditions of production are
reconstituted), the opportunity that now exists to
make a more fundamental and permanent intervention
into the process of capital accumulation should not
be squandered.

The contributions to this volume, as well as
the literature referred to in this introduction,
indicate that the theoretical and practical
development of an AES will be constrained by the
following caveats:
(i) that an AES must be nationally specific.
Because the patterns of industrial development,
institutional arrangements and political
sophistication differ substantially in various parts

of the world economy, any programme for expanded accumulation of capital under democratic control will obviously need to accommodate itself to local sectoral, conditions.

(ii)   that there will be limitations to the effectiveness of some parts of any such programme. Clearly not all distributive effects, nor impediments to growth, can be anticipated in advance. Even though inflationary consequences of growth, balance of payments effects, public sector borrowing requirements etc. can and should be incorporated into the strategy itself; there will be some aspects of social, political and economic transformation that will surely produce new conditions for which past experience and analytical premeditation cannot prepare us. That is why an AES is a 'strategy' for change and not a fixed 'blueprint' for the future. Judgments and adjustments will need to be made along the way; compromises will be inevitable.

(iii)   that traditional parliamentary institutions and strategies are insufficient to achieve 'full employment without inflation'. While public enterprise, public investment funds, prices and incomes policies, import controls, and a range of democratic sanctions can be legislated, the experience of reformism (101) strongly suggests that widespread and explicit labour movement endorsement of legislative change is essential to the transformation of state power and capitalist prerogatives that is implied by anti-recessionary policy. The conditions for transition are that a more permanent, extra-parliamentary degree of organisational cohesion, class unity and economic democracy be maintained (102).

(iv)   that the agenda will be to some extent structured by a pre-existing pattern of ruling class hegemony. These obstacles to such a programme need to be countered by a massive educational effort from as broad a base in progressive movements as possible. This requirement has been referrred to as a 'broad democratic alliance' which will transcend the present limitations and frustrations of labour politics. The call for mass participation is not merely to legitimate the institutional struggles that will be encountered, but to transform social relations in the family, workplace and political parties, etc. that currently mitigate against change (103). They should also include internal party democracy and the extension of unionism to the police and armed forces.

(v)   that differing needs of differing segments of the population have to be met.   If long term full employment is to be provided in a way which demands democratic   control   over   the   whole   economy, democratic   control   over   the   conditions   of   labour process   participation   will   also   need   to   be secured.   Permanent part-time work, recognition of the   role   of   unpaid   domestic   labour,   abolition   of gender   and   racially   segmented   labour   markets   and transformed   gender   roles   will   all,   of   necessity, need   to   be   embraced   by   an   AES.   In   so   far   as recessions   are   facilitated   by   working   class fragmentation,   alleviation   of   periodic   slumps   will necessarily   involve   elimination   of   any   place   for   a scapegoated   portion   of   the   workforce.   In   turn   this will   demand   a   significant   transformation   of   the realms   of   'political'   and   'private'   life.   An   AES could   not   be   achieved   without   wholehearted endorsement   of   the   economic   lessons   of   feminist struggles (104).

(vi)   that new forces must be inserted into the capitalist   state.   State   organisation   and   state power   must   be   mobilised   to   effect   capital accumulation   under   public   control   (i.e.   without representing   private   ownership).   The   state   must cease   to   be   a   capitalist   state.   In   the   past,   as   the specific   functions   of   the   state   have   been   to politically   articulate   economic   conditions   in   a diverse   number   of   ways,   and   as   the   problems   germane to   this   role   (e.g.   'class   struggle,   the   unity   of   the state   apparatus,   state   power   and   class   interests' (105)   have   themselves   been   subject   to   various, separate   determinations,   then   it   is   not   unreasonable to   suppose   that   the   conditions   of   existence   and effects   of   the   capitalist   state   can   be   transformed by a coherent AES.

The   essays   collected   here   reveal   aspects   of   the relation   between   the   state,   class   and   recession   as well   as   some   caveats   for   the   transformation   of   those relationships.   The   political   and   economic possibilities   for   a   restructuring   of   capitalist development   towards   capital   accumulation   under democratic   control   are   given   by   the   recession itself.   These   essays,   from   different   perspectives, are a contribution to its resolution.

NOTES

1.   For   a   brief   statement   of   this   argument, see   Joan   Robinson   'The   Second   Crisis   of   Economic Theory'   American   Economic   Review   (Papers   and

Proceedings) vol. 62(2), May, 1972.
2.   Some of these issues are canvassed by Michal Kalecki 'Political Aspects of Full Employment' Political Quarterly vol. 14, September-October, 1943; and also in Alfred S. Eichner (ed.) A Guide to Post-Keynesian Economics (Macmillan, New York and London, 1979).
3.   Immanuel Wallerstein 'Semi Peripheral Countries and the Contemporary World Crisis' Theory and Society vol. 3(4), Winter 1976.
4.   Ernest Mandel Late Capitalism (New Left Books, London, 1975).
5.   Andrew Gamble and Paul Walton Capitalism in Crisis: Inflation and the State (Macmillan, London, 1976).
6.   John Urry The Anatomy of Capitalist Societies: The Economy, Civil Society and the State (Macmillan, London, 1981).
7.   John D. Stephens The Transition from Capitalism to Socialism (Macmillan, London, 1979).
8.   Stuart Holland The Socialist Challenge (Quartet, London, 1975).
9.   See John Kenneth Galbraith The Age of Uncertainty (BBC and Andre Deutsch, London, 1977); and Joan Robinson 'The Age of Growth' Challenge: The Magazine of Economic Affairs vol. 19(2), May-June, 1976.
10.   For a prescient (1958) account by Joan Robinson, see 'Full Employment and Inflation' in Collected Economic Papers: Volume Two (Basil Blackwell, Oxford, 1960).
11.   John Maynard Keynes The General Theory of Employment, Interest and Money (Macmillan, London, 1936).
12.   For example, her essay 'What Has Become of the Keynesian Revolution?' in Joan Robinson (ed.) After Keynes (Basil Blackwell, Oxford, 1973).
13.   See Joan Robinson 'Michal Kalecki: A Neglected Prophet' New York Review of Books vol. 23(3), 4 March, 1976.
14.   Collected in Michal Kalecki Selected Essays in the Dynamics of the Capitalist Economy (Cambridge University Press, Cambridge, 1971).
15.   A contemporary version of this thesis can be found in Andrew Glyn and Bob Sutcliffe British Capitalism, Workers and the Profits Squeeze (Penguin, Harmondsworth, 1972); also published as Capitalism in Crisis (Pantheon, New York, 1972).
16.   Some recent empirical support for Kalecki's argument is discussed by Raford Boddy and James Crotty 'Class Conflict and Macro Policy: The

Political Business Cycle' Review of Radical Political Economics vol. 7(1), Spring, 1975; and 'Stagnation, Instability and International Competition' American Economic Review (Papers and Proceedings) vol. 66(2), May, 1976. An elaborated analysis of some theoretical complexities is given by Howard Sherman 'A Marxist Theory of the Business Cycle' Review of Radical Political Economics vol. 11(1), Spring, 1979.

    17.   For a brief summary, in the context of a discussion of the formulation of new avenues of analytical enquiry, see the editor's introduction to Alfred S. Eichner (ed.), 1979.

    18.   See the discussion of mainstream and Kaleckian growth (accumulation) models in Maurice Dobb Theories of Value and Distribution Since Adam Smith: Ideology and Economic Theory (Cambridge University Press, Cambridge, 1973), ch. 8.

    19.   For example, the theoretical argument for labour movement control of profits is put by Rudolf Meidner Employee Investment Funds: An Approach to Collective Capital Formation (George Allen and Unwin, London 1978), p. 14.

    20.   For two representative surveys, see Bob Jessop 'Recent Theories of the Capitalist State' Cambridge Journal of Economics, vol. 1(4), December, 1977; and Boris Frankel Marxian Theories of the State: A Critique of Orthodoxy (Arena Publications, Monograph no. 3, Melbourne, 1978).

    21.   James O'Connor The Fiscal Crisis of the State (New York, St. Martin's Press, 1973).

    22.   This position is re-endorsed in James O'Connor 'The Fiscal Crisis of the State Revisited: A Look at the Economic Crisis and Reagan's Budget Policy' Kapitalistate: Working Papers on the Capitalist State no. 9, 1981.

    23.   A further example is Gamble and Walton, 1976.

    24.   Ian Gough The Political Economy of the Welfare State (Macmillan, London, 1979); J.F. Sleeman Resources for the Welfare State: An Economic Introduction (Longman, London, 1979); and N. Ginsburg Class, Capital and Social Policy (Macmillan London, 1979).

    25.   Victor George Social Security and Society (Routledge and Kegan Paul, London, 1973); and F.F. Piven and R.A. Cloward Regulating the Poor: The Functions of Public Welfare (Vintage Books, New York, 1971).

    26.   Mandel, 1975.

    27.   Mandel, 1975, p. 483.

28. Mandel, 1975, p. 488.

29. O'Connor, 1981, p. 42.

30. As argued by Mike Campbell Capitalism in the UK: A Perspective from Marxist Political Economy (Croom Helm, London, 1981), Chapter 7.

31. Joachim Hirsch 'The State Apparatus and Social Reproduction: Elements of a Theory of the Bourgeois State' in John Holloway and Sol Picciotto (eds.) State and Capital: A Marxist Debate (Edward Arnold, London, 1978).

32. J.D. Kingsley Representative Bureaucracy (Antioch Press, Yellow Springs, 1944).

33. See, for example, Michael Meacher 'How the Mandarins Rule' New Statesman, 5 December, 1980.

34. Adam Przeworski 'Proletariat into Class: The Process of Class Formation from Karl Kautsky's 'The Class Struggle' to Present Controversies' Politics and Society vol. 7(4), 1977.

35. Folker Fröbel, Jürgen Heinrichs and Otto Kreye 'The World Market for Labour and New Industrial Sites' Journal of Economic Issues vol. 12(4), December, 1978.

36. Most aspects of this overt regionalisation of the world economy are discussed in Holly Sklar (ed.) Trilateralism: The Trilateral Commission and Elite Planning for World Management (South End Press, Boston, 1980).

37. Ajit Singh 'UK industry and the world economy: a case of de-industrialisation' Cambridge Journal of Economics vol. 1(2), June, 1977.

38. A point made repeatedly by Joan Robinson in her own critiques of Keynes. See Robinson, 1972.

39. See the discussion by Erik Olin Wright Class, Crisis and the State (New Left Books, London, 1978).

40. C.B. Macpherson Democratic Theory: Essays in Retrieval (Clarendon Press, Oxford, 1973, p. 6).

41. Robert A. Dahl Pluralist Democracy in the United States: Conflict and Consent (Rand McNally and Co., Chicago, 1967); and Seymour Martin Lipsett Political Man (Doubleday and Co, Anchor edition, New York, 1963).

42. Herbert Marcuse One Dimensional Man (Routledge and Kegan Paul, London, 1964).

43. Perry Anderson Considerations on Western Marxism (New Left Books, London, 1976).

44. Nicholas Abercrombie, Stephen Hill and Bryan S. Turner The Dominant Ideology Thesis (George Allena dn unwin, London, 1980).

45. Göran Therborn 'The Rule of Capital and

the Rise of Democracy' New Left Review no. 103, May-June, 1977.
46.   Tom Nairn The Break-up of Britain (New Left Books, London, 1977).
47.   Sheila Rowbotham, Lynne Segal and Hilary Wainwright Beyond the Fragments: Feminism and the Making of Socialism (Merlin Press, London, 1979). An argument has been put that 'party decomposition' is occurring, again as a concomitant of economic uncertainty, in Europe as well: see Gösta Esping-Anderson 'Social Class, Social Democracy and the State: Party Policy and Party Decomposition in Denmark and Sweden' Comparative Politics vol. 11(1), October, 1978.
48.   Philippe Schmitter 'Still the Century of Corporatism?' in Philippe C. Scmitter and Gerhard Lehmbruch   (eds.)   Trends   Toward   Corporatist Intermediation (Sage, London, 1979).
49.   Stuart   Hall   'Popular-Democratic   vs Authoritarian   Populism: Two   Ways   of   "Taking Democracy Seriously"' in Alan Hunt (ed.) Marxism and Democracy (Lawrence and Wishart, London, 1980).
50.   The relation between these arguments and Marx's analysis of Bonapartism should be noted. See Victor M. Perez-Diaz State, Bureaucracy and Civil Society: A   Critical   Discussion   of   the   Political Theory of Karl Marx (Macmillan, London, 1978).
51.   Marian Sawer (ed.) Australia and the New Right (George Allen and Unwin, Sydney, 1982); and Ian Gough, 1979.
52.   Bengt Abrahamsson and Anders Broström The Rights of Labor (Sage, London, 1980).
53.   See the more general discussion by Fred Block 'The Ruling Class Does Not Rule: Notes on the Marxist Theory of the State' Socialist Revolution no. 33 (vol. 7, no. 3), May-June, 1977.
54.   See Daniel Drache 'Resource Capitalism and the Making of the Quebec and English Canadian Working Class' Paper presented to Three Nations Conference Christchurch, New Zealand, November, 1980; and R.W. Connell and Terry Irving Class Structure in Australian History (Longman, Melbourne, 1980) for accounts of class formation in Canada and Australia.
55.   See   Michel   Aglietta   A   Theory   of Capitalist Regulation: The US Experience (New Left Books, London, 1979).
56.   See accounts by Winton Higgins 'Working Class Mobilisation and Socialism in Sweden: Lessons from Afar' in Paul Boreham and Geoff Dow (eds.) Work and Inequality - Volume One: Workers, Economic

Crisis and the State (Macmillan, Melbourne, 1980); Abrahamsson and Broström, 1980; and Gösta Esping-Anderson 'From the Welfare State to Democratic Socialism: The Politics of Economic Democracy in Denmark and Sweden' in Maurice Zeitlin (ed.) Political Power and Social Theory vol. 2, 1981.

57. See Stephens, 1979.

58. Block, 1977.

59. Holland, 1976.

60. Stuart Hall 'Moving Right' Socialist Review no. 55 (vol. 11, no. 1), January-February, 1981.

61. Stephens, 1979, p. 209.

62. Antonio Gramsci Selections from the Prison Notebooks (Lawrence and Wishart, London, 1971).

63. Nicos Poulantzas Political Power and Social Classes (New Left Books, London, 1973).

64. Claus Offe 'Crisis and Crisis Management: Elements of a Political Crisis Theory' International Journal of Politics no. 6 (3), Fall, 1976.

65. O'Connor, 1973.

66. Paola A. Farnetti 'Italy: The Response to Overload' in Richard A. Rose (ed.) Challenge to Governance: Studies in Overloaded Politics (Sage, London, 1980.

67. To appreciate this, Marx's classic analysis of the failure of the 1848-51 Constitutional Assembly in France still provides an appropriate model. See 'Excerpts from "The Eighteenth Brumaire of Louis Bonaparte"' in Lewis S. Feuer (ed.) Marx and Engels: Basic Writings on Politics and Philosophy (Fontana, London, 1969).

68. Alvin W. Gouldner 'Metaphysical Pathos and the Theory of Bureaucracy' in W. Chambliss (ed.) Sociological Readings in the Conflict Perspective (Addison-Wesley, Reading, Mass., 1973).

69. Krishan Kumar Prophecy and Progress: The Sociology of Industrial and Post-Industrial Society (Harmondsworth, Penguin, 1978).

70. For example, Daniel Bell The Coming of Post-Industrial Society: A Venture in Social Forecasting (Harmondsworth, Penguin, 1978); and John Kenneth Galbraith The New Industrial State (Harmondsworth, Penguin, 1967).

71. Herbert Marcuse 'Industrialisation and Capitalism' in Otto Stammer (ed.) Max Weber and Sociology Today (Basil Blackwell, Oxford, 1971).

72. Charles Perrow Complex Organisations: A Critical Essay (Scott-Foresman, Evanston, Ill.,

1971).

73. See, for example, Schmitter and Lembruch (eds.), 1979.

74. For example, Jack Winkler 'Corporatism' European Journal of Sociology vol. 17(1), 1976.

75. For example, in the latter days of the Heath government.

76. See Antony Cutler, Barry Hindess, Paul Hirst and Athar Hussain Marx's Capital and Capitalism Today: Volumes One and Two (Routledge and Kegan Paul, London, 1977 and 1978); and John Urry, 1981.

77. This extends an earlier account of such schemes in Britain. See Harvie Ramsay 'Cycles of Control: Worker Participation in Sociological and Historical Perspective' Sociology vol. 7(3), September, 1977; also see Paul Boreham and Geoff Dow (eds.) Work and Inequality - Volume Two: Ideology and Control in the Capitalist Labour Process (Macmillan, Melbourne, 1980).

78. See also Stewart Clegg and David Dunkerley Organisation, Class and Control (Routledge and Kegan Paul, London, 1980); Stewart Clegg 'Organisation and Control' Administrative Science Quarterly vol. 28(4), 1981; Graeme Salaman Work Organisations: Resistance and Control (Longman, London, 1979), and Stephen Hill Competition and Control at Work: The New Industrial Sociology (Heineman, London, 1981).

79. Walter Korpi and Michael Shalev 'Strikes, Power and Politics in the Western Nations, 1900-1976' in Maurice Zeitlin (ed.) Political Power and Social Theory vol. 1, 1980.

80. Anthony Giddens The Class Structure of the Advanced Societies (Hutchinson, London, 1973); and Michael Mann Consciousness and Action Among the Western Working Class (Macmillan, London, 1973).

81. Fully elaborated and coherent statements are given by CSE London Working Group The Alternative Economic Strategy: A Labour Movement Response to the Economic Crisis (CSE Books and Labour Co-ordinating Committee, London, 1980); Sam Aaronovitch The Road from Thatcherism: The Alternative Economic Strategy (Lawrence and Wishart, London, 1981); and Holland, 1975.

82. See, for example, Stuart Holland 'The New Communist Economics' in Paolo Filo Della Torre et. al. (eds.) Eurocommunism: Myth or Reality (Pelican, Harmondsworth, 1979).

83. Compare, for example, the Friedmans' attack on the unintended consequences of welfare

state income transfers in Free to Choose: A Personal Statement (Macmillan, London, 1980) with Ian Gough's (1979) criticism of welfare-spending's class bias.

84. Samuel Brittan and Peter Lilley's The Delusion of Incomes Policy (Temple Smith, London, 1977), while misrepresenting the case for political control over the class distribution of income, does none the less highlight some of the procedural and logistical difficulties that would attend any alternative anti-inflationary strategy.

85. See the defense of conservatism (against both liberalism and charges of theoretical shallowness) by Roger Scruton The Meaning of Conservatism (Penguin, Harmondsworth, 1980).

86. Daniel Bell The Cultural Contradictions of Capitalism (Basic Books, New York, 1976).

87. Samuel Brittan 'The Economic Contradictions of Democracy' British Journal of Political Science vol. 5(2), April, 1975.

88. A mild version of this argument can be found in Peter Self 'Resource and Policy Co-ordination under Pressure' in Richard Rose (ed.), 1980.

89. See Richard Rose 'The Nature of the Challenge' in Richard Rose (ed.), 1980.

90. Lord Hailsham of St. Marylebone 'Forward' to Lord Blake and John Patten (eds.) The Conservative Opportunity (Macmillan, London, 1976).

91. Bell, 1976, p. 239.

92. Bell, 1976, p. 257.

93. See discussions by Paul Ormerod 'Inflation and Incomes Policy'; and David Purdy 'Government-Trade Union Relations: Towards a New Social Contract', both in David Currie and Ron Smith (eds.) Socialist Economic Review 1981 (Merlin Press, London, 1981); and Roger Tarling and Frank Wilkinson 'The Social Contract: post-war incomes policies and their inflationary impact' Cambridge Journal of Economics vol. 1 (4), December, 1977.

94. John Kenneth Galbraith Economics and the Public Purpose (Andre Deutsch, London, 1974), especially Part 5; and Malcolm Anderson 'Power and Inflation' in Fred Hirsch and John H. Goldthorpe (eds.) The Political Economy of Inflation (Martin Robertson, London, 1978).

95. In The Wasting of the British Economy: British Economic Policy 1945 to the Present (Croom Helm, London, 1982), Sidney Pollard writes: 'Again and again in the course of the past thirty years,

governments have set out to discourage, cut back and stifle investment, and in the long run they have succeeded... The Treasury will always choose, from any set of options available the one which will do the most damage...' (p. 71).

96. See Jessop, 1977.

97. Bob Jessop The Capitalist State: Marxist Theories and Methods (Martin Robertson, Oxford, 1982), p. xiv.

98. Tony Benn 'The Regeneration of British Industry' (HMSO White Paper, 1974) reprinted in Challenge: The Magazine of Economic Affairs vol. 18(1), March-April, 1975.

99. A discussion of the permutations and ambiguties that can subsequently emerge is in Peter Kellner 'The coming U-turn - and why it will hurt' New Statesman vol. 100 (2590), 7 November, 1980.

100. Jessop, 1977, p. 365.

101. See Geoff Hodgson 'On the Political Economy of the Socialist Transformation' New Left Review no. 133, May-June, 1982, for a critique of easy dismissals of reformism. Hodgson shows that in both economic and political terms, both capital and labour can initially benefit from legislative reforms. An AES is not a programme of reforms, however, but a strategy for enabling economic expansion to transform the parameters of its historical incubator.

102. An indication of these conditions and of the likely consequences of failure to achieve them is provided by Esping-Anderson's (1981) discussion of strategies for economic democracy in Denmark and Sweden.

103. See, for example, Dave Cook '"Rocky Road Blues": The Communist Party and the Broad Democratic Alliance' in George Bridges and Rosalind Brunt (eds.) Silver Linings: Some Strategies for the Eighties (Lawrence and Wishart, London, 1981).

104. See Rowbotham et. al. (1979); and Anna Coote 'The AES: a new starting point' New Socialist no. 2, November-December, 1981.

105. Jessop, 1982, p. 259.

Chapter Two

COMPETITIVE PARTY DEMOCRACY AND THE KEYNESIAN
WELFARE STATE: SOME REFLECTIONS ON THEIR HISTORICAL
LIMITS

Claus Offe

If we compare nineteenth century liberal political
theory on the one side and classical marxism on the
other, we see that there is one major point of
agreement between the two. Both Marx and his
liberal contemporaries, such as J.S. Mill or
de Tocqueville, were convinced that, in their
contemporary societies, capitalism and full
democracy (based on equal and universal suffrage)
would not mix. Obviously, this analytical
convergence was arrived at from diametrically
opposed points of view: the classical liberal
writers believed that freedom and liberty were the
most valuable accomplishments of societal
development which deserved to be protected, under
all circumstances, from the egalitarian threats of
mass society and mass politics. Marx, on the other
side, analysed the French democratic constitution of
1848 as a political form that would exacerbate
societal contradictions by withdrawing political
guarantees from the holders of social power while
giving political power to subordinate classes;
consequently, he argued, democratic conditions could
bring the proletarian class to victory and put into
question the foundations of bourgeois society.
    Looking at the twentieth century experience of
capitalist societies, there is a lot of evidence
against this nineteenth century hypothesis
concerning the incompatibility of mass democracy
(defined as universal and equal suffrage plus
parliamentary or presidential forms of government)
and bourgeois freedom (defined as production based
on private property and 'free' wage labour). The
coexistence of the two is known as liberal
democracy. To be sure, the emergence of fascist
regimes in some of the core capitalist countries
testifies to the continued existence of tensions and

contradictions that prevail between the two models of economic organisation and political organisation, and to the possibility of the outbreak of such tensions under the impact of economic crises. But it is also true that most advanced capitalist countries have also been liberal democratic states throughout most of the twentieth century. In view of this evidence and experience, ours is in some way a problematic that is the reverse of that of the classical writers of both liberalism and marxism. While these prognosticised an incompatibility, we have to explain the coexistence of the two partial principles of societal organisation. More precisely, we want to know which institutional arrangements and mechanisms can be held responsible for a pattern of coexistence which has proved to be far more solid than any nineteenth century expectations would have predicted and what, if any, the limits of such arrangements are. These limits, or failures of mediating mechanisms would be defined analytically as those points at which either capitalist societies turn non-democratic or democratic regimes turn non-capitalist. It is these two questions with which I will be concerned in the following remarks.

To pose these questions at all is to presuppose, in accordance with both Marx and Mill, that there is some real tension between the two respective organising principles of social power and political power: market society and political democracy. This is a tension that must be (and possibly cannot indefinitely be) bridged, mediated and stabilised. Lenin and the Leninist tradition deny that there is such tension. They assume, instead, that there is a prestabilised harmony of the rule of capital and bourgeois democratic forms, the latter mainly serving as a means of deception of the masses. Consequently, it makes little sense to ask what makes democracy compatible with capitalism or what the limits of such compatibility might be, because democracy is simply seen to be the most effective and reliable arrangement of class dominance. Central to Lenin's position is an argument which states that the interests of the working class and the organisational form of the parliamentary democratic state are contradictory (1). Plausible and convincing as this view can be taken to be if based on the constitutional practise of Russia between 1905 and 1917, its generalisation to the present would have, among other and still worse political consequences, the effect of grossly

distorting and obscuring the very problematic which
we want to discuss (2).

The reciprocal distortion is the one
promulgated by the ideologists of pluralist-elitist
democratic theory. They claim (or more precisely,
they used to claim in the fifties and early sixties)
that the tension between the principles governing
capitalist market society and political democratic
forms had finally been eliminated in the American
political system. According to this doctrine, the
class struggle within bourgeois society had been
replaced by what Lipset calls the 'democratic class
struggle' (3). The underlying logic of this
analysis can be summarised in the argument: 'If
people actually wanted things to be different, they
simply would elect else other into office. The fact
that they don't, consequently, is proof that people
are satisfied with the socio-political order as it
exists'.

Both the Leninist and the pluralist-elitist
conception of democracy miss the point which
interests us here. The one dogmatically postulates
total dependence of democratic forms and procedures
upon class power, while the other equally
dogmatically postulates total independence of class
and democratically constituted political power. A
more modest question which seems more promising in
terms of developing insights of both intellectual
and practical significance would be: which
institutions and mechanisms regulate the extent to
which the two can become incongruent in a given
society, and what are the limits of such potential
incongruity - limits, that is, which would constrain
the range of potential variance of class power and
democratically constituted political authority?

MARKETISATION OF POLITICS AND POLITICISATION OF THE
PRIVATE ECONOMY

In what follows, I will argue that the continued
compatibility of capitalism and democracy that was
so inconceivable to both classical liberalism and
classical marxism (including Kautsky and the Second
International) has historically emerged due to the
appearance and gradual development of two mediating
principles, (a) political mass parties and party
competition and (b) the Keynesian welfare state.
Each of the two mediating principles has largely
taken shape in Europe during or in the aftermath of
the two world wars: democracy through party
competition after World War I and the Keynesian

welfare state after World War II. Each of these two principles follow a pattern of 'mixing' the logic of authority and the logic of the market, of 'voice' and 'exit' in Hirschman's terminology (4). This is quite obvious in the case of the Keynesian welfare state for which the term 'mixed economy' is often used as a synonym. But it is no less true for the political sphere of capitalist society which could well be described as a 'mixed polity'. The dynamics of this are often, and to a certain extent appropriately, described as the 'oligopolistic competition' of political elites or political 'entrepreneurs' providing public 'goods'. The logic of capitalist democracy is one of mutual contamination: authority is infused into the economy by global demand management, transfers and regulations so that it looses more and more of its spontaneous and self-regulating character, and market contingency is introduced into the state, thus compromising any notion of absolute authority or the absolute good. Neither the Smithean conception of the market nor the Rousseauan conception of politics have any substantial counterpart in the real world.

Let us now consider each of the two links, or mediating mechanisms between state and civil society in turn. Following the problematic developed above, we will ask two questions in each case. First, in what way and by virtue of which structural characteristics do political parties and the Keynesian welfare state contribute to the compatibility of capitalism and democratic mass politics? Second, which observable trends and changes occur within the institutional framework of both the 'mixed economy' and the 'mixed polity' that threaten the viability of the coexistence of capitalism and democracy?

STABILISATION THROUGH COMPETITIVE PARTY DEMOCRACY

The widespread fear of the German bourgeoisie during the first decade of this century was that, once the full and equal franchise was introduced together with parliamentary government, the class power of the working class would, due to the numerical strength of this class, directly translate into a revolutionary transformation of the state. It was the same analysis, of course, that inspired the hopes and the political strategies of the leaders of the Second International. Max Weber (5) had nothing but sarcastic contempt for both these neurotic anxieties and naive hopes. He was (together with Rosa Luxemburg (6) and Robert Michels (7) who conducted the same analysis with their own specific accents) among the first social theorists who understood that the transformation of class politics into competitive party politics implies not only a change of form, but a decisive change of content. It is probably not too much to say that the twentieth century theory of political organisation has been formed on the basis of the experience and the theoretical interpretation of these three authors who, interestingly enough, arrived at widely divergent political positions at the end of their lives: Luxemburg died in 1919 as a revolutionary democratic socialist and victim of police murder, Weber in the same year as a 'liberal in despair', and Michels in 1936 as an ardent admirer and ideological defender of Mussolini and Italian fascism. In spite of the extreme diversity of their political views and positions, there is a strong common element in their analysis. This element can be summarised in the following way: as soon as political mass participation is organized into competitive party democracy, the very dynamic of this organisational form contains, perverts and obstructs class interest and class politics in ways that are described as leading to opportunism (Luxemburg), oligarchy (Michels) and the inescapable plebiscitarian submission of the masses to the irrational impulses of the charismatic leader and a demagogic use of the bureaucratic party 'machine' (Weber).

According to this analysis, as soon as the will of the people is expressed through the instrumentality of the competitive party striving for government office, what is expressed ceases to be 'the will of the people' and is instead transformed into an artefact of the form itself and the dynamics put into motion by the imperatives of political competition. More specifically, this dynamic has three major effects. The first is the deradicalisation of the ideology of the party. In order to be successful in its electoral striving for government office, the party must orient its programmatic stance towards the expediencies of the political market. This requires a maximisation of votes by an appeal to the greatest possible number of voters and consequently a minimisation of those programmatic elements which could create antagonistic cleavages within the electorate. It also requires that any particular party be prepared to enter into coalitions and to restrict the range of substantive policy proposals to those demands which can be expected to be negotiable to potential coalition partners. The combined effect of these two considerations is to dissolve any coherent political concept or aim into a 'gradualist' temporal structure or sequence, giving priority to what can be implemented at any given point in time and with the presently available resources, while postponing and displacing presently unrealistic and pragmatically unfeasible demands and projects.

Second, the fully developed competitive party is forced by the imperatives of competition to equip itself with a highly bureaucratised and centralised organisation structure. The objective of this organisation is to achieve a dominant presence on the political market, just as the success of a business firm depends in part upon the size and continued presence of its marketing and sales organisation. The bureaucratic organisation of the modern political party performs the tasks of (a) collecting material and human resources (membership dues, other contributions and donations, members, candidates), (b) disseminating propaganda and information concerning the party's position on a great number of diverse political issues, (c) undertaking the exploration of the political market, identifying new issues and monitoring public opinion and (d) managing internal conflict. All of these activities are normally executed by a professional staff of party officials who develop a corporate interest in the growth and stability of the apparatus that provides them with status, and careers.

This pattern of internal bureaucratisation that can be found in parties of the Right and the Left alike, has two important consequences. One consequence is that the social composition (as measured by class background, formal education, sex, occupation, age etc.) of the party leadership, the officials, the members of parliament, and the government, is more and more at variance both with the social composition of the population in general and the party's electoral base in particular. That is to say, the professionalisation of party politics leads to the political dominance of professional and party personnel who, by their training and professional experience, typically come from such backgrounds as business administration, public administration, education, the media, or interest organisations. The other major consequence of this bureaucratic-professional pattern of political organisation is the de-activation of ordinary members. The more the organisation is geared toward exploration of and adaptation to the external environment of the political market, in what has been described as a virtually permanent electoral campaign, the less room remains for the determination of party policies by internal processes of democratic conflict within the organisation. The appearance of internal unanimity and consensus is what any competitive party must try to cultivate in order to become or remain attractive to voters. A consequence of this is that internal division, factionalism and organised conflict of opinion and strategy are not only not encouraged, but rather kept under tight control or at least kept out of sight of the public in a constant effort to streamline the party's image and to standardise its product. (It is tempting to compare, in this respect, the practice of some social democratic parties to the theory of the Leninist party; I suspect we would find some ironic similarities.) The highly unequal importance of external and internal environments frequently becomes evident when the results of public opinion surveys, which today are routinely commissioned by the party leadership, suggest positions and strategies which are in conflict with declared intentions of party members who then, in the interest of 'winning the next elections', are called upon to yield to political 'reality'.

A third effect of what may be called the modern 'catch-all-party' concerns the increasing structural and cultural heterogeneity of its supporters. This heterogeneity results from the fact that the modern political party relies on the principle of 'product-diversification' in the sense that it tries to appeal to a multitude of diverse demands and concerns. This is most obvious in the case of social democratic and communist parties which have often successfully tried to expand their base beyond the working class and to attract elements of the old and new middle classes, the intelligentsia and voters with strong religious affiliations. The advantage of this stragegy is quite obvious, but so is its effect in dissolving a sense of collective identity which, in the early states of both socialist and catholic parties, was based on a cultural milieu of shared values and meanings.

It is easy to see why and how the three consequences of the organisational form of the competitive political party that I have discussed so far - ideological deradicalisation, deactivation of members, erosion of collective identity - do contribute to the compatibility of capitalism and democracy. Each of these three outcomes helps to contain and limit the range of political aims and struggles, and thus provides a virtual guarantee that the structure of political power will not deviate so far from the structure of socio-economic power as to make the two distributions of power incompatible with each other. 'The party system has been the means of reconciling universal equal franchise with the maintenance of an unequal society', as Macpherson (8) has remarked. The inherent dynamic of the party as an organisational form which develops under and for politial competition generates those constraints and imposes those 'non-decisions' (9) upon the political process which together make democracy safe for capitalism. This conclusion, of course, is strongly supported by the fact that no competitive party system has so far ever resulted in a distribution of political power that would have been able to alter the logic of capital and the pattern of socio-economic power it generates.

In order to avoid misunderstanding, I should emphasise that I do not intend a normative critique of the organisational form of the political party which would lead to the suggestion of an alternative form of political organisation. Rather than speculating about the comparative desirability of anarchist, syndicalist, council-democratic or Leninist models of either non-party or non-competitive party organisation, let us look at the future viability of this organisational form itself - its potential to construct and mediate, as it did in the post-war era, a type of political authority that does not interfere with the institutional premises of the capitalist economy. The question is, in other words, whether the institutional link that in most advanced capitalist countries has allowed capitalism and political democracy to coexist for most of the last sixty years is likely to continue to do so in the future.

One way to answer this question in the negative would be to expect political parties to emerge which would be able to abolish the above mentioned restrictions and constraints, thus leading to a challenge of class power through politically constituted power. I do not think that there are many promising indicators of such a development in

spite of Eurocommunist doctrines and strategies that
have emerged in the Latin-European countries in the
mid-seventies, and in spite of the recently elected
socialist/communist government in France. The other
possibility would be a disintegration of the
political party as the dominant form of democratic
mass participation and its gradual replacement by
other forms which are less likely than party
competition to lead to 'congruent' uses of state
power. It is worthwhile exploring this possibility
a little further.

CAUSES OF THE DECLINE OF THE PARTY SYSTEM AS THE
DOMINANT FORM OF MASS PARTICIPATION

In my view, it is possible today to argue that the
form of mass participation in politics that is
channelled through the party system (i.e. according
to the principles of territorial representation,
party competition and parliamentary representation)
has exhausted much of its usefulness for reconciling
capitalism and mass politics. It is, therefore,
increasingly by-passed and displaced by other
practices and procedures of political participation
and decision making. It is highly doubtful,
however, whether those new and additional practices
that can be observed in operation in quite a number
of capitalist states will exhibit the same potential
for reconciling political legitimation with the
imperatives of capital accumulation, which has been,
at least for a certain period, the accomplishment of
the competitive party system. Three new forms of
political participation may be discerned: new
social movements, corporatism and repression - all
phenomena which tend to by-pass, restrict and
subvert the party system and its political
practices.
    In many capitalist countries, new social
movements which, for a number of reasons, are very
hard to absorb into the practices of competitive
party politics, have emerged during the seventies.
Such movements include ethnic and regionalist
movements, various urban movements, ecological
movements, feminist movements, peace movements, and
youth movements. To a large extent, all of them
share two characteristics. First, their projects
and demands are based not on a collective
contractual position on either goods or labour
markets, as was the case, for instance, with
traditional class parties and movements. Instead,
their common denominator of organisation and action

is some sense of collective identity (often underlined by ascriptive and 'naturalistic' conceptions of the collective 'self' in terms of age, gender and 'nation'). Closely connected with this is a second characteristic: they do not demand representation (by which their market status could be improved or protected) but autonomy. In short, the underlying logic of these movements is the struggle for the defence of a physical and/or moral 'territory', the integrity and identity of which is fundamentally non-negotiable to the activists of these movements. For the purpose of this defence, political representation and parliamentary politics is often considered unnecessary (because what is requested of the state, as can be illustrated in the issues of abortion or nuclear energy, is not to 'do something' but to 'stay out') or even dangerous, (because it is considered likely to demobilise and disorganise the movement). To the extent that such movements attract the attention and the political energies of people, not only individual political parties, but the traditional competitive party system as a whole will lose in function and credibility because it simply does not provide the arena within which such issues and concerns can possibly be processed

Secondly, many observers in a number of capitalist states have analysed the ongoing process of de-parliamentarisation of public policy and the concomitant displacement of territorial forms of representation through functional ones (10). This is most evident in 'corporatist' arrangements which combine the processes of interest representation of collective actors with policy implementation *vis-a-vis* their respective constituencies. The functional superiority of such corporatist arrangements, compared to both parliamentary-competitive forms of representation and bureaucratic methods of implementation, resides in their informal, inconspicuous, and non-public procedures and in the 'voluntary' character of compliance that they are said to be able to mobilise. Although the dynamics and limits of corporatist forms of public policy making, especially in the areas of economic and social policies, cannot interest us here, what seems to be clear is that there has been a trend toward such arrangements, most of all in countries with strong social democratic parties (such as Sweden, the UK, Austria and Germany) which has worked at the expense of parliament and the competitive party system. A number of marxist and non-marxist political scientists have even argued that 'parliamentary representation on the basis of residence no longer adequately reflects the problems of economic management in a worldwide capitalist system', and that a system of functional representation is more suited to securing 'the conditions of accumulation' (11).

Thirdly, a constant alternative to free party competition is political repression and the gradual transformation of democracy into some form of authoritarianism. In an analytical sense, what we mean by repression is exclusion from representation. Citizens are denied their civil liberties and freedoms, such as the right to organise, demonstrate, express certain opinions in speech and writing. They are denied access to occupations in the public sector, and the like. The expansion of police apparatuses and the practice of virtually universal monitoring and surveillance of the activities of citizens that we observe in many countries are indications of the growing reliance of the state apparatus upon the means of preventive and corrective repression. More important in the context of a discussion of the limits of competitive party democracy is one other aspect of the exclusion from representation. It is the *de facto* and/or formal limitation of competitiveness within the party system. This includes the strengthening of intra-party discipline and the sanctions applied against dissenters, the election campaigns from which substantive alternatives concerning the conduct and programmatic content of public policy often seem to be absent, and finally, at the level of parliament and parliamentary government, the increasingly frequent disappearance of the identity of individual (and only nominally 'competing') parties behind what occasionally is called the 'great coalition of the enlightened', inspired by some vague 'solidarity of all democratic forces'. Such phenomena and developments could well be described as the 'cartelisation' of political supply and the closure of market access.

If I am correct in assuming that the displacement of the role and political function of the competitive party system (as indicated by the emergence of new social movements, increasing reliance on corporatist arrangements, and self-limitation of the competitiveness of party systems) is a real process that could be illustrated by many examples in numerous advanced (and not so advanced) capitalist states; and if I am also correct in assuming, as I have argued before, that the organisational form of the competitive political party plays a crucial role in making democratic mass participation compatible with capitalism, - then the decline of the party system is likely to lead to the rise of less constrained and regulated practices of political participation and conflict, the outcomes of which may then have the potential of effectively challenging and transcending the institutional premises of the capitalist form of social and economic organisation.

THE KEYNESIAN WELFARE STATE AND ITS DEMISE

Let me now try to apply the analogous argument, in an even more generalised and schematic fashion, to the second pillar on which, according to my initial proposition, the coexistence of capitalism and democracy rests, namely the Keynesian welfare state. The bundle of state institutions and practices to which this concept refers has been developed in western capitalism after the Second World War. Until the decisive change of circumstances which has occurred since the decline of the post-war boom and which was marked by OPEC price policies, the end of *detente*, and the coming to power of Reagan in the US and Thatcher in the UK (to mention just a few indicators of this change), the Keynesian welfare state has been adopted as the basic conception of the state and state practice in almost all western countries, irrespective of parties and government and with only minor modifications and time lags. Most observers agree that its effect has been (a) to produce an unprecedented and extended economic boom favoring all advanced capitalist economies and (b) to transform the pattern of industrial and class conflict in ways that increasingly depart from political and even revolutionary radicalism and lead to more economistic, distribution-centred and increasingly institutionalised class conflicts. Underlying these developments (which constitute a formidable change if compared to the dynamics of the capitalist world system during the twenties and thirties) is a politically instituted class compromise or accord, which can be concisely described as the accord represented, on the part of labour, by the acceptance of the logic of profitability and markets as the guiding principles of resource allocation, international exchange, technological change, product development, and industrial location. In return, labour received assurances that minimal living standards, trade union rights, and liberal democratic rights would be protected, massive unemployment avoided, and real incomes increased approximately in line with labour productivity, through the intervention of the state, if necessary (12).

Again, it is easy to see why and how the existence of this accord has contributed to the compatibility of capitalism and democracy. By accepting the terms of the accord, working class organisations (unions and political parties) reduced their demands and projects to a program that sharply differed from anything on the agenda of both the Third and the Second Internationals. After the physical, moral and organisational devastation the Second World War had left behind, and after the discredit the development of the Soviet Union had earned for communism, this change of perspective is not entirely incomprehensible. Moreover, the accord itself worked amazingly well, thus reinforcing a deeply depoliticised trust in what one leading German Social Democrat much later arrogantly termed the 'German Model' ('Modell Deutschland'): the mutual stimulation of economic growth and peaceful class relations. What was at issue in class conflicts was not the mode of production, but the volume of production – and this type of conflict was particularly suited for being processed on the political plane through party competition, because it does not involve yes/no-questions, but questions of a 'more or less' or 'sooner or later' nature. Overarching this limited type of conflict, there was a consensus concerning basic priorities, desirabilities and values of the political economy – namely economic growth and social (as well as military) security.

This inter-class growth-security alliance does in fact have a theoretical basis in Keynes' economic theory. As applied to practical purposes of economic policy making, it teaches each class to 'take the role of the other'. The capitalist economy is a positive-sum game: this is the lesson to be learned from Keynesianism. Therefore, playing as one would in a zero-sum game is against one's own interest. That is to say, each class has to take the interests of the other class into consideration: workers must consider profitability, because sufficient level of profits and investment to secure future employment and income increases is necessary and capitalists' must consider wage levels and welfare state expenditures, because these must be sufficient to secure effective demand and a healthy, well-trained, and well-housed working class.

The welfare state is defined as a set of legal entitlements providing citizens with claims to transfer payments from compulsory social security schemes as well as to state organised services (such as health and education) for a wide variety of defined cases of need and contingencies. The means by which the welfare state intervenes are thus bureaucratic rules and legal regulations, monetary transfers and professional expertise of teachers, doctors, social workers etc. Its ideological origins are highly mixed and heterogeneous, ranging from socialist to catholic-conservative sources; its character, resulting from ideological, political and economic interclass compromises, is something the welfare state shares with the logic of Keynesian economic policy making. In both cases, there is no fast and easy answer to the zero-sum question of who wins and who loses. This is because, although the primary function of the welfare state is to cover those risks and uncertainties to which wage workers and their families are exposed in capitalist society, there are some indirect effects which also serve the capitalist class. This becomes evident if we look at what would be likely to happen in the absence of welfare state arrangements in a capitalist society. We would probably agree that the answer to this counter-factual question is this: first, there would be a much higher level of industrial conflict and a stronger tendency among the proletariat to avoid becoming wage workers. Thus, the welfare state can be said to partially dispell motives and reasons for social conflict and to make the existence of wage labour more acceptable by eliminating parts of the risks that result from the imposition of the commodity form upon labour. Second, this conflict would be much more costly in economic terms by its disruption of the increasingly complex and capital-intensive process of industrial production. Therefore, the welfare state performs the crucial function of taking part of the needs of the working class out of the arena of class struggle and industrial conflict, of providing the means to fulfil these needs more collectively and hence more efficiently (to make production more regular and predictable by relieving it of important issues and conflicts) and of providing, in addition, a built-in-stabilizer for the economy by partly uncoupling changes in effective demand from changes in employment

If all of this were true, today's ubiquitous critiques and political attacks directed at Keynesianism, the welfare state and, most of all, the combination of these two most successful political innovations of the post-war era, would be plainly incomprehensible. They are not. As in the case of competitive political parties, these innovations and their healthy effects seem to have reached their limits today. While the integrative functions of the party system have partly been, displaced by alternative forms of political participation, the Keynesian welfare state has come under attack by virtue of some of its less desirable side effects and its failure to correct some of the ills of an economic environment that has radically changed, compared to the conditions that prevailed prior to the mid-seventies. Let us look at some of the reasons why there are very few people left, be it in academia or politics, on the Left or the Right, who believe that the Keynesian welfare state continues to be a viable peace formula for democratic capitalism.

My thesis, in brief, is this: while the Keynesian welfare state is an excellent and uniquely effective device to manage and control some socio-economic and political problems of advanced capitalist societies, it does not solve all those problems. And the problems that can be successfully solved through the institutional means of the welfare state no longer constitute the most dominant and pressing ones. Moreover, this shift of the socio-economic problematic is an unintended consequence of the operation of the Keynesian welfare state itself. The two types of problems to which I refer are the production/exploitation problem and the effective demand/realisation problem. Between the two, there exists a trade-off: the more effectively one of the two is solved, the more dominant and pressing the other one becomes. The Keynesian welfare state has indeed been able to solve, to a remarkable extent, the problem of macroeconomic demand stabilisation. But, at the same time, it has also interfered with the ability of the capitalist economy to adapt to the production/exploitation problem as it emerged ever more urgently since the mid-seventies. The Keynesian welfare state, it might be argued, has operated on the basis of the false theory that the problems it is able to deal with are the only problems of the capitalist political economy, or at least the permanently dominant ones. This erroneous confidence is now in the politically and economically painful process of being falsified and corrected

To the extent that the demand problem is being solved, the supply problem becomes wide open. The economic situation has changed in a way that lends strong support to conservative and neo-*laissez-faire* economic theory. Far from stimulating production any longer, the governmental practice of deficit spending in order to combat unemployment contributes to even higher rates of unemployment. For this practice drives up interest rates and makes money capital scarce and costly. Also (and possibly even worse), the welfare state amounts to a partial disincentive to work. Its compulsory insurance schemes and legal entitlements do provide such a strong institutional protection to the material interest of wage workers that labour becomes less prepared and/or can be less easily forced to adjust to the contingencies of structural, technological, locational, vocational and other changes of the economy. Not only are wages 'sticky' and 'downwardly inflexible', but, in addition, the provisions of the welfare state have partly 'decommodified' the interests of workers, replacing 'status' for 'contract', or 'citizen rights' for 'property rights'. This change of industrial relations that the Keynesian welfare state has brought about has not only helped to increase and stabilise effective demand (as it was intended to), but it also has made employment more costly and more rigid. Again, the central problem on the labour market is the supply problem - how to hire and fire the right people at the right place with the right skills and, most importantly, with the right motivation and the right wage demands. Concerning this problem, the welfare state is, in my view to a large extent rightly, seen by business not to be part of the solution, but part of the problem.

Quite analogous difficulties are caused by the Keynesian welfare state (and the reformist policies to which it has given rise) in respect to the third supply category, or 'factor of production', namely nature. In many countries, regulatory policies concerning raw materials, industrial processes and products have been legislated in the sixties and seventies and today these are felt to severely limit and constrain the capitalist process of 'creative destruction'. In some countries at least, powerful political coalitions have emerged outside and sometimes even inside the political party system and these are inspired (by no means exclusively in the case of nuclear energy) by the view that the destructiveness of capitalist production today far surpasses its creativeness, and that therefore use value criteria of productive activity must win the upper hand over exchange value criteria. The obstacles to technical change that derive from these kinds of political motives and concerns (as well as from the concern for work humanisation) are often seen as a further inhibition to economic growth and exacerbate a situation that is already made difficult by the various waves of oil price hikes that were decreed by the OPEC cartel.

It does not concern us whether such charges, which today are ever more frequently directed against the Keynesian welfare state, are entirely 'true', or, in addition, partly the result of paranoic exaggerations or a conscious tactical misrepresentation of reality on the part of capital and its political organisations. For what applies in this context is a special version of a law known to sociologists as the 'Thomas-theorem': what is real in the minds and perceptions of people will be real in its consequences. The structural power position of the owners and managers and associational representatives of capital in a capitalist society is exactly their power to define reality in a highly consequential way, so that what is perceived as 'real' by them is likely to have very real impacts for other classes and political actors.

Without entering too far into the professional realm of the economist, let me suggest two aspects of what I consider a potentially useful (if partial) interpretation of this change. One is the idea, already alluded to, that the Keynesian welfare state is a 'victim of its success', the side-effects of its successful practice of solving one type of macro-economic problem has led to the emergence of an entirely different problematic which is beyond the steering capacity of the Keynesian welfare state. The familiar arguments that favour and demand a shift of economic and social policy making toward what has been baptised 'supply-side economics' are these: the nonproductive public sector has become an intolerable burden upon the private sector, leading to a chronic shortage of investment capital; the work ethic is in the process of being undermined, and the independent middle class is economically suffocated by high rates of taxation and inflation.

The other set of arguments maintains that, even in the absence of those economic side effects, the political paradigm of the Keynesian welfare state presently is in the process of definitive exhaustion for inherent reasons. The relevant arguments, in brief, are two. Firstly, state intervention works only as long as it is not expected by economic actors to be applied as a matter of routine, and therefore does not enter their rational calculations. As soon as this happens, however, investors will postpone investment because they can be reasonably sure that the state, if only they wait long enough, will intervene by special tax exemptions, depreciation allowances or demand measures. The spread of such expectations is fatal to Keynesianism, for, to the extent that it enters the calculations of economic actors, strategic behaviour will increase the problem load to which the state must respond. This pathology of expectations, of course, is itself known to (and expected by) actors in the state apparatus. It forces them to react either by acceding to ever higher doses of intervention or, failing that possibility for fiscal reasons, by giving up the interventionist practice that breeds those very problems that it was supposed to solve. This would lead us to conclude that state intervention is effective only to the extent that it occurs as a 'surprise' and exception, rather than being routinised.

A second inherent weakness of the Keynesian welfare state resides in the limits of the legal-bureaucratic, monetarised and professional mode of intervention. These limits become particularly clear in the areas of personal services, or 'people processing organisations', such as schools, hospitals, universities, prisons and social work agencies. Again, the mode of intervention generates the problems with which it is supposed to deal. The explanatation of this paradox is well known: the clients' capacity for self-help, and, more generally, the system of knowledge and meanings generating such capacity, are subverted by the mode of intervention. The suppliers of such services, especially professionals and higher level bureaucrats (which are in neo-conservative circles referred to as the 'new class') take a material interest in the persistence (rather than the solution) and in the continuous expansion and redefinition of the problems with which they are supposed to deal.

Thus, for reasons that have to do both with its external economic effects and the paradoxes of its internal mode of operation, the Keynesian welfare state seems to have exhausted its potential and viability to a large extent. Moreover, this exhaustion is unlikely to turn out to be a conjunctural phenomenon that disappears with the next boom of economic growth. For this boom itself is far from certain. Why is this so? Firstly, because it cannot be expected to occur as the spontaneous result of market forces and the dynamics of technological innovation. Secondly, it apparently cannot be generated and manipulated either by the traditional tools of Keynesianism or by its 'monetarist' counterpart. Thirdly, even to the extent that it does occur either as an effect of spontaneous forces or state intervention, the question is whether it will be considered desirable and worthwhile in terms of the side-effects it inevitably will have for the quality of life in general and the ecology in particular. This question of the desirability of continued economic growth is also accentuated by what Fred Hirsch (13) has called the 'social limits to growth' and by which he means the decreasing desirability and 'satisficing potential' of industrial output, the use-value of which declines in proportion to the number of people who consume it.

CONCLUSION

We have seen that the two institutional mechanisms on which the compatibility of the private economy and political mass participation rests, namely the mechanism of competitive party democracy and the paradigm of the Keynesian welfare state, have come under stress and strains, the order of magnitude of which is unprecedented in the post-war era. The political and the economic variants of the interclass accord that had gradually developed in all advanced capitalist states since the First World War and that had helped to make capitalism and democracy compatible are clearly disintegrating under the impact of the developments and paradoxes that I have discussed. Does that mean that we are back in a situation that supports the convergent views of Marx and Mill concerning the antagonism of political mass participation and (economic) freedom? Yes and no. I think yes, because we have numerous reasons to expect an increase of institutionally unmediated social and political conflict, the expression of which is not channelled through parties or other devices of representation, and the sources of which are no longer dried up by effective social and economic policies of the state. But I also think no, because there are strict limits to the analogy between the dynamics of 'late' and 'early' capitalism. One important aspect of these limits is that the forces involved in such conflicts are extremely heterogenous, both concerning their causes and their socioeconomic composition. This pattern is remarkably different from a 'class conflict' situation which involves few and highly inclusive collective actors who are defined by the two sides of the labour market. But, in spite of the highly fragmented nature of modern political conflict, its outcomes may well involve fundamental changes of either the economic or the political sphere of society, - changes that have, for a limited period of time, been inconceivable under the unchallenged reign of competitive party democracy and the Keynesian welfare state.

NOTES

1.   This argument is considered in B. Jessop, 'Capitalism and Democracy: The Best Possible Political Shell'. in G. Littlejohn *et al* (eds) Power and the State (Croom Helm, London, 1978), pp. 10-51; also see B. Hindess, 'Parliamentary Democracy and Socialist Politics', in M. Prior (ed.) The Popular and The Political: Essays on Socialism in the 1980s (Routledge and Kegan Paul, London, 1981) pp. 29-44.
2.   Lenin argued that a democratic republic provided the best 'political shell' for capitalism. Further he maintained that once this 'shell' was in existence no change in personnel, institutions or parties would crack it. V.I. Lenin, 'The State and Revolution', in Collected Works, vol. 25, (Foreign Languages Publishing House, Moscow, 1947). Bearing in mind this Leninist tradition of thinking of the state as a mere reflection of socioeconomic power structures, and the corresponding theorem of the withering away of the state after the revolution, questions of whether or not there is anything like a 'marxist theory of the state' conceptually equipped to grasp the 'specificity of the political' have been raised, by, among others, Norbeto Bobbio, 'Marxism and

Socialism', Telos, 39, 1979 pp. 191-200.

3. S.M. Lipset, Political Man, (Doubleday, New York, 1962).

4. A.O. Hirschman, Exit, Voice and Loyalty, (Harvard University Press, Cambridge, 1972).

5. M. Weber, Economy and Society (Bedminster Press, New York, 1968).

6. R. Luxemburg, Social Reform or Revolution, (Routledge and Kegan Paul, London, 1966). .

7. R. Michels, Political Parties: A Sociological Study of the Oligarchical Tendencies of Modern Democracy (Free Press, New York, 1962).

8. C.B. Macpherson, Democratic Theory: Essays in Retrieval (Clarendon Press, Oxford, 1973), . p. 69.

9. P. Bachrach and M.S. Baratz, 'Two Faces of Power', American Political Science Review 1962, 56, pp. 947-52.

10. One may consult, for example P. Schmitter and G. Lehmbruch (eds.), Trends Toward Corporatist Intermediation (Sage, London, 1978) which contains an important array of recent and comparative statements on 'corporatism', as well as O. Newman, The Challenge of Corporatism (Macmillan, London, 1981), and R. J. Harrison, Pluralism and Corporatism: The Political Evolution of Modern Democracies (Allen and Unwin, London, 1980).

11. Jessop, 'Capitalism and Democracy', p. 41.

12. I am grateful to Sam Bowles for this characterisation.

13. F. Hirsch, The Social Limits to Growth (Routledge and Kegan Paul, London, 1976).

Chapter Three

THE HISTORICAL FOUNDATIONS OF CLASS STRUGGLE IN LATE
CAPITALIST LIBERAL DEMOCRACIES (1)

Nixon Apple

In her contribution to the 1977 Michal Kalecki
Memorial Lectures, Joan Robinson correctly
identified 'the most famous of all Kalecki's
insights into the economics of capitalism' as his
analysis of business opposition to full employment
and the socio-economic dynamics of what Kalecki
called 'full employment capitalism' (2). In the
final passage of his 1943 article 'Political Aspects
of Full Employment' Kalecki argued:

> 'Full employment capitalism' will have of course
> to develop new social and political institutions
> which will reflect the increased power of the
> working class. If capitalism can adjust itself
> to full employment a fundamental reform will
> have been incorporated in it. If not it will
> show itself an outmoded system which must be
> scrapped... The fight of the progressive forces
> for full employment is at the same time a way of
> preventing the recurrence of fascism (3).

Having seen the rise and fall of 'full employment
capitalism' we can and should ask, what new social
and political institutions did emerge to reflect the
enhanced power of the working class in the fully
employed labour market, and what part did they play
in the collapse of full employment? These are
historical questions. Answering them requires a
description of the struggles to secure full
employment and an explanation of the manner in which
these new institutions, particularly those affecting
the labour market, developed in the way they did.
These historical questions must be approached
comparatively because particular national traditions
and patterns of development express themselves in
dissimilar conjunctural forms and produce different

types of class organisation and struggle. Such differences should be acknowledged by specifying the different forms of struggles to secure full employment that occurred in a number of countries and the various institutional linkages that evolved as a result of such differences. Different patterns of class mobilisation must be identified and related to variations in the balance of class forces, for class conflict was the key variable in deciding when, how and for how long, full employment was achieved.

In this essay an analysis is given of the struggles for full employment that occurred in western capitalist countries in the 1945-51 period. I will argue that the commitment to full employment was not a decisive working class victory of the 1940s. In virtually all countries the full employment commitment was watered down or defeated and the labour movement unable to sustain the strategy and organisation necessary to enforce permanent full employment. In a number of countries full employment was only secured during the late 1950s or early 1960s. In general terms 'full employment capitalism' only lasted from 1955 to 1965, primarily because the various roads to full employment capitalism were paved with a series of ideological and political defeats suffered by the labour movement in the 1945-51 period. These defeats weighed heavily on the working class by undermining the strength of its organisations and vitiating the benefits that otherwise would have been derived from full employment. Above all these defeats blocked the emergence of international and domestic institutions with the capacity to maintain full employment.

The chapter begins with post-war international monetary reconstruction, its effects on the balance of class forces and whether or not the new international monetary order was capable of supporting or even intended to support, full employment policies. Several different paths to full employment capitalism are then distinguished in terms of the different patterns of class mobilisation that emerged in the 1945-51 period. Having focused on the experience of the US, UK, Australia, Canada, Italy, France, Germany and Japan the paper concludes with an analysis of the long term consequences of the defeats suffered by the labour movement in the reconstruction period and how these defeats were averted in Sweden, resulting not only in the maintenance of full employment today, but also in a diverging pattern of class mobilisation.

INTERNATIONAL MONETARY RECONSTRUCTION 1940-51

During the 1940-51 period the basic sets of relations involving Western imperialism, the USSR and capital, labour and the state were reconstructed (4). The reconstitution of these basic sets of relations was mainly shaped by the changes that occurred in the institutional policies, rules and relations of class and state power underlying the international monetary system. While a number of factors contributed to these changes, the pattern of international monetary reconstruction was primarily affected by the relative power and conflicting objectives of British and American imperialism

In a number of respects international monetary reconstruction and Anglo-American rivalry reflected a clash between two different forms of capital accumulation. British superiority had rested on steam, the coal, textiles, shipbuilding, railroad industries, free trade, the gold standard and foreign portfolio investment. Upon this foundation Britain became the largest importer of food and raw materials, the major exporter of capital and manufactured goods, as well as the leading world power ruling over an empire which in 1914 encompassed an area of over 13 million square miles with a population of 400 million. With the world's capital and commodity markets centred in London and with the British merchant fleet carrying the bulk of world trade, international prices came to be expressed in sterling and foreigners increased their holdings of sterling to meet their obligations. Since Britain met her obligations in gold on demand, many observers saw the sterling based gold standard as an automatic stabiliser of the production, circulation and exchange of capital and commodities on a world scale.

The transition from competitive to monopoly capitalism (1890-1935) eroded the relations of class and state power that supported the sterling-based gold standard and British domination. The resulting fragmentation of power relations in the international monetary system led to its splitting into sterling, franc and dollar zones during the 1930s. The ascendence of American political and economic power during this period was based on the second technological revolution (auto, chemical, electrical manufacturing and engineering). Unlike the British pattern of foreign portfolio investment within a cohesive empire and the separation of banks and industry in the domestic economy, the American pattern of development was marked by the integration of banks and industry combined in an aggressive form of foreign expansion through foreign direct investment. While Britain had maintained an import surplus in a relatively open world economy (imports rising to 25% of GNP in late nineteenth century Britain), the United States maintained an export surplus during the inter-war years as well as achieving a high degree of self-sufficiency (imports rarely accounting for more than 4% of GNP) (5).

These differences between Britain and the United States made a vital contribution to the conflicts which arose out of the 1939-45 war economy. During the war the United States supplied Europe and the British Empire with an increasing share of exports so that the value of American exports during the war had increased from 3 to 15 billion dollars (6). This raised the question of whether Britain or the US would supply these markets in the post-war period, which had far reaching implications for their domestic levels of employment and income. This issue lay at the centre of the 1941-42 British-US negotiations on lend-lease arrangements and the conflicts over access to markets and raw materials during the drafting of Article 4 of the Atlantic Charter and Article 7 of the Mutual Aid Agreement. Moreover, the war economy had transformed Britain and the US into the major debtor and creditor nations respectively. Thus strongly opposed views emerged on how credit should be provided and domestic stabilisation policy regulated on an international basis.

A number of conflicting domestic pressures shaped the British position on these matters. For Empire Leaguers such as Beaverbrook and Amery, international monetary reconstruction involved seeking the ever elusive if not utopian Victorian restoration through protection of Empire and the imperial preference system. This was also a concern of British industrialists given the challenge of an expansive American capitalism, and the fact that in 1944 British exports were only a third of their pre-war level. It also figured in the strategy of London bankers who, while rarely heeding the requirements of domestic industry, clearly appreciated the link between London, the Empire, sterling and profits. This link was threatened by New York and the dollar system American bankers were advocating. For the governing British Labour Party, the problem of reconstruction presented itself in terms of arriving at a socialist solution to Empire and a domestic policy consistent with planning full employment and the welfare state (7). These perspectives provided the agenda for the Bretton Woods talks, especially Keynes' formula for creating international liquidity and balance of payment stability. The Clearing Union Plan that Keynes developed was considerably influenced by what he saw as three fundamental problems:

> First he placed the greatest importance on Britain's pursuing full employment policies after the war, and he opposed any international monetary order that would interfere with this goal. Second he recognised that the war had greatly reduced Britain's international investments and expanded her debts so that Britain would no longer be able to rely on investment earnings to finance her extensive imports of food and raw materials... This would make Britain dependent on international credit until exports could be expanded and it gave Britain an interest in international trade liberalisation. Finally, Keynes, like many others abroad, was concerned that the US economy would be allowed to slip back into depression or that the United States would again behave irresponsibly in its international transactions. He wanted to create a monetary order that was not dependent on the vagaries of American politics (8).

Keynes sought to solve these problems through regulatory bodies that would permit virtually unconditional expansion of international liquidity while maintaining exchange-rate stability. His plan meant that deflationary policies hindering domestic expansion and undermining effective demand would not be forced on deficit countries. But at Bretton Woods and subsequent negotiations US negotiators rejected Keynes' Clearing Union Plan. Access to IMF funds was severely restricted and no mechanisms created to force surplus countries to adjust their payments by domestic economic expansion. Such amendments extended to the International Bank for Reconstruction and Development which was given a more limited role dependent on the American capital market and the judgement of conservative bankers. With these developments, the spectre of instability and recurring unemployment that Keynes and many others had feared began to emerge in the form of a massive American trade surplus in the late 1940s. This American export surplus flourished during an acute dollar shortage, restricted access to liquidity, and the refusal of the United States to adjust its surplus position. Such were the obstacles to the employment policies of deficit countries (9).

The American export surplus represented a new relationship between the United States and the OEEC. Whereas in the United States industrial production had increased 65% between 1938 and 1947, it had fallen by 19% over the same period in Europe. With supply shortages, the separation of Eastern and Western European markets, and the deterioration of the consolidated European external balance (mainly because overseas income from investments no longer covered Europe's trade deficit), Europe depended on the US for exports and credit. While 24% of Europe's imports had come from the US in 1938, this quota had risen to 44% by 1947. During the same period America's share of European exports declined from 16% to 14%. While the European consolidated deficit deteriorated, the American export surplus grew, reaching 11.5 billion dollars in 1947, which represented a surplus of exports over imports of 58.1% (10).

Within the United States policy makers felt that the maintenance of this export surplus for as long as twenty years, would resolve the dilemma of achieving full employment in the US (11). But American proposals for the IMF and World Bank, persistent opposition to writing a commitment to full employment in the founding Charter of the United Nations and the Charter of the International Trade Organisation showed that the US was much less concerned than the British with the employment aspects of world trade, monetary adjustment and liquidity creation (12). With 60% of the world's gold stock, an economic infrastructure not ravaged by the war, and massive holdings of wealth and war debt credits, the US was the only country with a capital market adequate for international monetary reconstruction. But it also had a Congress still isolationist in outlook, dominated by the tariff lobby, and increasingly hostile to shouldering what it saw as the main burden of international reconstruction. Under these circumstances the American strategy for securing and maintaining an export surplus became the overriding factor in the conflict between domestic and international political pressures.

This strategy had been developing during the early 1940s with the efforts of the American State Department to dismantle Britain's imperial preference system by tying American loans to Britain's commitment to sterling convertibility. Unless sterling was convertible into dollars and sterling countries' foreign exchange earnings available for current transactions elsewhere, there was little chance that American exports could continue or increase their penetration of the British Empire. This commercial strategy received broad support from American industrialists and also enabled the State Department to secure the co-operation of American bankers whose opposition to a government commitment to full employment complemented their fear of IMF control over international liquidity. The strategy for American banking capital was developed by John Williams, Vice President of the New York Federal Reserve Bank in his 'key currency plan'. As F.L. Block has summarised it:

> At base, Williams' plan was a call for the restoration of the gold standard. It reflected the interests of the American international bankers, who opposed the IMF... They preferred the discipline imposed by the gold standard and they feared the access to the fund's resources would destroy that discipline forever... They feared that extensive national or international governmental intervention would eliminate the role that private international bankers had historically played... To deal with this problem, State Department planners devised a strategy that was ingenious in its simplicity. They would simply forget that Bretton Woods had ever occurred and pursue John Williams' key currency plan as though nothing else had happened. This meant offering Britain a substantial loan in exchange for British co-operation in restoring an open world economy (13).

By 1947 this strategy of opening the world economy on a multi-lateral rather than bilateral basis, securing an American export surplus, and by-passing the IMF and UN in favour of unilateral diplomacy had already gone a long way. But the limited recovery that was occurring within Europe from mid-1946 'was attained within a framework of national economic restrictions and bilateral payment treaties which had tripled in a year's time to over two hundred in 1947' (14). Such a recovery threatened the American export surplus by placing obstacles on both further dollar imports as well as hindering the liberalisation necessary for an open international economy. The problems of financing the export surplus also remained. Given the strength of the tariff lobby in Congress which virtually precluded a tariff trade-off acceptable to Europe, and Congress' reluctance to grant reconstruction funds, American strategy proceeded by implementing the Truman Doctrine and the Marshall Plan both based on two long-term assumptions.

According to the first assumption America could only maintain its export surplus if European dollar shortages were reduced by massive US loans. US policy makers feared that unless this was done the vision of an export surplus and an open international economy would be lost, as Europe resorted to even more extensive exchange controls, import restrictions or bilateral trade agreements through state trading agencies. It was also assumed that Britain's failure to resolve matters in Turkey or to reinforce fascism in Greece would require greater American intervention to incorporate Western Europe into an American bloc united against the Soviet bloc emerging in Eastern Europe. The flow of American dollars to Europe through the Marshall programme could open up export and investment outlets and block the advance of the Soviet Union. The ideological 'communist menace' device could secure congressional appropriations, thus pre-empting the European resort to international agencies (15).

American policy makers wanted to use unilateral diplomacy to by-pass international agencies, a choice that sealed the fate of the IMF. The United States was successful in blocking access to the fund and tightening up its rules so that drawings upon the fund did not go above the 1947 levels until 1956. In this way no precedents were established that could interfere with the deflationary discipline American bankers had in mind. The same strategy was used to force the IMF's rejection in 1949 of the United Nations Economic and Social Committee's proposals aimed at opening up world trade and maintaining full employment proposals that were not compatible with the free-trade multi-lateral trading system that the United States was developing (16). After the events in Czechoslovakia in February 1948 and Mao's victory in 1949, the Marshall Plan provided the means and the pretext for reintegrating Germany into the Western economic and military bloc.

By late 1948 and early 1949 however, the United States had entered a recession which saw unemployment in the US rise to a peak of 7.6%. The US recession and another crisis of the pound sterling forced American planners to search for the means to further liberalisation of the international capitalist economy. Their response was to combine the devaluation of other major world currencies against the dollar with support for European economic integration and a massive build-up of military production (17). Together these various strands of American strategy accelerated both trade liberalisation and the movement towards unfettered short, and long-term capital flows.

Central to this strategy was the devaluation of European and other currencies in 1949, which was achieved by forcing a British devaluation of the pound that other countries had to follow. But the devaluations stimulated something that continues to be a major destabilising factor in the international monetary system, short-term capital flows. In 1949, speculation over an impending devaluation led to a massive outflow of short-term funds from major European countries into Switzerland and the United States. It is estimated that the lack of controls on short term capital flows in this period allowed a net capital outflow from Europe that exceeded the inflow of funds from the Marshall Plan (see fn. 18).

This development was hardly a good beginning for what Keynes had termed 'the euthanasia of the rentier'. Nor was it a good beginning for general economic stability. After the devaluations the capitalist world's economies became export economies operating with fixed exchange-rates. Less scope remained for influencing the balance of payments or the creation of liquidity now dependent on the export of American dollars through the Marshall Plan, and after 1950, by American balance of payment deficits deriving from enormous military expenditures and foreign direct investment. Thereafter 'an export lobby of increasing importance came into existence in all European countries which prevented meaningful adjustments of European currencies until 1971' (18).

Currency convertibility, and greater multi-lateral trade liberalisation and a larger flow of

long term capital had to wait until the late
1950s. During the early fifties dollar shortages
and rises in the international price level in the
wake of the Korean war boom, forced western
countries to retain quantitative restrictions on
international transactions. Nevertheless the preconditions for liberalisation had been achieved in
the steps taken to consolidate the United States'
leadership in the western bloc. And a central part
of this process of reconstituting the international
balance of power were the struggles for
reconstituting the balance of authority and
domination within domestic labour markets.

For in a capitalist society it is by way of the
labour market that labour power and capital are
brought together.

> This market is the central structure of the
> capitalist system, the pivot on which the
> dynamic of the system turns. By 'labour market'
> we mean more than simply the employment bureaus,
> the pick up at the gates of the dock and the
> direct bargaining over the terms of the sale,
> the wages and the conditions to be gained. We
> mean the whole complex of institutions and
> arrangements that make labour power a commodity,
> and keep it a commodity - the fact of the
> ownership of the product by the capitalist, the
> dependence of the workers on wage income, and
> the possibility of the accumulation of capital
> out of the labour process.
> This structuring of production relations did not
> fall from the sky; it was produced historically
> by a long and often violent process (19).

Within this 'long and often violent process' there
is forged the capacity of the working class to
negotiate, strike, and organise its industrial
power. But in certain situations this process is
more intensively and extensively politicised. The
reconstruction of the social relationships of the
labour market from 1940 to 1951 took place in a
series of such situations thanks to the overriding
importance of a basic working class demand. It was
the demand for full employment to defend and
strengthen the organisations, solidarity, living and
working conditions of working class men and women.
It was a demand that was rooted within a cumulative
experience of social injustice and powerlessness
during the depression. The social and political
expression of this class experience generated

various forms of working class mobilisation to remove and democratise capitalism through a full employment economy. Such a demand could not be met in the labour market because it was a demand for social transformation. Ultimately it was fought out at the political level. But the manner in which full employment and social reconstruction was secured had tragic consequences for the solidarity of the working class because the various roads to what became 'full employment capitalism' were paved with a series of ideological and political defeats of the labour movement. And out of these defeats there emerged a reconsolidated bourgeois order both internationally and domestically, which reimposed the relations of domination and subordination of a capitalist labour market.

An examination of the different roads to full employment reveal their drastic implications for the working class' ability to mobilise.

DEBATES AND STRUGGLES FOR FULL EMPLOYMENT IN THE US AND UK 1940 TO 1951

The conflicts between Britain and the United States during the 1940-51 period resulted in the reconstitution of an international monetary system that was not supportive of the working class demand for full employment. Instead, American concern for price stability, an export surplus, liberalisation and rolling back the 'Soviet menace', led to the restoration of the disciplinary logic of deflation. This logic was expressed in the rules governing the creation of international liquidity and domestic adjustment by countries with balance of payment deficits. But the struggles between American and British planners of international monetary reconstruction reflected the ideologies and forms of political opposition that emerged within the United States and Britain, particularly domestic debates on full employment. The securing of a commitment to full employment in Britain, and its defeat in the United States, bore heavily upon the policies for restoring an international capitalist economy.

During the 1940s, the post-war debate on the commitment to full employment in Britain was focused on the work of the architect of British welfare policy, William Beveridge. While his contribution was well known it was not always welcomed by the British press, business, treasury officials or the still largely pre-Keynesian academic community (20).

The Treasury in particular feared the implications of Beveridge's 'more jobs than people' definition of full employment. It removed all the civil servants who had been assisting Beveridge's inquiry into full employment, so that a much milder commitment to full employment could appear as a coalition government White Paper before Beveridge's work was published (21). And it was not Beveridge's work but this milder, more ambiguous White Paper that committed the government to maintaining a 'high and stable level of employment'. This modest aim became the only reference to full employment in the Conservative Party's 1945 election Manifesto (22).

The British Labour Party, on the other hand, made a more extensive examination of full employment policy in documents such as 'Full Employment and Financial Policy' (1944), and the 1944 executive resolution to the party conference, 'Economic Controls, Public Ownership and Full Employment', which emphasised:

> Full employment ... can only be secured within a planned economy ... and above all by the transfer to the state of power to direct the policy of our main industries, services and financial institutions (23).

The trade union movement promoted public control as the precondition to full employment. It held that the fully employed society 'can only be adequately fulfilled within a system of public control' where 'the extension of public control must mean an increasing democratisation of economic life' (24).

This broader conception of full employment in the planned welfare state formed the core of the radical TUC 'Interim Report on Post-War Reconstruction' and the 1945 Labour Party election manifesto, 'Let us Face the Future', around which the working class mobilised in electing the first majority labour government. Working class mobilisation to secure full employment expressed strong opposition to returning to the conditions of the inter-war period when the annual rate of unemployment after 1920 never fell below 10% until after rearmament. Working class men and women bitterly remembered what had happened in the depression after World War One when sections of the governing coalition, employers and the treasury had united to dismantle controls and thwarted the reconstruction plans and promises of the Ministry of Labour (25). Securing the commitment to full employment in this new period of reconstruction was the result of working class efforts which transformed the balance of class forces in British society.

The Labour Party's plan to maintain full employment appeared more radical than Beveridge's proposals. Although the 1942 Beveridge Report emphasised that 'the plan for social security is first and foremost a method of income redistribution...' Beveridge's letters in the early 1940s suggest that he had already adopted a view that would link wage restraint and a system of comprehensive arbitration procedures to a model of 'socialism in one class' (26). This scheme suggested that a redistribution of income within the working class could abolish poverty while retaining capitalist relations of production and distribution virtually unchanged. Such a view naturally led Beveridge to place the responsibility for the maintenance of full employment on the action of trade union leaders who would be required to exercise wage restraint to secure price stability.

> So long as freedom of collective bargaining is maintained, the primary responsibility of preventing a full employment policy from coming to grief in a vicious spiral of wages and prices, will rest on those who conduct the bargaining on behalf of labour. The more explicitly that responsibility is stated - the greater can be the confidence that it will be accepted (20).

This was Beveridge's wage restraint - social control theory of 'full employment capitalism' which suggested that, 'if trade unions under full employment press wage claims unreasonably maintenance of a stable price level will become impossible; wage determination will perforce become a function of the state' (28). For a number of British economists the solution to this dilemma lay in redefining full employment. This was the position adopted by Jewkes in his famous right-wing polemic Ordeal by Planning (1948) which maintained that 'unemployment of 5 or 6 per cent should not be a matter of concern'. Even within the Labour government ambivalence existed on this point. The Chancellor of the Exchequor, Stafford Cripps, argued in the 1948 Economic Survey that the problem of labour mobility under full employment would have to be resolved by increasing the unemployment rate by

50% (29). Seldom was the connection between ruling class power, the investment function and full employment addressed as explicitly as in the following passage from the Fabian socialist, Thomas Balogh written during the economic crisis of the late 1940s:

> The resistance of the entrepreneurial classes to state measures calculated to maintain full employment is based on their correct intuition that such measures while they safeguard their short run profits, would in fact, undermine their ultimate source of power, the power to decide the level of business activity and thus their respective bargaining power as a class... Once the power of inflicting slumps is removed, the entrepreneurial classes lose their role as absolute rulers (30).

Faced with the forced convertibility of sterling in 1947 and the devaluation of the pound in 1949, the British Labour Party increasingly turned to Beveridge's wage restraint-social control theory of 'full employment capitalism'. It emerged in Labour's 1948-50 incomes policy which relied on the loyalty of the trade union leadership to the Labour Party. But such loyalty was granted at the expense of rank and file power in a fully employed labour market: 'union members were thus faced with a situation in which their executives were debarred by law from calling a strike while they were being constantly exhorted to exercise restraint and at the same time to help employers increase their output' (31). It was not government control of capital formation but trade union compliance with government objectives in wage formation that the Labour government secured. And throughout this period the Labour government watered down its commitment to planned full employment. It refused to return to the 1934 policy on nationalisation of the banks (32) or to implement plans for more extensive public control of business activity. Instead, the party increasingly adopted the posture of a national integrative rather than class-based party. Its subservience to the 'national interest' and an integrative ideology demobilised the working class on critical occasions (33).

Although the welfare state had been secured, and Britain, along with Norway and Sweden, were the only countries the United Nations regarded as having achieved 'stable full employment' by 1950, (34) the

British labour movement in reality had suffered a series of ideological and political setbacks. The radical conception of democratising the full-employment society had been urged in Labour's 1945 election manifesto on the basis that:

> The great inter-war slumps were not acts of God or of blind forces. They were the sure and certain results of the concentration of too much economic power in the hands of too few men... The price of so called economic freedom for the few is too high... (35).

But by 1947 the government's economic survey had amended the goal of democratising the full employment society:

> Under democracy, the execution of the economic plan must be much more a matter for co-operation between the government, industry and the people, than of rigid application by the state of controls and compulsion (36).

It was this type of ideological confusion about the nature of class and state power that provided the conservatives with the basis for launching a bourgeois counter offensive.

The 1945 electoral defeat had shaken the conservatives who saw that they faced an enormous legitimation problem over the issue of full employment. As R.A. Butler, Chairman of the Conservatives Advisory Committee on Policy and Political Education, expressed it:

> ... The conservative predicament (was) our need to convince a broad spectrum of the electorate ... that we had an alternative policy to socialism which ... would release and reward enterprise and initiative without abandoning social justice or reverting to mass unemployment... (thus) our first purpose was to counter the charge ... that full employment and the welfare state were not safe in our hands (37).

This problem of legitimation led to the formation of the Tories 1947 Policy Paper, 'The Industrial Charter' which Harold Macmillan claimed 'proved our determination to maintain full employment' (38). And in the 1950 election manifesto the Tories for the first time declared that 'we regard the maintenance of full employment as the first aim of a conservative government' (39).   In 1950-51, the Tories mobilised around the theme of 'set the people free' which argued that full employment had only been achieved because of American aid, but would be lost if reckless socialist controls and spending were not stopped (40).   While Labour's campaign linked the Tories to mass unemployment, the initiative had been lost.

The Tories only returned to power in 1951 after Labour's wage-restraint incomes policy broke down, and after the debate on planning and freedom had destroyed Labour's capacity to promote a socialist solution for achieving full employment.   This failure enabled the Tories to project their conception of an unequal hierarchical full employment society based on the logic of order, domination and the free market.   As Labour lost ground in the ideological struggle, the ground was prepared for an even closer alliance between capital and the Conservative Party.   As Jacques Leruez has argued in relation to the 1950-51 bourgeois offensive: 'The collusion between industry and the Conservative Party has never been more obvious. One could almost say that private industry fought the conservatives campaign for them' (41).   And so 'full-employment capitalism' was ushered into the 1950s, accompanied by the conservative rhetoric of 'a property-owning democracy'.   Thirteen years of uninterrupted Tory rule followed.

In the United States opposition to a state commitment to full employment was more broadly based and effective, resulting in the defeat and subsequent dismantling of Senator Murray's proposed Full Employment Bill (1945).   As Michal Kalecki had anticipated, American businessmen expressed their fears that full employment would undermine the discipline imposed by the reserve army of labour on the working class.   They also argued that it would improve labour's bargaining power (as well as ending the state's dependence on business confidence) by promoting a state guarantee of income and job creation (42).   With these themes in reconstruction policy to the fore a new right wing coalition of business leaders, fiscal conservatives, congressmen and civil servants emerged to oppose a government commitment to full employment

Included in this coalition were men such as Ira Mosher, President of the National Association of Manufacturers, who argued before the Senate Sub-committee that a full employment bill demonstrated groundless lack of faith in the dynamic of America's free-enterprise system, perpetuated class legislation on labour's behalf, and was based on unsound financial assumptions about deficit spending as a cure for unemployment. Sections of the academic community provided support for such views by redefining full employment as requiring an unemployment 'allowance of 5 or 6 per cent ... essential for flexibility and freedom' (43). However, the meaning of 'flexibility and freedom' was inevitably linked to the very nature of capitalism itself. For instance, the United States Chamber of Commerce stated that: 'Under a free voluntary society no one class or group is responsible for jobs. The job-making process depends on the maintenance of profit expectations and this in turn rests on a vast complex of forces and factors' (44).

More blatant examples of the 'class instinct' (as Kalecki termed it) that made capitalists oppose full employment were to be found in the 'Private Bulletin to Members' issued by the Ohio Chamber of Commerce which drew the connection between communism and a state commitment to full employment that 'would be the scaffold on which private enterprise could be dropped to its death...' (45). The reasons underlying the opposition of American bankers to a state commitment to full employment were bluntly expressed by William Kleitz, Vice President of Guaranty Trust Co. of New York:

> I oppose primarily the assumption by the federal government of the responsibility – practically a guarantee – of providing full employment because I feel that in order to make the programme effective, the government will step by step be led into a programme that will be the antithesis of private industry and a system of private enterprise ... leading toward an authoritarian form of government (46).

The eventual passage of the 1946 Employment Act was only secured through emasculating the content of the original bill. The phrase 'right to useful remunerative, regular and full-time employment' contained in the original Bill, was replaced by the phrase '... responsibility of the federal government ... to promote free competitive enterprise ... under which there will be afforded useful employment for those able, willing and seeking to work...'. Murray's proposed 'Full Employment Bill' became the

'Employment Act' and elsewhere in the text of the act the word 'full' as in 'full employment' was discarded. The words 'assure' and 'guarantee' that had originally expressed a strong government commitment were discarded as was the phrase 'investment and expenditure' which had originally expressed how the federal government was to sustain full employment. To secure the bill's passage in the senate, a number of limitations were placed on the action of the federal government so that it would be 'consistent with the needs and obligations of the federal government and other essential considerations of national policy'. As Senator Barkley admitted, all that the amended senate bill did was 'promised anyone needing a job the right to go out and look for one'. And even this bill was defeated by the conservative House Committee which led to another series of obfuscating amendments before the draft legislation became an Act of Congress (47).

In effect, as well as subsequent practice, what emerged was not a commitment to full employment, but rather an ambiguous statement of intent to consider possible means of promoting 'employment opportunities' through the state if and only if they proved consistent with the more 'essential' aspects of government policy. And these more 'essential' aspects of government policy were undergoing a fundamental transformation. The coalition of class forces that was uneasily held together in the New Deal Period was weakened by the defeats in the 1942 congressional elections, Roosevelt's death in April 1945, and the succession of the Truman administration.

A new coalition of class forces was forming around the issue of reducing the role of the state in general and a government commitment to full employment in particular. This also involved re-establishing market mechanisms by dismantling war controls, and support for the cold war strategy taking in the IMF, The Truman Doctrine and the Marshall Plan. With the weakening of the Treasury (where the strength of the Keynesian economic planners lay) and the re-affirmation of the state department's position of primacy in foreign policy (where the new coalition's power base lay), the consolidation of this new coalition was well under way (48).

But the defeat of the commitment to full employment in the United States must also be seen in terms of the changing patterns of class mobilisation, and the changing role of the state in the American political economy. During the progressive era, divisions within the ruling class generated several conflicting strategies for political mobilisation. In part this reflected opposing objectives of large scale industry and the banks, who sought federal-level government regulation, while small and medium-sized capital units tended to support the movement for a more decentralised form of state regulation (49). The movement towards political centralisation was also operative within the federal state system as seen in the 1920 Budget and Accounting Act which concentrated the responsibility for budget co-ordination within the executive, where the Bureau of the Budget assumed increasing importance particularly after the passage of the 1939 Reorganisation Act.

Accompanying this centralisation of economic policy co-ordination, was a shift in the form of state intervention. The New Deal strategy of rationalising separate branches of industry was gradually replaced by a more Keynesian aggregated approach to affecting economic fluctuations, focusing more directly on demand rather than supply for purposes of economic stabilisation (50). Given these developments, one can suggest that a congressional act committing the President and the Bureau to full employment through deficit spending would have seriously impaired monopoly capital's capacity to mobilise around the executive and the Bureau, which strategy was becoming more feasible. And such a constraint would also have seriously eroded the autonomy of the business groups that had emerged within the state apparatus during the New Deal period (51).

These changes in the relationship between patterns of class mobilisation and the institutionalisation of economic policy co-ordination were also affected by business objectives in relation to foreign commercial policy and domestic industrial militancy. These concerns were inseparable from the stagnationist tendencies that afflicted American capitalism during the 1930s. The severe depression which produced a 27% fall in GNP between 1929 and 1932 was not followed by a sustained recovery. The levels of capacity utilisation in industry which had averaged 94.5% during the 1920s had fallen to an average of 63.5% during the 1930s. Unemployment after a brief recovery during the first phase of the New Deal, had risen to 19% in 1938, 17.2% in 1939 and 14.6% in 1940, to fall again only with the stimulus of the war economy (52).

Such stagnationist tendencies had also been apparent in the last 25 years of the nineteenth century, when the depressions of 1873-78, 1882-85, and 1893-97 saw a violent outburst of class conflict culminating with the march of the unemployed on Washington in the 1890s. The class compromise that emerged in the 1886-1924 period when Samuel Gompers was President of the American Federation of Labour, involved securing labour's support for foreign expansion, the war effort and the attainment of an informal empire that would generate the export surplus required for domestic expansion and higher levels of employment (53).

In the 1940s, the concept of an export surplus once again played a central role in securing a domestic class compromise that linked the attainment of an export surplus to an aggressive expansion of American imperialism. This compromise was guided by a strategy for directing the form of European reconstruction, containing communism, defeating the left in Europe, re-integrating Germany and Japan within the international capitalist system and subordinating developing countries to the imperatives of American capitalism (54).

However, this was made possible by the historical failure of the American labour movement to translate intense and often violent class struggle at the level of the plant or region into nationally based mobilisations. This failure facilitated the defeat of the commitment to full employment as well as the implementation of the Taft Hartley Bill in 1947-48. This Bill eroded labour's mobilisation capacity by restricting the right to organise and empowering the state to limit the duration and spread of strikes. Thus the defeat of the commitment to full employment and the passage of Taft-Hartley re-initiated the long-term domestic solution to industrial militancy in the labour market. But this was in turn dependent on the maintenance of an export surplus. For many American capitalists this surplus was an alternative to state intervention in the economy to maintain full employment and alleviate stagnationist tendencies, thus ensuring the state's dependence on 'business confidence' and all that this notion entails for income distribution and the level of employment (55).

One can now explain the paradox between

business opposition to full employment and its occasional public support for it. This was a product of the diverse and often conflicting elements making up the new right-wing coalition, but also an indication that capital was prepared to accept full employment if, and only if, the ways and means of securing it were subject to the state's dependence on business confidence as well as labour's subordination to capital. And this made the achievement of an export surplus all the more important to the American ruling class, thereby focusing increasing attention upon the strategy for post war reconstruction of the international monetary order (56).

THE FULL EMPLOYMENT COMMITMENT IN AUSTRALIA AND CANADA

The struggles for full employment were also a central part of post war developments in Canada where the commitment to full employment and implementation of social security programmes was the bourgeoisie's concession to industrial militancy. The Liberals' fear of the co-operative Commonwealth Federation's growing electoral support, the mobilisation of the unemployed in demonstrations at the municipal level in the 1930s, as well as the strikes during the 1941-43 period of war control were all indications that the state could not avoid playing an increasing role in maintaining higher levels of employment (57). But as the 1945 White Paper on Employment and Income (which embraced the commitment to 'a high and stable level of employment and income') made clear:

> The Government will make every effort to create by all its policies favourable conditions within which the initiative, experience and resourcefulness of private business can contribute to the expansion of business and employment... As war time scarcities disappear, wartime controls will be relaxed and discontinued... The postwar employment problem is not to be solved by huge expenditures on public works... The problem of the transition is to maintain the level of employment while substituting private for a large part of public expenditure (58).

This private enterprise approach to full employment led writers during the 1940s to compare the

Class Struggle in Liberal Democracies

Canadian, Australian and British White Papers on
employment policy in the following manner: 'Canada
gives more prominence than either of the other two
White Papers to private enterprise... The Canadian
approach is that public investment must be
subservient to private expenditure' (59). And at
international conferences, the Canadian delegations
consistently supported the United States in arguing
against the inclusion of a commitment to full
employment in international agreements such as the
Founding Charter of the United Nations (60).
   The Australian case differed from the Canadian
experience. The Canadian working class, like its
American counterpart, lacked the mobilisation
capacity to enforce a more encompassing commitment
to full employment. Canadian working class
organisations were underdeveloped and fragmented
given the late arrival of a working class political
party (1932), the traditional ethnic and regional
cleavages that divided it, and the failure to secure
an alliance between the industrial and political
wings of the labour movement until the late 1950s
and early 1960s. The development of a broadly-based
and militant working class movement was also
inhibited by Canada's largely unindustrialised and
increasingly foreign dominated economy in which the
petite bourgeoisie in the form of the small rural
independent commodity producer remained the 'largest
subordinate class' in the period before World War II
(61). Australia on the other hand, had greater
levels of urban concentration and deeper traditions
of working class organisation (the Commonwealth
Labour Party was founded in 1902 and formed the
world's first National majority Labour government
elected in 1910) particularly at the local level.
Australia closely followed the British pattern both
in the level and form of working class organisation
and the labour party's holding office between 1943
and 1949.
   Despite these common factors, the struggle for
the commitment to full employment in Australia
differed from the British case in several ways.
Firstly, the Australian State had assumed powers
over prices, production and employment during the
war years, powers which were constitutionally vested
in the states rather than the Commonwealth except in
wartime. The Labor Party's attempt to mobilise
public opinion for a permanent transfer of these
powers to the central government (in a campaign
stressing the connection between these powers and
maintaining full employment) was defeated in the

Powers Referendum in 1944.   Following this defeat,
Labor's 1945 White Paper on Full Employment in
Australia went through a number of different
drafts.   Rather than attempting to compensate for
the defeat in the Powers Referendum, each draft
omitted more elements from the planning apparatus as
originally projected, including any reference to the
original scheme which had emphasised deficit
spending, and the creation of a planning office and
investment board (62).
     Both Labor's ideological confusion and business
opposition contributed to this result.   Leading
Labor Party planners such as H.C. Coombs had argued
with full employment, 'an employee does not fear
that if he loses his present job, he will be unable
to find another. Consequently the basic sanction of
labour discipline has been removed ... (and must) be
replaced by the self-discipline and co-operation in
common objectives' (63).
     This was one of many examples of the liberal
reformist tradition that had evolved within the
Labor Party as it came to adopt the stance of a
national integrative party at odds with its support
from and dependence upon, a working class base.
     In the struggles over how full employment was
to be achieved the party repeatedly returned to this
stance as in Labor Prime Minister Curtin's speech to
the businessmen at the Secondary Industries
Conference in 1945 where he emphasised that Labor
was committed to 'high' not 'full' employment, thus
making it easier for the bourgeois parties to make
the same commitment (64).   Australian businessmen
opposed full employment because they recoiled from
the measures necessary to achieve it.   Their
propaganda organ, the Institute of Public Affairs,
applauded the fact that 'the unattainable 'full
employment' was substituted in the White Paper by
the more modest but practical 'high employment'
because 'planned full employment is not possible
without power to direct everybody' (65).
Nevertheless, even the watered-down White Paper
which emerged was regarded as heresy by the
President of the New South Wales Chamber of Commerce
who stated that the White Paper should be renamed
'To Hell with Democracy' (66).
     Business spokesmen referred to the need to link
democracy to the 'competitive efficiency' of the
market economy. This link would be undermined by
'the equalising of incomes... which lead to all
sorts of ethical injustices and economic evils'
(67), but could be restored if the Labour Party

would 'assure private enterprise of the full co-operation of the government' (68). This opposition was channelled into a full-scale ruling class offensive when Labor passed legislation to nationalise the banks in order to promote full employment through control over the financing of investment. This mobilisation helped to defeat bank nationalisation and maintained its momentum through the 1949 election, ousting Labor and ushering in 23 uninterrupted years of conservative rule. In this respect the Australian working class achieved a formal commitment to full employment but without the controls over the level and form of investment necessary to guarantee it (69).

VARIATIONS IN THE 'DEMOCRACY FIRST' PATH TO FULL EMPLOYMENT CAPITALISM: THE CASE OF GERMANY, JAPAN, ITALY AND FRANCE

The Australian and British struggles for securing full employment had several common features: majority Labour governments in power, the bourgeoisie divided and facing legitimation problems, and major ruling class mobilisations in the late 1940s and early 1950s leading to the dismantling of war controls and ushering in a lengthy period of conservative rule. While full employment had been secured, the labour movement had suffered a series of ideological and political defeats which would later impair working class political mobilisation for two decades. The Canadian case came closer to that of the United States. The Canadian ruling class was not faced with a strong working class challenge and the war-time planning apparatus was thus more rapidly dismantled, the full-employment commitment explicitly relied more on the private sector, and unemployment in the fifties and sixties rose significantly higher than either Britain or Australia. But in Germany, Japan, Italy and France the labour movements' demand for full employment took second place to the struggle to gain the basic preconditions for working class mobilisation - the democratic right to organise. In these countries the class struggles of the post-war period revolved around rooting out the heritage of fascism. And in all four countries the ruling class turned to monetary deflation to stabilise the economy and demobilise a militant working class challenge.

    In Germany the preconditions for the deflation programme were established under American occupation in the 1945-48 period. A ban had been placed on political activities immediately after the war which seriously impaired the reconstitution of working class political activities (70). Such hindrances on working class organisation had been combined with American enforcement of plant-level rather than industry-wide unionism as well as the disbanding of workers' councils. With the SPD's main electoral base lying in East Germany (under Soviet occupation) the organisational capacity to revitalise the predominantly Catholic working class population in the western zones was severely restricted. At the same time the leadership of the SPD was being 'filled mostly by the old guard functionaries, who had either remained passive under the Nazi regime or escaped abroad to await the day they could return to political life' (71). The hopes of Party leader, Kurt Schumacher to develop a leading cadre among the younger generation who had fought fascism in the socialist youth groups and the resistance movement failed, and the party suffered the long-term consequences of being unable to mobilise and remould an entire generation of youth who had been socialised under fascism.

While the social democrats placed the goals of a socialist democracy and reunification at the forefront of their programme, the occupation forces and the Christian Democrats rebuilt the state apparatus. The popular demand for the socialisation of industry was frustrated and in 1947 the Bizonal Economic Council was formed (without popular elections) to preside over economic reconstruction. After the SPD withdrew its support for the council, the deflationary 1948 currency reform programme was launched. It was designed to '... increase savings through high profits and tax concessions for the upper class while low wages, the most regressive taxation system in Europe and mass unemployment were to reduce the 'propensity to spend' on the part of the working class' (72). In the process price controls were arbitrarily removed, the money supply drastically contracted and a further deflationary squeeze was imposed following a series of large strikes in November 1948. The result was mass unemployment which rose from 450,000 to 1.3 million during 1949 (73).

It was during this economic assault on the organisations and standard of living of the working class that the Federal State apparatus was reconstituted by the Basic Law of 1949. Federalism was designed to inhibit central economic planning thus curtailing the mobilisation capacity of labour and providing the ground for a synthesis of capitalism and Christian Democracy. This synthesis expressed the dogma of a 'social market economy' the ideological foundations of which were summarised by the Christian Democratic Chancellor, Konrad Adenauer in the following terms:

> Let me summarise the main features of the social market economy from a CDU/CSU pamphlet issued in July 1949... The 'Social Market Economy' produces the maximum economic benefit and social justice for all by letting free individuals make an efficient contribution to an order that embodies a social conscience. It combines freedom and obligations, genuine competition and an independent control of monopolies. Genuine competition is possible where there is a system that rewards the better performance in a framework of equal chances and fair conditions of competition. The proper market price gives the right direction to the co-operation of all concerned...The Social Market Economy renounces the planning and direction of production, labour or sales. But it favours the organic means of a comprehensive economic policy based on elastic adaptation to market research' (74).

A similar pattern of post-war reconstruction occured in Japan during the six year period of American occupation. Initially American plans for Japanese reconstruction centred on a programme for combining a decentralised competitive capitalism with a liberal democratic regime. The Japanese economy was based on the zaibatsu system, which, through vertical and horizontal integration of mining, manufacturing, commercial and financial enterprises, had concentrated control of roughly 75% of Japan's economy primarily in the hands of some 10 major families. Guided by the reports of the US Mission on Japanese Cartels, which pointed to the zaibatsu as the causal nexus within a system perpetuating low wages, concentrated profits, militarism and the growth of imperialism, the American economic planners initially opted for a programme of dissolving the zaibatsu system through the passage of the 1947 Monopoly and Deconcentration Laws. But by mid 1948 the plan and the application of the law had been halted before it really began. The list of 325 corporations originally scheduled for decomposition was cut to 19, of which only 9 were actually dissolved, and the purging of the business elite was largely avoided (75). American foreign policy opted for restoring rather than dissolving the zaibatsu system. Events in China as well as cold war hostility to the Soviet Union fostered American support for a powerful Japanese capitalism aligned to the US. With a small group of American capitalists fearing adverse consequences of zaibatsu dissolution for their own activities in Japan, a campaign was launched to present the dissolution plan as an un-American form of socialism. It was argued that unless it was halted Japan's capacity for self-sufficiency would be undermined, thus requiring further flows of reconstruction dollars and inhibiting the possibility of Japan developing as a bulwark against communism. Co-ordinated through sections of the media (Newsweek in particular), the campaign was supported by Japanese businessmen who emphasised the detrimental effects of disbanding the very organisational structure that could bring to a halt the upsurge of industrial militancy from the working class.

The reversal of zaibatsu dissolution also enabled an important link to be forged between Japanese recovery and America's export surplus strategy. During the immediate post-war period and for the next two decades, the United States enjoyed a large trade surplus with Japan, who became a major absorber of the large American agriculture surplus. This relationship was formalised in the subsequent negotiations surrounding the 1954 Mutual Defense Agreement, and became a vital American concern in later years, with the growth of the EEC Common Agricultural Policy which began to operate after 1962. But the preconditions for this development included crushing the militancy of the Japanese labour movement (76).

Lacking a strong wartime resistance movement, which was so important for the strength of the left in post-war Europe, Japanese labour was also weakened by war and nuclear holocaust as well as war time restrictions on the right of unions to organise. Trade union membership had fallen from 400,000 in the 1930s to less than 10,000 in 1940 and by 1946 real wages were between a quarter and one-third of their pre-war levels (77). The benefits from the American democratic reforms that enfranchised women, released political prisoners and extended the right to organise, were secured from above rather than through agitation and mobilisation from below. The result was that democratic reforms dampened rather than sustained extra-parliamentary political mobilisation.

Nevertheless working class militancy grew through the practice of 'production control' and factory occupation, the mass demonstration on May Day 1946 and the Tokyo Food Rally, as well as mass union drives to eliminate enterprise unionism and the election of the Socialist Party as the largest Party in the 1947 Diet.

A further significant move had come in July 1948, when in the face of calls for a general strike, all strikes by government employees were debarred, with the Socialist Party remaining in the government. But still in 1948 only one company was able to carry out discharges (layoffs of workers) and then only after the plant was surrounded by 'Four American Army tanks, one cavalry squadron, three airplanes and 1,800 armed police' (78).

But the passage of the 1946 Labour Relations Adjustment Law, the penetration of anti-communist 'mindo' cells within militant trade union organisations, and the ban on the general strike limited working class mobilisation and facilitated the employers' counter-mobilisation to restore their own system of enterprise unionism. The Dodge programme in 1949-50, (79) further strengthened the bourgeois offensive, and helped it to victory.

The Dodge programme spelled out the political, economic and social implications of the defeat of the commitment to full employment in the United States in 1946 as they were transmitted to other countries in the form of labour disciplinary and deflationary measures aimed at restoring private enterprise, opening up the world economy and containing the mobilisation of labour. In 1947, Dodge had argued:

...the world problem today is the extent to which government controls of ownership will replace private enterpise... Underlying these problems and trends, is the ultimate fact that the expansion of socialism and government control and ownership finally leads to some form of totalitarianism.

This attitude corresponded with his view that an 'increase in unemployment will in turn lead to increased efficiency of labour' and that

99

unemployment benefits meant 'no incentive to the individual to answer his own problem by seeking other employment'. He believed that what was required was '... a move away from over-employment to a reasonably defined full employment' in order to 'get the country into hard condition for the struggle in the export market'. To do this, Dodge unleashed an acutely deflationary policy through major cuts in areas of government expenditure such as school-building and unemployment benefits, along with monetary contraction to contain inflation, discipline labour and generate investment in the export sector (81). Japanese employers responded by hastening the return to enterprise unionism and with layoffs aimed at militant workers and unionists in particular, resulting in trade union membership declining by almost 900,000. With these developments, the preconditions for building the foundation of the Japanese 'miracle' were laid.

In Italy and France the post-war balance of class forces was fundamentally different than in Germany and Japan. The prestige of the Soviet Union, and the communists who led the resistance movement, made the PCF and PCI the primary agencies for working class mobilisation. Under their auspices the French and Italian trade union movements were reconstructed from the leading sections of the political and industrial arms of the labour movement (82). While fragmentation and splits emerged in labour organisations, this highly mobilised and militant communist bloc proved decisive in dismantling the fascist state apparatus and restoring democracy.

The participation of the PCF in government till April-May 1947 helped to achieve several important reforms. PCF demands were among those that led to the nationalisation of coal, electricity, gas and the banks, wage increases that the Resistance movement had promised, and the beginnings of a social security system. But the communists' decision to place the armed forces of the resistance under De Gaulle's control and the allied command, further diminished the Resistance organisation and the local and departmental committees of liberation. The party also failed to mobilise successful opposition to the French military's repression in Vietnam, Madagascar and Algeria. And compliance with Stalin's strategy for appeasement and co-existence under 'the Grand Alliance' made the Party a sheet-anchor to wage militancy and working class agitation under conditions of rampant

inflation and falling real wages. The PCFs
leadership of 'the battle for production' produced
very little in the way of a revolutionary advance or
even a tangible *quid pro quo* for the rank and file
(83).

American intervention also subverted working
class organisations, thus hindering the
communists. The CIO and the AFLs Free Trade Union
committee financially supported the Bothereau group
in the Force Ouvriere and the hiring of strike
breakers in the 1949-50 dock strike. The group
sought to split the CGT and destroy its links with
the PCF. American support for French post-war
planning also helped to protect the long term
investment plan by insulating it from the political
mobilisations of the immediate post-war period.
Nevertheless a capitalist recovery strategy which
sacrificed working class living standards was aided
by PCF co-operation in containing insurrectionism
until after the party left government in April-May
1947 (83).

On the other hand the restoration of bourgeois
democracy rather than totalitarianism depended on
the strength of the PCF which stood against
De Gaulle's mobilisation of the right through the
Rassemblement du Peuple Francais (RPF) in late 1947-
48: As one writer said of the 1947 municipal
election:

> Never in the whole of French history had a
> municipal election been of such national and
> international significance as the municipal
> elections in October 1947 when suddenly nearly
> 40% of France went what was loosely called
> 'Fascist'... Each of his (De Gaulle's) meetings
> with its many thousands of people, its flags,
> beacons and elaborate ceremonial was becoming
> more and more like a little 'Nuremberg' (with
> the Cross of Lorraine being used in much the
> same way as the swastika)... It was an
> emotional election, the nearest French approach
> to the German election of 1933 ...The
> fact...remains that for at least 3 months it
> looked as if France might turn Fascist (84).

The socialists rejected the PCF call for joint
action against fascism and while the RPF virtually
monopolised the right wing vote winning 39%, the
only party to achieve an electoral bloc greater than
20% were the communists with 31%. The PCF
maintained this support and prevented the RPF making

inroads into the working class. In November 1947, the communists organised a series of mass strikes, and the mobilisation of the left continued through the strikes of October-November 1948, which were brutally repressed, with 2,000 miners imprisoned and 6,000 dismissed. In 1949-50 the PCF launched its peace campaign and helped to mobilise the extensive dock strikes to prevent the shipment of war materials. Given the political instability of the 1944-52 period during which the French government was reconstituted on 13 occasions and De Gaulle supported the call for an amnesty for Petain and the Vichy collaborators, a militant communist-led working class bloc was the best defence against a resurgent fascism. While the PCFs policies may have prevented some form of revolutionary transition, the party did most to halt the RPF at a crucial time.

In Italy, (85) the post-war economy suffered from the structural distortions left from 21 years of fascist policy. These distortions overlay the traditional imbalances between development in the North and South. In 1945, *per capita* income was below the level of 1914, productive capacity in agriculture was more than 40% below pre-war levels, industrial output was 25% below the 1941 level, the transportation system lay in ruins and over 2 million were unemployed. Industry was particularly underdeveloped in the capital goods sector while the consumption goods sector remained largely unmechanised. These conditions were exacerbated by uncontrolled inflation (the retail price index 1938=100, had risen to 4844 by 1948), supply shortages and the bad harvests of 1947 (86). The economic crisis greatly complicated the task of rebuilding working class organisations. The fascists had established the Fascist Syndical Corporation in 1925, abolished the right to strike in 1926, introduced the Labour Charter in 1927-28 and imposed the passport system *(libretto di lavoro)* in the 1930s to control labour mobility (87). But under the leadership of the PCI, the resistance movement had liberated the main cities and towns of the North in April 1945, organising factory occupations and seizing control of government administration in the process. With the industrial bourgeoisie supporting fascism and the big southern agrarian interests seeking an alliance with the western occupation forces, the PCI and CGIL (formed in 1945) began to reforge the labour movements (88).

Workers set up 'internal commissions' inside

the factories of the north which became new organs of trade union organisations. The representatives of these commissions and those of the National Liberation Committees of North Italy united to plan for post-war reconstruction. But in the south the landed interests and the allied occupation forces were aligned in a conservative bloc.

The CGIL responded to this north-south dualism by encouraging in its own organisation a democratic centralisation to co-ordinate trade union action across the whole labour market. By securing escalator clauses *(scala mobile)* in wage contracts from 1946, it made an important advance in defending real wages against inflation. But working class organisations in the south met stiff resistance from the mafia who killed CGIL activists. To break the political deadlock De Gasperi reconstituted his government without the Italian communists in May 1947, paving the way for the 1947-50 deflation (89).

The Finance Minister, Einaudi, initiated the deflationary programme and the group of liberal economists linked to the Ministry of Finance restored market mechanisms, while keeping investment capital away from the state owned IRI. The deflation aided the recovery of the export sector (textiles in particular) and advanced productivity, but this was achieved at the expense of consumption and mass unemployment. Industrialists, the peasantry and sections of the middle classes were cushioned from the deflationary measures which helped to secure the alliance for the April 1948 'Christ vs Communism Election' (90). With the bourgeois parties secured in office, and with Marshall dollars building up foreign currency reserves rather than domestic purchasing power, an alliance between capitalism and Christian Democracy was forged which left the southern question unresolved.

The new regime subjected the communists to brutal repression prior to the Korean war:

> Between 1949 and 1950, 17 workers were killed by the police, 100 wounded, 13,000 arrested and there were 132 million hours of strikes, the highest level until 1961 (91).

Under these conditions Giuseppe De Vittorio, Secretary-General of the CGIL, led the largest working class campaign of the 1950s. It was a campaign for full employment and social transformation known as 'The Labour Plan' (1950-52):

It was a programme of irrigation and dam construction in agriculture, financed by national borrowing. At the same time production plans for the underutilised industries in the North were drafted in accordance with the needs of the agricultural sector. The Plan commanded deep respect also among Government observers, and when it was launched it mobilised millions of people, who in many cases started, in the south, building dams after occupying absentees' land. In the closing factories workers refused to discontinue production and tried to supply the peasants with industrial products (the famous RGO tractor produced by the workers occupying the Reggiance factory in Raggio Emilia). Some of these factories are nowadays co-operatives (92).

However as Joseph Halevi and other leading PCI-CGIL figures have argued, the plan (which was abandoned in 1952) underestimated the complexities of the structural imbalances within the economy, and serious divisions in the labour movement prevented this mobilisation from achieving a political victory. Nevertheless, in the face of repression and mass unemployment the organisations of the working class had stamped out fascism and resurrected a working class ethic of militancy and insurgency.

THE RISE AND FALL OF FULL EMPLOYMENT CAPITALISM: CONCLUSIONS AND CONJECTURES ON SWEDISH EXCEPTIONALISM

The various paths to full employment capitalism were paved with a series of defeats suffered by the working class. These defeats were domestically inflicted by ruling class mobilisations and/or externally induced by American occupation and American led international monetary reconstruction. The dismantling of war-time controls and deflation subverted the twin working class demands for full employment and social transformation. The labour movement was driven back, often in a violent manner, and these setbacks weighed heavily on the labour movement's capacity to mobilise during the fifties and sixties.
     The first casualty in these defeats was trade union solidarity. In Belgium, the Netherlands, Ireland, Italy and France the peak trade union

organisations were split with the creation or strengthening of anti-socialist catholic central trade union organisations. In Japan, ruling class measures destroyed the militant Sanbetsu, while promoting the formation of what was initially the ultra conservative Sohyo central trade union organisation. In Greece the fascists disbanded the Greek Confederation of Labour, only reconstituting it when the left was removed. In Australia, Britain and Germany the radical trade union programmes for post-war reconstruction (particularly 1944 TUC programme, 1947 ACTU programme and 1949 DGB Munich programme) were substantially modified during the cold war. In the US the AFL and CIO merged in 1955 after the expulsion of militants and on the basis of the AFLs conservative apolitical stance. Given the influence of the AFL and CIO upon the two central trade union organisations in Canada, (TLC and CCL) the merger of the latter bodies in 1956 signalled the emergence of a conservative form of international trade unionism that stunted the development of an autonomous Canadian trade union movement (93).

The deterioration of trade union solidarity occurred during a critical period. As the table 3.1 suggests, the level of trade union organisation increased substantially from 1930 to 1950. But the defeats of the reconstruction period were followed by declining or stagnating membership levels as a percentage of total labour force after 1950 (in Australia, US, Italy, France, Netherlands and Britain (in the 1950s) or advances under conditions of high unemployment which restricted their effects (Belgium, Germany). The only country to maintain a rapid rise in the level of trade union organisation over the 1950-75 period was Sweden. But this decline or stagnation in the level of trade union organisation was often far more serious in limiting socialist advances than the data indicates. For example, in Italy the membership levels of the CGIL (expressed as a percentage of the total labour force) declined from 43.4% in 1951 to 20.5% by 1961. This decline was even more serious in the strategically important metal industry where the CGILs Metal Worker Federation (FIOM CGIL) saw its share of the labour force decline from 52% in 1951 to 13.4% in 1961. At Fiat FIOM CGILs strength in elections to the internal commissions fell from 61% in 1954 to 21% in 1957 (95).

The second serious consequence of the defeats suffered by the labour movement in the reconstruction period was declining electoral support for working class political parties. In some cases party membership declined sharply. There was also the drastic decline of the communist vote. For example in France the PCFs share of the vote declined from 26.1% (1945) to 19.2% (1958). In Japan the communist vote averaged less than 3% in the fifties and sixties after reaching a high of 9.8% in 1949. In Denmark communist support fell from 12.5% (1945) to 1.1% (1960). Between 1951 and 1964 no working class political party ever held central office in Canada, France, US, Italy, Germany, Japan, Australia or Britain. While no working class political party has ever taken part in central level government in several of these countries, the non-existence of a working class party in office in any of these core OECD countries was more than symbolic in its effects on international working class solidarity. It also underlined the new marginality of working class politics. This meant that the crucial relationship between the trade union movement and working class parties evolved during a long period in opposition. The ensuing demoralisation contributed to the right wing drift of social democracy during this period (96).

Table 3.1: Trade Union Membership as a Percentage of the Total Civilian Labour Force

	1930	1940	1950	1960	1970	1975
Sweden	30	54	67	72	81	86
Denmark	36	45	53	63	61	62
Norway	17	-	47	65	62	58
Britain	30	-	46	45	49	52
Germany	46	-	38	42	37	39
Austria	39	-	62	63	62	66
Belgium	34	37	48	58	62	64
Netherlands	27	32	40	40	37	-
France	11	-	39	18	22	24
Italy	-	-	58	57	52	49
USA	11	27	32	31	27	27
Australia	53	48	58	58	54	-

Source: A. Kjellberg, 'Den Fackliga organisationsgradens utreckling i 12 lander 1930-1975' (Sociologiska institutioner, Lund University, 1979). (94)

This demobilisation of the working class accompanied the reconstruction of the capitalist state along two lines. Firstly the war-time institutions for economic regulation were abolished and new institutional linkages and formats of representation held sway over policy formation. Secondly the ideology of a democratic political system was redefined. Conservative parties and business interests had faced serious legitimation crises because of their association with mass unemployment or collaboration with fascism. But ruling class mobilisation emasculated the working class demand for a democratised full employment society. Working class strength in countries that followed variations of the 'democracy first' path to full employment capitalism, was largely responsible for dislodging the anti-democratic heritage of fascism. But bourgeois notions of democracy (the property owning democracy of British Toryism, the social market economy of German Christian Democracy etc) predominated, and combined with a bourgeois state apparatus with its newly forged linkages to the class structure (economic concertation in France, the sponsoring department system in Britain, the business committees in the American state, the reconsolidation of the zaibatsu and the network of connections with the Japanese state elite, the autonomous banker-controlled Bundesbank in Germany etc).

The third consequence of the defeats suffered by the labour movement from 1945-51 was that they facilitated the imposition of capitalist relations of authority in the labour market. This occurred during a crucial period when the war economy and working class militancy had fundamentally altered the wage and price formation process and the rules and relations of domination and subordination involved in hiring, firing, planning and directing work as well as the general mobility of 'factors of production' between different markets and regions. In short the rewards of labour were once again to be determined by 'market principles' after the defeat of trade union attempts to supplant these principles in the interests of social equity. During the next two decades the absence of a trade union strategy for mobilising in a fully employed labour market inhibited effective trade union activity.

Certainly, when full employment finally arrived, it enhanced trade union bargaining power. But this strengthening of the unions must be weighed against the deterioration of trade union solidarity and the electoral decline of labour which had already taken place. It must also be considered in terms of how much could have been achieved in transforming the labour market given the level of working class militancy and bourgeois disarray during the reconstruction period. And finally, trade unions' bargaining power must be weighed against their ineffectiveness when unemployment returned in the late sixties. For the defeats of the reconstruction period meant that no manpower policy evolved to prevent the working class from bearing the burden of the accelerated structural change accompanying full employment. Moreover, in the absence of an effective labour response to wage policy under full employment trade unions were drawn into state incomes policy especially in the sixties. Taken together, the adverse consequences structural change had on working people, and the divisive consequences incomes policy had within the labour movement, often led to a resurgence of working class militancy. But incomes policy and later monetarism would be utilised to contain this militancy at the same time as mass unemployment began to re-emerge. While it is beyond the scope of this chapter to analyse the rise and fall of full employment capitalism in any detail, there are several dimensions of this development which should be sketched.

Firstly the timing of the emergence of full employment capitalism is decisive. For it only occurred on a generalised basis during the 1955-65 period after the defeats suffered by the working class in the reconstruction period. This was certainly the case in the countries that followed the 'North American' path to full employment. In Canada unemployment averaged 6.6% in the 1958-62 period and only fell below 4% momentarily in 1965-66 (97). In the US unemployment (measuring from cyclical peak to peak) rose from 4.2% (1948-53 cycle) to 4.4% (1953-57 cycle) to 5.9% (1957-60 cycle) (98). Full employment was only temporarily achieved with the Kennedy administration's shift to Keynesian policies in the early 1960s, a shift which came after a period of economic stagnation with 4 recessions between 1945 and 1961.

In those countries which followed variations of the 'democracy first' path to full employment only Japan and France had achieved it in the reconstruction period at the same time as the working class was being demobilised. In Italy where deflation had increased unemployment to 17% in 1948, the level of unemployment remained near 10% during the 1950s. It was only in the boom years 1958-63 'that the Italian economy, achieved for the first

time in history a *quasi* full employment situation'
(99). In Germany and Belgium full employment was
not achieved till after 1955 (100). For those
countries such as Britain and Australia which
followed a 'social democracy' path to full
employment, the latter was achieved while labour
parties were in retreat during the 1940s. But other
countries which pursued the social democratic road
did not achieve full employment. In Denmark the
commitment to full employment was expressed in the
social democrats 1944 programme *Denmark of the
Future*. But despite the social democrat's influence
in post-war coalition governments, unemployment
amongst insured members of trade union funds never
fell below 8% in any year between 1950 and 1958. In
Ireland where nationalism and catholicism broke the
unity of the labour movement, unemployment averaged
8.3% in the 1950-58 period (101).

This leads us to a second aspect of the rise
and fall of full employment capitalism. The
generalisation of a regime of full employment
amongst industrially advanced countries arrived at
the same time as the second phase of the opening up
of the international capitalist economy between 1955
and 1965. In many European countries full
employment began with the investment boom in housing
and auto production. With another phase of trade
liberalisation between 1955-65 the rate of growth of
exports considerably exceeded the growth of
manufacturing output and 'high profit margins on
exports permitted continuing heavy investment and
the expansion of high productivity, capital
intensive industries dependent on export sales'
(102). This development was facilitated by a major
change in the composition of demand for exports
particularly in increased trade in technologically
advanced capital goods between the major industrial
countries. During the 1950s the UK, France, Germany
and the US absorbed 31% of the total increase in
world imports of capital goods, as against 6% in the
1899-1937 period (103). In other words the export
sector became increasingly important in sustaining a
full employment level and form of investment
(104). But this form of development in an
increasingly open world economy required (a) that
the desynchronisation of trade cycles between
countries be maintained to facilitate export led
recovery from countries under recessionary
pressures; (b) that the higher marginal propensity
to import that is characteristic of a full
employment economy be adjusted through a flexible

approach to the balance of payments; (c) that supply shortages and bottlenecks in the labour market did not drive up unit labour costs to the point of undermining a country's position in world markets; (d) that the institutional arrangements for creating international liquidity and maintaining exchange rate stability be made to operate in such a way that surplus countries did not force deflation on deficit countries.

But with the liberalisation of capital and commodity flows after the Treaty of Rome (1957) and currency convertibility (1958), a system of fixed exchange rates provided little flexibility for deficit countries to adjust without deflation and no measures to enforce pressure on surplus countries. Thus deficit countries resorted to raising the short term interest rate to attract capital inflow which soon deteriorated into destabilising interest-rate wars (105). Lack of a co-ordinated response to multinational corporations and to regulations of the eurodollar market further diminished governments' ability to influence the money supply. American militarism abroad and stagnation in the US economy defeated efforts to co-ordinate the balance required to support the American dollar. With the collapse of the Bretton Wood system in 1971 and the inflationary primary-commodity boom (1972-74), the industrial production cycles in the major industrial economies were resynchronised providing the preconditions for the generalised recession of 1974-75. In short, between 1966 and 1973 all of the preconditions for export led growth broke down and full employment capitalism fell with it after only a decade (106).

This collapse could only have been averted through co-ordinated domestic and international regulation of capital flows and balance of payment adjustments in all countries. This in turn would have called for liquidity creation on a basis other than the 'empire building expenses' of American militarism and foreign investment. An equitable solution to the agrarian question in Japan and Europe would have had to be found and existing relations between developed and underdeveloped countries overturned. Enforcing such solutions while maintaining full employment and a more equitable distribution of income would have required far reaching public control over investment. Only a politically ascendant labour movement could have implemented such a programme.

The real tragedy of the reconstruction period

is that this possibility was precluded by a series of ideological and political defeats that the labour movement suffered. While it is important to ask whether or not the various labour movements' strategies could have co-ordinated such an alternative we should not lose sight of the fact that the development of such a programme would have required a difficult working through process during the 1950s. By that time, however, trade union solidarity had been seriously eroded and working class parties removed from office. In the sixties and seventies the labour movement paid a heavy price for these early defeats, as an era of global disorder emerged, accompanied by the resurgence of unemployment, militarism and monetarism. In this climate bourgeois (and even working class) parties abandoned the objective of full employment. But the Swedish labour movement avoided this fate. The labour movement resisted the post-war bourgeois assaults and the trade unions enjoyed a new golden era containing ruling class mobilisation and underpinning 44 years of social democratic rule. Full employment was maintained. Sweden did not achieve a socialist transition but there did emerge a quite different form of full-employment capitalism. For this reason several aspects of Swedish development require elaboration.

The deterioration of bourgeois mobilisation at the political level and the development of a unique trade union strategy for maintaining full employment are the two main elements distinguishing the Swedish path to full employment from the 'social democracy' road followed by countries such as Australia and Britain. The bourgeois parties in Sweden and the central employers association (SAF) had been in a state of disarray since the early 1930s when the Agrarians had joined the Social Democratic Party (SAP) to form a coalition government. While this alliance constituted the first major break in the cohesiveness of the bourgeois bloc, the employers were also seriously divided between the economic policies and political strategies put forward by the home market sector (through SAF) and the more confrontationist strategy advanced by firms in the export sector and by their propaganda instrument, the Directors Club (107). These divisions cleared the way for the new government to break with deflationary economic orthodoxy in the 1930s and implement expansionary monetary and fiscal policy. But the new economic policy neither explictly aimed at nor achieved full employment. Such a commitment came later in the reports of the 'Myrdal Commission' on post-war reconstruction and the joint LO-SAP 'The Labour Movements Post War Programme' of 1944 (108).

Although labour's programme for reconstruction was ambiguous in many respects, its radical interventionist thrust provoked a counter offensive aimed at reconsolidating the bourgeois bloc and restoring the operation of 'free market' forces. Known as the Opposition to Economic Planning Movement, the bourgeois campaign found its leitmotiv in the works of von Hayek and Jewkes. But when the socialist bloc held its majority in the 1948 elections, the campaign to end sixteen years of social democratic government collapsed, unlike the bourgeois offensives in other countries which followed the 'social democracy' road to full employment. In Australia and Britain the mobilisations of the late forties ushered in a long period of conservative rule during which the divisions between the business and political leaderships of the ruling class were overcome by a shared ideology of developmentalism, moderate social welfareism and virulent anti-communism. While contradictory strategies for economic growth persisted this ideology produced a cohesive bourgeois approach to renovating relations between the state and class organisations. The lines along which these relations developed thus began to diverge from the dynamics of full employment capitalism in Sweden where the social democrats remained in office through the cold war till 1976. A more even balance of class forces accounts for the peculiarities of the Swedish development.

The Swedish social democrats reacted with excessive caution to the bourgeois offensive and the cold war. The priority they gave (in spite of the socialist majority) to resurrecting the coalition with the Agrarians, accomplished in October 1951, exemplifies this response. Associated with this cold-war mentality was an economic policy based largely on assumptions of overcoming economic instability through the trade union movement bearing the 'primary responsibility' for restraint. But unlike trade union movements abroad whose strategy was focused on maintaining an autonomy from conservative governments after the defeats of the reconstruction period, LO channelled its efforts into a trade union plan of action known as the Rehn-Meidner model. The LO strategy focused on the interdependent goals of ensuring stable full employment to enhance the organisational strength of the working class and advancing the cause of social justice. Such an objective required a quite different form and direction for economic policy, and it was around this that the trade union movement mobilised during the 1950s.

The immediate origins of the Rehn-Meidner model (named after the LO economists Gösta Rehn and Rudolf Meidner) was the trade union experience with incomes policy in the late forties. As Gösta Rehn has pointed out:

> That experience instilled in us LO economists the impression that incomes policy, whether through wage and dividend freeze or other similar measures, as a rule must be seen as actually politically and psychologically damaging in the struggle against inflation: government leaders are given the illusion that they themselves can avoid other unpleasant and awkward measures after the trade union movement freely or unwillingly pulled the chestnuts out of the fire (109).

Thus LO began to search for a new economic policy that would combine full employment and wage-price stability without provoking fatal tensions within and between the industrial and political wings of the labour movement. In this respect it is vital to understand that the economic debates (in the labour movement journals 'The Time' and 'The Trade Union Movement') leading up to the 1951 LO congress was an attempt to link the commitment to full employment with an economic policy that bolstered rather than undermined working class solidarity (110).

The basis of the new economic policy was outlined in section 5 of the 1951 LO Report, 'Trade Unions and Full Employment' which represented the trade union movement's commitment to full employment in the Rehn-Meidner model. The essence of the Report can be summarised as follows. In order 'to maintain full employment, profit prospects must be sufficiently good to incite industry to engage all available manpower' (111). But in a full employment labour market 'competition for manpower combined with a high level of profits, tends to press wages upwards irrespective of the content of the collective agreements' (112) because of 'so called wage drift'.

While wage drift has detrimental effects on class solidarity and the national economy because it promotes wage inequality and inflation, it cannot be cured by wage restraint along the lines Beveridge proposed through trade union restraint. This would abolish the *raison d'etre* of trade unions in a capitalist economy, to defend their members and fight for improved living standards. It would also ignore the fact that it is not wage drift but high profits which cause this problem.

High profits induce wage drift inflation and speculative investment in an unco-ordinated capitalist economy, and this threatens to undermine full employment which is the basis of democracy. Therefore the trade union movement must extend its 'responsibilities' to the working class and the national economy (113) by promoting the best means to 'remove the prospects private enterprise has of making exaggerated profits, by means of deliberate monetary, fiscal and wage policy' (114). This involves disciplining management and the forces that 'cause private enterprise to attempt to make more investments than is warranted by the supply of saved capital, raw materials and manpower' (115).

In other words to counter the irresponsibility of capitalist investment and high profits, the organised working class must assume new responsibilities. Not those discussed by Beveridge (116) but those that capitalists cannot fulfill. The trade union movement must adopt a solidarity wages policy to ensure that high profits neither cause inflationary wage increases nor hinder the redistributive effects of full employment. A solidarity wages policy (117) will require scrapping the market principle of 'capacity to pay' at the level of the firm and industrial sector because this principle enables inefficient firms to survive in spite of their inefficiency by paying less wages. Under such circumstances 'particular groups of workers are actually subsidising their industry by abstaining from the wages such an industry should normally have to pay' (118). This high wage policy in low wage industries enforces economic efficiency. In order to accomplish this, workers must accept the need to transfer out of firms and industrial sectors requiring rationalisation. This required wage earners to accept labour mobility and 'an active labour market policy'. According to the LO Report this programme would require more centralisation and co-ordination of trade union wage policy and responsible use of the strike weapon (119). Unlike the 1944 Post-War Programme which almost exclusively focused on the state's role in economic planning, the 1951 LO Report established an autonomous and formative role for the trade union movement in the fully employed labour market. In the Rehn-Meidner approach the state was to step up public savings through a restrictive fiscal policy. This policy would contain inflationary pressures by squeezing high profits which would otherwise generate excess demand. But the state was also to abide by 'the fundamental principle of trade union freedom from state intervention' in the labour market. In short the LO plan required the integration of wage policy with general economic policy with high wages and restrictive fiscal policy squeezing profit margins, and manpower policy facilitating an accelerated rate of structural change to promote stable growth increasingly financed from public saving. If the institutional support for this plan, centralised collective bargaining, could be secured, the plan itself represented a complete alternative to a state-led incomes policy which LO economists rightly saw as subverting the autonomy and solidarity of the labour movement (120).

The social democratic leadership adopted the Rehn-Meidner model in 1955, and permanent centralisation of collective bargaining began in the following year. The way was then open for a new electoral strategy for the labour movement. This new political strategy emerged from the labour movement's electoral campaign for a supplementary pension scheme funded by a graduated payroll tax on employers. The scheme would increase public sector savings, provide greater government control of the credit market (and therefore investment behaviour) and act as a vehicle for restrictive fiscal policy to squeeze 'excess profits' and demand inflation. Between 1957 and 1960, the intense conflict over the supplementary pension scheme led to a government resignation, a referendum and two 'pension elections'. Once again bourgeois political mobilisation was impaired as LO and SAP leaders mobilised sufficient additional support for the pension scheme within the central organisation for white collar workers (TCO). As a result the labour movement won the 1960 election convincingly, providing the first majority socialist government since the 1940s. Not only had the social democrats' dependence on agrarian support been broken, but LO had shown its ability to provide electoral support for its solidarity wages policy. The Rehn-Meidner model could now become the basis of economic policy in general (121).

Class Struggle in Liberal Democracies

The period from 1957 to 1961 saw the
introduction of the various elements of the Rehn-
Meidner Model in the form of an active manpower
policy in the 1958 recession, the introduction of
supplementary pension funds for expanding public
savings and a turnover tax in response to the 1960-
61 boom, as well as the effective use of the
investment reserve fund system to co-ordinate the
'time pattern' of investment behaviour. There were
two preconditions for those initiatives. Firstly
the trade union movement itself had developed the
programme for achieving full employment and relative
wage-price stability, which it had imposed on the
party, thus defeating the 'primary responsibility'
doctrine that forms the ideological basis of incomes
policy. Secondly, the unions had assisted the party
in linking what was to become an increasingly
important feature of the Rehn-Meidner model (pension
funds) to a political strategy for mobilising both
blue and white collar workers. This was done in a
manner and over an issue that provided the social
democrats with an electoral majority, while
preventing the party from undermining working class
mobilisation by straying from its class base and
adopting the posture of a national integrative
party, which, without a strategy of class conflict,
tends (to use Rehn's metaphor) to ask its trade
union base to 'pull the chestnuts out of the fire'
for the so called 'national interest'.
In Sweden these developments would shape the
scope of government policy and social democratic
electoral strategy during most of the sixties.
Elsewhere, the different paths to full employment
capitalism began to converge as a result of the
limited range of policies available to governments
responding to the pressures of trade liberalisation
and intensified international competition. Without
a more flexible system of international monetary
relations and without a viable working class
strategy for bolstering trade union autonomy under
full employment, incomes policy became the point of
this convergence. This policy was used to achieve
wage restraint and neutralise the strength that was
available to unions in the fully employed labour
market. In countries which followed the North
American path to full employment capitalism there
was no working class political party to mobilise
around an alternative to such policies, and the
modest consultative role that was offered to the
unions in exchange for compliance served to deepen
the gulf between the leadership and the rank and

file. In countries which followed variations of the 'democracy first' path to full employment capitalism there were similar attempts to secure institutionalised wage restraint (although an alternative began to emerge with the rise of eurocommunism in Italy and France). But incomes policy wrought most damage in countries where labour parties had returned to office. As Leo Panitch shows in his remarkable study *Social Democracy and Industrial Militancy: The Labour Party, the Trade Unions and Incomes Policy, 1945-1974* incomes policy was the major cause of the fracturing of working class solidarity in Britain. This occurred primarily (although certainly not exclusively) because the political party founded, financed, electorally dependent and morally nurtured by the trade union movement was in a unique position to secure wage restraint while abandoning progressive economic and social policies that it promised as the *quid pro quo* for the unions' co-operation. Since the historic role of incomes policy is· as a substitute for public control over capital formation it was also instrumental in the collapse of full employment in the late sixties and seventies and in leaving a demoralised labour movement to face the scourge of monetarism (122).

While similar pressures were brought to bear on the Swedish labour movement between 1966 and 1980 full employment was maintained despite the ascendance of a bourgeois coalition government in 1976. Maintenance of full employment has depended on a massive expansion of the public sector, particularly in the area of labour market policy, which absorbed 9% of government expenditure (3% of GNP) in 1977-78 (123). With profits being squeezed between high wages and a declining demand for Swedish exports, LO has responded to the combination of industrial militancy, rising prices and declining investment by pushing the logic of the Rehn-Meidner model a stage further in a programme for industrial democracy and wage earners funds. Just as the 1951 LO congress began a ten year struggle to institutionalise the solidarity wage policy and to combine this with government policies to support full employment and boost the strength of the working class, LOs congresses in 1971 and 1976 initiated a new phase of a much older working class struggle involving what Meidner has called 'the achievement of this most fundamental of all our aims ... the demand for full employment, or jobs for everyone' (124).

The basic pre-condition for this stragegy is working class solidarity in the labour market. The inequality in income distribution has constantly obstructed trade union efforts in this direction. The destabilising effects on LO wage policy of high profits in certain sectors of the economy, the burden of structural adjustment that the working class is no longer prepared to accept, and the inability to make wage earners' funds a positive issue in the 1976 election, have also plagued the movement. As a result LOs solidarity wages policy is now facing the most intense bourgeois assault since the forties. But the more even balance of class forces remains as the contrast in May 1980 between the dismal outcome of the TUCs Day of Action on the one hand and LOs defeat of the wage freeze that the government and SAF sought so strenuously to impose on the other, starkly demonstrates. While we must analyse these developments in terms of recent events, we cannot ignore the historical legacy of the reconstruction period and its contribution to enhancing or undermining the solidarity of the labour movement. The erosion of working class solidarity led to the series of defeats the working class suffered in the 1945-51 period throughout most of the OECD area. And with these defeats there emerged a domestic order and an international monetary system incompatible with long-term full employment and hence incompatible with the solidarity of the labour movement. The demobilisation of labour was a precondition for the development of an unplanned version of full employment capitalism and thus the crucial factor that accounts for why full employment only lasted a decade.

In the political class struggle of the 1980s another series of defeats of the organised working class may put full employment permanently out of reach and jeopardise democracy itself. To ensure that such defeats do not occur the labour movement must shoulder its responsibility to defend the organisations and standard of living of the working class against militarism and monetarism by developing a plan of action around which to mobilise. At the center of such a project there must be a labour movement strategy for advancing and securing the historical working class demand for full employment and social justice. Such a strategy would depend on trade union and state encroachments on the capitalist labour market and the prerogative of capital over investment. In other words, this

strategy calls upon the labour movement to pinpoint
and destroy the two institutions upon which capital
as a social relation stands or falls - a labour
market underpinned by unemployment and private
control of the means of production.

NOTES

1. I would like to thank Bob Connell,
Andrew Glyn, Joseph Halevi and George Warskett for
providing me with unpublished material and/or
comments on an earlier draft of this chapter. I
would also like to thank Leo Panitch and
Winton Higgins. They both spent untold hours
reviewing and developing a critique of the first
draft which was of considerable importance in my
rethinking the central arguments. An earlier
version of this chapter appeared in Studies in
Political Economy: A Socialist Review, 4, (1980),
pp. 5-39.
2. J. Robinson, 'Michal Kalecki on the
Economics of Capitalism', Oxford Bulletin of
Economics and Statistics, vol. 39, no. 1 (1977).
3. M. Kalecki, 'Political Aspects of Full
Employment', Political Quarterly, no. 4, (1943),
quoted in Robinson, 'Michal Kalecki', p. 16.
4. P. Armstrong, A. Glyn, J. Harrison,
B. Suttcliffe, 'Post War Reconstruction:
Metropolitan Capitalism from the Second World War to
Korea', unpublished paper, (Oxford, 1976). An
abridged version appeared in CSE Conference 1977.
Papers and Abstracts.
5. Ibid., p. 8., 1.
6. M. de Cecco, 'Origins of the Post war
Payments System', Cambridge Journal of Economics,
vol. 3, no. 1 (1979), p.54.
7. For the Atlee government's failure to
deal with these two concerns see R. Miliband,
Parliamentary Socialism, 2nd edn. (Merlin Press,
London, 1972) pp. 272-317. M. Amin and M. Caldwell,
Malaya: The Making of a Neo-Colony (Spokesmen
Books, London, 1977), Chs. 6, 7, and 9.
8. F.L. Block, The Origins of International
Economic Disorder: A Study of United States
International Monetary Policy from World War II to
the Present (University of California Press,
Berkeley, 1977) p. 47.
9. These developments are dealt with
extensively in R.N. Gardner, Sterling Dollar
Diplomacy (McGraw Hill, New York, 1969); Block,
Economic Disorder, R.F. Harrod, The Life of John

Maynard Keynes (Macmillan, London, 1951), pp. 525-650.

10.   Armstrong, _et   al_,   'Reconstruction:
Metropolitan Capitalism from the Second World War to
Korea', pp.1.19, 1.25, 8.1, 8.10; Block, _Economic Disorder_, p. 238.

11.   Block, _Economic Disorder_, p.36.

12.   For an excellent summary of American
opposition to an international commitment to full
employment see L.F. Crisp, 'The Australian Full
Employment Pledge at San Francisco', _Australian Outlook: Journal of the Australian Institute of International Affairs_, vol. 19, no. 1 (1965).

13.   Block, _Economic Disorder_, pp. 52 and 56.

14.   J. and G. Kolko, _The Limits of Power: The World and the United States Foreign Policy 1945-54_, (Harper and Row, New York, 1972), p. 337.

15.   _Ibid._, pp.329-383.

16.   Block, _Economic Disorder_, pp. 113-114.

17.   _Ibid._, pp. 94-108; M. de Cecco, 'Post War Payments System', pp. 59-60.

18.   M. de Cecco, 'Post War Payments System', p. 60.

19.   R.W. Connell and T.H. Irving, _Class Structure in Australian History: Documents, Narrative and Argument_ (Longman Cheshire, Melbourne, 1980), p.19.

20.   For good examples of opposition to a
state commitment to full employment from the press,
the academic community and the treasury see:
L. Panitch, _Social Democracy and Industrial Militancy: The Labour Party The Trade Unions and Incomes Policy 1945-74_, (Cambridge Univ. Press 1976), pp. 8-9; A.C. Pigou, _Lapses from Full Employment,_ (MacMillan, London, 1945); D.E. Moggridge, _Keynes_ (MacMillan, London, 1976), pp. 124-130. For the position of the FBI see:
S. Blank, _Industry and Government in Britain: The Federation of British Industries in Politics: 1945-1965_ (Saxon House, D.C. Heath Ltd. and Lexington Books, England and USA, 1963), pp. 35-37. For an
overview of the full employment debate see:
T.W. Huchison, _Economics and Economic Policy in Britain, 1946-66_ (George Allen and Unwin, London, 1968), pp. 19-37.

21.   H. Harris, _William Beveridge: A Biography_ (Clarendon Press, Oxford, 1977), Ch. 7.

22.   F.S.W. Craig, _British General Election Manifesto's 1900-1974_ (MacMillan, London, 1975), pp. 113-123 esp. 115.

23.   Labour Party Annual Conference Report

1944, p. 161, quoted in R. Miliband, _Parliamentary Socialism_, 2nd edn. (Merlin Press, London, 1972).

24.   General Council of the Trades Union Congress, _Interim Report on Post-War Reconstruction_ in Appendix D of the TUC 1944 Report London 1944.

25.   For the Treasury's role in this see: Rodney Lowe, 'The Erosion of State Intervention in Britain', _The Economic History Review_, vol. 31, no. 2 (1978).

26.   The 'doctrine of socialism in one class' is developed and related to the ideology of British Labour in: Panitch, _Social Democracy and Industrial Militancy_, p. 216 and passim.   For Beveridge's conception of this J. Harris, _William Beveridge_, p. 393 and passim.

27.   William Beveridge, _Full Employment in a Free Society_ (W.W. Norton, New York, 1945), p. 200.

28.   Quoted in Eric Wagham, _Strikes and the Government 1893-1974_ (Macmillan, London, 1976,), p. 95.

29.   Huchison, _Economics and Economic Policy in Britain_, pp. 32-34.

30.   Thomas Balogh, _The Dollar Crisis: Causes and Cure_ (Basil Blackwell, Oxford, 1950), p. 105.

31.   Wigham, _Strikes and The Government_, p. 102.

32.   See S. Pollard, 'The Nationalisation of The Banks: The Chequered History of a Socialist Proposal' in D.E. Martin and D. Rubinstein, _Ideology and the Labour Movement: Essays Presented to John Saville_ (Croom Helm, London, 1979).

33.   For an outstanding elaboration of this thesis see L. Panitch, _Social Democracy and Industrial Militancy_, esp. pp. 235-239; L. Panitch, 'Ideology and Integration: The Case of the British Labour Party', _Political Studies_, vol. 19, no. 2 (1971).

34.   United Nations, _Economic Survey of Europe 1949_, pp. 91-95.

35.   Craig, _British General Election Manifesto's_, pp. 123-24.

36.   Economic Survey for 1947 Cmd. 7046, p. 29.

37.   Lord Butler, _The Art of the Possible: The Memoirs of Lord Butler_, (Hamish, Hamilton, London, 1971), pp. 132 and 146.

38.   H. Macmillan, _Tides of Fortune 1945-55_ (Macmillan, London, 1969), p. 302.

39.   Craig, _British General Election Manifesto's_, p. 142.

40.   _Ibid._, p. 140-142.

41.   J. Leruez, Economic Planning and Politics
in Britain (Martin Robertson, London, 1975), pp. 70-
71.
42.   For Kalecki's argument and a discussion
of his work see M. Kalecki 'Political Aspects of
Full Employment', Political Quarterly, (1943);
G.R. Feiwel, The Intellectual Capital of Michal
Kalecki: A Study of Economic Theory and Policy
(University of Tennessee Press, 1975), Ch. 9 'The
Political Business Cycle'.
43.   Quoted in R.B. Duboff, 'Full
Employment: The History of a Receding Target',
Politics and Society, vol. 7, no. 1 (1977), p. 7.
44.   Quoted in S.K. Bailey, Congress Makes a
Law: The Story Behind The Employment Act of 1946,
(Columbia University Press, New York) (1965), p. 83.
45.   Ibid. , p. 141.
46.   For Ira Mosher's Testimony see: Full
Employment Act 1945: Hearings Before a Subcommittee
on Banking and Currency: United States Senate 79th
Congress first session of S380: especially pp. 462-
471.   For the quotation from Kleitz: Ibid.,
pp. 526-27.   For employers fear of 'planning' to
correct unemployment see the exchange between
Senator Taylor and James Donelly (Executive Vice
President Illinois Association of Manufacturers)
Ibid., pp. 665-676.
47.   Bailey, Congress Makes a Law, contains
both the original senate bill and the final act as
well as portions of the various drafts. Also see:
S.A. Alexander, 'Opposition to Defecit Spending for
the Prevention of Unemployment' in Income Employment
and Public Policy: Essays in honour of Alvin H.
Hansen (W.W. Norton, New York, 1948), pp. 177-198;
R. LeKeachman, The Age of Keynes (Allan Lane, The
Penguin Poress, Harmondsworth, 1967), pp. 140-149.
48.   For the development of this coalition and
domestic policy see D.A. Gold, 'The Rise and Decline
of the Keynesian Coalition', Kapitalistate, No 6
(1977).
49.   The theme of state and federal regulation
is dealt with extensively in G. Kolko, The Triumph
of Conservatism: 1900-1910 (The Free Press, New
York, 1963).
50.   D. Gold, 'The Rise and Decline of the
Keynesian Coalition', pp. 130-131; For the
development of class relations and the history of
the budget process see: J. O'Connor, The Fiscal
Crisis of the State (St. Martin's Press, New York,
1973), p. 64-96.
51.   For the development of new business

groups within the state, D.W. Eakins, 'Business Planners and America's Post War Expansion' in David Horawitz (ed), Corporations of The Cold War, (Monthly Review Press, New York, 1969).

52. For this data: G. Kolko, Main Currents in Modern American History (Harper and Row, New York, 1976), p. 155; and P.A. Baran and P.M. Sweezy, Monopoly Capital (Penguin Books, Harmondsworth, 1966), p. 236.

53. G.S. Jones, 'The History of US Imperialism' in R. Blackburn (ed), Ideology in Social Science, 3rd edn. (Fontana Collins, London, 1975), pp. 220-221. W. Lafeber, The Empire - An Interpretation of American Expansion 1860-1898 remains indispensible for the surge of American expansionism in the 19th century. R. Radosh, American Labour and US Foreign Policy (Random House, New York, 1965), pp. 4-25; for the incorporation of Gompers and the export surplus strategy.

54.   The best account of these developments remains: J. and G. Kolko, The Limits of Power: The World and United States Foreign Policy 1945-54 (Harper and Row, New York, 1972).   For the incorporation of the American labour leadership in this strategy see: Radosh, American Labour and US Foreign Policy esp. pp. 310-347.

55.   For the formation of the American working class and the reasons for the absence of co-ordinated nationally based working class mobilization see: Kolko, Main Currents in Modern American History, ch. 3 and 5; M. Shalev and W. Korpi, 'Working Class Mobilisation and American Exceptionalism', Economic and Industrial Democracy, vol. 1 (1980).

56.   For an alternative account focusing on 'the institutionalisation of the planning function in the Executive Branch' see: Bailey, Congress Makes a Law, chs. 8 and 9.

57.   CF: D. Swartz, 'The Politics of Reform: Conflict and accommodation in Canadian Health Policy', and A. Finkel, 'Origins of the Welfare State in Canada', both in L. Panitch (ed.), The Canadian State: Political Economy and Political Power (University of Toronto Pres, Toronto and Buffalo, 1977); C. Cuneo, 'State Mediation of Class Contradictions in Canadian Unemployment Insurance, 1930-35'. Studies in Political Economy: A Socialist Review, 3, (1980).

58.   Canadian White Paper on Employment and Income April 1945, Reprinted in The Federal Reserve Buletin, vol. 31 (1945), pp. 542, 543-44, 547.

59. D.H. Merry and G.R. Bruno, 'Full Employment: The British, Canadian and Australian white papers', Economic Record, vol. 21 Dec. (1945), pp. 226 and 229.

60. For Canada's opposition to an international commitment to full employment see: Crisp, 'The Australian Full Employment Pledge', p. 12.

61. For these developments see Panitch (ed.), The Canadian State: Political Economy and Political Power, pp. 20-21; L. Johnson, 'the development of class in Canada in the twentieth century' in G. Teeple (ed.), Capitalism and the National Question in Canada (University of Toronto Press, 1972), C.B. Macpherson, Democracy in Alberta (University of Toronto Press, 1953).

62. The best account of these developments is: S.J. Butlin and C.B. Schedvin, War Economy: 1942-45 (Griffin Press, South Australia, 1977), chs. 21-25 esp. pp. 673-680; L.F. Crisp, Ben Chifley: A Biography (Longmans, Green & Co., Victoria, 1963) esp. ch. 13-14; T. Rowse, Australian Liberalism and National Character (Kibble Books, Victoria, 1978), esp. ch. 4, pp. 127-188.

63. Quoted in Rowse, Australian Liberalism, pp. 131.

64. For Curtin's speech and the Liberal's pledge: Sydney Morning Herald June 2 1945, and Sept. 1, 1945.

65. Institute of Public Affairs, What is Ahead for Australia (NSW Sydney, June 1954), pp. 39 and 57.

66. Quoted in W.J. Waters, 'Australian Labor's Full Employment Objective, 1942-45', Australian Journal of Politics and History (1970), p. 64.

67. Institute of Public Affairs, Taxation in the Post-War Years (A Looking Forward Publication, Victoria, 1944), p. 40.

68. Institute of Public Affairs, What is Ahead for Australia, p. 8.

69. For the ruling class mobilisation of the 1940s and its historical setting see: R. Connell and T. Irving, 'Yes Virginia, there is a Ruling Class' in H. Mayer and H. Nelson (eds), Australian Politics: A Third Reader (Cheshire, Melbourne, 1973).

70. L.J. Edinger, Kurt Schumacher: A Study in personality and Political Behaviour (Stanford University Press, California, 1965), p. 105.

71. Ibid., p. 96.

72. Quoted in Kolko, The Limits of Power, pp. 432-33.

73. Edinger, Kurt Schumacher, p. 205.

74 Konrad Adenauer: Memoirs 1945-53 (Weidenfeld and Nicolson, London, 1966), p. 165.

75. The best accounts of the zaibatsu dissolution plan emphasising ruling class mobilisation are H.B. Schonberger, 'Zaibatsu Dissolution and the American Restoration', Bulletin of Concerned Asian Scholars, vol. 5, no. 2 (1973), pp. 16-31; J. Halliday, A Political History of Japanese Capitalism (Pantheon Books, New York, 1975), pp. 177-190.

76. Halliday, Japanese Capitalism, pp. 177-190, and 194-195.

77. Armstrong *et.* *al.*, 'Reconstruction: Metropolitan Capitalism from the Second World War to Korea', pp. 5.1 and 5.2.

78. *Ibid.*, p. 5.7.

79. For the development and opposition to working class militancy see Halliday, Japanese Capitalism, pp. 204-220; J. and G. Kolko, The Limits of Power, pp. 510-533. Eitaro Kishimoto, 'Labour Management Relations and Trade Unions in Post War Japan', Kyoto University Economic Review, (1968).

80. The quotations from Dodge are taken from Kolko, The Limits of Power, pp. 24, 522-524 and Halliday, Japanese Capitalism, p. 189.

81. D. Hine, 'The Labour Movement and Communism in France and Italy since 1945' in M. Kolinsky and W.E. Paterson Social and Political Movements in Western Europe (Croom Helm, London, 1976), p. 184.

82. F. Claudin, The Communist Movement from Comintern to Cominform (Penguin, Harmondsworth, 1975), pp. 316-43.

83. For the efforts to split the left in France and other parts of Europe, see: Radosh, American Labour, pp. 310-347; on the Monnet Plan: S.C. Cohen, Modern Capitalist Planning: The French Model (University of California Press, Berkeley and L.A., 1977), pp. 100-103.

84. A. Werth, France 1940-55, 1966 edn. (Beacon Press, Boston), pp. 361, 370-71, 373.

85. I am indebted to Joseph Halevi for providing me with his unpublished paper on the Italian Reconstruction henceforth referred to as 'The 1945-50 Reconstruction Period and the Foundation of Class Unionism'.

86. Halevi, 'The 1945-50 Reconstruction Period', pp. 3-6; K.J. Allen and A.A. Stevenson, An

Introduction to the Italian Economy (Martin Robertson, London, 1974), pp. 8-11; J. Halevi, 'Italy and the EEC', _World Review_, vol. 18, no. 4 (1979), pp. 71-73.

87. S. Ricossa, 'Italy 1920-1970' in _The Fontana Economic History of Europe_, vol. 6, (Harvester Press/Barnes and Noble, Brighton, 1977), pp. 286-290.

88. Claudin, _The Communist Movement_, pp. 344-369.

89. Halevi, 'The 1945-50 Reconstruction Period'.

90. M. De Cecco, 'Economic Policy in the Reconstruction Period' in S.J. Woolfe (ed.), _The Rebirth of Italy 1943-50_ (Longman, London, 1972).

91. Halevi, 'The 1945-50 Reconstruction Period', p. 9.

92. _Ibid._, p., 12.

93. Various aspects of these developments are discussed in W.E. Paterson and A.H. Thomas, _Social Democratic Parties in Western Europe_ (Croom Helm, London, 1977); E. Jacobs, _European Trade Unionism_ (Croom Helm, London, 1973); W. Kendall, _The Labour Movement in Europe_ (Allen Lane, London, 1975), S. Barkin (ed.), _Worker Militancy and its Consequences_, (Praegar Publishers, New York, 1975); J. Hagen, _The Australian Congress of Trade Unions: A Short History_ (Reed, Sydney, 1977), G. Horowitz, _Canadian Labour in Politics_ (Univ. of Toronto Press, 1972); J. Halliday, _The Political History of Japanese Capitalism_.

94. A. Kjellberg, 'Den fackliga organisationsgradens utveckling i 12 lander 1930-1975' (The Development of the Level of Trade Union Organisations in 12 Countries 1930-1975) (sociologiska institutionen, Lund University, 1979). Because of problems in establishing a directly comparable data base, this data must be understood cautiously, even though it very accurately depicts the major trends and differences between countries.

95. Halevi, 'The 1945-50 Reconstruction Period', pp. 10-11.

96. All electoral statistics in this section are taken from T.T. Mackie and R. Rose, _The International Almanac of Electoral History_.

97. J.O.N. Perkins (ed.), _Macro-Economic Policy: A Comparative Study_ (Allen and Unwin, London, 1972), p. 58.

98. F. Paukert, 'Technological Change and the Level of Employment in Western Europe', _British

Journal of Industrial Relations, vol. 6, (1968), p. 140.

99. J. Halevi, 'Italy and the EFC', p. 75.

100. B. Hansen, *Fiscal Policy in Seven Countries*, (OECD, March 1969).

101. *International Labour Office Report* Geneva, vol. 77, (1958), pp. 112-113.

102. A.R. Braun 'The Role of Incomes Policy in Industrial Countries since World War Two', *IMF Staff Papers*, March (1975), p. 15.

103. A. Shonfield, *Modern Capitalism* (Oxford University Press, 1970), p. 429.

104. T. Barker, 'International Trade and Economic Growth: an alternative to the neo classical approach', *Cambridge Journal of Economics*, p. 169 *et passim*.

105. E. Chalmers, *International Interest Rate War* (Macmillan, London, 1972), pp. 62-120.

106. F.L. Block, *Economic Disorder*, chs. 5-8; V. Cheick, *Transnational Enterprises and The Evolution of the International Monetary System* (Research Monograph No. 5, Transnational Corporations Research Project, University of Sydney, 1976).

107. S.A. Soderpalm, *Direktorsklubben-Storindustrinisvensk politik under 1930 och 1940 talen* (The Directors Club - Big Business and Swedish Politics in the 1930s and 1940s) (Stockholm Zenit Raben Och Sjögren, 19760.

108. The following section draws on research compiled in conjunction with the 'Sweden Under Social Democracy' project: N. Apple, W. Higgins, M. Wright, *Changing Patterns of Class Mobilisation in Britain and Sweden: 1930-1980* (forthcoming).

109. G. Rehn, 'Finansministrarna, LO-ekonemerna och arbetsmarknodspolitiken' (Finance Ministers - LO Economists and Labour Market Policy): *Ekonomisk debatt och ekonomisk politik: National ekonomiska Foreningen* (100 ar Stockholm, 1977), p. 210.

110. For a reprint of parts of this debate R. Turvey, *Wages Policy Under Full Employment* (William Hodge, London, 1972).

111. 1951 LO Report - English Translation (1953), p. 92.

112. *Ibid.*, p. 92.

113. *Ibid.*, p. 87.

114. *Ibid.*, p. 90.

115. *Ibid.*, p. 89.

116. *Ibid.*, pp. 85-87.

117. *Ibid.*, pp. 94-97.

118. *Ibid.*, p. 96.
119. *Ibid.*, pp. 99-106.
120. N. Apple and M. Wright, 'European Lessons for Australian Incomes Policy', Paper presented to Section 28 Jubilee ANZAAS Conference, Adelaide 12-16 May 1980, pp. 18-22.
121. *Ibid.*
122. For a useful survey of Incomes Policy in the OECD A.R. Braun, 'Incomes Policy'; A. Blyth, 'The interaction between collective bargaining and government policies in selected member countries', OECD Collective Bargaining and Government Policies (OECD, Paris, 1979); P.S. Andersen, 'Incomes Policy: The Overseas Experience' paper presented to the working party No. 4 of the Economic Policy Committee of the OECD.
123. Labour Market Policy in Transition: Summary of a report from the Expert Group for Labour Market Research at the Swedish Ministry of Labour (Stockholm 1978), p. 5.
124. R. Meidner, Employee Investment Funds: An Approach to Collective Capital Formation (George Allen and Unwin, London, 1978), p. 16.

Chapter Four

THE INSTITUTIONAL TRANSFORMATIONS OF THE POST
LAISSEZ-FAIRE STATE: REFLECTIONS ON THE ITALIAN CASE

Franco Ferraresi

STATE TRANSFORMATIONS IN RECENT DISCUSSIONS

To my knowledge, no comprehensive reconstruction of
the institutional transformations connected with the
emergence of the post *laissez-faire* state exist,
although the state is a crucial object of interest
in contemporary debates. This lapse is probably due
to a curious form of schizophrenia that (at least in
Europe) afflicts this area of study. On the one
hand, disciplines like Government, Public
Administration, Public Law, etc. have devoted much
attention to the study of specific public
institutions and agencies, producing an impressive
wealth of very useful materials. These studies,
however, very rarely attempt to link the analysis of
institutions with the broader social context in
which they operate: economic and political causes
of institutional transformations, social effects of
administrative acts, etc., are typically considered
outside the scope of pure juridical inquiry. On the
other hand, the social sciences (especially
Sociology and the 'new' Political Economy,
particularly in their neo-marxian versions), after a
long period of neglect have in recent years shown
great interest in the role of the state in
contemporary society; by and large, however, such
interest has not extended as far as the institutions
and apparatuses that constitute the 'secular arm' of
the state: hence the abstract and disembodied
character of much contemporary theorising on the
subject.
    If the above is true in general, it tends to
apply also to discussions on recent state
transformations, where institutional analysis, when
present, is often indirect and partial, while
different authors focus on different aspects and

make use of analytical frameworks belonging to different conceptual traditions, schools of thought and frames of reference. Not surprisingly, the resulting picture is scattered, heterogeneous and often contradictory. Semantic heterogeneity reflects this state of affairs. Discussions whose main object is the state make use of terms like welfare state, interventionist state, social state, monopoly state, and the like; studies focussing on the economic system employ such terms as monopoly capitalism, state capitalism, assisted capitalism, late capitalism and neo-capitalism; discussions focussing on the political system and decision-making processes talk of neo-corporatism, political exchange, overload, governability and so on. There is probably only one major point of agreement, and it regards an empirical datum, namely the fact that over the last forty to fifty years there has been a dramatic increase in public interventions and in the number of agencies carrying them out. Interpretations of this datum, however, differ widely. A major distinction can be drawn between those that link this development to an increase in the power, authority and force of the state, and those which maintain that the sprawling growth of agencies and tasks goes together with a withering away of state authority.

A cursory review of some arguments on both sides of this debate will provide some useful insights into present discussions of the state and related matters.

AN INCREASE IN THE FORCE OF THE STATE

Interpretations that see a reinforcement of the state frequently take the form of a before-after model, focussing on the transition from a nineteenth century *laissez-faire* state, operating in a mode of competitive capitalism, to a contemporary interventionist state, corresponding to late (monopoly) capitalism.

The former situation is usually described in terms of a rigid distinction between the state and civil society, between the role of the state and that of the market. In this perspective, society is organised according to the principle of 'equivalent exchange' carried out through the use of instruments belonging largely to the private sphere (stock market, company law, contracts, regulation of competition, etc.). Such instruments are sufficient for the performance of the major social transactions, namely the 'mediation' between production, saving and consumption. Thus, this also shapes social stratification; that is, the relationships between producers, intermediaries and consumers, between capitalists and rentiers, between capital and labour.

The main task of the state is to provide external support for this pattern: it becomes a 'guarantee state'; it grants that the law and the principle of the 'exchange of equivalents' be respected. The law is defined as abstract and universal, issuing mainly procedural-formal commands, defining the external conditions which enable (economic) acts to be carried out. It draws the boundaries between spheres of competence (between public and private spheres, between the spheres of different private actions); typically, it does not carry substantive contents (for example, the reduction of social inequality). Other complementary functions are performed by the state which, however, do not go so far as directly supporting accumulation: modifying the supports for production, intervening in the economic cycle, etc.

This situation undergoes drastic changes when the capacity of the market to function as the chief regulatory mechanism of society declines, due to the advent of monopoly capitalism, while cyclical crises jeopardise economic stability. The state must then 'step in', increasing both the number and the scope of its interventions.

The above is the perspective wherein some of the most interesting contributions to contemporary state theory can be seen: theories of fiscal crisis (1); theories of crisis management (2); French structuralist theories (3). One major point these theories have in common is the belief that, in late capitalist society, state intervention is necessary both to sustain accumulation and to ensure the legitimation of the system as a whole. This implies the performance of activities directed at rationalising and homogenising heterogeneous and conflicting capitalist interests, going perhaps so far as 'sacrificing' some such interests — typically, the most backward ones. In so doing the state acquires a variable degree of relative autonomy *vis-a-vis* capital.

Beyond this general area of agreement, the theories mentioned disagree on several issues, at least one of which is rather important: some authors, such as O'Connor and Poulantzas, believe that the harmonisation-rationalisation of interests

carried out by the state favours one dominant
fraction of capital (usually monopoly); others, like
Offe, see state action as favouring the capitalist
mode of production or system as a whole, by
functioning as a comprehensive ideal capitalist.

As stated these models do not show much
interest in institutional dynamics; in all of them,
however, there is a more or less implicit notion of
a process of politico-administrative centralisation,
necessary for the performance of the rationalisation
tasks that characterise state interventions in this
stage of capitalist development. The most explicit
statement can be found in O'Connor's paradigm,
according to which the principal (capitalist)
solution to the fiscal crisis is a co-operation
between the state and monopoly capital, in order to
increase productivity in private and state
sectors. A centralised administrative control of
the budget, and centralised planning are required,
implying significant transformations because (in the
US) monopoly capital does not bear a necessary link
with the agencies that control budgets (4).
Traditionally, a multitude of interest groups
clustering around several regulatory agencies have
been able to control portions of the budget,
operating without 'sense of responsibility', that is
without class consciousness. During the course of
the century, a 'conscious political directory' has
been emerging, aiming at the unification of
capitalist interests. Institutionally, such
development has brought about a centralisation of
decision-making powers in the hands of the executive
branch of government (Cabinet and the Presidency),
one able to encompass 'the system as a whole'.
Correspondingly, there has been a weakening of the
legislature, and in general of the agencies that
correspond to local and regional interests; this has
brought about a decline in the democratic character
of government.

A centralisation of political decision-making
is also implied by Poulantzas' work: that sector of
the state apparatus which prevails and acquires
superior decision-making capacity is that which is
most closely linked to the dominant capitalist
fraction. (What constitutes the nature of such
linking representation is a moot point in
structuralist paradigms). No concrete institutional
analysis is carried out by Poulantzas although some
(questionable) efforts in this direction have been
performed by his disciples and associates (5),
especially in the realm of urban studies.

Even without explicit institutional analyses however, Offe (6) does provide some most useful insights into the mechanisms through which the *spatkapitalistische Staat* operates. Present society is composed of a multitude of interest groups, none of which is strong or dominant enough to subordinate the state to its own needs, while all pose competing claims on the state. Together with the withering away of class cleavages and struggles, this creates a situation where the state allocates priorities, according to how close groups and needs are to certain general systemic imperatives. In order to achieve this result, the most effective proposals are those 'strategies of the state apparatuses which are not promoted by expressed interests, thus coming from 'outside', but originate in structures and routes belonging to the state organisation proper' (7).

Several points in this conception are worth stressing. First, the state performs a crucial, directive role. Secondly, it does this by selecting which needs are to be privileged or sanctioned, and, by allocating resources accordingly, the *spatkapitalistische Staat* carries out substantive (material) interventions, which set it apart from the formal-procedural measures of the *laissez-faire* state. (Hence legitimation problems, etc.) But these substantive interventions are also different from those of the neo-corporate state that Offe discusses in his more recent work. Here the main feature is the establishment, on the part of the state, of decision-making bodies in which the groups whose resistance could become critical to the implementation of policies, are represented: 'after the establishment of such bodies, the government is less likely to be held responsible for material outcomes of intergroup negotiations for which only the procedural rules, not the concrete results, are decided upon politically' (8).

The difference between these two formulations is undeniable; the question is whether it can be attributed to some inconsistency in Offe's theories, or whether it refers to different forms of the state, whose reciprocal relationship has yet to be worked out. The above formulation, especially in the early version, implies that the state enjoys a significant degree of autonomy *vis-a-vis* capitalist interests. But whereas other authors (especially structuralists) take for granted that the state, albeit autonomous, is subordinate to capitalist needs/interests, this possibility is problematic for

Offe: 'there is no superior, *a priori*, guarantee that recourse to the state as a directing mechanism will not, at the same time, reinforce its character as an 'extraneous body' and so become relatively independent' (9). In other words, a 'particularisation' may occur in administrative processes (their exclusion from the production of commodities), rendering them uncontrollable from the viewpoint of the needs of valorisation. The apparatuses may become so 'independent' as to use autonomy in order to pursue their own ends. The importance of this point is obvious, and it is all the more regrettable that Offe does not really pursue it, for example, in an analysis specifying under which conditions the state apparatuses utilise their autonomy in 'particularistic' forms. A more direct concern with institutional matters is to be found in Offe's article 'The Theory of the Capitalist State and the Problem of Policy Formation' (10) but it does not deal with the problems outlined above.

A partially differing view emerges from the analyses carried out during the middle 1970s by some Italian jurists connected with the Communist Party (11). The main interest of these authors is in the significance of the sprawling parastatal sector, which constitutes the main agents of the state's intervention in the Italian economy. What contradictions are caused by such structures in a representative system?

As long as the state does not intervene in economic matters, representative democracy does not severely hamper bourgeois domination: the distinction between the economic and political sphere allows private capital to control the really crucial economic decisions, without undue interference from political (representative) bodies. The spread of state interventionism implies that the economic organisation of society is no longer immune from the possibility of popular control via representative assemblies. The only non-authoritarian way in which the bourgeoisie can keep control of crucial decision-making powers is by dislocating such powers outside the reach of representative controls. This attempt was carried out in Italy after the Second World War, with a strong effort made to compress the powers of Parliament and of elected local governments, at the same time as statutory agencies were multiplied, their powers increased, and representative control over them rendered largely symbolic.

This set of cirumstances, however, opens up a new set of contradictions. State intervention in the economy is supposed not only to rationalise the capitalist system, but also to provide possibilities for popular access to the management of the economy. These are the tenets of (bourgeois) interventionist ideology itself, and they constitute some sort of 'rules of the game' that 'capitalist classes can and must be compelled to follow' (12). According to this view, in the past few years workers have gained important positions in this struggle, especially with the establishment of a new tier of government, the Regions, which have in this view, multiplied the centres for expression of popular sovereignty. In sum, the autonomy of the state from the capitalist classes is possible: state interventionism produces democratic needs which require a multiplication of decision-making loci that can be operated in a dialectical manner against the institutions of centralism. The analogy between these positions and the PCI strategy of the mid-seventies is quite obvious.

Precisely this analysis, and the kind of political conclusion it leads to, are hotly disputed by radical leftists like Negri (13). According to this author, the expansion of public interventions in the economy indicates the highest possible degree of penetration of the state in civil society. The state takes the place of market mechanisms in order to regulate class relationships, but it does so from a position which identifies its role with that of capital. Thus the state is now a direct organiser of exploitation, which rules out, as an illusion, the possibility of a working-class strategy based on the democratic seizure of single sectors or agencies of the state, to be used in the struggle against monopolies.

THE DECLINE OF THE FORCE OF THE STATE

Neo-Corporatist Models
Neo-corporatist models are well known and widely discussed. Only some aspects of them will be mentioned here - those that have immediate relevance for the purposes of the discussion.

The starting point is usually the acknowledgment of a decreasing capability of contemporary politico-bureaucratic systems to produce and implement coherent alternative policies. The state is then led to delegate decision-making powers to bodies where the interested parties are represented. Neo-corporatism thus appears as a method for absorbing the resistance of groups whose hostility could become critical for the implementation of policies (14).

Bargaining and negotiating agencies, whose characters, institutional features, powers and scopes vary according to context, multiply. The morphology of political and economic systems is altered, and so is the policy-making structure: bargained decisions acquire immediately authoritative effect. A new decision-making circuit is added to the one foreseen by constitutional documents; most of those actors, who as groups operate within this circuit, cannot be sanctioned by the electorate at large.

Opinions on the force and effects of the state within these patterns vary considerably. According to some authors (15), its role is still a crucial one, because the state is in charge of attributing political status to relevant groups, of regulating the procedures for access to the bargaining table, and, in general, guarding the rules of the game. This, then, is a major function, although it is admitted that the state, through its mainly procedural interventions, does not carry out a comprehensive development strategy, but one oriented to the attainment of consensus and avoidance of conflict.

Other authors argue that neo-corporatism is causing a much more radical decline in the state's role (16). The state ceases to be a unitary, autocephalous subject, capable of planning and enforcing major strategies for the regulation of social dynamics, and the maintenance and reproduction for social formations. Rather, it is reduced to being a partner in a bargaining circuit, and not even a unitary partner, because corporatisation implies that the apparatuses are disjointed into a multitude of different actors, each with its own *enjeus*, resources, or veto powers.

Political assessments of neo-corporatism are ambivalent. According to some it is the winning strategy of dominant classes, relegating the electorate to a purely symbolic role, and the labour movement to permanently subordinate status. Others see it as a step forward towards some kind of economic-political democracy; a step forward which, not without reason, is presently undergoing worldwide challenge.

A similar reasoning characterises 'overload' models, where the conclusions, however, are often quite different.

The Overload Models

Readings of governmental 'overload' vary according to whether the focus is more on political aspects, such as the Trilateral Commission (17), or on systemic features, but one major element is common to most statements: welfare democracy produces severe destabilising effects, because it poses an excess of demands that systems are unable to satisfy.

The argument can be stated approximately as follows: technical-scientific progress increases system-complexity, produces an enlarged number of interactions and alternatives, but also of interdependencies, thus rendering the system more vulnerable. Class distinctions wane, new collective identities emerge, new forms of conflicts and needs, linked to 'vital worlds', arise. The state's interventions in favour of accumulation and legitimacy give rise to new needs and interest groups which place upon households increasing welfare demands, that in turn, become irreversible social rights.

The functions of the state grow, its authority fades; the decision-making capacity of governmental elites decreases. Public philosophies and ideologies lose vigour, in favour of an 'exchange culture' which reduces all public interactions to commodity exchanges. Parties, trade unions, intermediate groups lose aggregative capacity; groups move from solidarity-orientation to interest-orientation, from universalism to particularism. Politics is by-passed in favour of administration. The resulting governability deficit becomes critical when inflation and zero-growth all but wipe out the resources to be distributed on the political market.

Conservative recipes for overcoming this situation include a reduction of complexity via political 'decisionism'; and bureaucratic engineering, in order to filter political demands, to reduce alternatives, to lower the level of mass requests, to reduce the 'excess' of democracy, to re-establish the boundaries between the political and social sphere (between state and market), to reinforce decision-making centres, to encourage apathy and to discourage participation. So far the left has answered these attacks only by issuing manifestos and declarations of principle asserting, for example, that mass democracy is sacrosanct, the market must undergo political control, and so on.

Some Open Questions

The above survey points to a series of unresolved dilemmas, which can be briefly summarised as follows:

> On the overall role of the state *vis-a-vis* civil society: is the state the chief governing and ruling agency in society, and one whose power and authority have strengthened as a result of the emergence of post *laissez-faire* patterns of intervention; or is it reduced to being a partner in some sort of a bargaining circuit, where its authority is faded and diluted? In this second case, is the circuit a neo-corporatist one, or one where 'overload' and 'ungovernability' prevail?

> Concerning administrative apparatuses: does bureaucracy operate within the logic of accumulation, that is, in the service of capitalist interests, be they the interests of capital as a whole or of one dominant capitalist fraction; or does it extend its relative autonomy to the point of putting itself outside the logic of accumulation, thus following a 'private', 'particularistic' logic?

> Concerning recent institutional transformations, linked to the emergence of the interventionist, post *laissez-faire* state: can these be seen as rationalisation processes that follow some sort of a unified, centralising pattern (as implied by structuralists); or do the new agencies and institutions multiply at random, in a disjointed, non-rationalised form?

> If this random alternative holds, does the multiplication of organs and agencies open up, however chaotically, political spaces for democratic participation, or does it merely entail a kind of fragmentation without pattern, where the 'law of the jungle' prevails, favouring the non-mediated predominance of the strongest interest groups?

Variations in the answers to these questions reflect both different contextual situations, and different theoretical and methodological approaches, – raising the problem of whether a unitary reconstruction of the post *laissez-faire* state is possible at all.

My present interest is more limited, and regards the possibility of charting the transformations that the Italian state has undergone in the postwar years. The discussion developed so far has brought up certain issues and indicators that can be used as benchmarks for such an exploration. Firstly, we can consider the extent of changes in the character and significance of the law, as indicators of the shift in the boundary line between market mediation and state mediation of social relationships. Secondly, we can consider the extent of transformations of constitutional organs, concerning especially the relationship between the legislative and executive branches: does a possible decline in the power of Parliament correspond to a reinforcement of central government and cabinet? Thirdly, considering transformations of administrative apparatuses: how far has there been a move away from a purely law-and-order function of public administration, towards one more oriented to the management and mediation of social relationships? What has been the significance of new public agencies and corporations, as distinct from traditional structures of public administration? How developed has been the establishment of bargaining and negotiating agencies representing the major interest groups? How extensive are their powers? Finally, we can consider transformations in the structure and powers of local government. We can analyse recent transformations of the Italian administrative/state system, along these lines. In what follows I will provide some rough indication of my reasoning and findings thus far.

TRANSFORMATIONS OF THE ITALIAN STATE

Historical Peculiarities
A purely non-interventionist state never existed in Italy, even in classical *laissez-faire* times. Since the unification of the country, in the 1860s, the state has intervened heavily in social and economic matters, for a set of interrelated reasons, that can be indicated only sketchily here. They included the need to bring about some social and economic integration in a deeply fragmented texture which had achieved political unity after centuries of separation; the problems of industrialisation, in a system that featured 'latecomer's problems' (18),

and the lack of a strong moderate party, capable of aggregating the heterogeneous bourgeois interests and which hence threw on the state responsibility for such aggregation.

Although structured and organised in rigorous law-and-order patterns (19), public administration has always performed an important role of social mediation and intervention. For instance, one may consider the role of the Prefects, at least until the First World War, as major protagonists of political life at the local and sometimes national level; the role of public administration on the labour market, where it absorbed intellectual and manual unemployment, especially in the South. This was especially true of *petite-bourgeois* strata whose support was necessary for the maintenance of the system of domination, and which were being expelled from the market by capital concentration. Awareness of these dynamics receives surprisingly similar expression in as distant observers as Gramsci and Mussolini:

> The Mezzogiorno was reduced to the status of a semi-colonial market, a source of savings and taxes, and was kept 'disciplined' by measures of two kinds. First, police measures ... Secondly, political-police measures: personal favours to the 'intellectual' stratum or *paglietta* (pettifogging lawyers), in the form of jobs in public administration and of licence to pillage the local administration with impunity... that is incorporation of the most active Southern elements, 'individually', into the leading personnel of the state, with particular 'judicial' and bureaucratic privileges etc. Thus the social stratum which could have organised the endemic southern discontent, instead became an instrument of Northern policy, a kind of auxiliary private police (20).

Mussolini replying to a Minister who was submitting a plan for extensive restructuring of the administration, noted that

> Your suggestions would severly reduce the employment in state jobs of graduates from the South, thus damaging southern white-collar-and-tie proletariat. These people are very much to be feared - they possess a natural gift for propaganda, which has much effect in places

where friendship and kin relationships play a great role in creating emotional currents that spread like fire, especially when they are supported by disappointed bourgeois elements, which in the South carry much more weight than in Milan or Turin. We must adopt a policy of maximum job availability in the state bureaucracy, unless we want to have on our hands an insurrection, the insurrection of hungry - I repeat, hungry - intellectuals, the most difficult insurrection to placate. Besides, it is a duty to take care of them (21).

Data on the present situation confirm the persistence of this trend. In 1954 the percentage of administrative class employees in the state bureaucracy coming from the South was 56.3% of the total, while southern population was 37.3% of the national; in 1964 the percentage had reached 62.7%, while the southern population had in fact decreased *vis-a-vis* the national (36.7%), although minimally.

As for the general growth of public employees, between 1881 and 1971, the ratio of state employees to 100,000 population increased from 338 to 3,294. Between 1951 and 1972 the percentage of persons employed by Public Administration, of the total occupied, went up from 5.8% to 9.7%. Of course, the enormous increase in state functions over this period renders it impossible to maintain that employee growth was an answer only to occupational problems. It is hard, however, to deny that throughout Italian national history bureaucracy has performed a crucial role in absorbing (intellectual) unemployment, and is still one of the chief protagonists in the labour market.

Changes in the Character and Significance of the Law
The decline of the generality of the law is by now a classical *topos* of legal philosophy which tends to attribute it to the passage from a freely-competitive system to one ruled by state capitalism and monopolies (22). Different kinds of legislation prevail in different contexts and times. What features appear in recent Italian law? Some items which require further investigation, include the following. First, the establishment of new intervention mechanisms, supposed to perform the mediating functions once belonging to the market, requires a new kind of legislation, which is different from abstract-universal law, from social legislation and from *ad*

hoc, specific provisions (*leggi provvedimento*). It is a form of law that creates new juridical subjects, endowed with special powers and duties. The so-called 'individual-abstract' law is characterised also by the fact that its implementation is postponed in time (*attuazione differita*) (23); the laws that regulate rapports and sanction accords among the most important social groups are typically negotiated outside parliament, the latter being merely required to approve such bargained and negotiated laws. What features and contents do these laws present in procedural, substantial, terms? The great legislative *corpora* tend to be reduced, if not disaggregated, as general codes are substituted by a number of micro-systems (24) The above tendencies entail a high degree of fragmentation and particularism in parliament's legislative activity, whose main and best known indicator is the enormous number of micro-acts (*leggine*) that make up a disproportionate part of legislation. Their scope, mode of production, significance, have been explored in depth by a number of studies (25) and will not be discussed here; but a further development has emerged in the last years: an increasing resort to Executive Decrees as a form of legislative production. (Government, in the case of 'necessity and urgency', may issue acts (decrees) carrying the force of laws. Such acts must then be 'converted' into laws by parliament, within a specified deadline). During the first 24 years of parliamentary activity, 291 Decrees were issued, of which 280 were converted into laws; in the last eight years, 360 were issued of which 285 obtained conversion. In 1979-1980, out of about 300 legislative measures, 90 (almost 30%), were Decrees. A content analysis of them reveals that they are concerned largely with controversial and conflictual matters, the ones that governments do not like to submit to regular parliamentary scrutiny. Parliament is left with trivial legislation (26).

Parliament and Public Corporations

The last paragraph points to a marked decline in the role of parliament, a development that can be observed in most advanced capitalist systems (27), although the extremes it has reached in Italy are probably unknown elsewhere. The reasons for such decline have been extensively studied (28); though one point should be mentioned here, namely the fact that Parliament's decline has been in part a consequence of the growth and expansion of the public sector of the economy (public corporations, parastatals and the like).

In turn, in the growth of the parastatal sector (caused by a general trend towards 'welfare' inefficiency in traditional administrative structures), one purely political factor should be mentioned: namely the strategy of the ruling Christian Democratic (DC) party in the immediate post-war years. Christian Democracy was then a recently founded party (1944) with neither a solid political base nor organisation (it had to rely on the church structure), and without preferential links with the state apparatus. At the same time, parliamentary opposition from the left was very strong, because of the strength of the workers' movement, of the moderate-conservative policies of the DC, the Cold War atmosphere, etc. The DC as a party needed to set up its own power base and to curtail the spaces available for parliamentary opposition. The establishment of the parastatal system answered both needs: holding managerial positions within parastatals as a rigorous party monopoly, Christian Democrats provided themselves with a loyal network of public institutions, which proved to be an invaluable source of power and funds. By keeping controls over parastatals cumbersome, formalistic and inefficient, parliament was bypassed, thus effectively emptying the main forum of the left. As a consequence, the most dynamic instruments of the public sector of the economy, the most characteristically post *laissez-faire* ones, have operated largely outside parliamentary (and often governmental) control.

Local governments have also been heavily affected by the growth of public corporations and statutory agencies - a development which was taking place at a time in which the powers of municipalities were anyhow weakening (29). Especially in the less developed southern regions, the huge development corporations like *Cassa per il mezzogiorno* (Southern Development Agency), richly endowed with state funds, could apply enormous pressure on impoverished municipalities, thus effectively cancelling local autonomy. (The newly established regions have not really been able to redress the balance).

The decline of parliament, and in general of elective bodies, appears then to be hardly in doubt. The problem, however, remains: does this development correspond to a reinforcement of central government (Council of the Ministers and Presidency of the Council), much in the same way as, allegedly, is happening elsewhere? Before tackling this question, a further exploration will be needed, concerning the role and significance of those corporate administrative bodies (Boards, Committees, Colleges, Councils, etc.), that represent one of the most characteristic features of post *laissez-faire* states, especially in their neo-corporate version.

Administration by Boards

Recent empirical enquiries have provided much new information on these developments (30). The establishment of boards and committees acquired relatively significant dimensions at the turn of the century, when the new, emerging social interests were found to lack adequate representation in the channels provided by the law-and-order administrative structures. A large number of boards was then set up, very soon eliciting a barrage of criticisms centring on their number (too many), dimensions (too large), and, more importantly, on the fragmentation of political and administrative responsibility they were alleged to provoke.

This latter aspect also holds the foreground concerning contemporary developments. Between 1943 and 1976 about 1600 new boards have been set up, with peaks in the 1943-48 and in the 1963-68 periods, that is, the periods registering the major institutional transformations. Let us briefly sketch some features of this corporate population.

Placement within the administration: most boards are located within, and are responsible to, single ministries: the importance of the presidency of the council as a 'parent' organisation has decreased, both in quantitative terms (the number of boards referring to the presidency has gone down from 15.6% in 1948 to 10.5% in 1976) and in qualitative terms (only 4% of the boards operating with the presidency perform co-ordinating functions, whereas 45% of them carry out active administrative duties).

Scope of activities: each group of boards operating within each ministry performs the whole spectrum of possible functions (boards concerned with personal services operate within 14 different ministries; boards concerned with production operate within 17 ministries, and so on). This imples the following: a minute fractioning of interventions, a reassembly of powers within each ministry and a very low level of co-ordination.

Activities performed: there has been a congealment of the fields of activity, whereby 'classified' activities (production, real services, personal services) have taken the largest share, while non-classified, heterogeneous activities are in decline. This is taken to indicate that in the former sector (especially regarding production), autonomous mechanisms of interest selection and articulation are gradually being substituted by administrative mechanisms. The interpretation is confirmed by data regarding membership.

Membership: criteria are becoming more rigid. Board membership tends to be more and more specified by statutes and acts; the boundary between the 'ins' and the 'outs' is thus sharpening; appointments left to 'free' choice of political organs decline, while appointments controlled by interest groups grow (abdication of state authority?). Where the boards' activity deals with matters internal to the politico-administrative system, politicians are by far outnumbered by bureaucrats, 70% against 18% (and this does not take into account boards concerned with public employment matters).

Interests represented: economic interests are on the increase, especially in the area of productive activities, the share of transactions regulated by market mechanisms is decreasing, to the advantage of administrative regulations; differences among capital and labour are marked; the two are represented in around 120 boards, but labour alone in 23, capital alone in 82, both in 112.

Some sketchy conclusions appear obvious: administrative regulation of social interests grows in most social areas, but it does so in a fragmented, unco-ordinated way, without any overall strategy; the leadership functions of the state are in fact declining. The very sharp definition of membership criteria reduces the possibility that boards perform a 'democratic' role, admitting new, disaggregated, emerging social interests: the Labour Unions are the only grass roots interests which find systematic representation. Nevertheless capital's representation continues to be numerically much stronger. Similar features (stifling of popular participation) can be found at the regional level.

Is there any *locus* where this fragmentation may be overcome? Attention must obviously turn to the central governmental apparatuses.

Government and Cabinet

The general weakness of government as an effective controlling and co-ordinating agent is a well-known fact of Italian politics. The reasons for this are both political and institutional. Institutionally, the central governmental structure appears as a loose and disjointed swarm of ministries lacking coherence and co-ordination, as a result of a growth process that has taken place through the decades, with no real effort at rationalisation. Fragmentation, overlapping and conflicts of competence are the normal condition. For example, financial matters are apportioned amoung three ministries (Treasury, Finance, Budget), a situation without parallel in modern parliamentary systems. Industrial policy is handled by at least three ministries; those concerning public transporation amoung four; and so on. Some efforts towards co-ordination have been attempted by way of interministerial committees, most notably in 1967-68 through the Economic Planning Committee, but the results have been disappointing.

Overall co-ordination should be the responsibility of the presidency of the council, one of the major victims of the system's lack of capacity or will to amend itself. For at least a century the need to rationalise the powers and means of the presidency has been acknowledged by all political parties and groups, yet no reform of the office has been carried out (even though an article of the 1948 Constitution requires it). The president is charged with the obligation to co-ordinate government but is given no formal instruments (aside from those accruing from his personal political position) to do so. At present each ministry tends to go its way, and is run as a fiefdom by the politicians and the small top level oligarchy of senior administrators (31).

The Bureaucratic Structure

The difficulties encountered by the Cabinet in performing a truly governing role are also due to the low efficiency of the bureaucratic structure (32). The prevailing conceptions of the state and the bureaucratic structure are still those of the nineteenth centry *laissez-faire*, law-and-order state, and they permeate most crucial aspects of the system. Thus the basic legislation relating to such matters as the budget, public accounting, contracts and controls is primarily concerned with formal legality, and provides no instruments for socio-economic intervention. Likewise, the provisions and regulations for personnel management and organisation are concerned with powers, obligations and spheres of competence, while neglecting such matters as job content or the adequacy of available skills. For example, economic skills are still extremely scarce and poorly utilised, while juridical preparation is still predominant (33). The result is rigidity, fragmentation, inadequate professionalisation and skilled technical personnel, low morale and motivation, and strong arbitrary powers wielded by senior officials.

Many attempts have been made to reform the apparatus, but instead of a comprehensive reorganisation the basic structures and principles have continued unchanged, while time and again legislative bodies, agencies and institutes have been added to satisfy the demands of various political regimes. Thus Giolitti's 'assistance state', at the beginning of the century, nationalised railroads and established the first major social security agencies; fascist corporatism established a score of special purpose agencies for the assistance of a multitude of groups and categories (war orphans, workers' children, etc.), while, under pressure from the 1930s economic crisis, it initiated a massive process of state intervention in economic matters. After the Second World War, 'welfare state' agencies were expanded and multiplied to cover previously excluded categories (artisans, shopkeepers, farmers, etc.), while interventions and regulations of the economy became daily occurrences. However, the new bodies were not grafted on to the old, but were suddenly introduced as partial modifications, exceptions and waivers which have undermined the old structures, without creating consistent new ones.

The results are easily predictable. The arbitrary powers of the senior ranks are enhanced and the irrationality of the system strengthens the postions of those who can provide the *interpretatio authentica* of norms, and decide which regulations can be evaded with impunity, and which must be enforced.

SUMMARY

It is obvious that the Italian situation does not quite fit in any of the models described by the literature. Firstly, no strengthening and reinforcement of the state's authority has taken place; no centralistic rationalisation of the apparatuses, either towards a comprehensive ideal capitalist function, or towards support for a capitalist fraction. Secondly, it is also difficult to see the emergence of neocorporatist developments, for lack of at least two conditions: the capability of the state to enforce and guarantee the 'rules of the game' and the willingness on the part of the major social groups to strike a 'social pact', at least until recent years. Thirdly, 'overload' models present external similarities with the Italian situation, but one major difference obtains: demands on the state to distribute resources easily predate that villain of overload tales, welfare democracy, and have been advanced most extensively by bourgeois interests.

A peculiar pattern prevails, one which becomes most explicable if one examines the very intimate link existing between the administrative and the political system. The dominant feature in the latter is a deep socio-economic fragmentation, due to historical factors arising from the distorted pattern of capitalist development. In order to overcome the resulting cleavages, it would have been necessary to carry out structural, system-wide reforms, which would inevitably have hurt some interests belonging to the dominant groups (e.g. urban speculators). This is why reforms have never really been on the ruling class agenda. The dearth of really hegemonic groups has left the power bloc with insufficient force to cut off parasitic branches; at the same time, fragmentation has made it possible to manage the system not via universalistic programmes, but via particularistic allegiances, obtained through client dealings.

Within this framework, the role played by the state and its apparatuses has been crucial (34). If personnel, resources and patterns of behaviour had been efficient, coherent and aggressive, probably the administration would have attempted to achieve some form of rationalisation of political demands, or, at least, to act as a filter for the aggregation of the most sectoral and particularistic handouts. On the other hand, *vis-a-vis* such logic, the existing irrationality turns out to be functional, because it is easily amenable to dealings with clientele. The bureaucratic machine itself becomes a party to such dealings, since the general inefficiency allows the senior ranks to transform into negotiable items what should be institutional duties.

This is the sense in which the notion of 'relative autonomy' of the state acquires a meaning in the Italian case. It is not so much that an overall guidance and rationalising function regarding the needs of capitalist accumulation has appeared (in spite of the existence of a most impressive arsenal of intervention instruments of all sorts, the economic system remains one of the most unregulated and anarchic in advanced capitalist countries) but rather that bureaucracy occupies a crucial bargaining position, which allows it to reap (short term) benefits for itself and its kin.

As to the former (benefits for bureaucracy), it should be sufficient to point out that between one-fourth and one-third of all bills submitted to parliament after the war have dealt with salary and employment conditions of civil servants. As to the latter, a new social stratum is supposed to have been the result of increased public intervention in the economy. It takes on different names: 'state bourgeoisie', 'assisted bourgeoisie', 'dependent small bourgeoisie', and the like. The nature and boundaries of this stratum are unclear, but its position at the centre of a major vicious circle of contemporary development cannot be reasonably disputed. Resources absorbed by the 'assisted state bourgeoisie' are subtracted from productive utilisation, which weakens the productive basis of the system; this, in turn, creates the need for more assistance, which further reduces the productive utilisation of resources. For how long the system will be able to suffer from this drainage, is again, an open question.

NOTES

1. J. O'Connor, The Fiscal Crisis of the State (St. Martins Press, New York, 1973).
2. C. Offe, 'Crises and Crisis Management: Elements of a Political Crisis Theory', International Journal of Politics, 6, 1976, pp. 29-67.

Institutional Transformation of the Italian State

3.   N. Poulantzas. State Power Socialism, (New Left Books, London, 1974).

4.   See·A. Negri, *La forma stato* (Feltrinelli; Milano, 1979) for a consequent critique of the structuralist position.

5.   R.   Dulong,   'La   Crise   du   rapport etat/societe locale vue au travers de la politique regionale' in N. Poulantzas (ed.), La Crise de l'Etat (P.U.F., Paris, 1976); M. Castells, 'Advanced Capitalism,   Collective   Consumption   and   Urban Contradictions' in L.N. Lindberg, *et.al.* (eds.), Stress   and   Contradiction   in   Modern   Capitalism (Lexington, Massachussetts, 1975).

6.   C. Offe, 'Klassenherrschaft und Politisches System: Die Selektivitat politischer Institutionen' in Strukturprobleme des Kapitalistischen Staates (1972), (the pages referred to in the text are those of the Italian collection which contains this and other   articles   under   the   title   Lo   stato   nel capitalismo maturo, (Milano, 1977)).

7.   Offe, 1972, p.129.

8.   C. Offe, 'The Attribution of Political Status to Interest Groups: The West German Case', mimeo, (1978), p.22.   (Since published in S. Berger (ed.), Interest Groups in Western Europe, (Cambridge University Press, 1981)).

9.   Offe, 1972, p.72.

10.   C. Offe, 'The Theory of the Capitalist State and the Problem of Policy Formation' in L.N. Lindberg, *et. al.* (eds.), 1975).

11.   See, for instance, P. Barcellona, 'Legislazione e stratificazione sociale', Democrazia e Diritto, 3, 1975; P. Barcellona, Oltre lo stato sociale, (De Donato, Bari, 1980); F. Galgano, Le istituzioni dell'economia capitalistica, Zanichelli, Bologna, 1974).

12.   Galgano, 1974, p.34.

13.   Negri, 1979.

14.   Offe, 1978.

15.   C. Offe, 1978; M. Regini, 'I rapporti tra sindacati e stato nella formazione della politica economica   in   italia: verso   un   sistema neocorporativo?'   mimeo, 1978; and G.E. Rusconi, 'Scambio politico', Laboratorio politico, 2, 1981.

16.   S.   Belligni,   'Governi   privati   nel capitalismo   maturo: a   proposito   di   neo-corporatiismo', Democrazia e Diritto, 4-5 1979.

17.   S. Belligni, 'Teori della governabilita e postulati della democrazia', Introdpction to: Il governo del territorio, Turin, forthcoming; and M. Crozier, S.P. Huntington, J. Watanuki, The Crisis of

Democracy: Report on the Governability of Democracies to the Trilateral Commission, (The Trilateral Commission, New York, 1975).
18. A. Gerschenkron, Economic Backwardness in Historical Perspective, (Harvard University Press, New York, 1962).
19. F. Ferraresi, Burocrazia e politica in Italia, (Il Mulino, Bologna, 1980).
20. A. Gramsci, Prison Notebooks, (Lawrence & Wishart, London, 1971), p.94.
21. Mussolini as quoted in Ferraresi, 1980, p.113.
22. F. Neumann, The Democratic and the Authoritarian State, (Free Press, Glenroe, 1957).
23. Barcellona, 1975.
24. P. Rescigno, 'I mutamenti nelle vie del potere', Progetto, 1, 1981.
25. See G. di Palma, Surviving without Governing, (Free Press, New York, 1978); A. Predieri (ed.), Il parlamento nel sistema politico italiano, (Comunita, Milano, 1975); and G. Sartori (ed.), Il parlamento italiano, (ESI, Napoli, 1963).
26. F. Cazzola and M. Morisi, 'La decretazione d'urgenza 'continua: da Andreotti a Cossiga', Laboratorio politico, 1, 1981.
27. G. Poggi, La vicenda dello stato moderno, (Il Mulino, Bologna, 1979).
28. See di Palma, 1978; Predieri (ed.), 1975; and G. Satori (ed.), 1963.
29. F. Ferraresi, 'Crise de la ville et politique urbaine in Italie', Sociologie du Travail, No.2, 1979.
30. Especially M. Cannelli, L'amministrazione per collegi. (Il Mulino, Bologna, 1981).
31. Ferraresi, 1980.
32. Ferraresi, 1980.
33. F. Ferraresi and G. Ferrari, 'Italy: Economists in a Fragmented Political System', History of Political Economy, Fall 1981.
34. Ferraresi, 1980.

Chapter Five

TECHNOCRACY AND LATE CAPITALIST SOCIETY: REFLECTIONS ON THE PROBLEM OF RATIONALITY AND SOCIAL ORGANISATION

H.T. Wilson

INTRODUCTION TO TECHNOCRACY

'Technocracy' is a concept which both resists formal definition and cries out for it. To the extent that it stands for process as well as structure, Nietzsche's point about the elusiveness of concepts that are shorthands for process is particularly well taken. To be sure, the concept's inability to appropriate its object – the phenonmenon itself – argues for its status as a universal substantive rather than a mere term whose meaning is dependent on its reduction to 'concrete' functions and operations (1).

On the other hand, conventional standards of intelligibility cannot be totally ignored. In a society which honours the norm of adequacy, with its emphasis on identity, a correspondence theory of knowledge and truth, and an empirical convention which views the whole as an abstract concatenation of 'concrete' parts-as-facts-as-events, it is difficult to analyse technocracy and allied concepts without acquiescing, at least initially, in the idea of knowledge as a grasp, an appropriation.

It becomes all the more necessary to honour such a convention when it is remembered that by 'technocracy' is understood not only observable (or observable in principle) structures and processes but ideology or doctrine as well. Compared to these considerations, the assertion that 'technocracy' functions as a condensational as well as a referential symbol for those either supportive or critical of it appears trifling. Nevertheless, the fact that it is employed in both a laudatory and a pejorative way provides an important insight into its origins and variegated meanings (2).

One way of approaching the task of analysis

might include the construction of an 'ideal type' paralleling Weber's well-known formulation of modern Western bureaucracy (3). The objective here would be not only to follow Weber's advice on type construction in order to generate a comparative tool sitting somewhere between an operational definition and no definition at all (4). It would also permit 'technocracy' itself to emerge as an ideal type which could be compared on substantive grounds to Weberian bureaucracy and associated phenomena.

Another aspect of the analytical task relates to the already-noted fact that technocracy denotes both structure and process and ideology or doctrine. In effect, we need a complementary focus to that provided by the Weberian technique of type construction and the bureaucratic ideal type itself. The distinction in the study of the professions between professionalisation as a process, profession as a structure, and professionalism as an ideology or doctrine either supportive or critical of the process of professionalisation is a useful one for this purpose (5).

The tension between hierarchy and professional specialisation continues to be of central significance to an understanding of contemporary work organisations and their role in advanced industrial societies (6). It would be surprising if an analysis of technocracy in these societies could be carried out without attending to this particular problematic. In what follows, we shall be concerned not only with structural and processual attributes but attitudinal attributes of individual technocrats in the midst of bureaucratic formal organisation and professional specialisation (7).

This tension between the managerial and the technical, between power and the responsibility for its exercise and knowledge, is fundamental to any adequate understanding of technocracy. The same can be said for the very different, and often conflicting, imperatives of rationalisation and innovation (8).

This chapter will proceed as follows. First, it will elaborate the concept of technocracy using the Weberian ideal type as a model, and the type formulation of bureaucracy as a basis for substantive comparison in the ways already indicated, in order to discuss reasons why technocracy has been variously described on the one hand as a spectre and on the other as a myth. Second, we attempt to relate technocracy to some key concepts (including class, elite, meritocracy, rationalisation and social formation) and conclude by assessing the significance of technocracy for the analysis of the twin problems of rationalisation and legitimation.

BUREAUCRACY: SCALAR, FUNCTIONAL AND CAREER ASPECTS

The continuing substantive value of Weber's ideal typical 'bureaucracy' only serves to support further the comparative method for which it is ideally to be used. When the ten key characteristics cited in *Theory of Social & Economic Organisation* are scrutinised carefully, they can be seen to reduce to three basic aspects or clusters: (1) the scalar cluster (hierarchy, discipline, formal authority, rule orientation); (2) the functional or technical cluster (defined sphere of competence, selection and advancement mainly on the basis of technical qualification); and (3) the career cluster (free selection and contract, separation from means of administration with no right of appropriation, full-time salaried career based on appointment and tenure) (9).

What we shall discover in our effort to formulate a parallel ideal type is the extent to which technocracy continues to be grounded in the tensions and accommodations worked out between these three clusters. This , of course, is not to say that no novel characteristics serve to distinguish technocracy from bureaucracy, even in its contemporary variant. Clearly we need to take account of several important society-wide developments if we are to meaningfully assess the present and future role of technocracy.

They include the following: (1) the increasing role of the state and the virtual collapse of the public-private distinction in property, contract, commercial, urban and administrative law; (2) the ever greater role of the large corporations, particularly multi-national corporations, in an emerging world economy; (3) the now central role of science and science-based technology in production, research and development, and administration and service activities; (4) the 'socialisation' of functional and technical modes of rationality; and (5) the emergence of operations research, systems, and game-theoretical modelling as a complement to increased dependence on automated-electronic and robot technologies (10).

To admit that these developments have occurred,

and are absolutely central to any adequate understanding of technocracy, is not to argue that the conflicts embedded in bureaucratic formal organisation have been superseded and are no longer relevant. This is particularly true when we realise the importance of the conflict between authority and knowledge which Weber thoroughly anticipated, and which is well captured by the contrasting imperatives of the scalar and functional-technical clusters. There is an overwhelming body of research and scholarly work on one variant or another of this basic problem, but rarely has it been tied to technocracy as an elite class fragment in late capitalist society (11).

BUREAUCRACY, KNOWLEDGE AND POWER

If we look first at the central role of the state, either in terms of sponsorship, corporate regulation and taxation or the more ominous development of corporatism (12), we can see that the collapse of the public-private distinction so central to differentiating public from private functions in the common law merely confirms Weber's point about the relationship between bureaucratisation and the so-called rationalisation process in all industrial and urban societies. 'This type of organisation is in principle applicable with equal facility to a wide variety of different fields', including profit-making enterprises, charitable organisations and political and religious organisations (13).

The point here is that size, scale and complexity can only partly explain recourse to the formal bureaucratic model (14). This was the point of Weber's analysis of the relation between bureaucracy and money economies of all types, and it confirms the close tie between his ideal type and all forms of capitalism, whether state or corporate in animus and structure (15). To a significant extent, one must acknowledge the interdependence between bureaucracy as a form of organised goal-functional rationality and the issue of legitimacy and legitimation which surrounds his entire discussion of the ideal type, if one is to make sense of technocracy as a structure favouring certain norms and behaviours (16).

We would argue that it is to some extent the 'socialisation' of certain values associated with the growth of a labouring and consuming (but not necessarily an investing) class, who find their separation from the means of administration almost totally unproblematic, which is one essential property of the technocratic elite as a class fragment. Not that they are hard-nosed producers, battling the parasitic financiers and investors, as Veblen and his followers fancied when they first formulated the term technocracy (17). It is rather their wholesale lack of interest in problems and issues surrounding the ownership and disposition of property which is of central significance.

In a sense, their very sponsorship by the state either directly, or indirectly as decision-makers and problem-solvers in large corporations, guarantees the society-wide impact of their efforts to preserve the basic features of Western political economy, even while adjusting to new political, economic, and military realities. From the standpoint of contemporary sociological understandings, we would have to describe technocrats in late capialist society as that elite fragment of a labouring and consuming class who have been subjected to 'secondary socialisation', not only with regard to specific and general knowledge-claims, but also by reference to basic values, norms, biases and preferences, including most importantly, the ideology of objective knowledge itself (18).

Another issue also arises out of bureaucratisation and the emergence of technocratic norms of rationality in all sectors of organised activity in late capitalist society. Here we have in mind, first, the crucial distinction already suggested between class, class fragment and elite (19). We purposely ignore the ideologically conflicting origins of class and elite concepts in, respectively, marxian and Paretian analysis in favour of comparing and contrasting the two notions along the following lines. By elite is meant a fragment of a class, a fragment whose secondary socialisation in this case has led them to favour certain goals for capital, certain approaches and techniques of decision-making and problem solving, and certain views about the nature of the ideal society and the role of the state and corporations therein (20).

By class is meant a specific segment of the social structure related in one or another way to the means of production through their occupational, organisational or career status. Technocrats are tied to the production system, at the outer perimeter, by the law of value itself, if not in more direct ways. It is the technocratic defence of objective unbiased knowledge and the notion of 'knowledgeableness' as an objective property of the well-trained and well-disciplined observer which marks off technocracy's more specific base for domination in and through the auspices of a meritocratic 'stratarchy' premised on formal training and certification rather than 'experience' (21).

The second point is a corollary of the first. It concerns the distinction pointed out by Giddens, among others, between the argument that a 'new class', whether of managers (Veblen; Burnham) or technocrats (Meynaud; Dreitzel) is emerging, and Galbraith's claim since 1967 that power, is in fact, being dispersed downward in large corporations because 'knowledge' is alledgedly displacing capital as the central factor of production, that is, the one most scarce 'at the margin' (22). Galbraith's arguments, in both *The New Industrial State* and *Economics and the Public Purpose*, provide an eloquent testimonial to the extent to which the ideology of objective knowledge and knowledgeableness has permeated the higher circles of American intellectual opinion (23).

Apart from the absurdity of so dissociating knowledge from other factors of production as to argue that it can stand on its own in the absence of goals, priorities, values and images of the ideal and real in collective life, there is also the strategic question of just how far such a downward dispersion would be understood to go. Even if such a dispersion of the knowledge once allegedly possessed by the capitalist few could be argued to have taken place, it is the basis for participation and membership *now* which serves to set the contours for defining inclusion and exclusion.

Ignoring the matter of secondary socialisation in career, bureaucratic, meritocratic and technocratic values completely, Galbraith sees the marginality of knowledge as a key factor of production to have increased as a result of the downward dispersion already noted! (24) This suggests a rather peculiar conception of knowledge, one which is only valid as a 'key factor' so long as it can be seen to be thoroughly distended from the activity of individuals engaged in accumulation, profit maximisation (whether short or long-term in nature), or forms of comparative advantage involving the ownership, manipulation and control of other factors of production as well.

In his more recent *Economics and the Public*

Purpose, Galbraith appears to have revised a hope expressed in *The New Industrial State* that somehow, at some point in time, the so-called 'educational and scientific estate' could be counted on to bail out the 'techno structure' which is the alleged result of this dispersion of knowledge-as-power downwards. He now seems to realise that such a hope is far less realistic than the totalisation of narrow rationality norms that is the hallmark of such thinking, albeit now within an operational, game theoretical and/or systems framework (25).

It may be that Galbraith's conception, far from simply being mistaken, is in fact an indication of 'American uniqueness' relative to the other advanced industrial societies. It is far more likely, however, that any American uniqueness found in Galbraith's claims resides in the arguments as 'rationalisations' in their own right. This is in contrast to the claim that they constitute accurate depictions of the American industrial and social structure as a culturally unique configuration not amenable to inclusion in generalisations about European 'class' societies (26). In one sense, it is not too much to say that Galbraith's thesis about the technostructure and 'knowledge' as a key factor of production attempts to turn a sow's ear into a silk purse. This becomes all the more apparent when we examine the position which Robert Lane and Daniel Bell take regarding knowledge and 'knowledge-ableness'.

In what follows, it is their claim to have overcome the tension and distinction between the knowledge possessed by the 'technostructure' and that held by the 'educational and scientific estate' which marks off the work of Lane and Bell. On the order of Mannheim in *Man and Society in an Age of Reconstruction*, but lacking Mannheim's understanding of expert knowledge, judgement and decision, Lane and Bell make what is perhaps the strongest case on record for knowledge as an independent objective entity which has been purged of all doctrinal and ideological remnants.

The excerpt by Robert Lane which follows clearly expresses the point of view of Daniel Bell as well, and indeed has been cited favourably by Bell in *The Coming of Post-Industrial Society*. It shows how much more than merely relations between the economy and the state, technocratic thinking comprehends in its frameworks, models and games.

Knowledge, of course, is a broad term and I mean to use it broadly. It includes both 'the known' and 'the state of knowing'. Thus a knowledgeable society would be one where there is much knowledge, and where many people go about the business of knowing in a proper fashion. As a first approximation to a definition, the knowledgeable society is one in which, more than in other societies, its members: (a) inquire into the basis of their beliefs about man, nature, and society; (b) are guided (perhaps unconsciously) by objective standards of veridical truth, and, at the upper levels of education, follow scientific rules of evidence and inference in inquiry; (c) devote considerable resources to this inquiry and thus have a large store of knowledge; (d) collect, organise and interpret their knowledge in a constant effort to extract further meaning from it for the purposes at hand; (e) employ this knowledge to illuminate (and perhaps modify) their values and goals as well as to advance them. Just as the 'democratic society' has a foundation in government and interpersonal relations, and the 'affluent society' a foundation in economics, so the knowledgeable society has its roots in epistemology and the logic of inquiry (27).

Lane's attitude to these alleged 'developments' was written sixteen years ago (1966). At that time he believed that the increasing concern for knowledgeableness would lead to a society denuded of ideological factionalism concerning the proper goals of collective life and their rank-ordering. Lane's position is reminiscent of Karl Popper's to the extent that both accept the Enlightenment view of knowledge as an independent and objective property standing in a zero-sum relation to dogmatism of all kinds. The idea that 'knowledge' can not only serve and express different ideologies and world-views, but can itself constitute an ideology of no ideology ('knowledgeableness') is anathema to both. Like Mannheim in *Man and Society in an Age of Reconstruction,* Lane sees people (not just 'intellectuals') 'getting behind' ideologies and dogmas, thereby undoing 'a kind of disequilibrium' that dogma is in the main responsible for (28).

Daniel Bell, in *The Coming of Post-Industrial Society,* carried this argument one step further by arguing that a new 'politics' beyond dogmatic partisanism would arise out of the ascendancy of knowledgeableness as a society-wide property or attribute. According to him

> the major source of structural change in society...is the change in the character of knowledge, the exponential growth and branching of science, the rise of a new intellectual technology, the creation of systematic research through R & D budgets, and, as the calyx of all this, the codification of theoretical knowledge.

Bell displays an eminently technocratic refusal to see in the alleged 'progress' of these various forms of 'objective' knowledge at least the possibility of competition and conflict. The reluctance to do so indicates how substantial was his commitment to the premise that a mesh between literacy, increasing levels of education, and the integration of economy, culture and polity would produce an 'open society'.

In place of Popper's vaunted 'unity of method', Bell puts the unity of knowledge in knowledgeableness as the essence of the ideology of no ideology. In place of 'piecemeal social engineering' and the reformism so characteristic of interventionism and 'social technology', Bell offers us a meritocratic 'stratarchy' and 'civic culture' whose politics have been reduced to administration, organisation, labour and consumption, and socialisation in the values of these pursuits.

In place of critique, reflection and analysis, Bell by-passes even Popper's tirades against holism, historicism and 'utopian' thinking to promote our acquiescence in instrumental and strategic conceptions of rationality premised on managerial notions of decision and action. In place of individuated and incremental approaches to societal problem-solving based on an extrapolation of ends-means linear thinking, Bell posits the requirement that such approaches be bounded by frameworks and models (OR, systems, game theory) whose alleged 'heuristic' purposes only underscore their essentially prescriptive character as visions of the ideal society for technocrats. And finally, in what can only be termed the grandest of Bonapartist (or Gaullist) gestures, Bell cites 'as the calyx of all this, the codification of theoretical knowledge' (31).

What is signally important about the claims of Lane and Bell is less their fanciful views of knowledge, knowledgeableness and the unity of knowledge than the fact that they constitute the consummate expression of technocratic ideology itself. In their way of overcoming the tension still evident in Galbraith's work between intellectual and managerial/professional models of knowledge and knowing, they provide an updated attempt to realise the project inaugurated by Mannheim. In no sense critical, it is thus their status as technocratic ideology rather than simply their absurdity as depictions of actual and probable future states of affairs in American (and perhaps other) late capitalist society which is of the greatest significance.

We can now perhaps better see the seamy side of the social intellectual's unremitting (but understandable) desire to have an impact and be taken seriously. On the other hand, there is the early Mannheim of *Ideology and Utopia*, fearful in ways that would never again bother him so much that intellectuals were in danger of losing their independence (32). Ironically, it is precisely Galbraith's support for their recognition as the possessors of an independent and centrally valuable 'factor of production' standing on its own ('knowledge') which nowadays functions as such a strong justification (and temptation) for their necessary absorption into technocratic rationality norms (33).

The ideology of objective knowledge now goes far beyond the notion that knowledge functions (or should function) as the property of an intellectual caste, as Mannheim in proposed *Ideology and Utopia*. It now is argued to be a societal property in the sense that it constitutes both the objective and the result of proper socialisation in the urban centres of late capitalist society. Such an ideology is the product, more than anything else of the generalisation of bureaucratic norms of rational behaviour and decision, so that they now encompass the large majority of societal members. The knowledgeable society is bureaucracy writ large in the sense that its picture of its real and ideal self takes its point of departure in the objectivity, neutrality and detachment produced by disciplined observation. Such observation is nowadays the essence of both responsible practice and responsible theory in these societies (34).

To the extent that the attitudinal, behavioural and decisional attributes of technocracy build upon bureaucratisation and rationalisation so conceived, they participate in, and express the reality of, this development. But technocracy, while dependent in many important ways on the persistence of bureaucracy as a structure and bureaucratisation as a process, means more. It is in the claim to have overcome the tension still prominent in Galbraith between intellectual and managerial/professional modes of thought, rather than solely in and through its commitment to the notion of objective knowledge and knowledgeableness, that technocracy as late capitalist ideology makes its most sustained impact.

To the extent that this vision has been realised in practice through the ongoing linkage of instrumental and strategic modes of rationality and operational, systems, and game-theoretical frameworks in an organisational setting, it is no longer accurate to treat technocracy solely as an ideology with inconsistent and discontinuous impacts on managerial and bureaucratic decisions and actions. Technocracy as an elite class fragment appears to increasingly constitute a structure for socialising, reinforcing and rewarding such behaviours and norms, one more than capable of tempting social intellectuals to acquiesce in the fiction of that very 'rational domination' that should now ideally become the centre of a critical agenda for those who refuse such co-optation (35).

TECHNOCRACY AND FUNCTIONAL ASPECTS OF BUREAUCRACY

Let us now return in a more concerted way to the Weberian bureaucratic ideal type, in particular to the functional and technical aspects, in an effort to compare bureaucracy and technocracy. Following this, we shall attempt a similar comparison with the scalar and career aspects respectively. This exercise should serve to complement our discussion of the role of the state and the belief in objective knowledge and knowledgeableness by directing our attention to the more specific continuities and discontinuities between bureaucracy as a structure and technocracy as an ideology seeking to embed its values and practices in permanent structures of power, authority and influence.

As already suggested, the objectives of those who support technocracy and the process of 'technocratisation' can be usefully compared to the activities of occupations imbued with an ideology of professionalism in search of professional (and semi-professional) status. While both professionalising occupations and supporters of technocracy seek to sediment their values and norms of action in permanent structures, whether bureaucratic or otherwise, only supporters of technocracy explicitly seek to supplant existing managerial orientations, values and norms of action with their own.

This indicates both the strengths and the weaknesses of technocracy relative to professionalising occupations. Technocracy is strong in the sense that it can attempt such a supplanting of now-conventional managerial values with its own, but weak to the extent that it lacks an optional power base independent and distinct from large scale corporate and state bureaucratic structures (36). Indeed, it is precisely this option as an actual or credible state of affairs perceived by professionalising occupations which constitutes one basis for their claim of objective knowledge, competence, and skill standing apart and distinct from the scalar structures that technocrats appear to require, no less than conventional managers, whether they occupy positions in corporate or governmental and state sectors (37).

On the other hand, it is the very technocratic pretensions to 'rational domination' which give present and future substance to Weber's pessimistic anticipations of rationalisation and disenchantment at the same time that they preserve and defend the idea not only that knowledge and power should in fact be merged in economic, political and administrative practice, but that this merger includes the already noted reconciliation between intellectual and mangerial/professional modes of thought and rationality (38).

If, from the standpoint of the scalar cluster, bureaucracy is best comprehended as a power and authority structure, from the standpoint of the functional, technical cluster it is best understood as a peculiarly modern form of division of labour seeking to reconcile authority and knowledge in a system of 'rational domination' (39). Weber points to 'a clearly defined sphere of competence' as one of the key elements of the functional cluster. Here he alludes to the fact that the incumbent not only has a power of action but a requirement both to act and to take responsibility for his actions (40).

Even though bureaucracy as a structure has clear collective properties for Weber, he tends to downplay this collective and corporate character when discussing the central characteristics of his ideal type. Indeed it is not too much to argue that Weber's pattern of analysis is straightforwardly

Technocracy and Late Capitalism

individualistic inasmuch as it addresses specific
positions and the individual's role therein. This
is important in light of the emphasis on team and
group decision-making and forms of 'collective
responsibility' in the work of Whyte, and
thereafter, of Galbraith and Wilensky (41). To the
extent that technocracy comprehends a group and
corporate dimension as both the instrumental basis
of its claim to knowledgeableness, and the society-
in-microcosm that rewards and sustains proper
socialisation manifested in correct decisions and
actions, it underscores the continuing dilemma posed
by absentee ownership for both public and private
property in late capitalist society (42).

Central to the ideal of 'a clearly defined
sphere of competence' is not only the relation of
the individual to group and collective
decision-making and responsibility, but the kind of
secondary sector relationships 'available' for
incumbents. Today it is necessary to realise that
bureaucracy on its own is simply not capable of
integrating technical and professional competences
into a standard hierarchy of superior-subordinate
relationships as Weber had suggested it might at the
turn of the century. Thus we have the line-staff
distinction inscribed throughout contemporary
bureaucratic structures, albeit, a solution with
problems of its own (43).

How does technocracy deal with either or both
of these problems? The answer lies in the ideology
of knowledgeableness, group decision-making and
collective responsibility, and the socialisation
processes that both initiate and reinforce
appropriate modes of decision and action in modern
large-scale organisation. To the original problem
for which the line-staff distinction was supposed to
be a solution, technocracy obliterates formal
individual responsibility in favour of the formal
properties of group decision-making and collective
responsibility. It no longer really matters to this
elite class fragment's particular 'social ethic'
that in a conflict on 'the facts' between a superior
and his subordinate in a conventional bureaucratic
structure, the subordinate is increasingly likely to
be 'correct' (44).

As for the 'solution' to this problem, numerous
writers have noted that the line-staff distinction
isolates staff specialists in all non-professional
organisations in 'second-class' statuses. Here it
is the absence of a hierarchy running parallel to
that of the formal bureaucratic structure, and the

fact that it is in these latter 'generalist' positions that real decision-making power and authority is supposed to inhere, that concerns supporters of professional specialists working in large-scale organisations (45). Technocracy's ideological commitment to smoothing over this tension is no doubt aided in the contemporary context by the sheer progress of societal specialisation, relative to the sort of specialization of tasks historically generated by the work organisation. Indeed, it would be difficult to make sense of group decision-making and collective responsibility in the absence of the decline of a model of individual responsibility premised on property ownership which was in earlier times transferred to work and labour activities. Paradoxically, this is one way that the absence of election may come back to haunt those who support the revival of more individualistic models of responsibility for decision and action (46).

Thus a strong case could be made for the argument that individual responsibility for the practices associated with occupancy of a bureaucratic 'office' with a 'specified sphere of competence' must be transcended for the contemporary conception of qualification and expertness to prevail at all. It is as a consequence of the pre-eminence of modes of training and education outside the ambit of organisational control, in the societal division of labour, that expertness loses its distinctly individualistic stamp (Weber) and takes on a clear collective character. That this group process of 'problem-solving' appears to have supplanted the more conventional top-down model of 'decision-making', only speaks to what must be the basis for the established or emerging system of 'collective responsibility', such as it is (47).

Our point is only underscored when we go beyond the distinction between task (organisational) and person (societal) specialisation to ask how the discretionary properties of technocratic positions in the structure relate expert knowledge to decision and action (48). Here we encounter a major dilemma for the contemporary effort to make higher level positions 'responsible', one which is perhaps insoluble within the present economic and social system. Thompson put the matter succinctly twenty years ago when he noted that the higher one goes in most bureaucratic structures, the higher the percentage of discretionary role responsibilities and the lower the percentage of routinised and fixed non-discretionary tasks (49).

'Specified sphere of competence' for Weber meant not only acknowledged expertness, as attested to by certifications and degrees, but evidence of this competence in and through individual decisions and actions. To be sure, competence in this case was more than casually tied to the well-known rule orientation for which public bureaucracies, in particular, are legitimately notorious (50). But, nevertheless, it remained the individual incumbents in their day to day decisions and actions who generated, or rather 'built up', the bureaucratic structure as an organised group *(Verband)* (51). This reflected the continuing central role of pre-industrial and pre-urban traditional values and modes of behaviour in the early twentieth century, and the fact that formal organisational rationality at that time constituted both an exception to the rule and as-yet-unrealised model for the further development of collective life.

Nowadays it is the reversal of this situation, with bureaucracies obliged to keep pace with models of knowledge, process and decision all too often generated extraneous to them which set the contours for the desired and contemplated technocratic ascendancy over modern organisation. It is this fact which sustains the gradual erosion of individual responsibility for decisions and actions, and replaces it with a form of collective responsibility which is substantively meaningless though processually and 'formally' impressive (52). The all-too-typical response to the fundamental irrationality of corporate and state organised managerial capitalism, characterised as it is by ever-increasing, non-specific, and discretionary role responsibilities as one ascends the hierarchy, is to widen the ambit of the tenure or security principle so that it comprehends everyone not subject to near-instant dismissal at *either* end.

As tenure and the security principle (*de facto* if not *de jure*) have served to frame the problem posed for society by the very success of technocratic (or technostructural) ideology, a thoroughly irrational form of retribution has emerged as a poor substitute for responsibility. This retribution applies to the political, super-bureaucratic or executive 'chiefs' standing outside and above the system of collective non-responsibility, and it is the price they must be prepared to pay in order to reconcile the interests of publics and shareholders in punishment for 'alleged' incompetence, and society's interest in preserving and extending the tenure and/or security principle (53).

Originally generated in the public sector in order to protect 'merit' as it sought to displace spoils, amateurism or traditional administration, tenure and job security now express the commitment of neo-Keynesians to the priority of consumer over producer roles, on the presumption that technical progress is given and that social welfare comprehends work and labour activities as well as unemployment, illness and retirement (54). The fact that collective responsibility is a clear fiction only becomes the more problematic when it is realised just how totally the tenure principle and job security generally, express the presumption of competence attested to by prior training and certification. Here occupancy of a given position with a 'specified sphere of competence' is a reward for exhibiting one's intellectual capabilities in formal examinations and the associated paraphernalia of 'secondary socialisation' in a professional (or professionalising) occupation (55).

Discretion loses its status as a property of individual decision-making for higher-order incumbents to the extent that its 'other side' – responsibility – is itself collectivised and formalised through group processes reflecting proper socialisation in the idea of objective and impartial expert knowledge. In this way, the fundamental distinction between the task-specific and the role-discretionary is substantially lessened, since it is no longer possible to trace decisions and actions to individuals. To say this, is not, however, to make a claim of conspiracy, but instead simply to draw attention to the extent to which expert knowledge and technical qualification have become such important and central attributes of decision and action as to be no longer meaningfully comprehended as the property of individuals, no matter how well trained and qualified (56).

The irresistible logic of the commitment to objective knowledge and knowledgeableness completes itself in the notion that such knowledge can only be mastered, corporatively and collectively, through group problem-solving processes. It is absolutely essential to an understanding of technocracy that this distinctively corporate and institutional dimension be appreciated as the basis of its claims as a collectivity to the possession of objective knowledge. This is the real reason that technocracy ultimately follows a managerial rather than a professional model in its attempt to co-opt bureaucratic decision hierarchies (57). The idea that a given office or position exhibits a specified sphere of competence becomes substantively meaningless relative to the idea of decisions and actions based on knowledge in such an equation. What persists for the petty-bureaucrat (or manager) is only a generalised and formalised orientation to impersonal rules rather than a specific, non-formalised orientation to other technocrats whose collective presence both permits and requires group problem-solving, whether within or in tandem with conventional managerial and bureaucratic structures (58).

Let us now turn to that aspect of the functional/technical cluster which is perhaps most readily called to mind by the merest mention of the word 'technocracy' - technique, the technical and technology. Weber's emphasis on 'selection on the basis of technical qualifications ...tested by examination or guaranteed by diplomas certifying technical training, or both' has already been discussed as it bears on the 'clearly defined sphere of competence' of bureaucratic positions. Here we are interested in Weber's corollary point to the effect that 'the role of technical qualifications in bureaucratic organisations is continually increasing' (59).

While this claim is clearly implied by our argument regarding increasing societal specialis-ation with the 'progress' of the industrial and urban division of labour, we did not attempt to isolate what exactly are alleged to be the uniquely technical properties of technocratic capabilities. It is here, not surprisingly, that we discover the distinctly organisational and formal/functional character of technical qualification. Weber's allusion to the superiority 'from a purely technical point of view' of 'the monocratic variety of bureaucracy' is instructive in this regard (60).

What really serves to demonstrate the organisational character of technocratic qualification and capabilities however, albeit as a reflection of the process of social specialisation and concomitant secondary socialisation, is Mannheim's discussion of functional rationality. In particular, that aspect which considers the conflict between its imperatives and the capacity for intelligent judgement in new or unexpected situations is the essence of what he terms 'substantial rationality' (61). From the standpoint of any meaningful understanding of 'technical rationality', Diesing is quite correct to take issue with Mannheim's (and Weber's) tendency to use terms like technical, functional and bureaucratic interchangeably (62). At the same time, there can be little dispute about the prescience of both writers when they implied that real technical capabilities could be nothing short of collective and corporate in their ambit.

Perhaps we should once more underscore our earlier point regarding what precisely there is in technocracy which constitutes its basic differences with conventional managerialism and bureaucracy. Bureaucrats, according to Weber, may have combined their individual competences to produce an organisational and formal/functional or structural effect as suggested. Weber makes reference to this when he states that: 'Bureaucracy is superior in knowledge, including both technical knowledge and knowledge of the concrete fact within its own sphere of interest' (63). The issue is less whether this combination occurred than the fact that the objectivity and neutrality of such knowledge appears increasingly to be externally (that is, socially) produced rather than generated predominantly inside the organisation.

This means that society, instead of merely respecting the difference between itself and bureaucratic incumbents, now sees decision-making-cum-problem-solving processes in large organisations as more formally rigorous versions of what is required of all labouring and consuming denizens in late capitalist societies (64). Technical qualifications, tied as they are to formal certification, coupled with proper socialisation in values, attitudes, and world-views takes virtual possession of key organisational positions from 'outside'. To be sure, this presumes the givenness of technical progress, itself increasingly dependent upon applied science and the science-based technology produced through corporate, state and military R and D (65).

It is the way that technocracy trades on the clearly scientistic ideology of science in its relation to technique which serves as the almost unchallengeable basis for its claims to the objectivity and neutrality of its knowledge (66). 'Knowledgeableness' gains in its claim to credibility, as Veblen pointed out, the more readily it can point to its knowledge as ' peculiarly matter of fact' and to its standards of reasoning as premised on 'opaque and material cause and effect'. Public attitudes toward the technocratic control and disposition of human and material resources are undoubtedly improved by this association of knowledge with hard-nosed technical rationality and technical rationality and technique with 'science' (67).

Indeed it was precisely this association, originally formulated by Frederick Taylor and Henry Gantt, which led to the term 'technocracy' first being coined by W.H. Smyth of Berkeley, California in 1919 (68). Smyth was a follower of Thorstein Veblen and Morris Cooke who had read several installments of what would later become Veblen's *The Engineers and the Price System* in *The Dial* (69). Smyth's original definition of technocracy was 'the organisation of the social order based on principles established by technical experts'. Here it is the backward reference to the work of St. Simon, Fourier, Comte, Enfantin and the Ecole Polytechnique in the period between 1820 and 1848 which is far more important than the brief vogue which the technocratic movement enjoyed in the United States between 1931 and 1933 (70).

Close scrutiny of the concept of technocracy from the vantage point of either 1919 or 1931-1933 only underscores our earlier point about the central role of knowledgeableness as a presumption held by supporters of technocracy. Our preference for a more critical, less affirmative, conception of technocracy can perhaps be better understood by turning to the question of just who these technocrats are and what it is about their knowledge (besides its alleged objectivity and neutrality) which is thought to be so valuable to urban industrial societies. As it turns out, it is mainly on the matter of their joint understanding of the rarely articulated goals or objectives of technocracy as the late capitalist ideology of objective knowledge and knowledgeableness that supporters and critics are able to agree (71).

Probably the best way to attempt to isolate who the technocrats are, is to examine their present relation to other occupations and functions in advanced societies. Here it will be necessary to keep in mind the capitalist role of the state and its virtual supersession, along with large corporations, of the traditional distinction between public and private functions in the common law.

Thus technocrats are an elite class fragment whose socialisation, including 'technical qualifications', is seen to equip them for group problem-solving in many or most types of formally organised settings where they often pool their individual capabilities and competences. In this respect, the claim of technocratic applicability to a large number of organisational endeavours clearly parallels Weber's oft-quoted statement regarding bureaucracy's applicability 'with equal facility to a wide variety of differenct fields', and in fact builds upon it in significant ways (72).

At the same time, we must be clear on the ways in which technocracy stands apart and distinct from, even while it is interdependent with, other occupations. Technocrats are neither engineers as a group, nor specific subgroups of practitioners (civil, mechanical, electrical, chemical, ceramics, nuclear), even though engineers since St. Simon and Enfantin have been viewed as a group trained to deal in the understanding and manipulation of the material facts of external nature (73). Ironically, it was precisely their alleged lack of political and/or 'pecuniary' concern which led Veblen to equate their hardheadedness with an objective manifestation of the instinct of workmanship. In this, alas, Veblen and his followers seemed seriously out of touch with the values of most engineers and the reasons behind the interests of those few who did complain and organise during the 1920s and early 1930s. In fact, supporters of Veblen's 'soviet of technicians' were drawn, in the main, from intellectual and literary, rather than technical and professional, fields. Almost none of them were engineers (74).

As Layton points out, engineers during the period from 1900 to 1920 attempted to generate an ethic of 'social responsibility' principally in order to underwrite and legitimise their attempts to gain professional status and recognition by big business interests. Nothing could more readily point to the gap between Veblen's ideal and reality than this fact. At the very time he was contrasting the workmanlike discipline of the engineer and the pecuniary predation of business and finance capitalism, the engineering societies, inspired by the examples of Taylor, Gantt and Cooke, were attempting to achieve professional status in the eyes of these very interests! This is not to say that there was no dissatisfaction in the ranks, as well as at the top in the engineering societies, but rather to suggest that whatever dissatisfaction there was was related far more to concerns about professional status and recognition than the desire to dispossess big business with the help of the industrial workers in the name of higher productivity (75).

In the period since the 1920s, it is interesting to note that it is engineers, more than almost any other occupation, that have been ready, willing, and able to integrate themselves into line positions of managerial authority in particular in large-scale business organisations. This would not be at variance with our earlier point about technocracy as a product of certain values favouring group decision-making on the basis of 'objective knowledge', were it not for the fact that in the process of taking on these managerial positions, engineers are notorious for being an occupational group perhaps more ready to accommodate to managerial 'generalist' values and attitudes than practically any other (76).

As a consequence, they often jettison their professional ties altogether, and in any case rarely either return to the technical specialism in which there were trained or make use of the knowledge this qualification initially provided them with in their managerial work. As Layton points out, it would have been almost impossible to come up with a less revolutionary group than Veblen did (77). It was his failure to understand the real reasons for their discontent, coupled with this rigid bifurcation between industrial and pecuniary employments, which led a man with such a clear picture of many features of the social landscape to such unfulfilled expectations (78).

Other occupations from which technocracy draws its members, as well as its ideological support, but from which it differs substantially, would include: applied scientists and technologists in R and D settings; other professional and technical specialists including economists, social scientists and experts in administration, functioning in line or staff (advisory) capacities in large organisations, and salaried managers and bureaucrats in *de jure* or *de facto* tenured positions (79).

In all these instances it is the role of applied science and science-based technology in production and innovation, fortified by a scientistic ideology asserting a deterministic linkage between these activities, which underwrites more specific claims by technocracy to have substantially overcome the tension between bureaucracy and professional and technical experts in large organisations without in the process turning away from technical specialisation like engineers (80). It is technocracy's designs upon management and their claims on the bureaucratic apparatus of large organisations to which we shall need to address ourselves as we turn to the scalar and career clusters of Weber's ideal-typical bureaucracy for further analysis.

TECHNOCRACY AND SCALAR ASPECTS OF BUREAUCRACY

Perhaps the most important matter to address at the outset is the issue of how technocratic domination differs from the sort of domination which Weber attempted to capture in his discussion of the bureaucratic scalar cluster. There are some who would argue that technocracy is apolitical even while readily admitting that it constitutes a type of domination and control unique to both capitalist and other advanced industrial societies. Here it is significant that technocracy's claim to being apolitical can only have meaning inasmuch as this claim is understood to be a property of the ideology of objective knowledge and knowledgeableness so central to the idea of 'rational domination'.

To the extent that technocracy, so understood, finds it possible to enter into a vast continuum of 'mixed' political-economic systems like those delineated by Lindblom (81), and have a significant and continuing effect in all or most cases, the claim to apolitical status can be seen to mask the reality of domination rather than dispute it. No elite class fragment, socialised into certain specific values, attitudes, and worldviews in the matter of technocrats, should be allowed to explain their own ascendancy in modern organisations by reference to such a self-serving view of group process as a self-justifying requirement which ties knowledgeableness to decision and action (82).

Yet there are undeniable aspects of technocratic thinking and behaviour which take the idea of a 'knowledge' component far beyond Weber's discussion of the functional/technical cluster. Instead of simply being tied to a knowledge of rules, procedures and the files, technical qualification becomes a property of collective activity in the form of group process, with the result that traditional bureaucratic management based on a fixed or specified 'sphere of competence' is either complemented in fundamental ways or transcended in certain of its aspects altogether.

Technocratic emphasis on group *process* is the action prerequisite to knowledgeableness in the form of professional and managerial capabilities which alledgedly reconcile technical/technological and intellectual/critical knowledge. This impression is clearly aided and abetted by the scientistic ideology, now well accepted, which argues that the role of applied science and science-based technology in R and D activities can only be linked in an on-going way to production and innovation by technocratic intervention as the truly 'rational' approach to organisation and management. Technocrats become the great integraters and synthesisers in this equation, and their greatest achievement is their ability to point to this alleged reconciliation of affirmative and critical forms of knowledge, not only in all areas of organisation activitiy, but in other sections of collective life as well (83).

When we turn to the scalar cluster in order to continue our comparison along Weberian lines, we discover that its properties reduce to four – hierarchy, discipline, formal authority, and rule-orientation (84). We also discover that it is not as easy to distinguish scalar from functional/technical attributes as one might have thought it would be. Indeed, it is this very failure to make a clear distinction which underscores the limits of the ideology of objective knowledge and knowledgeableness itself. Only by accepting central assumptions of this ideology would it be possible to defend the idea that the fully functional and technical, after all, stood on its own apart from domination in the form of hierarchy, discipline, formal authority and rule orientation (85).

In the case of hierarchy, and, to a lesser extent, other elements of the scalar cluster, we are dealing with one of the most persistent characteristics of collective life – the idea of a pecking order. The scalar cluster as a whole is cited by Weber as the most 'traditional' one of the three, and is argued to be characteristic of all forms of collective activity. This even holds for rule-orientation inasmuch as such an orientation is absolutely necessary if we are to give any credence to the idea of an organised hierarchy as a collective enterprise 'built up' out of individual office-holders *(Verband)*. More to the point is the observation that the functional/technical cluster itself can only be considered unique to modern bureaucracy in urban industrial societies to the extent that it too presupposes an ideology of objective knowledge and knowledgeableness.

Like Galbraith's mistaken idea of 'knowledge' as a newly emerging factor of production standing apart from land, labour and capital, this view would have us believe that past societies possessed nothing that could be meaningfully understood to constitute technical knowledge relative to less specific capabilities in the culture at large. While such a tendency is evident in Weber's discussions of competence, knowledge and the technical in several parts of his analysis of bureaucracy, it clearly contradicts his view, expressed in *The Protestant Ethic and the Spirit of Capitalism* and elsewhere, that one can only seek to meaningfully understand other (and earlier) cultures by viewing them in terms of their own standards, understandings and problems (86).

To meet this requirement, Weber would have to admit that competence, knowledge and the technical is a possession of all cultures, and one which is relative to commonsense capacities and traditional and customary understandings (87). The fact that he often does not do this when discussing bureaucracy points to his own ambivalence on the matter of the objectivity of knowledge and technique, and suggests that Weber the sociologist was often more supportive of this ideology than many interpreters of his pessimisic rationalisation thesis would have us believe. It was all the more incumbent on Weber to take the *verstehen* requirement seriously, given his thoroughgoing knowledge of the origins of technique in religion and art at the dawn of human history. For these reasons, and others, it is difficult to ignore the presence of indisputable aspects of technocratic thinking alongside a generalised fear of technocracy in the work of Weber himself (88).

Perhaps it is the clear persistence of hierarchy throughout the history of human collective life which justified the emphasis placed upon it in Weber's bureaucratic formulation. After all, 'rational domination' is still a form of domination and the word 'rational' remains the modifying element in the term. Does this tell us something about the meaning of contemporary rationality as Weber understands it? The answer would seem to be 'yes', when we recall that, for Weber, bureaucracy constitutes the organisational expression of the legal-rational form of authority. Thus 'legal' authority or 'legality' means impersonality, objectivity *sine ira et studio*, and the idea that no person is above the law in its application and enforcement (89).

What follows from this is an argument for the collective rationality of the hierarchical structure which has been organised on the basis of individual offices, each with an allegedly fixed and specified sphere of competence. Weber's basic presumption in his application of the bureaucratic ideal type is that what is formally required of individual office-holders provides the parameters for their actual behaviour in the form of decisions and actions. Thus his emphasis on the need for job and task descriptions to include not only the application of what he called technical knowledge and skills but strict discipline under a regimen of formalised superior-subordinate relations. Looked at on a system-wide basis we realise that virtually *every* 'office' or position in a bureaucracy must include not only a task or technical component but also an authority component, if the idea of a collectively rational *structure* is to have any meaning (90).

This also helps us place the issue of discretion and its unavoidable relation to authority in better perspective. Such a formalised system of positions in the form of *statuses* makes it easy to see how the 'legal' demand for objectivity and neutrality invariably serves the interests of the structure as a collectivity. Only if each position couples responsibility for its own discretionary behaviour with strict discipline to superiors is the exercise of discretionary authority in each instance reconcilable with the interests of the structure as a whole (91). The lynchpin in many or most cases is 'rule orientation': it provides the illusion of technical capability, and equates the technical with that which is alleged to be neutral and 'objective'.

More significantly, 'rule orientation' provides a basis in bureaucratic *practice*, as well as theory, for hiding the clearly scalar properties of such a behaviour pattern. Weber, after all, often treated 'rule orientation' more as an attribute of the functional/technical cluster than the scalar one, and for good reasons. As a clear improvement over arbitrary bases of decision, it was problematic for him only from the standpoint of what we nowadays call'equity'. Thus Weber's preference for certain features of 'Khadi justice' on grounds of its greater capacity for 'individualization' in his discussion of formal and substantive rationalisation in the law (92).

When organisational members can turn to rules, procedures and records which *they themselves have created*, and call this not only an exercise in objectivity and neutrality but also one which evidences their possession of technical skills and specialized knowledge, they have laid a central part of the groundwork for an emergent meritocratic order where their own processes and decisions will constitute the essence of 'rational domination' itself. To be sure, rule orientation means nothing if it fails to comprehend an incumbent's approach to the rules governing their *own conduct* of their office. Only by his willingness to accept the responsibility that goes with discretionary action would it be possible for one to favour a broad interpretation of one's job requirements over a narrow one in any particular situation (93). It is nowadays difficult to dispute the claim that this rule orientation, with its emphasis on objectivity and neutrality, and their alleged relation to technique and the technical, provides a model of secondary socialization which has since 1950 gradually become society-wide in its ambit. From the standpoint of what technocracy means, and what the key components of its ideology-become-structure are, it is therefore what bureaucracy and the increasingly organized professions have *in common*, rather than, what distinguishes them which is most important (94).

Technocracy builds upon, and simultaneously expresses, this interdependence between scalar and functional/technical clusters which was already apparent when Weber formulated his bureaucratic ideal type. Hierarchy relates individual positions and groups of positions to goals and sub-goals so that the bureaucratic form of the division of labour can appear to function as a collectively rational unit whose work has a beginning and an end. Discipline relates each incumbent to someone above him or her in order to compensate for the separate problems of discretion each one is invariably involved in (95). Formal authority, which invokes the idea of objective competence by equating prescribed, expected and required behaviours found in job descriptions with 'technical' capabilities, makes merit and tenure seem inseparable and 'rational domination' the only desirable basis for organised decision and action (96).

The result is a structure made up of groups of

individuals whose differences are so miniscule when
compared to the matters on which they are like-
minded, that it only makes sense to treat them as a
single collection. The idea that a rule orientation
is needed if individual incumbents are to overcome
their 'natural' disposition to decide and act in
particularistic and ascribed ways is dealt with by
treating proper secondary socialisation in
professional and managerial institutions as the
guarantee that those so trained have internalised
both the values and the 'technical' knowledge on
which their application is to be based (97). This
means that, in response to Merton's question forty-
five years ago, nowadays bureaucracies are less to
be counted as places where secondary socialisation
moulds individuals and more as structures which
receive individuals already schooled and certified
to be the possessors of the correct values, and the
competences or skills which apply them (98).

Related to rule orientation in important ways
is the parallel issue of *jurisdiction* as the basis
for delineating and denoting an incumbent's fixed
and specified sphere of competence (99). Here also
we discover how fundamentally scalar in character
are the capabilities which an individual possesses
as an organisation member. What appears to 'fix'
the specificity of the occupant's sphere of
competence is not the training and socialisation
which he has gone through prior to (or during) his
incumbency. Only his job description can claim to
do this, and can only succeed in doing it to the
extent that by specificity we have in mind not
'technical' knowledge as we nowadays understand the
term, but technical knowledge as Weber understood
it, that is, knowledge of rules, procedures and
files (100).

At the same time, it is the collective
character of bureaucracy as a *social structure*
comprised in part of like-minded individuals, who
constitute an elite class fragment, which makes the
contemporary notion of technical competence at all
comprehensible as a potential and actual basis for
managerial decision and action. This is not to give
technique and the technical anything approaching
objective status, but only to underscore the role of
secondary socialisation and training in the society
at large. To our way of thinking, it is the
obliteration of the tension between functional and
substantial rationality, (cited by Mannheim in
1935), with the transformation of capitalist
industrial societies into meritocratic and

credentialist 'stratarchies', which is supremely problematic (101).

What replaces it is a collective structure whose group processes underscore the extent to which the 'technical', (as we, not Weber understand it), has become unhinged from any single line position in the hierarchy of modern organisation and management. Fixed sphere of competence as a consequence now relates as much to the limi s of decision and action imperatives in the form of responsibility for the exercise of one's own authority and that of others to whom authority has been delegated as it does to bureaucracy as a *technically* superior method of dividing . and organising work and labour activities. Indeed, one might even argue that today the two are virtually indistinguishable. The very ubiquity and (alleged) objectivity of technical and technological considerations make the idea of their posession by individuals as individuals faintly absurd (102). Jurisdictional boundaries only underscore further the scalar nature of the idea of limit, that is, as a property of the structure as a system of authority and responsibility. To note the collective character of bureaucracy as an apparatus whose central characteristic today is 'control based on knowledge' is to go beyond the secret knowledge of rules, procedures and files that Weber had in mind. Ultimately it means nothing less than the ongoing effort to reconcile this structure with the technical and professional values and knowledge which is the hallmark of technocracy itself.

Weber's discussion of bureaucracy clearly realises that what is central to an understanding and appreciation of this new collective form of division of labour is precisely the way it appears to reconcile the three clusters, particularly the functional/technical and scalar clusters. Indeed, I have argued elsewhere, and shall take up again further on, that it is the career cluster more than anything else which provides the basis for the illusion that formal authority and expert knowledge have in fact been reconciled. Weber's great strength in this regard was to have brought together in one construct a whole host of factors that had been, and still were being, treated as if they were not intimately related to, and interdependent with, one another. Thus, changes in the structure of capitalist economies, the increasing role of the state, technologicial advance, and the so-called 'managerial revolution', are dealt with by Weber as factors demonstrating larger order developments in which all are directly implicated in both a structural and a processual way (103).

'Bureaucratic administration means fundamentally the exercise of control on the basis of knowledge' (104). With this statement Weber summarises what for him is prototypical of both the great achievement and the great problematic contained in the modern organisation of work and labour activities. The idea, already noted, that 'knowledge' is a unique property of modern or contemporary administrative decision-making is itself problematic. It is not just that 'knowledge' is a value-laden term whose use in this fashion has the effect, (if not the intent), of downgrading all other (and all previous) forms of decision-making as automatically arbitrary. Also important is the way that such a posture functions as ideological legitimation by leading us to rank-order general and specific knowledge claims on the basis of the extent to which their assertions of objective status can be seen to possess a basis in technique and the technical.

Even more central than these considerations is the already-mentioned achievement of the appearance of unity that bureaucracy realises. By what is now a culturally ingrained view that it is *more likely* to constitute 'the exercise of control based on knowledge' than any other social institution (105). No longer standing against an order where its structures are an exception to the rule, even in the world of work and labour, bureaucracy is now the established prototype of a society which has 'generalised' several of its most central attributes, and the relations of interdependence between them, to forms of life formerly subject to traditional modes of behaviour. It is nothing less than the dialectical reflex of our highly organised society of labourers, consumers and spectators back upon the now-conventional structures, (that earlier functioned as the prototype for societal development), that helps explain present technocratic claims on management as an occupation, and bureaucracy as a form of organisation (106).

The real question we must ask in light of the foregoing is this: what is it that makes it possible for such large collectivities of persons operating as incumbents in bureaucracies to maintain the continuing illusion of conflict-free decision processes based on objective technical grounds, and what is their motivation for allowing this illusion to continue? Here it is necessary to disavow any notion of conspiracy by technocrats even while admitting that they constitute an elite class fragment in the advanced societies, a fragment which finds expression by seeking to revamp management as an occupation and bureaucracy as a method of dividing and organising work and labour activities. The tentative answer to this question has to be that, in the main, technocrats, either singly or as a collectivity, are simply unaware of the problematic status of their claim to objective knowledge and its equation with technique and the technical. This is the essence of the process of successful secondary socialisation itself.

The essence of decision and action in a collective setting where general and specific 'goal orientation' sets the organisational and occupational parameters of behaviour must be the claim to 'rational grounds' or 'rational processes' (107). In this sense technocracy, even though more the product of societal processes of specialisation combined with the increasing role of applied science and science-based technology in production, administration and innovation, depends heavily upon the original claim to 'rational domination' first articulated by Weber on behalf of modern (now 'classical') bureaucracy. Even the technical or technological component which is a property of the widening ambit of applied science and science-based technology expressed in R and D activities becomes part of a technocratic claim to superior knowledgeableness only in the sense that doctrine seizes on aspects of the changing stock of commonsense knowledge in support of an ascending group (108).

We already noted the crucial contribution that scientism makes to technocratic thought. As the ideology supporting a deterministic linkage between science and technology, coupled with the idea that certain groups possess special knowledge of how to facilitate this linkage organisationally, it allows technocracy to underscore the need for 'professional' management trained in the potential or actual 'concrete facts of the case'. At the same time it maintains and improves upon the bureaucratic control structure which has been so central to managerial dominance over professional and technical specialists, particularly in staff functions, but also in subordinate line positions (109). Of the utmost importance to technocrats have been the many and varied 'overlays' on the formal bureaucratic structure, like task forces, project teams and matrix grids. These overlays have spoken less to professional needs for collegiality to complement hierarchy, authority and discipline than they have to the apparent demands for objective knowledge and knowledgeableness given in the nature of the new scientific, social-scientific and technical/ technological inputs to organised decision and action (110).

The fact that technocracy has built upon bureaucracy, while at the same time developing a body of doctrine of its own in concert with the professional and managerial training schools, often makes it difficult to understand what there is about it which is so central to the study of collective behaviour in the advanced societies. As a leading exponent of the idea and possibility of rational domination, technocracy presents its credentials as a basis for its 'right' as a *group*, rather than an elite class fragment, to function as the central steering component of societies dominated by large-scale corporate and state bureaucratic structures (111). It is the way that these structures increasingly seek to govern the pace and development of applied scientific and technological knowledge which is especially important, as much because of the *absence* of (former) working scientists amongst the technocracy as because of the threat this development poses for both science and technology in the future (112).

To argue that most technocrats sincerely believe all or almost all of what we have presented here as doctrine or ideology is not to say that certain developments have not occurred and have not changed the social and organisational role of management. It is rather to scientism and to the twin beliefs regarding knowledgeableness and the reconciliation of affirmative and 'relevant' critical knowledge that we must turn to comprehend the more contentious aspects of technocratic justification and legitimation. Indeed, we would argue that what has supplanted a managerial model in technocratic thought and ideology is less a professional model than a *social-scientific* one. When we contrasted Bell and Popper earlier, we did not intend to play down or ignore the fundamental continuity between Popperian 'social technology' and the idea of society as a *system* in more recent social-scientific and managerial/professional parlance (113).

It is precisly this perception employed as a

frame of reference in discussions of societal strategies by firms and organisations, and elsewhere, which sets the contours for the operation of the piecemeal method itself. The attempt by Popper to make Mannheim, in particular, appear an historicist in *The Poverty of Historicism* can only dispute the complementary character of their models of society as structure and process to the extent that 'piecemeal social engineering' is seen to function in an unorganised, negatively individualistic, way. Our point was made convincingly twenty years ago in Diesing's discussion of 'social rationality', in particular the relation between equilibrium and integration in *Reason and Society*. The system framework is a perception of society so highly compatible with Popperian social technology that one rarely finds them separated from one another in technocratic ideology (114).

It is this combination of piecemeal incrementalism and a systems framework which 'is the essence of the contemporary division of labour in the social, behavioural and administrative-managerial disciplines, no less today than when C. Wright Mills contrasted 'grand theory' and 'abstracted empiricism' in *The Sociological Imagination* over twenty years ago (115). Only a systems framework, premised on the essential 'functionality' of existing structures, can provide the theoretical ballast for organising and justifying social science interventionism in or alongside large-scale organised activity (116). Without the view of social structure as a system, the piecemeal method could not become the ideological lynchpin of social scientism as a formal discipline, combining respect for science and technology with professional status. It would remain a commonsense approach to problem-solving carried out by negative individuals in Popper's fictional society, one possessing process but no structure (117).

System theory as a normative, rather than simply a heuristic, framework thus provides a thoroughgoing legitimation of society as a functional structure whose key firefighters include not only managers and professionals, but also social, behavioural and administrative/managerial 'scientists'. The system concept is the ideal way that society *should* interrelate as interdependent parts of a whole, and piecemeal incrementalism is the ideal method by which such functional

articulation between the parts can be improved and
maintained. Far from simply constituting a separate
discipline with opportunities for sporadic
intervention on a piecemeal and incremental basis,
however, the social sciences and related disciplines
have increasigly become models of *practice* which go
beyond support for disciplined observation in the
advanced societies to encourage the obliteration of
critical/theoretical   reflection   and   the
reconstitution of commonsense practices themselves
(118).

It is in this unmistakable development that we
see the overwhelming threat posed by 'rational
domination'   to   the   continuing   autonomy   of
symbolically mediated interaction in the form of
commonsense and analytical/critical discourse.
While Weber anticipated this development to some
small   extent   in   his   discussion   of   world
demystification, it is Habermas, in particular, who
has drawn out the significance of this all-too-
ubiquitous form of 'rationalisation' (119).   The
'independence' of speech from the non-speech of
closed systems of doctrine, while always a problem
for human collective life, takes on certain unique
properties in the contemporary context with the
ascendancy of an elite class fragment that claims
its sanction from a *culturally* accepted notion of
objective knowledge and knowledgeableness, including
the knowledge of what is worthwile in both
commonsense and critical discourse.

It is the view that technocrats constitute the
leading edge of a *socially produced and sanctioned*
idea of knowledgeableness which allows them an
ascendancy all out of proportion to what their
socialisation has actually done to them. The fact
that their form of thinking and talking is highly
respected, albeit in the abstract, by lay members of
the society at large, allows their training and
certification to function as more than just a
substitute for 'mere' experience. In effect this
preparation, and the world views that it supports
and sustains through a more technically
sophisticated version of the social scientism spoken
(or respected) in the society at large, permits the
illusion   that   these   individuals   both   differ
fundamentally from and 'represent', in ways that
owners, proprietors, even managers and professionals
cannot claim to represent, key interests central to
the good health of the system (12)). Experience,
especially where continuing socialisation and
training is required, operates in the new equation

less as a basis for changing attitudes, values and ways of doing things than as something to be reconstituted in line with the claim that the incumbent is already in possession of objective knowledge, and the group processes which can be counted on to guarantee knowledgeableness in any given situation, where it is not collectively self-evident.

TECHNOCRACY AND CAREER ASPECTS OF BUREAUCRACY

Weber's third cluster - full time salaried career, free selection and contract, and separation from the means of administration with no right of appropriation - is the basis for any understanding of the relation of bureaucracy to the subsequent emergence of a society of labouring, consuming and spectating job-holders. Indeed, career is a key concept through which the fiction of a stable, conflict-free social structure expresses itself (121).

Here it is the assumption that society is sufficiently stable and predictable, at least in its general outlines, coupled with the social *duty* of full-time job-holding as a basis of the right-become-duty to consume and spectate, which is central to the idea of career. The notion that someone's primary socialisation is succeeded by a process which begins wih secondary socialisation and leads on into a temporal succession of positions, each linked logically and developmentally to one another, is only possible or conceivable for a majority of individuals in a highly organised social structure whose form of collective life is premised mainly on status rather than contract (122). It is no accident that sociology uses the terms 'position' and 'status' interchangeably in its discussion of social and organisational roles.

The view of society as a form of collective life based increasingly on status rather than contract is thoroughly prefigured in the emergence of formal bureaucratic organisation. What is important is the idea that a position with pre-formed task and authority/responsibility components *already exists* in advance of any particular occupant, as well as in concert with this incumbency. Organisation tables and procedure manuals provide a basis for the fiction not only that positions 'exist' independently of any particular occupant, but that the organisation itself possesses a formal existence (123).

Even though commentators frequently resist admitting it, it is difficult to ignore the fact that, for most individuals, tables of organisation and manuals of procedure function as normative and prescriptive ideals, or at least guidelines, rather than descriptions of actual states of affairs. The fact that it is the non-formalised everyday life aspects which impart reality to organisations as collective entities does not fundamentally challenge the claim that formalisation in advance makes sense. For purposes of analysis, Weber realised that such formal maps must be treated as heuristic devices regardless of their normative and prescriptive animus. Only if they are treated as a tool for comparative analysis can we in fact discover the extent to which the 'real' organisation differs from the formal model standing as a prescriptive ideal (124).

Whereas, for Weber, career denoted a less than commonplace approach to what had earlier been sporadic administration by aristocrats and nobles in what remained, on the whole a 'traditional' society, today we use the term career to refer to anyone's work life seen prospectively or retrospectively as a succession of possible or actual statuses. Whereas for Weber it was bureaucratic administration that pioneered the idea of a succession of full-time salaried positions leading up to retirement with pension, today we realise how much more general in its ambit the career concept has become.

It is for these reasons that it makes limited sense to speak of bureaucracy as a model for the development of advanced industrial societies, albeit one presently in the midst of responding to processes of specialisation generated in the larger society (125). To say that society has become a bureaucracy *writ large* has not just become a cliche, but also an inaccurate picture of the advanced societies as well. However, at the same time, it is clearly the now-accepted notion that society should function as a *rational social organisation* which is absolutely central to technocratic ideology and practice. This notion also helps us appreciate the significance of the work of intellectual precursors like St. Simon, Fourier, Enfantin and Comte as well as the subsequent furor over technocracy in the United States (126).

Thus there is a clear and unambiguous connection between St. Simon's view of the ideal society as a rational social organisation along the general lines suggested earlier by Maistre and

Bonald, the rise of the engineering profession in the United States and the importance of its differences with business as perceived by Thorstein Veblen and his followers and supporters, and present day affirmations and fears regarding technocracy in North America, Western Europe and the Eastern bloc countries. It is the convergence of and conflict between, large-scale organisation and secularised occupations as joint bases for full-time salaried careers which is so central to an understanding of contemporary technocratic developments in the advanced societies today (127).

The concept of a full-time salaried career based on free selection and contract where the incumbent is separated from the means of administration may have once been a unique property of bureaucracy, and may even today be principally found in organisational life. What has changed fundamentally as a result of the impact of the 'free' occupations, particularly those with professional or scientific/technological status, is the nature of career routes and timetables. Weber's bureaucratic career was played out mainly or exclusively in one organisational setting, while careers today often take shape over time in many different contexts spanning production and service organisations in both public and private sectors (128).

Through a process of societal specialisation never really controlled by large-scale economic and administrative organisation, certain occupations-become-professions have been able to secure a base point independent of bureaucratic salaried employment even though a large segment of their members depend directly upon such employment for their livelihood. This base point has allowed these occupations to generate their own notions of proper secondary socialisation and their own ideas of career development even though they lack the sort of public recognition and some of the controls typical of the established 'fee-for-service' professions (129). Indeed, it was the very dependence of management on professional and scientific-technological specialisation and specialists in standard bureaucratic structures in the corporate and state sectors, which has made it possible for these occupations to combine favoured status with not-inconsiderable functional autonomy (130).

It is in the area of research and development activities that we see what is perhaps the most current instalment in the ongoing battle between bureaucratic management and the free occupations, with their independent secondary socialisation processes, for control of the pace and character of specialised knowledge. Whereas, up to twenty years ago, technocratic elements were still mainly represented by members of the free occupations, today it is the attempt by *management* to develop an occupational-become-professional base (one more independent of bureaucracy than has been seen since the collapse of the scientific management movement), which points to the presence of an emerging technocratic bias here as well.

Even though bureaucratic formal organisation continues to combine a hierarchy of superior-subordinate relations with a functioning line-staff distinction, it is management's perceived need for *competence* in types of knowledge produced extra-bureaucratically, rather than simply control of those who are seen to possess it, and for the status associated with a collective stature somewhat independent of bureaucracy, which has led them to develop an extra-bureaucratic career orientation. It is not that management does not continue to operate out of formal bureaucratic organisation, but rather the combined effect of its changing career patterns and its increasing identification with specialised knowledge of a technical rather than a purely administrative kind, which sets the contours for present-day analyses of the role of technocratic values and ideology in the advanced societies (131).

It is somewhat ironic that the occupation which has been most ready to yield up its specialised competence to managerial careers – the engineering profession – appears in retrospect the leading edge of a development which has more recently captured other specialised and professionalising occupations. To be sure, here it is necessary to distinguish occupancy of superordinate line positions, where there is frequent and continuous reference to technical and professional training from occupancy where no such reference occurs (132).

While many engineers clearly meet the requirements of frequent and continuous reference to their knowledge base as functioning managers, bureaucrats, and executives, many have simply chosen to leave their training behind them in order to enter superordinate line positions. This was probably more true in the past than it is today. The only other major free occupation whose membership counts a large percentage of salaried organisational employees – accounting – provides a more recent example of a trend also visible amongst engineers, namely, a concerted movement into upper-middle and upper-level line positions in response to direct *managerial* dependence on such extra-bureaucratically produced kinds of knowledge. It is the perception that this dependence can no longer be dealt with *within* the line/staff format which provides the strongest impetus moving public and private management in a technocratic direction (133).

Nevertheless, the basic tension between capital and the idea that hard, objective knowledge in the possession of scientists, technologists, engineers and other professionals is the key to a 'rational' society still remains. The fact that management is 'professionalising', and that professionally, scientifically and technologically trained persons are moving into high-level managerial positions, simply means that the tension has taken on new forms. It is the clear successes that technocracy has achieved in its impact on traditional management and bureaucracy which requires us to look carefully at its claims to objective knowledge and knowledgeableness once again. For it is only by doing this that we can realise the real significance of challenging an updated version of Weber's argument regarding the superiority of administration based on knowledge in the contemporary context.

The question of the role of special skills, training and competences in 'rational' decision-making cannot be decided on an either/or yes or no basis. No less than in the case of St. Simon and Veblen is there a peculiar ring today to the argument that a rational social order can only be realised by the application of objective knowledge. It ignores the difference between goal-setting and prioritising on the one hand, and technical rationality in the efficent utilisation of means, given goals and their rank-ordering, on the other (134).

It makes too much of the idea of knowledge as a newly independent factor of production standing on its own apart frm other factors as it (allegedly) never has before. As a consequence it ignores the distinct possibility that knowledge has always been required for intelligent decisions, but that it is only as a consequence of its *conscious production and proliferation* that it has become distended from other factors to become the alleged property of specialists and professionals standing on their own. In effect, the theory of social specialisation

in the division of labour could be seen to account
for the independently 'knowledgeable' themselves
(135).

This point is all the more significant when we
recall that it is to metaphorical appeals to the
superior concreteness and hardness of a knowledge of
external nature that supporters of technocratic
ideology ultimately turn to buttress their claim to
the superior objectivity of scientists,
technologists and engineers. Even those
technocrats, and aspirants to technocratic
positions, from the social, behavioural and
administrative/managerial disciplines invoke a
not-dissimilar scientism when speaking of their own
actual or contemplated contribution to group
problem-solving and decision-making. Technocratic
ideology depends fundamentally for its claim to
uniqueness, superiority, and indispensability on a
scientistic conception of objectivity, and on public
acceptance of knowledgeableness as a societal
property only possessed in its more specific
variants by technocrats representing the leading
edge of what is presumed to be both a property of
the culture and a developmental trend (136).

While the distinction noted above between goal-
setting and technically rational behaviour may
appear facile in an age of organised systems of
interdependence, it is still necessary to
distinguish the rank-ordering of ends given scarce
means from the efficient utilisation of means given
ends. It is a distinction that continues to have
institutional and collective, as well as individual,
significance, and it is one which serves to
underscore the priority within any finite decisional
mode of the first to the second (137).

In fact, it is the tension between economising
and technically rational functions and activities
which expresses in decisional terms the tensions
between the scalar and functional/technical clusters
within large organisations, as well as between
bureaucracy and the free occupations as social
institutions competing for control of
organisationally relevant technical and professional
knowledge. Just as the career notion is central in
an analytical sense to resolving the tension between
scalar and functional/technical clusters, so also
does technocratic ideology *and practice* argue for
its unique capacity to achieve the sort of 'control
based on knowledge' which formalised (Weberian)
bureaucracy lost with the emergence and
proliferation of socially specialised technical and

professional knowledge by both the free, and fee for service, occupations (138).

Perhaps the best way of addressing critically the notion that objective knowledge on its own can provide society with a self-steering capacity is to point to the role of capital in economic allocation decisions and politics and the political in governmental and public secor activities. While it is obvious that capital and politics are relevant to government in the first instance and to economic activity in the second, it is the ideal of decision, and responsibility for decision, which helps put the doctrine of group problem-solving in better perspective. The fact that discretion and the rise of group processes have changed operative notions of decision and responsibility in fundamental ways does not alter the fact that such processes and decisions must take place somewhere, sometime. Our problem today is not that these processes and decisions have ceased to take place, but rather our frequent inability to know where and when this is happening and who to assess with 'responsibility' (139).

Without falling back into the sort of decisionism implicit in Weberian (and Popperian) analyses of the role of facts and values in politics, it must be clear that we are concerned here about the issue of objectivity and neutrality rather than the question of whether or not knowledge itself is present (140). Everett Knight drew attention over twenty years ago to a central problem faced by any collective which views itself as an 'objective society', namely, that objectivity is meaningless, even absurd, in the absence of the object that simultaneously completes and negates it. In the case of knowledge claims, it is essential that earlier arguments for a knowledge base on the part of other (and earlier) social actors be premised on the commitment to rationality as necessarily first and foremost a *commonsense* possession of human beings as human beings (141).

More specifically, it is the 'rudderless' character of any specialised knowledge claiming objective status apart from decisions, actions and policies which is more evident from an analysis not only of the way Marx and Engels refuted St. Simon, and the Ecole Polytechnique, but of the fate of the technocratic movement in the United States between 1919 and 1933 (142). Both in theory and in practice the idea of a social order based on the principle of 'rational social organisation' covers over the mainsprings of collective life itself. It does this because at base it relies on an ultimately untenable distinction between business and industry.

It fails to realise the way that rationality, organistion, and productivity so understood, express and promote the deepest values of dominant classes instead of standing in opposition to them. By failing to see society as a totality, it simply provides an ideology-become-practice for completing the existing socioeconomic order rather than challenging it analytically or transcending it in practice (143). The hoped-for alliance between engineers, scientists and technologists, on the one hand, and the workers on the other, proposed by St. Simon, then Veblen a century later, alarmed no thoughtful member of the capitalist investing and controlling class, and for good reason.

It is supremely indicative of the hopelessness of Veblen's view of engineers as a potential 'revolutionary' class that American economic and business interests were more worried about attempts by the engineering societies to gain professional recognition by developing an image of 'social responsibility' through public service than they were about efforts to displace owning and controlling groups through appeals to heightened efficiency and productivity (144). In the final analysis resort to these values was regressive inasmuch as it relied on a distinction between industrial and pecuniary employments whose empirical validity and normative relevance was thoroughly refuted by the real interests and experiences of engineers themselves (145).

It is to society as a totality that the student of technocracy must turn if he is to mount a critique of its most fundamental cultural and historical properties and values. Only in this way is it possible to point to objectivity and neutrality as 'observer's rules' in a culture where the observer, disciplined or otherwise, has displaced both theorists and practitioners (146). As essential tools of the culture, objectivity and neutrality underscore the uniqueness of advanced industrial society as an historically specific cultural configuration whose essence as a form of life is the belief that there are objective, neutral and independent facts of life. We thus make use of one of Wittgenstein's key distinctions without accepting his view that each side stands in a relation of mutual exclusivity, as for example in his attitude to 'progress' as a form *rather than* a fact of life. It must be clear that the doctrine of progress is *both* a 'fact' of life and (as a consequence) a form of life (147).

Only by remaining conscious of advanced industrial society as a historically and culturally specific form of collective life rather than a synonym for it can we see the way that appeals to diligence and industry have served the interests of capital, just as support for 'rational bureaucracy' has served as tacit support for governmental machinations (148). Technocratic ideology and practice combine the appeal to diligence and industry with the commitment to organisational and systems models of rational planning and behaviour. They do this in and through a career orientation which tries to resolve the competition between bureaucracy and the free occupations for control of existing technical and professional knowledge and the processes of innovation which will produce new knowledge (149).

In both public and private sectors of the social economy technocracy functions as an elite class fragment aiding and abetting the interests of capital and a politics of notables (150). Its reconciliation of the free occupations and large scale organisation has not resulted in an erosion of the sort of subordination to groups and classes standing above and outside these structures that Weber noted in the case of both public bureaucracy and economic organisations. At the same time, it is increasingly clear just how difficult a thoroughgoing refutation of Weber's pessimistic rationalisation thesis is going to be in light of the increasingly closed and uninnovative character of the emerging meritocratic 'stratarchy', and the central role of its class fragment as it appears in the organisational milieu-technocracy (151).

While it is easy to argue that the socially specialised knowledge provided by technical, professional and scientific and social-scientific training is more and more central to 'rational' problem solving and decision-making in advanced industrial societies, this says nothing about what the reference for such knowledge is supposed to be. What exactly are the reasons why this is the case, and to what extent can knowledgeableness, and its organisational embodiment, technocracy, be seen to denote yet another phase of the mystification engendered by a form of life determined not to recognise itself as a culturally and world-historically specific whole? (152).

It is an indication of the imperative need for

critique that the social division of labour is so capable of producing these continuing rationalisations of its own rationality in the face of the consequences of this false objectivity. Knowledge claims do not require a corollary assertion of certainty in order to validate them (153). Indeed this is precisely what reveals their partiality, inasmuch as it is only technical and professional knowledge which can seem to make such assertions without embarassment.

To the extent that advanced industrial societies remain commited to the idea of meritocracy as an objectively rational stratification order, they will fail to see the irretrievable damage being done to the possibilities for political and economic transformation still present in the culture by this devotion to objectivity, knowledgeableness and the unity of knowledge in positive, or effectively positive, affirmation. To the extent that they invoke a technocratic ideology such as that found in the work of Galbraith, Lane and Bell, they will be unable to resist the argument that ours is, after all, a post-capitalist social structure, rather than a social economy which has generalised secondary group statuses and observers' rules so far beyond the confines of work and labour settings that capitalism only appears to be nowhere because it is everywhere (154).

Galbraith's 'technostructure' has a lineage that goes back to Veblen's view of the engineers as the 'indispensable general staff' of the industrial system (155). Veblen's conception, based as it was on the distinction within capitalism between business and industry, commerce and production, in turn derives from St. Simon's and Fourier's proposals for European industrial reorganisation in the 1820s and the recommendation of Enfantin and the Ecole Polytechnique a decade later. In the case of these latter thinkers, it is difficult to ignore their *counterrevolutionary* pedigrees as exponents (through Maistre and Bonald) of Burkeian ideas and sentiments in post Napoleonic France (156).

The fact that sociology, in particular, originates in this counterrevolutionary animus rather than constituting an enlightenment discipline favouring individual liberty over social order, may compel one to wonder how its priorities are connected with present efforts at technocratic legitimation in all the advanced societies. Take the residual tension which Weber could still notice in the relation between free contract and selection on the one hand, and a salaried full-time career with no right of appropriation on the other. Here it was Durkheim's discussion of the conditional liberty of the individual prior to this 'initial choice' of occupation which served to underscore the greater emphasis on duties and responsibilities to his occupation once he had decided (157).

As compensation for his ever-faltering autonomy the occupational in question is virtually guaranteed some position in the status order for life. Closure is evident in the way that meritocratic requirements are effectively formalised with the ascendancy of objectivity, neutrality and knowledgeableness to the status of observers' rules. This, combined with *de jure* and/or *de facto* tenure under the guise of protecting impartial administrators from the pressures of 'politics' guarantees the triumph of the career concept, but only at the price of the demise of conditions making for real innovativeness in political life no less than in the economy, in science and in technology (158).

Powerful agencies of secondary socialisation, coupled with general support from the culture as a whole, continue to produce cadres of individuals committed to social-scientific and managerial approaches to policy-making and problem-solving. Their knowledgeableness will almost certainly possess a technical component, and it may even be the centrepiece of their training and qualification. The dilemma lies in the ease with which they, and almost everyone else, have been convinced that knowledgeableness can stand on its own as a basis for self-evident rational decisions and policies at the same time that this knowledge is alleged to stand apart from any specific used by anybody, including those allegedly in possession of it at any given time.

The reconciliation between business and industry which Galbraith claims to have perceived since 1967 in the United States papers over the concerns voiced in what is clearly an updated version of Veblen's tension. Here it is the lobby for professional and technical specialists in possession of training and certification from extra-bureaucratic (and extra-managerial) sources which trades on objectivity and knowledgeableness while mobilising the distinction between producers on the one hand and financiers and investors on the other. Adapted to the present context of large-scale organisation in the advanced societies, it is an argument for overcoming the second class status

195

imposed upon specialists by the line/staff distinction (159).

Yet it ignores Veblen's notion of trained incapacity insofar as it applies to *specialists*, rather than classical bureaucrats, by focussing exclusively on *managerial* pathologies as they are reflected in dependence upon formal authority mechanisms and guarantees (160). The fiction of objective knowledge and the ideal of rational organisation which it points to constitutes a microcosmic version of the idea first worked out and advocated by St. Simon - society as a rational social organisation (161). Wilensky's discussion of technical and professional specialisation as potentially and actually pathological aside, (162) it is the undeniable connection between technocracy and meritocracy which underscores the extent to which openness is illusory.

The 'open society' is increasingly contradicted by the emergence of a social structure whose essence is its generalisation of that 'closed body of office-holders' that Weber dreaded in his analysis of bureaucracy eighty years ago. The rhetoric and dogma is there in all cases, to be sure, covering over the fact that the social levelling that bureaucracy initially helps realise is stopped dead in its tracks by the very dependence on a money economy which made modern administration both possible and necessary (163).

The technostructure can double as a legitimate version of technocratic theory in the final analysis because the 'dispersion of power', as noted, can only go so far and no further (164). It allows for the consolidation of a vastly bloated salaried class of administrators and managers by provisionally reconciling the needs of extensive and far-flung organisational networks in both public and private sectors with certain of the free occupations claiming to possess objective knowledge of a technically specific and professionally valuable kind.

The occupationally specific jargons that have become a hallmark of these activities bespeak a new phase in the development of repressive communication beyond working class exclusion and consequent deprivation (165). The non-speech of such closed systems of symbolically mediated interaction confirms that version of Weberian world de-enchantment so well captured in Habermas' analysis of the demise of the practical and its absorption into the technical and strategic (166).

It cries out for for the emergence of the very sort of commonsense mediation of their 'objectivity in exclusivity and perpetuity' which they revile as an unfit basis for any meaningful knowledge claims.

Technocracy thus turns out to be both a myth and a spectre. It is a myth because it cannot hope to keep its promises for reasons that were suggested long ago by Crozier and Meynaud (167). It is a spectre because its ideology is a more successful basis for claims on management and bureaucracy today than at any time in its on-again off-again past. It serves the interests of late capitalism while arguing for its independence from all partisanship but that of objective knowledge and knowledgeableness itself.

This illusion only appears to be contradicted by the disdain with which its practitioners react to concern about technocratic separation from the means of administration with no right of appropriation. Guaranteed, or virtually guaranteed, full-time salaried careers underwritten by a view of tenure as the key to meritocratic performance and capped by adjusted or indexed retirement pensions, more than compensate for the absence of such irregular and undependable rewards. Commitment to objectivity in the absence of the object of all this knowledgeableness becomes a central factor in the emergence of a culture where rationality, history and progress are only facts of life because they are the essence of our form of life. Yet this suffocation of political possibility, combined with the decreasing likelihood of revolutionary transformation in the advanced societies, can only give the interests of capital and their technocratic henchmen temporary respite (168). Their most pressing question now becomes whether the advanced societies themselves can survive the last phases of modernisation in the face of Third World pressures on their claim to global leadership (169).

RATIONALISATION

In this concluding section we discuss the concept of rationalisation. Apart from .its status as perhaps the key concept in Weber's analysis of modern Western civilisation, an understanding of rationalisation is absolutely essential in comprehending technocracy as an ideology and practice seeking thoroughgoing societal legitimation (170). Technocratic commitment to objectivity in the absence of the object is premised on a view of rationality which equates it with technique and the technical. Both supporters and critics of technocratic ideology have referred to this type of rationality as *instrumental* reason, and its central assumption in all cases is that social and organisational goals are either given or unproblematic (171).

This does not mean that technocratic decision-making ignores ends, but instead points to the difference between proximate ends and longer-term, more astract (thus more *basic*) goals and values. The essence of instrumental reason is precisely its joint concern for *both* proximate ends and available means. Indeed, the uniqueness of this type of reason lies in the fact that its concern for the efficient utilisation of available means in any particular instance depends on a *prior* assessment of possible and desirable ends, however immediate they may be relative to more basic values presumed and/or accepted in the culture at large (172).

In equating instrumental reason with ends/means rationality in this way, we necessarily draw attention to the *contrast* between more abstract social values and goals and the kind of proximate ends which simply constitute a necessary prerequisite to any effort at efficient utilisation of means. The more abstract social values and goals referred to here may be thought of as core values of society as an historical and cultural collective, or they may be understood to constitute a reference point for organisational and political practices at any given time. Thus it is the interplay between the abstractness/concreteness and temporal dimensions which allows us to see rationalisation as a cultural property and phenomenon going on at a number of levels over time (173).

There is another, equally important, facet of rationalisation that arises out of what Weber believed to constitute its most important emergent property as a collective phenomenon - totalisation and closure. Originally, rationalisation had depended for its development on instrumentally rational *individuals* asserting new, basic values *against* the general culture through ends/means thinking in the context of emergent institutions like science, capitalism and the rule of law (174). But gradually significant resistance to these emerging institutions from the general culture was isolated where it did not collapse altogether.

This occurred in tandem with, and largely as a consequence of, the 'success' of capitalism and science in particular, but also as a result of the central role of constitutionalism and the rule of law. Over the past two centuries, modern Western civilisation, already in possession of these three key institutions, has seen their defenders vindicated by the following developments. First, capitalism extended its ambit from merely trading things produced by non-capitalist, guild methods to production processes themselves. Industrialisation, dependent in the main on the discovery of steam power and allied inventions in the technology of mining and textile manufactures, gradually turned the capitalist's attention away from the durability of the thing produced toward the processes used to produce it (175). The result was *commodities*: end products whose use value was more than matched by their exchange value as vehicles or means for the accumulation of capital.

A second major development tied in significant ways to the success of capitalist industrialisation was the extension of representative political democracy, first to the bourgeoisie, and thereafter to non-property holders, including the proletariat (176). This extension, though anchored historically in the bedrock of the principle of limited government and the rule of law, provided early evidence for the yet-to-emerge consumer society of advanced capitalism. Extension of the franchise and the right to the free vote clearly constitute a political prerequisite for the development of the society of free consumers. It is the notion of proximate preference ordering within a framework of now unchallenged basic cultural values by free *individuals* which is a central characteristic of both voting and consuming (177).

The final development concerns the success of capitalist industrialisation even more directly, even though it bears upon relations between science and technology. It is the emergence of science-based technology itself, in contrast to 'traditional' techniques based on experience, trial and error and rules of thumb (178). The emergence of *science-based* technology means that science and technology are brought into a continuous articulation with one another of as a consequence of entrepreneurial, then managerial and corporate (and state), capital allocation decisions. This is no argument for a deterministic linkage between science and technology, since it depends on the continuing role of economic (and later political) interests. They achieve, and thereafter sustain, an articulation between two institutions which had managed to coexist with at best sporadic connections for a period of almost 250 years after the development of modern experimental science (179).

In all three instances cited above we are speaking of developments central to the process of rationalisation and its corollary world of de-enchantment. From capitalism to industrialisation, from the rule of law to mass representative democracy, from science and traditional technology to science-based technology. While the last is clearly more immediately relevant to an analysis of technocratic ideology and practice, all three processes of institutional rationalisation are important to an understanding of the values of this elite class fragment, in part because of their close interdependence. Taken together, they help make it plain why rationalisation tends to totalisation and consequent closure (180).

It is the already-widened ambit and resulting complexity of advanced industrial societies as *cultures* characterised by the emergence of consumer over producer roles, near-total bureaucratisation in urban centres, and science-based technology arising out of corporate (and state) R and D infrastructures which underscores the residual character of traditional attitudes and structures as little more than vestiges of the past. But the sort of individualism which the original three institutions of Western modernity help produce and sustain is reversed by the very 'success' of the Western project seen in terms of the consequences of rationalisation. The instrumental rationality of individuals commited to overcoming traditional ways of doing things is gradually institutionalised with the acceptance of their claim to objective success as it is manifested in rising living standards, increased life spans, better working conditions, and surpluses generally.

At the juncture at which it becomes possible to point to agencies of secondary socialisation as evidence of the completion of the Western project as a unique cultural whole, individual support for instrumental rationality in both theory and practice looks more like a reflection of successful norm internalisation than anything else. Here it is the societal whole, with its interdependent but capitalisatically functional subsystems, which seems to provide the real point of reference for instrumentalism (181). The difference between proximate ends and core cultural values evident in individual efforts at ends/means rationality in the contemporary context can now be reconceptualised in terms of the contrast between the aggregated systemic whole and its individual 'parts' reflecting the system's basic values at many different levels in and through its 'individuals' labouring and consuming, functioning, behaving and spectating (182).

One problem in conceptualising the link between rationalisation and technocracy relates to our dependence on concepts from the very social, behavioural and administrative/managerial disciplines which function as central legitimising agents of technocracy itself. This was why we distinguished between supporters and critics of instrumental reason earlier, and why it is necessary to see in 'objective' sociological accounts of the role of instrumental reason in the advanced societies a form of affirmation rather than 'neutrality' toward the phenomenon (183). Only a dialectical analysis of disciplines which thoroughly repudiates the idea that their findings may be both 'correct', given certain assumptions and untrue by reference to standards of true objectivity can show why such an analysis is always on the side of content rather than form (184).

One of the most prominent examples of such a sociological analysis in the recent history of the discipline is provided by Talcott Parsons' alleged 'overhaul' of Weber's typology of action in *The Social System*. Arguing that the system concept had superseded that of action on practical as well as analytical grounds, Parsons went on to make a point of incontestable significance for our discussion:

> Contrary to the view held by the author in *The Structure of Social Action* (Parsons), it now appears that this postulate (subjective interpretation) is not essential to the frame of reference of action in its most elementary form. It is, however, necessarily involved at the levels of elaboration of systems of action at which culture, that is, shared symbolic patterns, becomes involved. It is, that is, a consequence of the fact that action comes to be oriented in terms of symbols which also serve to communicate with other actors (185).

Parsons' acknowledgment and endorsement of the totalisation of society as a rational social organisation is evident throughout *The Social*

System. To point out that system supersedes action in analytical terms is to insist that sociological theory keep 'current' with observable practical realities. Action, in line with the supersession of Weberian (and Marshallian) negative individualism by Durkheimian positive individualism, now becomes analytically relevant solely at the level of the subsystem of society which Parsons calls 'culture'.

It has always been Parsons' willingness to allow an anthropological conception of culture – the core of shared values held by a given collective – to be displaced by a view of culture as at best a 'subsystem', where action as intendedly-rational behaviour functions in an increasingly ritualistic and conformist way, which gives his theoretical work so much of its uniqueness. We have pointed out elsewhere in considerable detail how significant the societal cooptation of goal-rational action and the consequent isolation of value-rational action in Weber in fact was. First Mannheim, and thereafter Parsons, make plain how total has been the societal cooptation of goal-rational action in the form of 'instrumental rationality' (186).

In the case of Parsons, this cooptation is evident in the way 'norm internalisation' shifts the negatively individualistic emphasis away from intent as the basic (Weberian) criterion in assessing the reasonableness of behaviour-as-action toward *consequences* as a reflection of proper secondary socialisation.

> Institutionalisation of cultural patterns means...internalisation of the same patterns in the personality. Psychologically an internalised pattern is no longer an object of the situation. It is not possible to treat it as an instrumental means or condition. There is a specific mode of cathectic integration of the actor's need dispositions with an internalised pattern. This fact has a fundamental methodological significance. It means the orientation of 'instrumental rationality' cannot be the attitude defining the actor's orientation to internalised patterns (187).

When Parsons reformulates Weberian individual actors as 'personalities', he not only subsumes them into society's cultural subsystem, but redefines rationality itself. It now becomes a property of *Society* – that individual 'rational social organisation' in its own right with 'parts' in

continuous need of attention - just as it had become
for the more prescient Mannheim earlier in *Man and
Society in an Age of Reconstruction* and in later
studies (188).

It is the alleged 'complexity' both in
technical/scientific and relational terms of the
emergent whole - society - which becomes the basis
for subsequent claims to legitimacy by technocratic
ideology. Technocracy seeks legitimacy in the first
case by . pointing, as noted, to the need for
objective knowledge and knowledgeableness as a
collective property of group problem-solving and
pooling given the progress of societal
specialisation and the need for those trained in
matter-of-factness and opaque cause and effect
(189). It seeks legitimacy in the second case by
noting the continuing need for what Weber called
'imperative co-ordination' in the bureaucratic
context given the emergence of society as a process
of ongoing interdependence between numberless
corporate and state/governmental organisations
(190).

Analytically, Parsons allows the 'individual'
to reappear in other than exclusively non-rational
guise when he speaks of 'three levels of the
organisation of rational actions in action systems'
(191). But this supreme effort at preservation
cannot mask the fact that all three 'levels' - the
individual actor, the economy, and the political
system - are really collapsed into a thoroughly
amorphous new organism - society as a 'social
system'. This new whole is so total in its
socialising ambit, Parsons implies, as to render
completely meaningless political economy's
distinction between the economic substructure and
the political and cultural (ideational-artistic)
superstructure (192).

Like Durkheim before him, Parsons fails to see
how his determination to defend the idea that there
is a 'collective sociological reality' not reducible
to psychological terms acts to legitimise society's
claim to objective status as a synonym for
collective life rather than one historically and
culturally produced form of it (193). It is
Durkheim's view of 'everyone else' as a culture
which is at the root of this propensity on Parsons'
part, even though Parsons clearly jettisons
Durkheim's essentially anthropological notion along
with that of political economy when he speaks of
culture as a 'subsystem'.

To the extent that normative socialisation

occurs in the cultural sub-system, and produces individual actors as 'personalities' out of its efforts, one can see the clear drift of sociological theory as an ideology affirming actual developments. Add to this the fate suffered by residual socialisation processes standing as traditional or eccentric remnants in opposition to societal pre-emption, and the conditions requiring that empirical accuracy correlate with affirmation become even more difficult to deny (194).

Parsons makes the fate of the individual actor and culture clear enough when he tells us that 'sociological theory is...for us that aspect of the theory of social systems which is concerned with the phenomena of the institutionalisation of patterns of value - orientation in the soial system' (195). It is out of this theoretical grounding for disciplined observation and resulting objectivity and knowledgeableness that technocracy mounts its claims to legitimation as that set of group practices whose training, certification and resulting competence can be counted on to reconcile the technical/functional and scalar clusters beyond the capacities of either professionals or conventional managers and bureaucrats (196).

Central to these claims, as already noted, is the idea of normative socialisation. Here only the narrowly 'technical' aspects of specialised training are carried out exclusively by agencies of 'secondary socialisation'. As for 'norm internalisation', it is the mark of society as an emergent totality that it is more the *application* of *already internalised norms* 'available' in the general culture-as-civilisation than a first awareness of them that is accomplished by agencies of secondary socialisation like schools, professional training institutions and organised work and labour contexts.

This, to be sure, says nothing about the all-too-obvious discrepancies between the professional ideology of autonomy and self-control in return for service and the reality of institutional delivery systems (197). It only points to organised work and labour contexts as places where already diffuse and amorphous 'norms' appear even less contravened by managerial and bureaucratic practice than they do in professional fee-for-service situations. Indeed, in organisational settings norms themselves cease to constitute mainly values to be assessed as present or absent to varying degrees on the basis of individual actions, and come to constitute instead formal properties said to be present in persons who are, after all, 'qualified' (198).

The presence of this particular form of the 'Peter principle' as a central characteristic of technocratic management in large organisations today underscores further the consequences for innovative rationality in the midst of all-pervasive rationalisation of the already noted overhaul of Weber, first by Mannheim, then by Parsons. In the case of both writers, it is the conformity to internalised values which in every case of possible or actual practice are alleged to be 'rational' only to the extent that they serve the societal whole *through organised work and labour contexts* which defines technocratic claims to expertise.

Expertise in the new equation *means* a collective system of management whose group processes of problem-solving combine specialised knowledge and imperative co-ordination in a new objectivity characterised by disciplined observation and a more occupationally specific form of knowledgeableness, in short, a form of domination which is both socially and organisationally rational, no matter where it is carried out (199).

In turn, this requires that Weberian goal-rationality undergo two significant changes. First, it is hypostasised in order to constitute an ideal and actual property of collective structures, and second, its continuing source in individuals thereafter can only be attested to the extent that they reflect the norms of these very collective structures. This was anticipated by Weber in his discussion of rationalisation. So also was the fate of value-rationality, which is now absorbed into these collective structures as a synonym for normative socialisation. Values too, lose their anchorage in the individual, except to the extent that one also reflects proper socialisation in the form of norm internalisation. This was anticipated by Weber in his discussion of the de-enchantment of the world. Thus the fate of each of his two forms of individual rational action in the world - goal and value rationality - is the basis for comprehending rationalisation in the first case and world de-enchantment in the second (200).

It may seem fatuous or unnecessary at this point to turn our attention to an analysis of more empirically concrete manifestations of rationalisation in particular, but important aspects of an adequate understanding of technocracy require it. Just as the objectivity of disciplined

observation and resulting knowledgeableness
constitutes an apotheosis of world de-enchantment
expressed in the fate of value-rationality, so also
does the fate of collectivised goal rationality in
and through rationalisation as an empirical process
help us understand the socio-economic and political
basis of technocracy (201).

As a matter of fact, Weber himself gives us an
indication of how important it is to be aware of
rationalisation when he discusses what would later
become one of several significant points of
departure for the phenomenological clarification of
everyday life, particularly in the work of Schutz
(202). In the excerpt which follows Weber plainly
addresses rationalisation as that process in
collective life which displaces individual conscious
intentions, therefore rationality itself, with
organised routine and repetition.

> In the great majority of cases actual action
> goes on in a state of inarticulate half-
> consciousness or actual unconsciousness of its
> subjective meaning. The actor is more likely to
> "be aware' of it in a vague sense than he is to
> "know" what he is doing or be explicitly self-
> conscious about it. In most cases his action is
> governed by impulse or habit. Only occasionally
> and, in the uniform action of large numbers
> often only in the case of a few individuals, is
> the subjective meaning of the action, whether
> rational or irrational, brought clearly into
> consciousness. The ideal type of meaningful
> action where the meaning is fully conscious and
> explicit is a marginal case (203).

What is important in any analysis of the meaning
of this statement is that we forego the temptation
Weber elsewhere encourages us to yield to.
Rationalisation only appears to be different in type
from traditional routinisation as it is understood
in his discussion of forms of collective behaviour
because of our infatuation with the idea of
rationality as a unique property of collectives as
well as individuals (204). But the impact on given
individuals of structural predefinition of task-
specialised non-discretionary routines is the
same. Only what Parsons calls the 'peculiar goal-
orientation' of organised work and labour activities
themselves is different from more 'traditional'
structures, and even then probably only in degree
(205).

Modes of socialisation in values (norms) and techniques taking place outside the confines of work and labour settings, on the other hand, have already been cited as external in all significant aspects to the rationalisation process understood in its most empirically concrete sense. This is the essentially Durkheimian argument put forward perhaps most articulately by Victor Thompson and Georges Friedman (206). Only a broader more abstract notion of rationalisation can capture such person-specialised professional and managerial activities as well as those characterised by specialisation of tasks. This is the view of the social division of labour as a process whose further development is seen to be synonymous on the whole with 'progress', and its most passionate exponent remains Emile Durkheim (207).

It is only by treating rationalisation as a property of society as a culture that it can be seen to comprehend the generation of new knowledge within the urban and industrial division of labour, though external on the whole to specific work and labour settings. The difficulty with the notion that such developments lie 'outside' organisational contexts must be plain. It is increasingly the case that the new knowledge which is found external to one organisation was produced, generated, or simply 'come upon' in another.

This argues for a more societally *total* notion of rationalisation as well as an organisationally specific one, inasmuch as it is the very interdependence among vast networks of organised activity that explains *both* rationalisation *and* innovation in advanced industrial societies (208). It is precisely this tension in specific organisations between rationalisation and innovation which has led Crozier in particular to characterise technocracy as a myth. His major argument depends on the relationship between social specialisation and rationalization as a society-wide phenomenon anchored in specific events and developments. He dismisses the idea that 'the complexities of our technical age' necessitate the ascendancy of a tecnocratic group holding 'more and more power in society as a whole' as a 'misunderstanding of the situation created by technical and scientific progress'.

Crozier's perception of what is taking place is very different from those most concerned about technocracy, and on the whole is probably closer to Max Weber than anyone else, as the following except makes clear.

    The invasion of all domains by rationality, of course, gives power to the expert who is an agent of this progress. But the expert's success is constantly self-defeating. The rationalisation process gives him power, but the end results of rationalisation curtail this power. As soon as a field is well-covered, as soon as the first inventions and innovations can be translated into rules and programs, the expert's power disappears.

    As a matter of fact experts have power only on the front line of progress - which means they have a constantly shifting and fragile power. We should like to argue even that it can be less and less consolidated in modern times, inasmuch as more and more rationalised processes can be operated by non-experts. Of course, experts will fight to prevent the rationalisation of their own tricks of the trade. But contrary to the common belief, the accelerated rate of change that characterises our period makes it more difficult for them to resist rationalisation. Their bargaining power as individuals is constantly diminishing (209).

    What makes this assessment so similar to Weber's, albeit in the absence of any apparent pessimism regarding the pace and direction of industrial societies, is the role of rationalisation as a process which not only keeps pace with the production and generation of new knowledge in the society at large but now seems to be outpacing it. Crozier uses the process *as a whole* to overcome technocratic fears, arguing that there is an irresistible tendency in profit-making organisations in particular, as well as in state and governmental bureaucracies in capitalist societies, to try to 'rationalise' person-specialised dependencies requiring extensive discretion (210).

    Thus it is a two-phased process, with the latter phase in a certain sense cancelling out the first, the more so with the ever-greater organisation of society as a whole. Technocratic fears, he argues, depend for their substance on acknowledging only the first phase of this process, and thus, we might surmise, are probably more valid for state socialist than capitalist systems (211). It is as a consequence of giving due consideration to both phases that we allegedly realise the

groundlessness of our fears, since the result of the
latter phase appears to be routinisation in the form
of rules, programs and task-specialised job
descriptions.

Victor Thompson's approach to the problem is
somewhat differenct inasmuch as his contrast between
task and person-specialised activity sees them as
mutually exclusive, the first an organisational
approach and the second a societal one (212).
Thompson sees person-specialists as second-class
citizens that organisations nevertheless need, but
who suffer greatly from both the superior-
subordinate hierarchical structure of bureaucracies
and from managerial cooptation of line positions
(213). Relegation to staff positions only
aggravates the issue, since the line-staff
distinction itself was really only generated to
compensate for the problem of the subordinate being
increasingly more likely to be 'technically correct'
in a confrontation wih his superior. Thompson has
more faith in specialism, particularly person
specialisation, than Crozier. Where Crozier invokes
a Weberian analytic, Thompson abjures it in favour
of Durkheim. Also, Thompson tends to see person
specialists increasing their power relative to
organisational processes of task specialisation with
the onset of automation, in clear contrast to
Crozier (214).

Present day technologies are at a state of
development that can fairly be termed 'nearly
complete' according to Thompson, because little
portions of individual task specialists are still
required to complete production functions carried
out in the main by mechanised technologies. Since
the tremendously productive machine was incomplete,
little bits and parts of man had to be used to
complete it...The completed machine, automation,
will eliminate the industrial worker; it will
require skilled technicians (215).

This notion of a normal(ised) division of
labour on the model of Durkheimian 'organic
solidarity' almost totally ignores the contingent
character of technological progress in favour of a
belief in its inevitability, objectivity, and
goodness. By ignoring the 'other side' of
rationalisation, it plays down the essential
complementarity of person and task specialisation
both within the same position and between positions
(216). Thompson's confidence that automation can
and will automatically invade most areas of
organised work and labour evidences no appreciation

209

whatsoever for the role of capital allocation and oversight functions even in state socialist, but certainly in advanced capitalist societies, while his near-religious commitment to person-specialised professionals and semi-professionals, and his rage at managers and formal authority, harks back to Thorstein Veblen's attack on non-productive 'vested interests' (217).

While Crozier does take account of the tie between organisationally specific tensions between new knowledge and rationalisation and larger societal effects, he misses the essence of what exactly technocracy is and what technocrats do. Technocrats, as noted earlier, may and usually do possess some form of person-specialised training, but their main responsibilities lie in the exercise of a collective management through group problem-solving processes based on the ideology of objective knowledge and knowledgeableness. It is the way that their claims to legitimation depend on the notion of 'rational domination' expressed in and through their alleged reconciliation of authority and knowledge – in a 'knowledgeable' society stratified on a *formally* meritocratic basis which is of central importance in assessing their societal and organisational impact.

It is the new organisational requirements for *managers* capable of maintaining a continuing equipoise between the production of new knowledge through R and D and allied innovative activities, and the subjection to rules, routines and technology, *given incipient rationalisation* as the necessary 'other side' of innovation, that is central to comprehending technocratic indispensability in the advanced societies (218). Crozier chooses to formulate the idea of a ruling class or group demographically, then argue that present experts will in due course be displaced by more technically and professionally 'knowledgeable' successors trained in even more advanced developments given the continuous and permanent character of both phases of the total process already cited.

But this begs the issue, namely, that we now must acknowledge an apparent dependence on managers trained in a society-wide version of Weber's more oganisationally localised notion of 'control based on knowledge'. Yes, experts change is what constitutes expertise shifts, but this is simply a temporal version of the unmistakably collective properties of decision and action already alluded to as being the essence of technocracy. We are discussing not individuals qua individuals here, but an ideology-become-practice through its persistent and increasing sedimentation in organisational structures. Thus rationalisation cannot be put forward as evidence that technocracy is a myth for two reasons.

First, because experts who are allegedly rendered obsolete by the progress of knowledge and technique are simply replaced by other technocrats with the success of sedimentation and structuration, and second, because the essence of technocracy is not in the final analysis the mere possession of objective technical and professional knowledge, but collective control through managerial decision and action processes which make use of it in one way or another. It is rather to the idea of this institutionalisation of organised structures both within and outside of work and labour settings which facilitate such developments that we must turn for an understanding and an assessment of technocracy (219).

Max Weber in so many ways remains our best guide here, as Crozier more than most others seems to realise. When rationalisation becomes societally indistinguishable from routinisation, then 'rationality' itself will have become a tradition, perhaps the pre-eminent tradition of society, that culture whose essence is its refusal to recognise itself, in contrast to 'all others' as such (220). At this point the idea of knowledgeableness and objectivity, refined into a formal craft of behaviour by those allegedly in possession of capacities for 'rational domination', will eventually be seen for what it is. This, to be sure, will require the dethronement of technique and the technical, which in any case is more and more subservient as knowledge to pure and applied science and as process to capital allocation decisions in the political economy of advanced industrial societies (221).

As an elite class fragment of the new middle class salaried-but-propertyless group in a society increasingly stratified in a formally meritocratic way, they show the prospects for what is left of unorganised and unstructured rationality with the unrelenting movement toward totalisation and closure (222). Everything depends on our breaking through the fictions created out of commonsense worship of the false concreteness of technique by many or most in both the advanced and the developing countries.

211

The real question is whether and to what extent this will either require or create the conditions for new socio-economic and political possibilities in the process.

NOTES

1. Herbert Marcise One Dimensional Man (Beacon Press, Boston, 1964), pp. 84-120, 203-224; and T.W. Adorno, 'Society', in R. Bayers (ed.), The Legacy of the German Refugee Intellectuals, (Schocken Books, New York, 1969), pp. 144-153.

2. Murray Edelman, The Symbolic Uses of Politics (University of Illinois Press, Urbanay, 1964); and M. Edelman, Politics as Symbolic Action (Markham Press, New York, 1969), for a non-dialectical partial explanation.

3. Max Weber, Theory of Social and Economic Organisation, edited and introduced by Talcott Parsons, (Free Press, Glencoe, 1947), pp. 324-341 and particularly p. 329; and M. Weber, 'Bureaucracy', in H. Gerth and C. Wright Mills (eds.), From Max Weber, (Oxford University Press, New York, 1946), pp. 196-244.

4 Weber, Social and Economic Organisation, pp. 92-93 and pp. 109-112. Also, see generally Herbert Blumer, Symbolic Interaction: Notes and Readings, (Prentice Hall, Englewood Cliffs, 1969).

5. Harold Wilensky, 'The Professionalisation of Everyone', American Journal of Sociology. May (1964). H.W. Vollmer and D.L. Mills (eds.), Professionalisation (Pentice Hall, Englewood Cliffs, 1966), remains an excellent, though somewhat dated, sourcebook of readings. Particularly useful for our analysis are the contributions by Greenwood, Caplow and Scott.

6. Victor Thompson, Modern Organisation, (Alred Knopf, New York, 1961); V. Thompson, Bureaucracy and Innovation (University of Alabama Press, Alabama, 1968).

7. The well known study by J. Meynaud, Technocracy (Faber, London 1965) though consulted, has not been employed in any direct way in this study. While helpful in some general respects, it is both too diffuse in its focus within the French situation, and too dependent on this very situation for most of its generalisations. Also see Jacques Ellul, The Technological System Continuum Books, New York, 1980), particularly his discussion of the following works: Henri Le Febvre, Position, Contre les Technocrates (1970); John Joli Bennet

Technisation (1973); Radovan Richta, Civilisation at the Crossroads (1960); Schon, Technology and Change (1967); and Habermas, Toward a Rational Society (1968). While correctly noting his own priority to Habermas' susequent discussion of the phenomenon of technocratic consciousness, he ignores Weber's priority to his own work, concentrating on Weber's discussion of technology rather than rationalisation and de-enchantment. I have taken this up in 'The Sociology of Apocalypse', Human Context, Vol.7, No.3 (1975), pp. 474-494.

8.   See forthcoming H.T. Wilson, Tradition nd Innovation: Weber and Wittgenstein on Civilisation as Culture (Routledge and Kegan Paul, London, 1982).

9.   See Weber, Social and Economic Organisation, pp. 330-334; Weber, From Max Weber, pp. 196-204.

10.   See generally H.T. Wilson, The American Ideology (Routledge and Kegan Paul, London, 1977).

11.   Thompson, Modern Organisation; Michel Crozier, The Bureaucratic Phenomenon (Univesity of Chicago Press, Chgicago, 1964); Charles Perrow, Complex Organisations (McGraw Hill, New York, 1972); Harold Wilensky, Organisational Intelligence Basic Books, New York, 1966); Corinne Gilb, Hidden Hierarchies (Harper & Row, New York, 1966); and Meynaud, Technocracy. See Wilson, The American Ideology, ch. 7 for a detailed discussion of the concept of 'rational domination' in a formaly organised context, and its implications for 'rationalisation' in late capitalist society.

12.   R.E. Pahl and J.T. Winkler, 'The Coming Corporatism', Challenge, March/April (1975), pp. 28-35; J.T. McLeod, 'The Free Enterprise Dodo is no Phoenix', Candaian Forum, August, (1976), pp. 6-12. Compare to Charles Lindblom's analysis of the mix of political authority and economic organisation in Politics and Markets (Basic Books, New York, 1977).

13.   Weber, Social and Economic Organisation, p. 334.

14.   In this sense, modern 'rational; bureaucracy is a cultural artifact. This is discussed in Wilson, Tradition and Innovation, ch. 6.

15.   Compare Weber's discussion in Social and Economic Organisation and From Max Weber to the following studies: W. Muller and C. Neususs, 'The Illusion of State Socialism', and Habermas and Offe's reply, all in Telos No. 25 (1975), pp.

13-111. The larger framework guiding Habermas, and
to some extent Offe, can be found in J. Habermas,
Legitimation ·Crisis (Beacon Press, Boston, 1975).
The Telos essay reproduces pp. 50-60 of this latter
work.   Compare to Donald Hodges, The
Bureaucratisation of Socialism (University of
Massachusetts Press, Boston and Amherst, 1980),
where Hodges cites organisation itself as a fourth
factor of production. All these studies repeat
Weber's point about both the formative and
developmental role of organisational structure
throughout the history of Western capitalism,
including political authority and the bureaucratic
organisation behind it. To the extent that this
required (and requires) managerial capacities in
both the general and specific senses, the work of
Lindblom, Politics and Markets, and Alfred Chandler,
The Visible Hand (Belknap Press, Cambridge, 1977),
is instructive in assessing the long-term dependence
of industrial capitalism on state, bureaucratic and
managerial support almost since its inception in all
the advanced societies.
    16.   Weber, Social and Economic Organisation,
pp. 324-329. Habermas thus continues this focus as
one of the pre-eminent problematics in Western
social analysis in his Legitimation Crisis.
    17.   The term was first formulated by W.H.
Smyth of Berkeley, California in 1919, after reading
several articles by Thorstein Veblen in The Dial,
later collected together and publised as The
Engineers and the Price System. This is discussed
at pp. 169-71 of this study. Technocracy is defined
in the Shorter Oxford English Dictionary 1967
edition, at p. 2140 as 'the organisation of the
social order based on principles established by
technical experts'. This definition highlights the
two most important properties of technocracy as an
ideology and a movement, namely, its reference to
Society rather than simply work and labour contexts,
and the commitment to the idea of technique as
concrete, objective and impartial knowledge so
central to meritocracy as the modern day version of
the concept of 'rational domination' - the key to
legal-rational authority in Weber. Note Habermas'
acquiescence to this notion in 'Technology and
Science as Ideology', in J. Habermas, Toward a
Rational Society (Heinemann, London, 1971), pp. 81-
122 at pp. 104-106 and my response in 'Science,
Critique and Criticism: the "Open Society"
Revisited', in J. O'Neill (ed.), On Critical Theory,
(Seabury Press, New York, 1976), pp. 205-230 at pp.

217-224.

18.   Habermas, in 'Technology and Science as Ideology', pp. 111-114 notes that technocratic consciousness is not, after all, only ideology, but is now supported by the performance of the substructure without recourse to either utopian hopes or illusory forms of legitimation. We think this itself may constitute a form of technocratic thinking no less problematic than the inverted workshop evident in Ellul's view of technique and technology as a satanic phenomenon moving toward self-propelled totalisation and closure. It is not just totalisation and closure, but objectivity within the observed cultural reality which evidences the presence of this phenomenon. On this latter score, Habermas' analysis cited above is consonant with central features of technocratic thinking. See particularly H.P. Dreitzel, 'Social Science and the Problem of Rationality', Politics and Society, vol. 2, no. 2 (1972), pp. 165-182. Note especially in this regard Ellul's definition of technique 'in his earlier Technological Society (Vintage, New York, 1964) XXV, taken from Lasswell: 'the totality of methods rationally arrived at and having absolute efficiency (for a given stage of development) in every field of human activity', and my analysis in Wilson, 'The Sociology of Apocalypse'.

19.   See generally C. Wright Mills, The Power Elite (Galaxy, New York, 1956), especially reference 6, ch. 1, in footnotes, and the two studies by Wallace Clement, The Canadian Corporate Elite (McClelland and Stewart, Toronto, 1975), and Continental Corporate Power (Macmillan, Toronto, 1978). Also see John Porter, The Vertical Mosaic (University Press, Toronto, 1964), Robert Presthus, Elite Accommodation in Canadian Politics (University Press, Cambride, 1973) and Presthus, Elites in the Policy Process (University Press, Cambridge, 1974).

20.   Clement, The Canadian Corporate Elite. The central role of the idea of objective expertise in economics and the social, behavioural and administrative/managerial disciplines is central to technocratic self-legitimation and is discussed further on. For an application to Canadian politics and government as it has recently taken shape in the continental and Western context, see H.T. Wilson, 'Parties, Elites and Bureaucracies in the Canadian Political System: Some Implications for Political Leadership', G.H. Massey (ed.), Political Leadership in Canada, (McClelland and Stewart, Toronto, 1983).

22.   Anthony Giddens, The Class Structure of

the Advanced Societies (Hutchinson, London, 1973),
pp. 255-264. Also see Thorstein Veblen, Absentee
Ownership and Business Enterprise in Recent Times
(Huebsch, Boston, 1923); James Burnham, The
Managerial Revolution (John Day, New York, 1941);
Jean Meynaud, Technocracy; Dreitzel, 'Social
Science'; J.K. Galbraith, The New Industrial State
(Houghton and Mifflin, Boston, 1973).
    23. See Charles Kadushin, The American
Intellectual Elite (Random House, New York, 1973).
    24. Galbraith, The New Industrial State, chs.
1-6; Giddens, Class Structure, p. 263.
    25. Indeed Galbraith's focus has shifted
significantly from secondary manufacturing to
tertiary economic activity in the later book. See
The New Industrial State, pp. 282-295 and compare to
the absence of any reference to an 'educational and
scientific estate' in Economics and the Public
Purpose. Our argument is that this absence is more
indicative of the sterility of this 'estate' than of
its absorption by technocratic consciousness for
Galbraith.
    26. Giddens, Class Structure pp. 66-68.
    27. Robert Lane, 'The Decline of Politics and
Ideology in a Knowledgeable Society', American
Sociological Review, vol. 31, no. 5 (1966), pp. 647-
662.
    28. See Wilson, The American Ideology, chs. 2
and 9. Also compare Karl Mannheim, Ideology and
Utopia (Routledge and Kegan Paul, London, 1954),
originally published in 1929, to Mannheim, Man and
Society in an Age of Reconstruction (Routledge and
Kegan Paul, London, 1940), originally published in
1935.
    29. Bell, The Coming of Post-Industrial
Society, p. 184. Compare to Habermas' reference to
post-capitalist social formations in Legitimation
Crisis, p. 17.
    30. Wilson, 'Science, Critique and Criticism'.
    31. Wilson, The American Ideology, chs. 2, 5
and 10.
    32 Compare to his later attitude not only in
Mannheim, Man and Society in an Age of
Reconstruction, but in Diagnosis of Our Time 9RKP,
London, 1947), in Freedom, Power and Democratic
Planning (Routledge and Kegan Paul, London, 1951),
and in Essays in Sociology and Social Psychology
(Routledge and Kegan Paul, London, 1953). See John
Heeren, 'Karl Mannheim and the Intellectual Elite',
British Journal of Sociology, vol. 22, no. 1 (1971),
pp. 1-15.

33.   Galbraith, The New Industrial State, ch. 5.

34.   Wilson, The American Ideology, chs. 8, 9.

35.   This 'structure' is a property of the interpenetration of societally based norms and the authority that goes with occupancy of top managerial positions in large organisations. What gives priority to society over the organisation in this relationship, however, is precisely the collective character of this authority, and its expression in and through group problem-solving. See particularly Dreitzel, 'Social Science'.

36.   Here we note the diffuseness of technocracy's normative base in society. Lacking specific professional and semi-professional structures and processes, its societal character, while real, depends on generalised public respect for a range of white collar occupations, some with professional and semi-professional status, others without it. See Wilensky, 'The Professionalisation of Everyone', and the essays by Greenwood and Caplow in Vollmer and Mills (eds.), Professionalisation

37.   It is the still-existent difference between technological, managerial and social-scientific conceptions of scientism which help account for the diffuseness of technocracy's normative base in society, and the fact that neither the managerial nor the social-scientific notions have a sufficiently specific technical basis in public thinking and attitudes to sustain a professional or semi-professional perception. In the case of these latter two notions, it is the discrepancy between managerial rationales for their power and authority, and social-scientific scientism as a research and policy ideology which constitutes both the dilemma and the challenge for technocracy.

38.   Technocrats can be said to bear the same relation to society as a rational social organisation that Weberian bureaucrats did to conventional organisations only if we acknowledge the continuing tension between professional-technical and administrative-technical activities. See Perrow, Complex Organisations for a discussion of these two types of specificity. As to why only the former is in a position to secure public support as a professional or semi-professional occupation, Wilensky, 'The Professionalisation of Everyone?' Seen in this light, the alleged need for collective activity through group problem-solving in an organisational context can be understood as much as a compensation for the lack of a collective

occupational image in the society at large as a
necessary response to the complexity of contemporary
technology and science. See particularly William
Goode, 'Community within a Community', American
Sociological Review, vol. 22 (1957), pp. 194-200,
and Gilb Hidden Hierarchies.
    39   Thompson, Modern Organisation. This is
evident from much of Weber's analysis at several
levels on the political economy of capitalism and
the role of science and technology relative to
religion and magic.
    40.   Weber, Social and Economic Organisation,
pp. 333, 339, 340; Weber, From Max Weber, pp. 196-
198, 212-216, 228-230, 235-239.
    41.   William Whyte, The Organisation Man
(Doubleday, Garden City, 1956); Wilensky,
Organisational Intelligence. For one of the most
passionate overall defences of the group and
collective principle, all too prescient it turns
out, Mary Parker Follett, The New State (Longmans,
New York, 1918).
    42.   The idea of individual responsibility for
job activities is closely tied to the concept of
private property in capitalist society. Technocracy
completes the severence of activity and
responsibility initiated by absentee ownership and
the so-called managerial revolution noted by Veblen
and Burnham.   See also Adolph Berle and Gardiner
Means, The Modern Corporation and Private Property
(Macmillan, New York, 1932), G. Means, The Corporate
Revolution in America (Crowell-Collier, New York,
1962), and Berle, Power (Harcourt, Brace and World,
New York, 1969).   Thus, Veblen and Smyth were
premature in their reference to technocracy in the
period after 1919, since the other side of absentee
ownership in the person of both propetylessness and
the decline of contract relative to status for these
salaried groups had not developed so far. See Gilb,
Hidden Hierarchies, the final chapter on contract
status.   Propertylessness and the emergence of a
meritocratic status society where property and
contract is less and less a principal basis of power
in the societal division of labour makes the claim
to objective knowledgeableness and impartial
expertise all the more important, and helps explain
why aspects of collectivity and group process must
appear in the organisational context of work and
labour activities in the absence of a perceived
collective character in the society at large.
    43.   Thompson, Modern Organisation; Thompson,
Bureaucracy and Innovation.

44. Weber never specifically stated that this conflict might well be between two types of expertise rather than between the expert and the non-expert, while Thompson clearly opts for the latter interpretation sixty years later. it is in this sense that Thompson's approach, following Durkheim, is meritocratic and even technocratic in some of its aspects. Thompson fails to distinguish the multiplicity and complexity of salaried status occupations in large organisations combining properties from both managerial/bureaucratic and professional/technical occupations. On the 'social ethic', see Whyte, Organisation Man. On these jobs as two types of expertise, Perrow, Complex Organisations.

45. Thompson, Modern Organisation, and Peter Blau and W. Richard Scott, Formal Organisations (Chandler, San Fransisco, 1962). Also see Talcott Parsons numerous essays on business and the professions in Essays in Sociological Theory (Free Press, Glencoe, 1942).

46. Weber, in the relevant sections of both Social and Economic Oganisation and From Max Weber, makes a great deal out of the fact that bureaucrats in his ideal type are appointed. From the standpoint of state and governmental apparatuses, this fact has two quite separate and distinct aspects. It means a salaried career with no hereditrary right of appropriation and/or responsibility, but it also means appointment rather than election. It is the fact that tenure places such positions outside the control of elected officials which gives the notion of objective competence and merit such a hollow ring, one favouring collectivity and status over traditional individuality and contract and property. Their presence speaks to the limit of the electoral principle and their further extension to corporate economic organisation, in contrast to entrepreneurial and small business activities, shows the accuracy of Weber's forecast already noted, and the increasing similarity between organised action, whether in the public or private sector, relative to the traditional distinction between government and the economy. Nevertheless, technocratisation has probably gone further in the state and government sectors in the West because of tenure, combined with the persistence of 'the market', with its demand for non-technocratic decisional capacities, in the 'private' sector. In this regard see Lindblom, Politics and Markets; and Wilson, 'Parties, Elites,

and Bureaucracies'.

47. H.T. Wilson, 'The Dismal Science of Organisation Reconsidered' Canadian Public Administration, vol. 14, no. 1 (1971), pp. 82-99.

48. H.T. Wilson, 'Discretion in the Analysis of Administrative Process', Osgoode Hall Law Journal, vol. 10, no. 3, (1972), pp. 117-139; and H.T. Wilson, 'The Problem of Discretion in Three Languages', Proceedings of the International Congress of Legal Science (The Hague, 1977).

49. See particularly Richard Cyert and Kenneth MacCrimmon, 'Organisation', Handbook for Social Psychology, vol. 1; in G. Lindzey and E. Aronson (eds.), (Addison-Wesley, Reading, 1968), pp. 561-611.

50. Weber, From Max Weber, pp. 196-201, 214-221; Weber, Social and Economic Organisation, pp. 329-341. Note Weber's appreciation of the dominant role of rule orientation' not only in bureaucratic relations with clients and customers, but in the area of superior-subordinate relations inside the bureaucracy itself. Thus 'rule orientation' comprehends not only the secondary group pattern-variable orientations cited by Parsons in The Socal System (Free Press, Glencoe, 1951), pp. 58-67, but also 'formalism', 'strict discipline', 'control on the basis of knowledge', 'technical knowledge', 'knowledge of the concrete fact within its own sphere of interest', 'clearly defined sphere of competence' etc. Weber realises how central to 'rule orientation' both administrative rules and regulations following from legislation or executive orders (or procedure manuals) and organisational rules relating task performance and responsibility in bureaucratic organisations are. Also see Alvin Gouldner, 'On Weber's Analysis of Bureaucratic Rules', and 'Red Tape as a Social Problem', in R. Merton, et. al., Reader in Bureaucracy edited (Free Press, Glencoe, 1952), pp. 48-51 and La Paperasserie' in R. Merton et. al., Reader in Bureaucracy, pp. 407-410. On the distinction between meritocracy in theory and in practice, see Wilson, 'Parties, Elites, and Bureaucracies', where the ideal of ongoing performance assessments is contrasted to the reality of formal certification as a self-sufficient criterion for presuming capability in advance.

51. Weber, Social and Economic Organisation, pp. 124-132, and pp. 136-143, but especially pp. 145-157.

52. Weber From Max Weber, pp. 216-239; Weber

Social and Economic Organisation, pp. 329-333. See generally M. Weber, Law in Economy and Society, edited by Max Rheinstein (Harvard University Press, Cambridge, 1954).
53. Weber, Social and Economic Organisation, pp. 335.
54. Wilson, The American Ideology, ch. 8; Habermas, Toward a Rational Society, pp. 50-61.
55. Weber, From Max Weber, pp. 240-244. See John Findlay Scott, The Internalisation of Norms (Prentice Hall, Englewood Cliffs, 1973).
56. Technical ingenuity might be the result of specialised technical knowledge without prior awareness of situationally specific applications. In this case a significant individual component could be maintained because of the apparent lack of predictability of 'experience'. Nowadays situationally specific applications are a central part of the managerial training required of technocrats themselves. This means that the world is seen as a place to apply what is 'known' ideally without needing to have recourse to ingenuity at all. On how technocratic models are replacing decisionistic models of bureaucratic management, see Habermas, Toward a Rational Society on the matter of the possibility and desirability of a 'scientific politics'. On ingenuity as it relates to discretion, Wilson, The American Ideology. On ingenuity as it relates to exceptions challenging job rationalisation, Charles Perrow, 'A Framework for the Comparative Analysis of Organisations', American Sociological Review, vol. 32 (1967), pp. 194-208. The root association between ingenuity and engineer (Fr. ingenieur) is highly relevant, given the central role of individuals with engineering training in technocratic structures. This is only underscored by the post war subordination of engineers to technologies which are often replaced rather than repaired, thus eliminating opportunities for ingenious, though incremental, improvements in productivity, not to speak of new adptations. Managerial expectations regarding prior (and continuing) off the job training indicate how few exceptions they want to have to face. This is readily supported by their aversion to risks (like public sector bureaucrats) as evidenced in tests carried out in numerous MBA/MPA programmes in North America. Managerial ideology still places them with their very distant private-sector relations in small business and entrepreneurship, of course, rather than with public sector bureaucrats and technocrats

where they belong. See Alvin Gouldner, Studies in Leadership (Harper, New York, 1950) for an early post war indication of this development, and Thompson, Modern Organisation, pp. 114-177 for more extended commentary.

57. Here it is the conditional reality of the claim, coupled with collegiality within the work setting as a compensation for its absence in the eyes of publics and their governments in the society at large, which creates and sustains the idea that objective technical knowledge is so complex as to require a collective-cum-institutional dimension.

58. See Weber, Social and Economic Organisation, pp. 337-340. Also see Wilensky, Organisational Intelligence, pp. 75087, 110-129; and H.T. Wilson, 'Rationality and Decision in Administrative Science', Canadian Journal of Political Science vol. 6, no. 3 (1973), pp. 271-294.

59. Weber, Social and Economic Organisation, pp. 335-340; Weber, From Max Weber, pp. 214-216 and pp. 233-244.

60. Weber, Social and Economic Organisation, p. 337.

61. Mannheim, Man and Society in an Age of Reconstruction, pp. 49-60. For a comparison between Weber and Mannheim on this score, H.T. Wilson, 'Reading Max Weber: The Limits of Sociology', Sociology vol. 10, no. 2 (1976), pp. 297-315.

62. Paul Diesing, Reason in Society (University of Illinois Press, Urbana, 1962), pp. 3-13.

63. Weber, Social and Economic Organisation, p. 339.

64. See Weber, From Max Weber, pp. 240-244 for the tension between bureaucratisation and rationalisation given the increasing role of technical training and certification through 'universities and business and engineering colleges, and the universal clamour for the creation of educational certificates in all fields', which 'make for the formation of a privileged stratum in bureaus and in offices', (p. 241). Also see Weber, Social and Economic Organisation, p. 335.

65. Habermas, Toward a Rational Society, p. 64; and H.T. Wilson, 'Science, Technology and Innovation, The Role of Commonsense Capacties', Methodology and Science, Fall, (1982).

66. Trent Shroyer, 'Toward a Critical Theory for Advanced Industrial Societies', Recent Sociology, No. 2 (Macmillan, New York, 1970) pp. 210-234.

Technocracy and Late Capitalism

67.   T. Veblen, 'The Place of Science in Modern
Civilisation', American Journal of Sociology, vol.
11 (1906), pp. 585-609.   Compare to Weber, From Max
Weber, pp. 215-216 and pp. 240-242.
68.   See reference no. 17, this chapter.
69.   T. Veblen, The Engineers and the Price
System (Huebsch, Boston, 1921); Morris Cooke, How
About It? (N.D., N.P., 1917) and Snapping Cords
(N.D., N.P., 1915).   Particularly helpful on this
aspect of the study was Edwin Layton's unpublished
Ph.D. dissertation.   'The American Engineering
Profession and the Idea of Social Responsibility'.
(University of California, Department of History,
Los Angeles, 1956).
70.   See Sheldon Wolin, Politics and Vision
(Little, Brown, Boston, 1960), pp. 352-434,
including references, for a very useful analysis of
the growth of technocratic thinking and its tie from
the very beginning in St. Simon's predecessors to
the social sciences.   Sociology emerges from the
study far less as a creature of liberalism and the
enlightenment than as a counter-revolutionary force
seeking the recollectivisation of human beings that
had been sundered in France by the Revolution and
Bonapartism.   Also see the work of Frank Manuel,
Albert Salamon, and Robert Nisbet.
71.   Meynaud, Technocracy; Dreitzel, 'Social
Science'.
72.   Weber, Social and Economic Organisation,
p. 334.   In one sense, technocracy has helped
generate, with the help of public belief in
scientism, what amounts to a self-fulfilling
prophecy.   See reference no. 56, this chapter.
73.   Layton 'American Engineering', pp. 32-94.
74.   Ibid., p. 211.
75.   Ibid., Compare pp. 126-149 to pp. 150-199,
where Layton shows the tensions between liberal and
conservative wings of the professional societies,
the first favouring democracy, progressivism and
social responsibility, the second efficiency,
productivity and 'business as usual'.   Only after
1929 did a significant if temporary (1931-33) group
emerge favouring social planning.
76.   Here it is the lack of intensity and
continuity of professional-bureaucratic tensions,
coupled with a specific need for engineering trained
managers, which was instrumental in their ascendancy
in private, and to a lesser extent, governmental,
organisations in the period between 1929 and 1960.
See particularly D. Noble, America by Design:
Science, Technology and the Rise of Corporate

223

Capitalism (Oxford University Press, New York, 1977).

77. Marx, by this comparison, is far less fanciful, but then we need to be clear on what 'revolution' means when we can speak of a 'managerial revolution'. Both Veblen and Taylor, for example, had stressed the need, reminiscent in some ways of St. Simon and the Ecole Polytechnique, to bring the workers and engineers/technocrats together to confront and/or overthrow various 'vested interests', whether the landed nobility (St. Simon; Comte), financiers and investors (Veblen) or, in the contemporary context, managers whose formal authority and overly-wide discretion puts them beyond performance assessment (Thompson).

78. Veblen, *The Engineers and the Price System*.

79. This group coincides quite closely with one of Galbraith's definitions of the 'technostructure' in *The New Industrial State*, compare pp. 71 and 59 on this score.

80. Meynaud, *Technocracy*.

81. Lindblom, *Politics and Markets*.

82. Here we refer once again to the complex role of economics and the social, behavioural and administrative/managerial disciplines for technocrats. They simultaneously provide the basis for a world-view, an approach to and method of problem-formulation and solution, and both a generalised and specific form of legitimation. See Dreitzel, 'Social Science'.

83. Habermas, *Toward a Rational Society*, pp. 33, 63-67, 111; Shroyer, 'Critical Theory for Advance Industrial Societies'; Meynaud, *Technocracy*.

84. Weber, *From Max Weber*, pp. 196-198; Weber, *Social and Economic Organisation*, pp. 329-334.

85. See in this regard Guy Beneveniste, *The Politics of Expertise* (Croom Helm, London, 1973). Weber seems to realise this when he characterises bureaucratic 'rational domination' as 'control on the basis of knowledge' in Weber, *Social and Economic Organisation*, p. 339.

86. M. Weber, *The Protestant Ethic and the Spirit of Capitalism* (Scribners, New York, 1952). See also Weber, *Social and Economic Organisation*, pp. 87, 94-96.

87. H. Barnett, *Innovation: the Basis of Cultural Change* (McGraw Hill, New York, 1953); H.T. Wilson, *Tradition and Innovation:* and Wilson, 'Science, Technology and Innovation'.

88. Frederic Jameson, 'The Vanishing Mediator:

Narrative Structure in Max Weber', New German Critique, vol. 1 (1973), pp. 52-89; Wilson, 'Reading Max Weber'; Wilson, The American Ideology, chs. 2, 6 and 7.

89. Weber, Social and Economic Organisation, pp. 131-132 and pp. 328-333.

90. Weber's model of action may be decisionistic inasmuch as it depends on a rigid distinction between facts and values, but 'rational domination' premised on the idea of 'control based on knowledge' is ideally supposed to make this gap not only bridgeable, but non existent. It is at his point that a contrast can be observed between Weber's analysis of politics and science as vocations (From Max Weber, pp. 77-156) and his discussion of bureaucratic office holding as a vocation From Max Weber, pp. 196-244; Social and Economic Organisation, pp. 324-341. Decisionism in the strict sense really only applies to politics, and in an inverted form, to science, never to bureaucracy. Weber's different handling thus allows us to see how well he anticipates subsequent phases and levels of rationalisation in the West when he implies that the rationalisation of the functional/technical cluster can only be achieved by the emergence of collegial groups and even institutionalisation . See From Max Weber, pp. 235-242; Social and Economic Organisation, pp. 402-404.

91. Weber, From Max Weber, p. 214. In citing bureaucracy's technical superiority, Weber states: 'Precision, speed, unambiguity, knowledge of the files, continuity, discretion, unity, strict subordination, reduction of friction and of material and personal costs -- these are raised to the optimum point in the strictly bureaucratic administration and especially in its monocratic form'. Weber's remarks on material costs, here and elsewhere, thus make evident how factors other than size and complexity could guarantee bureaucratisation. He also indicates the way that even greater social organisation makes monocracy *vis a vis* collegiality less and less desirable.

92. Weber, Law and Economy and Society, pp. 198-255. But note Giddens' claim Class Structure pp. 275-276, that Weber was more concerned with administrative than actual technical expertise in his discussion of the functional/technical cluster. We have taken issue with this by noting the presence of both in Weber's discussion, in order to indicate his awareness of their essential

difference. At the same time, however, Weber was aware that scientific and technical knowledge is relative to time place, culture and circumstance. This is evident from Weber, From Max Weber, pp. 128-156 at pp. 138-139, where he discusses science's fate -- its tie to progress. For the full implications of this see Wilson, The American Ideology, pp. 51-54; and Tradition and Innovation, chs. 1, and 4-6.

93. Wilson, 'Discretion in the Analysis of Administrative Process'; 'The Problem of Discretion in Three Languages'.

94. Parsons realised this in Essays in Sociological Theory in his discussion of the similarities and differences between business and professional orientations, as well as in The Social System nine years later. The real difference between the two is the motive for objectivity, neutrality and calculation -- profit vs. performance -- not the fact that only the professions ideally exhibit it. See Weber, Social and Economic Organisation, pp. 158-171, 181-202, 209-225, and Weber, From Max Weber, pp. 215-216, 235.

95. Thompson, Modern Organisation, pp. 10-24 and pp. 58-80 on subfactoring and reassembly thereafter under the auspices of hierarchy, authority, discipline and rule-orientation. On the relation of rule-orientation to files, records, permanence, and secrecy, Weber From Max Weber, pp. 228-229 and pp. 233-235, and Stanley Raffel, Matters of Fact (Routledge, London, 1979).

96. It is the inseparability of merit and tenure which is the real basis for the collective-cum-institutional character of bureaucratic technical and administrative expertise. Technocracy expresses the societal basis of person specialisation while it succeeds in achieving an equipoise between the two types of expertise through the operation of group process. It is this active expression of collectivity which differentiates it so thoroughly from conventional bureaucracy. See Wilensky, Organisational Intelligence and Perrow, Complex Organisations, ch. 1.

97. Parsons, The Social System; Scott, The Internationalisation of Norms.

98. Robert Merton, 'Bureaucratic Structure and Personality', in R. Merton, Social Theory and Social Structure (Macmillan, New York, 1957) pp. 195-206.

99. Weber, Social and Economic Theory, pp. 330 and 340; Weber, From Max Weber, pp. 196-198, 215-216, 220, 228-229 and 237-239.

100. Thus 'real' technical qualifications as a feature of the functional/technical cluster are today collective, speaking organisationally, and are societally-based in terms of origins, in contrast to Weber's time. Though rules, files and procedures are preordained in the sense of being fixed, at least formally, their execution remains an individual exercise once they have been either learned or there is awareness of where they can be found when the situation requires it. In the latter instance, we have Weber's well-known understanding of 'de-enchantment', namely, that we can now 'find out' everything that interests us even though we need not even 'really' know because presumably someone else does. Weber discusses this in the context of a streetcar's operation in From Max Weber, pp. 137-139.

101. Mannheim, Man and Society in An Age of Reconstruction; Wilson, The American Ideology, chs. 8 and 10; Derek Phillips, The Credentialist Society (N.Y.: 1979).

102. Compare to Thompson, Modern Organisation, pp. 25-57.

103. See Wilson, The American Ideology, ch. 7.

104. Weber, Social and Economic Organisation, p. 339.

105. Ibid., pp. 118-120 on the basis of social relations in 'chance' or 'probability'; Weber, From Max Weber', p. 214 on 'unity'.

106. Weber, From Max Weber, pp. 228-241.

107. Ibid., pp. 216-219, 229, 240. Also see Parsons, Structure and Process in Modern Societies (Macmillan, New York, 1960), chs. 12 and 2 on 'goal orientation').

108. H.T. Wilson, 'Science, Technology and Innovation: The Role of Commonsense Capacities', (unpublished essay); Wilson, 'Rationality and Decision in Administrative Science'.

109. Weber, Social and Economic Organisation, p. 339. Thompson, Modern Organisation, would naturally exclude scientism from his list of ideologies since it lies at the heart of his own technocratic advocacy in the Veblenian tradition, rather than constituting a bulwark for the exercise of formal authority in the absence of objective specialised technical knowledge by managers. Compare to Wilensky, 'The Professionalisation of Everyone?' particularly pp. 48-58 and pp. 175-178 on the alleged objectivity of professional and technical specialisation as itself pathological. On this score, also see Chester Barnard, 'Functions and

Pathology of Status Systems', in C. Barnard Organisation and Management (Harvard University Press, Cambridge, 1948).

110. See Weber's anticipation of this development in Weber, From Max Weber. pp. 237-239.

111. Galbraith admits this in both The New Industrial State and Economics and the Public Purpose. Our difference with him is based on the far less cohesive character of his 'technostructure', which for him in fact embodies the sort of technical, scientific and managerial knowledge needed to run large corporations under conditions of high, and seemingly autonomous, technological change. But it is precisely his failure to link this group to the conditions of its emergence and sustenance which makes his position eminently technocratic. Its collective and group character thus lacks all points of reference in the larger society, and no interest is taken in addressing interpenetration and reciprocity, and along with the absence of publicly acknowledge professional status and recognition, as an issue for this elite class fragment.

112. See H.T. Wilson, 'Innovation: the Practical Uses of Theory', in Social Change, Innovation and Politics in East Asia (Asian Research Institute, Hong Kong 1980), pp. 9-29; H.T. Wilson, 'Attitudes toward Science: Canadian and American Scientists', 'International Journal of Comparative Sociology, vol. 18, nos. 1 and 2 (1977), pp. 154-178; The American Ideology, ch.

113. See Wilson, The American Ideology, chs. 2 and 5.

114. Diesing, Reason in Society; Wilson, The American Ideology, ch. 8.

115. C.W. Mills, The Soliological Imagination (Grove Press, New York, 1959).

116. Note the contrast between true and false function in H.T. Wilson, 'Functional Rationality in "Sense of Function": the Case of an Indeological Distortion', International Yearbook of Organisation Studies, 1980 (Routledge, London, 1981).

117. Wilson, The American Ideology, chs. 5 and 10.

118. Ibid. Also see H.T. Wilson, 'The Meaning and Significance of "Empirical Method" for the Critical Theory of Society', Canadian Journal of Political and Social Theory vol. 13 (1979), pp. 57-68; and H. Wilson 'Social Science and Social Change: An Analysis and Critique of Some 'Methodical Practices' and an Alternative' (unpublished essay).

119. See J. Habermas, 'Aspects of the Rationality of Action' in T.F. Geraets (ed.), Rationality Today, (University of Ottawa Press, Ottawa, 1979), pp. 185-212; and the earlier, J. Habermas, Technology and Science as Ideology' in Toward a Rational Society pp. 81-122.

120. This 'representative' principle through socialisation rather than formal election is addressed by Weber in From Max Weber, pp. 224-225 and pp. 242-244. Norton Long views the issue far more optimistically in 'Bureaucracy and Constitutionalism' in Long, The Polity (Rand McNally, Chicago, 1962). But see Wilson 'Parties, Elites and Bureaucracies', for a discussion of the relation between representative bureaucracy, and technocracy and meritocracy, which is more compatible with Weber's analysis.

121. Hannah Arendt, The Human Condition (University of Chicago Press, Chicago, 1958), chapters on 'the public and private realms' and 'labour'; Shroyer Toward a Critical Theory for Advanced Capitalist Societies, and Claus Muller, 'Notes on the Repression of Communicative Behaviour', Recent Sociology, No. 2 (Macmillan, New York, 1970) and Wilson's reply, 'Notes on the Achievement of Communicative Behaviour and Related Difficulties', Dialectical Anthropology (forthcoming).

122. Karl Mannheim, Essays on the Sociology of Knowledge Routledge and Kegan Paul, London, 1953)), pp. 235-249; Arendt, The Human Condition, on 'labouring in an artificial realm', and Gilb, Hidden Hierarchies, pp.215-226.

123. See Weber, From Max Weber, p. 228, where he discusses bureaucracy as 'the means of carrying "community action" over into rationally ordered "social action", thus as an instrument for "societalising" relations of power'.

124. We can thus compare the ideal typical focus on structure embodied in the exaggeration of key characteristics of a whole which sociology can only hope to represent, never describe, to Weber's reminder that such structures have a human basis in individual thoughts, beliefs and actions which build up wholes out of chance and probabilities.

125. Thompson, Modern Organisation. Here, however, it is necessary to be more precise about 'filling in' what otherwise might stand as a reification in the best tradition of interpreters of Durkheim, and possibly Durkheim himself. See Wilson, 'The Sociology of Apocalypse?;

126. Wolin, Politics and Vision. Also see Frederick Hayek, The Counterrevolution of Science (Macmillan, New York, 1955).

127. Meynaud, Technocracy; Dreitzel, 'Social Science'.

128. See generally, B. Glaser (ed.), Organisational Careers, (Aldine, Chicago, 1968).

129. This is discussed off and on throughout Professionalisation Vollmer and Mills and by Wilensky in 'The Professionalisation of Everyone?'

130. See Wilensky, 'The Professionalisation of Everyone?'; and Thompson, Modern Organisation on this score.

131. Thompson, Modern Organisation could not see this, but would have been able to anticipate management's eventual detachment from bureaucracy had he not dismissed Weber's rationalisation thesis as 'dubious' in favour of an explicit committment to Durkheim and a tacit one to Veblen and technocracy itself.

132. Layton, 'American Engineering'.

133. See the recent article by Barnaby Feder, 'Training Managers to Manage Technology', N.Y. Times Magazine, Sunday June 21, 1981.

134. On the difference between technical and economic rationality applied to individual decisions, see Diesing, Reason in Society, pp. 1-64. Also H.T. Wilson 'Values: On the Possibility of a Convergence Between Economic and Non-economic Decision-Making', in Proceedings of the Conference on Management under Differing Value Systems (Walter de Gruyter, Berlin, 1981), forthcoming.

135. Thompson, Modern Organisation, is a good case in point. See also H.T. Wilson, 'The Dismal Science of Organisation Reconsidered', where the writer falls for a different, but equally facile 'resolution' of the problem a decade ago. Compare to Wilson, The American Ideology, ch. 2.

136. Wilson, 'The Meaning and Significance of "Empirical Method" for the Critical Theory of Society', Wilson 'Social Science and Social Change: An Analysis and Critique of Some "Methodical Practices" and an Alternative'. Here we address the empirical/normative mix, contrasting commonsense conceptions comprised mainly of normative support in the form of internalised values, and technocratic assumptions, derived from a distinct, yet derived and continuously interdependent, idea of 'stock of knowledge' taking its point of departure in the objectivity of technically specific 'knowledgeableness'. See Wilson, 'Science,

Technology and Innovation: The Role of Commonsense
Capacities'.
137. Diesing, Reason in Society; Dreitzel,
'Social Science'.
138. See generally Parsons, The Social System
and Vollmer and Mills (eds), Professionalisation.
139. This is an 'update' of the problem of risk
and responsibility addressed by Berle and Means in
The Modern Corporation and Private Property. We are
not defending such a reduction, the essence of
nascent capitalism, but are rather pointing out the
problem a society faces when such notions continue
to exist in the absence of the conventional
reference points for assessment. This suggests that
positive individualism in Durkheim's sense is
dysfunctional from the stand-point of such a
standard. See Wilson, The American Ideology,
chapter 8.
140. This addresses the idea of knowledge and
knowing itself, and suggests some fundamental
disjunctions between scientific, social-scientific,
commonsense and theoretical/reflexive practices.
The requirement that knowledge evidence causes, good
reasons, 'motivational understanding' and
predictability recasts it in the direction of
objectivity. See Paul Feyerabend, Against Method
(New Left Books, London, 1975) and P. Feyerabend,
Science in a Free Society (New Left Books, London,
1978). I attempted to deal with many aspecs of this
problem in Knowledge and Totality: A Critical
Analysis of the Causal Principle in Science and Life
(unpublished manuscript).
141. Everett Knight, The Objective Society
(Braziller, New York, 1960). Also Alfred Schutz,
'The Problem of Rationality in the Social World',
Collected Papers, Vol. 2 (Martinus Nijhoff, The
Hague, 1964), pp. 64-87; Harold Garfinkel, 'The
Rational Properties of Scientific and Commonsense
Activities', Studies in Ethnomethodology (Prentice
Hall, Englewood Cliffs, 1967), pp. 262-283; and
Wilson, 'Rationality and Decision in Administrative
Science'.
142. See Layton, 'American Engineering' and
Veblen, The Engineers and the Price System,
including the introduction by Daniel Bell to the
Harbinger edition.
143. Marcuse, One Dimensional Man; Adorno,
'Society'.
144. Layton, 'American Engineering'.
145. See T.W. Adorno, 'Veblen's Attack on
Culture', in Adorno, Prisms (Neville Spearman,

London, 1967).
    146. Wilson, The American Ideology, chs. 2, 5,
8, 10. Also Pierre Bourdieu, An Outline of a Theory
of Practice (Cambridge University Press, London,
1976).
    147. Ludwig Wittgenstein, 'Remarks on Fraser's
Golden Bough', in The Human World Vol. 3 (1971), pp.
18-41. See M.O.'C. Drury, The Danger of Words
(Routledge, London, 1973) pp. 1-4. Also, Wilson,
Tradition and Innovation:.
    148. Adorno, 'Society'.
    149. See Wilson, 'Innovation: The Practical
Uses of Theory', for a critique of the technocratic
approach premised on the functionalist conception of
innovation.
    150. The idea of stability through apathy is a
fundamental characteristic of the political theory
of technocracy, premised as it is on the idea of
society as a functional system. As the false whole
becomes more and more technically complex and
relationally interdependent, politics and the
political must resign itself to redistribution under
the doctrine of inevitable technical progress. See
Muller, 'Communicative Behaviour'; Habermas,
'Technical Progress/Social Life World', in Toward a
Rational Society. The two best primers for an
introduction to the political theory of technocracy
remain Gabriel Almond and Sidney Verba, The Civic
Culture (Little, Brown, Boston, 1963) and Bernard
Crick, In Defense of Politics (Penguin,
Harmondsworth, 1960).
    151. Wilson, The American Ideology, ch. 9.
    152. See Wittgenstein, 'Remarks on Fraser's
Golden Bough'. Wilson, Tradition and Innovation;
Alfred Kroeber, Configurations of Culture Growth
(University of California Press, Berkeley, 1944);
Barnett, Innovation.
    153. See Ludwig Wittgenstein, On Certainty
(Basil Blackwell, Oxford, 1975).
    154. Wilson, The American Ideology, chs. 6 and
8. In this sense ours is a capitalist society, and
it is the absence of several of the formal
characteristics of a capitalist economy which is a
prerequisite for this development.
    155. Veblen, The Engineers and the Price
System; Layton, 'American Engineering'.
    156. Wolin, Politics and Vision; Hayek, The
Counterrevolution of Science; Adorno, 'Veblen's
Attack on Culture'.
    157. Emile Durkheim, The Division of Labour in
Society (Macmillan, New York, 1952).

158. Thus society as a formally meritocratic stratarchy can be seen to generalise bureaucratic attitudinal and structural attributes in the sense that the tenure for merit arrangement available to all members once in the buraucracy is now socialised in the form a of tacit 'collective agreement' -- work and labour seniority and continuity for the promise mainly of consumption from the societal member and only tangentially 'production'. The compromise of merit by tenure in the bureaucracy is more than paralleled by the shift away from production to consumption as the principal duty of the societal member. The fact that this applies neither to domestic nor to Third World underclasses suggests the class basis of technocracy as an elite class fragement in the advanced societies. See Wilson, 'Notes on the Achievement of Communicative Behaviour and Related Difficulties'.

159. Also see Thompson, Modern Organisation.

160. Wilensky, Organisational Intelligence; Wilson, The American Ideology, ch. 7.

161. Wolin, Politics and Vision; Hayek, The Counterrevolution of Science.

162. Wilensky, Organisational Intelligence.

163. Weber, From Max Weber, pp. 204-209, 224-244; Weber, Social and Economic Order, pp. 340-341.

164. Giddens, Class Structure p. 260-264.

165. Muller, 'Communicative Behaviour', Wilson, 'Notes on the Achievement of Communicative Behaviour'.

166. Habermas, Toward a Rational Soceity; Habermas, 'Aspects of the Rationality of Action', Habermas, Legitimation Crisis.

167. Meynaud, Technocracy; Crozier, The Bureaucratic Phenomenon.

168. Krishan Kumar, 'Revolution and Industrial Society', Sociology, vol. 10, no.2 (1976), pp. 245-269; Wilson, 'Social Science and Social Change: An Analysis and Critique of Some "Methodical Practices" and an Alternative'.

169. Marion Levy, Modernisation: Latecomers and Survivors (Basic Books, New York, 1972).

170. Wilson, The American Ideology, ch. 7; Habermas, Toward A Rational Society, pp. 33, 63-65, 111; Habermas, Legitimation Crisis, p. 37; Habermas, 'Aspects of the Rationality of Action'.

171. Compare Diesing, Reason in Society; chs. 1 and 2 to Max Horkheimer, The Eclipse of Reason (Seabury Press, New York, 1974). Also, H.T. Wilson, 'The Significance of "Instrumental Reason" for the Critical Theory of Society', (unpublished paper).

172. Wilson, 'Values: On the Possibility of a Convergence Between Economic and Non-economic Decision-Making'; Dreitzel, 'Social Science' on the technocratic decision mix and its relation to the social, behavioural and administrative/managerial disciplines.

173. Eddington, as quoted by J.W.N. Sullivan in Limitations of Science (Merton, New York, 1956), p. 141, cited the paradox of instrumenation. Its claim to objectivity and priority lies in its alleged autonomy from the human agency which built it. Yet the meaning of what instrumentation records must be provided by human beings. This is what caused Weber to revert to decisionism in the polital field -- the fact that the resulting 'labyrinth of instrumentation' can only be put in its role as a means by reference to some standard, some rank-ordering of values. It seems problematic that by instrumental rationality we presume to include economising behaviour, but only because the method of valuing and prioritising is foreordained as a prerequisite to subsequent acts of technical rationality. Eddington, as quoted in Limitations of Science, stated that scientific knowledge of the universe is based on the way things and events affect the instruments used to measure their qualities. See Hannah Arendt, The Human Condition, pp. 261; and Diesing, Reason in Society, Chs. 1 and 2, pp. 1-64.

174. See Karl Loewith, 'Weber's Interpretation of the Bourgeois-Capitalistic World in terms of the Guiding Principle of Rationalisation', in D. Wrong (ed.), Max Weber, (Prentice Hall, Englewood Cliffs, 1970), pp. 101-122.

175. See Arendt, The Human Condition, pp. 136-167.

176. C.B. Macpherson, Democratic Theory (Oxford University Press, Londin, 1972), pp. 3-38; Wilson, The American Ideology, pp. 200-208.

177. This is the hidden truth standing behind Anthony Downs, An Economic Theory of Democracy (Harpers, New York, 1957). It is as if non-critical liberal analysis must use the method of inversion and disciplinary disorientation as a substitute for critique which yet reveals the need for critique by what such analysis does to possibility.

178. Wilson, The American Ideology, pp. 61-65; Wilson, 'The Sociology of Apocalypse'; Wilson, 'Science, Technology and Innovation'.

179. Wilson, 'Science, Critique and Criticism'. See also Sandford Lakoff, 'Scientists,

Technologists, and Political Power', in J. Spiegel-Rosing and D. de Salla Price (eds.), Science, Technology and Society, (Sage, London, 1977), pp. 367-385.
180. Wilson, 'Social Science and Social Change'.
181. See The American Ideology, ch. 5, and Adorno, 'Society'.
182. Wilson, Knowledge and Totality; Wilson, The American Ideology, ch. 8.
183. Marcuse, One Dimensional Man
184. Adorno, 'Scientific Experiences of a European Scholar in America', in D. Fleming and B. Bailyn (eds.), The Intellectual Migration, Europe and America, 1930-1960 (Belknap Press, Cambridge, 1968), and his contributions to The Positivist Dispute in German Sociology, translated by Glyn Adey and David Frisby (Heinemann, London, 1976).
185. Parsons, The Social System, pp. 543-544.
186. Wilson, 'The Significance of "Instrumental Reason" for the Critical Theory of Society'; Wilson, 'Reading Max Weber: The Limits of Sociology'; Mannheim, Man and Society in an Age of Reconstruction.
187. Parsons, The Social System, p. 551.
188. This is not to ignore Durkheim's anticipations in The Division of Labour in Society as a central inspiration for Parsons. See Parsons, The Structure of Social Action (Free Press, Glencoe, 1937), sections on Durkheim.
189. See Veblen, 'The Place of Science in Modern Civilisation'.
190. This is importantly related to Mannheim's observations regarding the disjunctions between what he termed functional rationality and the capacity for independent judgement on the part of individuals facing new situations. Technocracy mobilises the generalisation of this complexity/integration and heterogeneity/homogeneity tension as a key rationale for their necessary ascendancy as socially rational actors, with the aid of the social, behavioural and administrative/managerial disciplines.
191. Parsons, The Social System, p. 549.
192. The result is the emergence of sociological rationality. See Wilson, The American Ideology, ch. 8.
193. Parsons, The Social System, p. 555.
194. Wilson, 'The Meaning and Significance of "Empirical Method" for the Critical Theory of Society'.
195. Parsons, The Social System, p. 552.

196. They thus purport to reconcile formal authority and person specialisation in ways more reminiscent of Weber's prognostications than Thompson's fifty years later in <u>Modern Organisation</u>.

197. Wilensky, 'The Professionalisation of Everyone?'; Haug and Sussman, 'Professional Autonomy and the Revolt of the Client', <u>Social Problems,</u> vol. 17, (1969), pp. 153-161.

198. This is an inescapable upshot of the obsession with objective technical competence and qualification, suggested by the prefix qual... itself, namely, the tendency to formalise and internalise the idea of objectivity (like merit). Weber strongly suggests this in <u>From Max Weber,</u> pp. 214-216, 235-244, and <u>Social and Economic Organisation</u> pp. 335-340 when he uses the term 'knowledge' as a formal property of experience as well as training. See also note 173, this chapter.

199. This means that increasingly competence for those everywhere but at the apex or the base of large organisations is exhibited in the combination of (1) formal training and certification and (2) conformance to correct rules and procedures rather than outcomes. This is explained by the complexity of the social system, which frustrates the best laid plans or makes it impossible to determine with confidence that such and such an action did (or did not) lead to some desired outcome which in fact took place.

200. Wilson, 'Reading Max Weber'; Wilson, 'The Significance of "Instrumental Reason" for the Critical Theory of Society'; Weber, 'Science as a Vocation', in <u>From Max Weber,</u> pp. 129-156; Loewith, 'Weber's Interpretation of the Bourgeois-Capitalist World. Weber also sees value-rationality dissolving either into goal-rationality when the values are appropriate, or into affectivity. Compare <u>Social and Economic Organisation.</u> pp. 115-118, where he discusses 4 types of social action, to *ibid.*, pp. 324-329, where he discusses 3 types of legitimate authority. While traditional action corresponds to traditional authority, affective action to charismatic authority, and goal-rational action to legal-rational authority, only value-rational action lacks a type of legitimate authority, for the above reasons, reasons which clearly bespeak the serious consequences of rationalisation and de-enchantment.

201. See Georges Friedman, <u>Industrial Society</u> (Macmillan, New York, 1955); and G. Friedman, <u>The Anatomy of Work</u> (Macmillan, New York, 1961).

202. Alfred Schutz, <u>The Phenomenology of the</u>

Social World (Northwestern University Press, Evanston, 1967); A. Schutz, *Collected Papers*, 3 Volumes (Martinus Nijhoff, The Hague, 1962-1967).

203. Weber, *Social and Economic Organisation*, pp. 111-112.

204. Wilson, *Tradition and Innovation*, chs. 5 and 6.

205. Parsons, *Structure and Process in Modern Society* (Macmillan, New York, 1960), chs. 1 and 2.

206. Friedman, *The Anatomy of Work*; Thompson, *Modern Organisation*.

207. Durkheim, *The Division of Labour in Society*.

208. Thompson, in *Bureaucracy and Innovation*, misses this point, again because of his bias for Durkheim over Weber. The tension between rationalisation and innovation is itself a *social* process, even though it occurs in organised settings. One might even say especially because it occurs in these settings, for reasons which Thompson himself had addressed in his earlier *Modern Organisation*, pp. 55-57. See James Q. Wilson, 'Innovation: Notes Toward a Theory', in J. Thompson (ed.), *Approaches to Organisational Design* (University of Pittsburgh, Pittsburgh, 1966).

209. Crozier, *The Bureaucratic Phenomenon*, p. 165.

210. See *Ibid.*, pp. 296-300.

211. See Donald Hodges, *The Bureaucratisation of Socialism*; and Habermas, *Legitimation Crisis*.

212. Thompson, *Modern Organisation*, p. 27.

213. *Ibid.*, pp. 58-113.

214. *Ibid.*, pp. 27-33, 46, 52-57.

215. *Ibid.*, p. 55.

216. See Perrow, 'A Framework for the Comparative Analysis of Organisations'.

217. Veblen, *Theory of the Leisure Class* (Huebsch, Boston, 1899); Veblen, *The Vested Interests and the Common Man* (Huebsch, Boston, 1919).

218 Dreitzel, 'Social Science'. See Barnaby Feder, 'Training Managers to Manage Technology'.

219. Parsons, *The Social System*, remains the social scientific 'bible' in this respect.

220. Wilson, *Tradition and Innovation*.

221. Wilson, 'Science, Technology and Innovation'.

222. Adorno, 'Society'.

223. This workshop of technique and the technical as the objective and concrete basis for rational decision and action is problematic, but

Ellul's analyses in <u>The Technological Society</u> and the recently published <u>The Technological System</u> are an inverted form of technocratic thinking in their own right. Thus such thinking would include those obsessed with technique and the technical, whether because they love it or hate it. What is important is the framework and logic of arguments not the 'outcome' on its own. On Ellul's parallels with St. Simon, Comte and Durkheim based on the logic and structure of thinking of 'French sociology', Wilson, 'The Sociology of Apocalypse'.

Chapter 6

THE CRISIS OF REPRESENTATION IN CLASS-ORIENTED UNIONS: SOME REFLECTIONS BASED ON THE ITALIAN CASE

Marino Regini

TRANSFORMATIONS OF EUROPEAN CLASS-ORIENTED UNIONS, AND THE ITALIAN CASE

In many central and western European countries since the war (especially in those periods when working class parties have been in government) there has been a general transformation of class-oriented unions (1). Many observers of industrial relations emphasise as central to this transformation the tendency towards union involvement in the political system. Indeed some of these observers, taking up the prediction made many years ago by Franz Neumann, speak of tendencies towards 'incorporation of unions in the State' (2). The main indicators of these tendencies would be the enhanced institutional recognition of unions, the delegation to them of public functions and the concession to them by the state of a monopoly over worker's representation. To adopt an expression of Claus Offe (3), one could say that there has been either a *de facto* or a legal 'attribution of political status' to unions. In exchange for this alteration in their status, the unions have been induced to offer relative moderation of wages (even though the incomes policies of the 'sixties formally failed, in all the north and central European countries the unions in fact under-utilised their market power, which had been enhanced by the adoption of Keynesian policies) and subordinate participation in the control of economic policy. These tendencies were, in addition, according to this view, the origin of the growing bureaucratisation of union organisation, and of the notable centralisation of their structure and activity.

To summarise these transformations one might consider the following list of characteristics towards which, according to Schmitter (4), there is a general tendency in all interest organisations: centralisation, bureaucratisation, co-optation of leaders, professionalisation of representatives and the use of experts, enhanced aggregation of demands, official recognition of their status, interdependence with public power, and long-term calculation of interests.

According to the critics of these 'neo-corporatist tendencies' in advanced capitalism, however, these transformations - which I have indicated in a rather brief and general way - in the structure and functions of class-oriented unions change the nature of their relationship with the membership, and inevitably provoke detachment from the workers' interests and their active or passive oppositional stance (5). It is therefore rather easy for those who describe the evolution (or involution, since such descriptions are often implicit criticisms) of class-oriented unions in a summary fashion, to detail the characteristics and origins of the crisis of representation which currently hits many of them. This crisis becomes reducible to an increasing divergence between the interests of the membership and those of the union organisations, which may be expressed as conflict between leaders and membership or, simply, increasing apathy and distrust, whose causes are none the less sought in the transformations I have described.

It is not possible to discuss here the extent to which the tendencies I have indicated effectively correspond to reality in the countries being examined. Instead I shall attempt to demonstrate that the problem of the crisis of representation should be seen in rather more complex terms than those proposed by the critics of neo-corporatist tendencies.

Before embarking on this discussion it is necessary to outline how the Italian situation fits these tendencies.

First of all, I would point out that the process of union involvement with the state which has also happened in Italy in recent years, has occurred under rather different circumstances. This process of involvement has appeared under pressure from, and to a certain extent within the control of the unions; it has been the outcome of union action rather than an initiative or concession of the governments.

Once the political isolation of the 1950s had

been broken, institutional recognition and the monopoly of representation were in fact gains made by the unions using the membership's capacity for mobilisation, prior to their being definitively sanctioned in the Workers' Statute enacted in 1970. In this manner unions became involved in the institutions which implement social and labour policies (e.g. the National Institute for Social Security) in the formation of economic policy. This was, in effect, the result of their tendency to act as political subjects as the spaces for negotiation with enterprises became gradually restricted, rather than the outcome of state efforts at incorporation.

Though the relations between unions and the state in Italy have come to resemble more and more the concertative model prevalent in north and central European countries, the differences remain rather significant (6). In the first place, the institutionalisation of these relations is not advanced; the unions thus retain full autonomy and are far from being transformed into 'anomalous organs of the state'. Further, the unions have not accepted a sectional and subordinate vision of their participation in the formation of economic policy: their vision remains tied to objectives for transformation and to a total strategy. Finally, whilst Italian unions have been by no means immune from the processes of increasing bureaucratisation and centralisation, the persistent vitality of the decentralised structures of union activity (Factory Councils and enterprise agreements) has up to now constituted a real bulwark and an element of permanent tension.

THE CRISIS OF THE REPRESENTATIVE RELATION

Having emphasised these undoubted differences, it is, none the less, necessary to recognise that in Italy too, the unions are experiencing a crisis of representation. We need therefore to clarify in what ways this is manifested and to what extent it is effectively related to the tendencies we have described.

In order to analyse this crisis we need firstly to note that any relation of interest representation inevitably faces the fundamental problem of the transmission of demands (7) from those being represented to those who are in the position of taking decisions concerning those interests (that is, in the case of trade unions, to the opposing parties: firms and public institutions). The process of transmitting demands is a problem for all representatives (in this case, for all union organisations), because in this process the demands of the membership are inevitably subject to selection, mediation and therefore to modification. A crisis of representation is thus potentially always present, taking the form either of those being represented reacting to the modifications that their demands have suffered, or of the representatives being unable to overcome the inherent difficulties of the process.

None the less, this problem can normally be discounted if at least one of the following conditions is present: a) if the representatives limit modifications to the specific and explicit requests of the membership to the indispensable minimum (so that they do not subject them to more general objectives or to their own interests); b) if they have access to efficient means of control over the membership (or at least means of retaining a high level of adherence); c) if the representatives manage to obtain indirect results, that is results which although they are different from the specific and explicit requests, none the less satisfy in a meaningful way other potential needs or objectives which are generally thought to be important.

Those analyses which relate the crisis of representation in the unions to the tendencies described earlier, in fact concentrate their attention exclusively on the fact that corporatist arrangements do not allow unions to meet the first of these conditions. Centralisation and bureaucratisation of the trade union organisations, their involvement in the state and their pursuit of semi-public functions result in fact, so it is said, in an excessive distancing from the demands of the membership, and even a substitution of the representatives own interests in place of those demands. Workers would however, sooner or later react to the subversion of their demands and the crisis which is always latent in the representative relation would thus become manifest.

The thesis which I shall attempt to develop in the following pages is rather, that in contrast to associational unions (see note 1), class-oriented unions always carry out a profound modification of the specific and explicit demands of their membership, even when they are not involved in corporatist relations. But this does not necessarily expose them to a crisis of representation. As far as Italian unions in particular are concerned, it would be difficult to explain the present crisis in their relations with workers simply as an effect of the transformations that have occurred in their functions and structure, given, (as I have argued beforehand), that other unions have gone further with this process without having experienced a graver crisis. If the first of the three conditions I mentioned is thus always absent in class-oriented unions, the crisis of representation will tend to afflict them when the other two conditions are not met either. Let us now discuss these three conditions separately.

First, we need to subdivide the process of demand transmission into the various stages in which it is analytically articulated. The process involves basically two stages: 1) the determination, interpretation and collection of demands; 2) their aggregation and articulation with those of other social groups which are potential allies, and their insertion into a long-term strategy.

THE CAPACITY TO DETERMINE AND 'GIVE VOICE' TO MEMBERSHIP DEMANDS

The determination, interpretation and collection of membership demands inevitably involves a measure of selection and modification. Nevertheless, it is possible to reduce this phenomenon to a low level if the representative structure is highly ramified thus allowing for frequent contact with the workers, if the institutionalised channels of communication within the trade union organisation are not blocked, and if there are effective procedures for verifying the wishes of the membership.

I believe that one can say that, all in all, the Italian unions satisfy these conditions rather better than many other European unions. The network of delegates and Factory Councils is now so complete (8) as to exclude the possibility that any large percentage of unionised workers are unable to make their demands known to their representatives. From this point of view, the situation today is very different from that of the 1950s and 1960s when it was very difficult for the members of the factory internal commissions (few in number, highly ideological, and frustrated by management) to maintain contact with a working class that was heterogeneous and subjected to rapid transformations.

Furthermore, the fact that the Factory Councils are considered for all purposes by the unions as their own organisms at the level of the firm, means that the rate of internal communication and therefore knowledge of membership demands is intense. In this respect, the Italian situation today is different not only from the period of the internal commissions but also from those countries where worker representation is (whether institutionally or *de facto*) dualistic; that is, where the factory representative body is not an organ of the trade union (as is the case with the German *Betriebsrate*) and does not therefore communicate membership demands through internal and institutionalised channels.

Finally, although the procedures for verifying the wishes of the membership are little formalised in Italy, and pose serious problems of internal democracy (9), one cannot say that they are, for this reason, non-existent. Despite the obvious ritualisation and decreasing participation, general assemblies remain significant occasions for various groups of workers to make their demands to their own representatives.

THE MODIFICATION OF DEMANDS FOR THE PURPOSES OF AGGREGATING THEM, AND THE RISKS OF DILUTING THEM INTO GENERAL INTERESTS

Once they have been determined and collected, the demands of various groups of workers must be co-ordinated with those of others. Aggregating demands is a necessary function of all unions. But whilst associational and trade unionist organisations confine themselves to co-ordinating the requests of rather similar groups (workers in the same firm or sector, or belonging to the same occupation in the case of craft unions) for class-oriented unions operating in the political arena, this process is considerably more complex.

Already their orientation towards the class as a whole, rather than to a particular group of workers makes the necessary mediation between demands more difficult. Even when demands are being made at the level of the individual firm, the class-oriented union will be alert to their compatibility with the interests of workers in other firms and regions, of the unemployed and so on. In addition, because the union is operating in the political arena as well, and not only in negotiating with firms (10), it will try to connect the demands with those of social groups not forming part of the working class but potential allies of it (pensioners, various categories of the middle class, etc.). Finally, as bearer of an ideology of transformation, a class based union will tend to insert the short-term demands of the membership into, or make them compatible with, a long-term strategy. It will do this rather more than a union which is intent on maximising the immediate interests of those it represents.

For these reasons, class-oriented unions will *always* profoundly modify the specific demands of their membership. That is why the possibility of a crisis of representation may appear in this phase of the transmission of demands precisely as a problem of aggregating membership demands, of co-ordinating them with those of other social groups and inserting them into a long term coherent programme.

However,various indicators suggest that this is an increasing problem: without doubt the most significant indicator is the explosion of particularist claims and the wage spiralling which already characterises various industrial relations systems including the Italian one.

One could certainly argue, as certain people do that such phenomena have to be seen in the context of changes in the socio-cultural composition of the working class, which tends to fragment their interests whilst at the same time provoking rising expectations and the capacity to pursue them in an organised fashion. But, against this argument, it is possible to postulate identical objections to those which others (11) have raised against the theory that democratic societies are becoming increasingly ungovernable because of the 'overload of demands' directed at the government. In other words, one cannot explain the crisis solely by reference to changes in the characteristics of those being represented (or ruled), one has also to explain why the representatives (or rulers) are unable to find adequate responses to these changes. Specifically, why are the unions increasingly less able to carry out the aggregation and co-ordination of demands in ways which are both effective and acceptable to the membership?

In most European countries this diminished capability should probably be examined in relation to the limitations that have been put on wage claim strategies in exchange for political recognition of the unions and the delegation to them of public functions. The chief limitation on the unions is the subordination of their day-to-day activities to a supposed general interest (12): what governments demand of them is that they behave like 'responsible social partners', that they recognise the interdependence of their interests with those of other public and private economic actors, and that, they therefore accept the pursuit of common interests rather than the maximisation of partisan ones. When these limitations are accepted by unions, there is an excessive enlargement of their function of co-ordinating the demands of workers with those of other social groups, which goes much further than the aggregation of demands carried out by all working class unions.

In other words, whilst working class unions always modify membership demands to co-ordinate them with those of groups who are potential allies, the modifications which are necessary to render them compatible with the 'general interest' (with which the union must be inspired in order to be admitted into political participation) are by nature and content very different. It is one thing, for example, to accept a certain moderation of wage demands in a factory in exchange for the maintenance of jobs in another factory of the same company. It is quite another to do so in order to contribute to a 'general interest' such as lowering inflation, especially when the unions have to conform to this as a government directive as a condition for participation in economic policy choices.

In contrast to some other Western European countries, in Italy governments have not been powerful enough to impose proscriptions and limitations of this kind. None the less one can say that in recent years Italian unions have autonomously developed a strategy which tends to privilege the country's 'general interests', and that it has, in some cases, led them to adopt a stance similar to that of other European unions. In the 'seventies the Italian unions have been reminded of their working class origins and thus of the need to represent the interests, not of the employed only (besides that of providing economic development which is not guaranteed by a weak bourgeoisie) and so it has progressively transformed its demands from the 'particular' to the 'general'. Objectives such as, firstly, social reform and employment, investment and development of the south to follow, and lastly productivity of enterprises and the economy have been the stages in an attempt to take on that role of 'representative of the general interests of the collectivity' which, according to the classic approach, ought to be the business of political parties (13).

There is no doubt that this process reflects objective needs which cannot be easily neglected by union organisations. It is, however, equally clear that, as a result, the process of demand transmission from the membership is expanded well beyond the simple mediation normally required to collate demands and put them in negotiable terms. It is for this reason that it meets with strong resistance from the membership, even when they are accustomed to profound alterations to their original demands.

Particularistic claims do not, therefore, in my view, mean a refusal of any aggregation or co-ordination of demands or of their being included in a long-term strategy which all working class unions have always had. They mean instead refusing an excessive enlargement of the process of demand aggregation, such as to divert union action from a coherent representation of the entire working class to that of even more general interests, those of the entire collectivity.

THE CRISIS OF THE MEANS OF CONTROLLING THE MEMBERSHIP

This displacement of the process of representation which the Italian unions have undergone in the 1970s explains, I think, why particularistic claims have exploded in number in recent years, where they were almost unknown before. The historical record of the protagonists demonstrate how the CGIL (Communist-Socialist trade union conferation) in the 1950s carried out an equally pervasive modification of membership demands (14). This was not only because the CGIL was, at that time, less equipped to select the demands of various groups of workers, out of which developed the self-criticism of the second half of the 1950s, but also because the need to include them in a long-term strategy was felt acutely by an organisation trying to survive in a hostile environment (15). Even so, particularist claims and wage escalation were rather limited, if not indeed unknown at that time.

Of course, the quite different situation pertaining today can to some extent be reduced to the relatively greater market power of workers who fall under the terms of the Statute, in contrast with the situation in the 1950s, and the logic of imitating wage demands which became widespread amongst all categories of workers following the

247

successes of the workers' mobilisation in 1968-72. But this is not enough to explain the difference between the two periods.

In fact, despite the defeats at Fiat and in other factories subjected to management repression, during the 1950s the CGIL did manage to avoid a more serious crisis of representation because it had a powerful means of controlling the membership: the ability to provide an ideology which emphasised the identification of workers with the organisation and its objective (16). This kind of identification is, to a certain extent, *independent of the satisfaction of membership claims.*

The more a demand is subjected to ideological confirmation, the more likely it is to become abstract, in that ideology discourages recognition and verification of the demand. When [instead] the ideological synthesis ceased to operate, the work of aggregating and co-ordinating the demand becomes much more difficult and particularism tends to predominate (17).

It was therefore the CGIL's ability to provide 'incentives for identification', in other words a sense of identification by means of a shared ideology, which allowed the CGIL in the 1960s to make a broad interpretation and aggregation of claims, the ideology in fact acted as a means of control and indeed as a way of preventing any possible crisis of representation.

However, and this is the important point, this ability was closely tied to a logic of class action: the ideology could work because the objectives which the union pursued and the potential interests which it represented, appeared strictly coherent with the ideology. When, however, the objectives became enlarged so as to conform with those of the entire collectivity, alongside the developing legitimacy of the concept of the general interest there inevitably developed amongst workers the idea of the particular interest. In a period of increasing secularisation of the society in which we live, this process led to a deep crisis of control based on ideological cohesion, that is, a crisis of identification with the organisation and its objective.

Quite naturally, the associational unions which were not oriented towards the entire working class, never had this means of control. These however, had less compulsion to modify their memberships'

demands, not having to aggregate and co-ordinate
them with those of other groups of workers.
Besides, these associational unions had developed
another means of control, that of 'selective
incentives', (18) in which particular benefits which
accrue only to members and sanctions exist against
not joining. By reserving certain rights to members
only, and even limiting the application of
agreements, and by promoting a series of services
for members only, some unions have become simply
service agencies for their own members. If interest
organisations become increasingly only service
agencies and increasingly less the centres of
political aspirations or personal identity, the need
for participation and solidarity will become
directed towards other movements and organisations,
and commitment to unions will become simply
instrumental (as Goldthorpe and Lockwood have
already shown in their research on the British
working class (19)). Like any other service agency,
such unions come to be considered by the workers as
something external, and belonging to them or not
becomes simply the outcome of a rough cost-benefit
calculation. Membership demands can then be
adjusted by the organisation without creating any
crisis of representation, as long as the total
benefits of belonging outweigh the costs.

Even those unions which are oriented towards
the working class as a whole have moved in the
direction of selective incentives in order to
counter-balance the decline in identification
incentives. Even in Italy there are examples of
this kind of control over the commitment of the
membership, even though there is no form of 'closed
shop' or explicit sanctions against non-members. If
social assistance services are generally an
incentive to join, some particular unions, such as
that of the agricultural workers

> have for some time recruited their members on
> administrative and assistance grounds rather
> than those of struggle...the most important
> point of contact, if not indeed the only one,
> between the union organisation and the labourers
> has been reduced to the business of despatching
> assistance forms...(20)

In this instance the claims for agricultural
unemployment benefit have become the organisational
nexus between members and union.

All in all, however, the Italian unions

demonstrate a strong resistance to following this route to its logical conclusion. The risks which this would involve are quite clear: bureaucratisation of the union, and an absolute decline in its ability to mobilise workers on issues which concern the entire working class. It is probable that an awareness of these risks encourages some union leaders to turn back from, rather than to follow, this path. One could interpret in this way the recent proposal by the CGIL that members should periodically be asked about their intentions to renew their membership. This proposal aims at transforming the decision to join into an act of identification with a representative organisation, rather than a bureaucratic routine which emphasises the externality of card-holders.

The two traditional instruments of control over the membership appear therefore to be largely unsuitable for present use by Italian unions. The crisis of the 'identification incentive', and the uncertainty or outright resistance to following the method of 'selective incentives', would expose them to the risk of losing control over the workers at the very moment when the enlargement of demands is producing unrest and opposition amongst the membership.

MEMBERSHIP DEMANDS AND THE LACK OF RESULTS

The two processes I have described seem to me quite inevitable. There is little that the unions can do about the crisis or the impracticability of controlling the membership. Also, the fact that the unions wish to maintain the power acquired both in the factories and in the political arena, despite the period of deep economic crisis, makes it difficult to avoid the enlargement of the process of aggregation and co-ordination of demands. If such a union leadership asks itself about the consequences of its own action should it decide to adopt a purely trade-unionist model, not to modify membership claims and not to take account of more general interests, it will tend to come to the following conclusion (even if significant internal minorities are of a different view) : that such a decision would weaken the union, because it would contribute to a worsening of the crisis and thus of its market power, and it would imperil its alliances and thus also its political power.

Should the unions, despite difficulty retrace their steps in these processes, is it inevitable that this will produce or increase a crisis of representation? I have already said that in my opinion such a crisis will appear only if a third condition becomes less salient : that is, the ability of trade unions to obtain by negotiation with their public and private counterparts results which, though they are different from the specific and explicit requests of the membership, none the less satisfy in a meaningful way other potential or objective needs which are widely felt to be important.

In modifying workers' demands to bring them into line with the so-called 'general interest', unions implicitly accept or propose a trade-off between the renunciation of certain benefits and the acquisition of others. The most obvious example of this in the Italian context (but also in other European countries) has been the practice of moderating wage claims in exchange for an anticipated increase in investment and employment.

One could argue that what is causing the explosion of the crisis of representation today is not so much the constriction of the wage demands of the membership which this line has led to, so much as the lack of investment and employment results which would have compensated for the non-satisfaction of the explicit claim. The trade-off thus appears unacceptable to the workers, and of dubious value to the unions themselves, not because it demands self-sacrifice but because they have not managed to get what was expected in exchange for the sacrifice.

The problem of the outcome of political exchange is a delicate one, because there is always a time-lag between the short-term advantages which have to be foregone and the kind of advantages one can obtain in exchange. In fact these come to fruition only in the long term, and are thus uncertain (21). The experience of those European unions which, in the 1950s and 1960s, accepted concertative policies, was that this time-lag could be bridged by the confidence that unions had in the good faith of their counterparts in government and enterprises, and in the possibility of actually gaining favourable results in the long term. This confidence allowed them to overcome a purely wage-claim strategy. The trade-off mechanism (or the social contract) could thus operate for most of the 1950s and 1960s. The benefits which accrued in the long term to workers, in terms of the growth of real wages, of full employment and of social policy prevented the occurrence, up to the 1970s, of a serious crisis in the representative relation, and this despite .the profound modifications made by the unions of those countries to their memberships' demands.

On the other hand, the confidence was not the result of the greater benevolence or optimism of the unions, but was due to the existence in those countries of a series of conditions which were perceived as guarantees of the trade-off. In the first place, the experience of steady economic growth, which at the time seemed inexorable, appeared to guarantee the continuation of full employment and redistribution of the fruits of accumulation. Secondly, the ability to predict long term trends, given the almost total absence of inflation, was an indispensable condition for calculating the long term advantages. Finally, the presence over long periods of working class parties in government or governing coalitions, constituted a political guarantee that the 'general interests' did not simply coincide with those of the ruling class, and even the unions could be assured of the positive results implicit in the trade-off.

It is easy to see how one or more of these conditions were diminished in the 1970s. As a result, the trade-off began to produce fewer advantages for the workers, and the 'crisis of results' exposed the unions to the dissatisfaction or revolt of the membership. It was only at this point that the modification of explicit demands, which had always gone on, provoked a crisis of representation.

It is equally. easy to see that the third condition that a workers' party be in power has never been present in Italy and that this is why the first two conditions are experiencing a crisis more serious than elsewhere. It is not just that there has never existed in Italy a public counterpart to the unions able to make political guarantees to the unions of favourable long term outcomes, there has hardly been a credible counterpart *tout court*, that is, one capable of achieving its own state objectives. The unions have had, and could only have had, little recompense in exchange for a willingness to co-ordinate specific membership demands with the 'general interests'. There have been very few results which might have demonstrated to the workers the acceptability of the trade-off.

But, if the first two processes that can bring about a crisis of representation are largely inevitable, then the unions cannot do other than concentrate once again on indirect results in order to re-establish their relationship with the workers. The increasing demands for control over enterprise decisions and economic policy could be read as a search for a direct guarantee, in the absence of those conditions which promote confidence in the counterparts, that union involvement in concerted policy-making will, in the long run, bring favourable results to the workers, and thus inhibit a crisis of representation.

The European class unions are still moving rather timidly in this direction. To those unions accustomed to predominantly collective bargaining activity, such as the Italian, British and French, it is difficult to accept that the co-ordination of particular demands with general interests can be any more than the result of autonomous and untrammelled choices.

On the other hand, a request for a concertative action based not on simple confidence in long-term outcomes, but on powers of control as a guarantee of such outcomes, might seem too radical to unions in social-democratic countries which already operate in a concertative system. In a somewhat hostile economic and political climate, such a request for guarantees would in fact take the unions to a level far removed from the traditional neo-corporatist order, in which their participation in economic policy decisions is sectionalized and subordinated (22). For example, straightforward rights to information about enterprise decisions or the practice of consultation by the government certainly do not constitute a sufficient guarantee, especially when the crisis of representation becomes acute. A guarantee of long-term outcomes can be given only through the conquest of real powers of control over fundamental enterprise decisions and economic policy (in the first place, over investment decisions); that is to say powers of control over the effective fulfilment of these decisions, such that they produce the desired results and not others.

CONCLUSIONS

The Italian unions appear hesitant at present and more divided than ever over what response to give to the crisis of representation which has hit them. Protracting this situation can do nothing but aggravate it, and at the same time produce the economic and political conditions for their total defeat. Aside from that eventuality, there appear to be three possible developments.

The first is a neo-corporatist one. At some years distance, the Italian solution might duplicate that of the social democratic countries, without, however, the conditions which made for relative success there. Without being able to render notable advantages for the workers, this solution will encounter a much deeper crisis of representation; it may be possible only at the price of a radical transformation of the nature of the unions in bureaucratic organisation, which will have to resort to selective incentives to obtain the minimum necessary commitment of the membership.

The second development would be that of a return to an insistence on wage claims, to its 'general interests' of the collectivity, not to be involved in concertative policies, and to transmit therefore with few modifications the membership's demands. Without doubt this policy would enable the unions to reinstate their relations with the workers. Indeed, this seems to be the only solution to the crisis of representation envisaged by those who criticise the neo-corporatist tendencies. But it would seem to be an impraticable policy at this historic stage of economic and political relations.

The third possible development, that of obtaining effective powers of control, is thus the only one which in the long term could prevent either a political defeat for the union or a crisis of representation. It is also clear that this would mean equally as much as the second an accentuation of social and political confrontation, not a reduction of it. It would also require of all the economic and political actors a notable capacity to innovate, to experiment with possible solutions, and to revise their own ideological conceptions (23).

NOTES

1. I use here the term 'class-oriented unions' without any evaluative connotations, simply to distinguish them from another kind of union, which is called 'associational'. The first, in contrast with the second, seek systematically to represent social groups on a wider scale than their own membership, strictly speaking. For a discussion of the two types of union and their respective strategies see A. Pizzorno "Fra azione di classe e sistemi corporativi' in A. Feltrinelli (ed.), Problemi del Movimento Sindacale in Italia 1943-73

(Mazzotta, Milano, 1976), and G. Esping-Andersen and M. Regini 'Trade Union Strategies and Social Policy in Italy and Sweden' in J. Hayward (ed.), Trade Unionsl and Politics in Western Europe (F. Cass, London, 1980).

2. W. Muller-Jentsch, 'Il rapporto fra Stato e sindacati' in L. Basso (ed.), Stato e crisi delle istituzioni (Mazzata, Milano, 1978).

3. C. Offe, 'The Attribution of Political Status to Interest Groups' in S. Berger (ed.), Organising Interests in Western Europe (Cambridge University Press, New York, 1981).

4. P. Schmitter, 'Interest Intermediation and Regime Governability in Contemporary Western Europe and North America' in Berger (ed.), Organising Interests.

5. The works which most clearly articulate this argument of the intrinsic contradictions of the neo-corporatist tendency are those of C. Sabel, 'The Internal Politics of Trade Unions' in Berger (ed.), Organising Interests; and of L. Panitch, 'Trade Unions and the Capitalist State', New Left Review, No. 125 (1981).

6. For an analysis of the relations between unions and state in Italy, see M. Regini 'Changing Relationships Between Labour and the State in Italy: Towards a Neo-Corporatist System?' in G. Lehmbruch and P. Schmitter (eds.), Patterns of Corporatist Policy-Making, (Sage, London, 1982).

7. For an analysis of the process of transmission of demands by political parties see A. Pizzorno, I soggetti del pluralismo (Il Mulino, Bologna, 1980), pp. 11–49.

8. According to estimates, the number of Factory Councils has increased from 8,101 in 1972 to 32,000 in 1978; that of delegates from 82,923 in 1972 to 210,000 in 1978 (Quanderni di Rassegna sindacale No. 51, (e La Republica, 1 November 1978).

9. On this point there is an interesting debate in Mondoperaio, No. 9, (1979); 'A dieci anni dall'autunno caldo'.

10. For these concepts see A. Pizzorno, 'Political Exchange and Collective Identity' in C. Crouch and A. Pizzorno (eds.), The Resurgence of Class Conflict in Western Europe Since 1968 (Macmillan, London, 1978), Vol. 2.

11. See Schmitter, 'Interest Intermediation'.

12. This appears particularly clear in the German Konzertierte Aktion. See C. Offe, 'Attribution of Political Status'; G. Lehmbruch, 'Liberal Corporatism and Party Government',

Comparative Political Studies, Vol. 10 (1977).

13. Those parties, as we know, often 'do not present only general demands, inspired by the 'common good', but also, to a greater or lesser extent, and sometimes exclusively, demands inspired by the 'good of a few' (Pizzorno, I soggetti p. 17).

14. See A. Accornero, Gli anni '50 in fabbrica (De Donato, Bari, 1973).

15. For the logic behind CGIL action in those years Pizzorno's analysis remains fundamental, and is now gathered in I soggetti pp. 99-190.

16. In what follows I shall refer to this instrument of control also as the capacity to provide 'identity incentives'. This concept is taken from a typology proposed by P. Lange, 'La teoria degli incentivi e l'analisi dei partiti politici', Rassengna Italiana di Sociologia Vol. 18, No.4 (1977), which takes up the theory of incentives developed by Clark-Wilson, Wilson and Schneider.

17. Pizzorno, I soggetti, p. 39.

18. For the concept of 'selective incentives' see M. Olson, The Logic of Collective Action (Harvard University Press, Cambridge, 1965), p. 51 *et passim*.

19. See in particular the introduction to J. Goldthorpe *et. al.*, The Affluent Worker in the Class Structure (Cambridge University Press, London, 1969).

20. E. Reyneri, La catena migratoria (Il Mulino, Bologna, 1979), p. 302.

21. See Pizzorno, 'Political Exchange'.

22 See Regini, 'Labour and the State in Italy', p. 59.

23. This chapter was initially translated from the Italian by Caroline White and corrected by Marino Regini.

Chapter Seven

AN INTERNATIONAL PARTICIPATION CYCLE: VARIATIONS ON
A RECURRING THEME

Harvie Ramsay

INTRODUCTION: CYCLES OF PARTICIPATION

This chapter is one of two sequels to an article
written some years ago in which I sought to argue
that the conventional wisdom on worker participation
in Britain was seriously flawed (1). Far from there
being an evolution of participation, as seems to be
assumed by almost all politicians, business
spokesmen and trade unionists (even if the form and
direction of evolution is not always the same for
all these), I suggested that history held a
different story. The picture of evolution has been
imposed by academics employing teleological
reasoning, cutting the cloth of history to suit an
ideology of gradual social progress and
development. 'Advances' are looked for, and all
events are interpreted as favourable or obstructive
factors accelerating or delaying the rational end-
state of 'constructive' management-labour
relations. A prescriptive 'recipe-book' approach to
participation results, stressing the 'good' (which
offers progressive lessons) and ignoring or seeing
as quirkish the 'bad' (which contains at most
negative lessons for the future).
   Once this ideological overlay is removed,
however, the path from past to present appears less
as a set of stepping stones and more as a series of
waves or cycles of interest in and decline of
participation schemes. This pattern was found to
follow periods of greater and lesser challenge to
management control. Management were attracted to
the notion of participation at times when they felt
the legitimacy of their dominance challenged, or
when the pressure on them to increase control over
labour intensified (e.g. when international
competition squeezed profit margins) but workers

257

were in a position to resist simple coercion. These
two aspects of control, ideological and direct
manipulation of effort, generally coincide, though
my own analysis has stressed the former for reasons
discussed elsewhere.

The perspective which offered most explanatory
power in accounting for the historical pattern was
argued to be marxism. Industrial relations are seen
as a struggle for control of the labour process and
over the distribution of the value created by the
application of labour power to capital; in other
words, a class relation. As agents of capital,
management are in fundamental conflict with
labour. In this scenario, participation is seen as
a conservative force, seeking to evade demands to
change the *status quo*, and if possible to extend
management control. In one British industrialist's
words, it would be a 'counter-force to shop floor
power' (2), or in the well-worn words of the British
pluralist academic, Allan Flanders, it sought to
'regain control by sharing it' (3). Notwithstanding
the demands from the labour movement for some forms
of participation (more usually termed by them
'industrial democracy'), those schemes which gain
'public' approval and are introduced in practice are
shaped by management's powers of initiative and
gatekeeping. They are thus overwhelmingly
consensus-oriented, purporting to herald a new dawn
of management-labour harmony and co-operation in
each new period of interest.

I have argued further that in the real world
the outcomes of participation schemes belie the
supposed success of these consensual goals (4) which
is clamorously proclaimed by media, government and
business spokesmen, and feared by the left haunted
by a spectre of incorporation. While management may
succeed in increasing control of labour, or, less
likely by far, labour may succeed in encroaching on
management power, other results have been far more
probable in practice. Triviality, in which the
scheme has no significant powers and no impact on
labour relations, doing little for either side, is
one likely outcome. Others are instability, where
schemes disintegrate and may even exacerbate
conflict, and change of status of the scheme into a
de facto negotiating body. The circumstances in
which each of these outcomes is particularly likely,
and the evidence supporting this disillusioned view
of schemes in Britain, are presented at length
elsewhere (5). The point to be emphasised here is
that participation does not fulfil the historic

mission to which it is assigned by its disciples. It does not transform the nature of management-labour relations. On the contrary, it reverberates with all the shocks and fissures which afflict those relations in capitalist societies.

Two points concerning the cycles arguments should be made before proceeding. Firstly, it is not argued here that cycles are the 'inevitable' pattern of participation over time, only that given the nature of changes in the socio-economic context and of related factors correlating with the degree of challenge to their authority which managers experience, there has been an understandable tendency for a cyclical configuration to emerge, as indicated by a recent historical study of strike activity (6). What is none the less indicated by this pattern is the underlying analysis of conflict and so of participation; the evolutionary account of an inevitable upward trend can only retain any credibility by trying to recast downturns in interest as temporary setbacks, and it is then hard put to reconcile such explanations either with its own assumptions about the supposed transformation in the nature of society and of labour or capital, or with any stipulations concerning an acceptable historical method.

Secondly, the analysis offered here is not an economic determinist one, in the sense that shifts in some technical-economic 'base' are then echoed in various political 'superstructures', including participation as part of the politics of the firm. I stress this because the argument has been reduced to this and criticised as such in some accounts. Causal models of this sort - which would reduce participation to a reflex of the trade cycle - are neat but unhelpful and analytically unsound (8). Briefly, my own argument is that changes in interest in participation schemes accompany changes in the state of the struggle between classes, and the ways this is experienced and perceived. This approach sees 'ideological', 'economic', 'cultural', 'social' factors, so conventionally categorised, as a nexus rather than split into a 'base' and 'super-structure'. Participation itself is, if one examines it closely, an ideological-social-economic etc. relation; so are most phenomena. Having said this, I will leave methodological formulations on one side, and proceed with the main argument.

There is one possible exception to the criticism of evolutionism. It may be evaded by the argument that cycles have been the dominant pattern

in the past, but this no longer holds true.
According to this position, the present era
represents a qualitative break with the past, and
the forces which previously led to the abandonment
of participation by management have been superceded
by new laws of motion in social development. It is
this 'new era' argument to which the second sequel
to the cycles paper is addressed (9), and I shall
deal with it only briefly in the conclusions to this
chapter, and in the light of the information
presented below.

A BRITI-CENTRIC ANALYSIS?

According to recent analysis by Daniel, all the
trends point to a growth of industrial democracy,
and, 'The tide appears irresistible' (10). But
Britain is a laggard whose 'industrial relations
traditions are alien to those which developed worker
directors and works councils' (11). Frankly this
last assertion is misplaced - as 'Cycles' has shown,
worker directors and works councils are nothing new
or 'alien' to British experience, though enforcing
legislation has not existed to date, at least
outside the public sector (12). None the less, this
caveat raises an important question - has the
'Cycles' analysis been developed to account for the
history of an *atypical* national experience? Is it
presumptuous to expect so quirkish a case as Britain
to provide lessons for an international analysis of
participation? In particular, how can a cyclical
interpretation apply in a case like West Germany,
where legislation has ensured the continuity of
participation arrangements since the early 1950s?
      Such a criticism has been hinted at in a recent
major piece of work which has carried out a survey
of practices and perceptions in a dozen countries in
a co-ordinated international project (13). The
authors offer as an alternative the possibility
that, with the added impetus provided by demands for
workers' control from below, participation assumes a
momentum giving it a permanancy, and they ask the
reader to consider whether this view is superior to
the 'cyclical' account from their evidence and
conclusions (14). Unfortunately, the authors offer
no historical account of their own (15), and so,
disappointingly the cyclical explanation is never
confronted. Their method of analysing the extent
(and so 'growth') of participation is also admitted
to be suspect (16). Hence this major research
project leaves us little further forward.

In the remainder of this chapter I shall seek to give an abbreviated justification for thinking that a cycles-type analysis of participation can be fruitfully applied *internationally* within the capitalist world. My account will be restricted almost exclusively to the current 'cycle' (if such it be), and will in the process offer an epilogue to my earlier analysis of British experience.

Primarily, the argument rests on the fact that the analytical foundation from which the predictions of the 'cycles' pattern is derived is an analysis of *capitalism*. As such, and given the increasingly visible bonds which tie separate nation-states together into a world capitalist system it can be expected that the analysis should have far more than parochial relevance. Rather, a degree of uniformity of motion, however different the surface institutions of industrial relations, seems a reasonable expectation. Moreover, the system linkages might well lead one to expect a marked simultaneity and hence, perhaps, an international cycle. Indeed, Cronin has argued for such a pattern stretching back into the nineteenth century as far as working class militancy and social movements are concerned, relating these to 'long cycles' of economic activity (17).

Extending this argument, it seems all too easy to retreat from comparative analysis and to account for everything in terms of 'special' local circumstances and culture. Thus West Germany experienced fascism and the possibility of starting anew after a war; the United States is a 'superpower' with a history shaped by the frontier, waves of immigrants, and an extreme entrepreneurial ideology, producing 'business unionism'; France and Italy are countries split by acute political consciousness and so divided by ideology; Sweden has had democratic socialist rule for a great swathe of time, and further has an exceptionally powerful union movement and centralised bargaining set-up; Israel has zionism, beleaguered nationalism and a union owning a major portion of industry ... and so on. Obviously to impose a rigid interpretation on all of these, to treat all differences as merely superficial, would be absurd. None the less, I believe that the degree of common ground between the examples discussed below is more striking than the differences, and that the differences can readily be encompassed within the analysis.

To take an example cited earlier, the fact that West Germany has had the institutions of participation, backed by statute for three decades, does not automatically preclude a cyclical analysis unless purely formalistic measures and an analysis going no deeper that these phenomenal features of the real world are adopted. The same argument, it is worth observing, could be advanced in relation to the public sector industries in Britain, which were required to establish bodies for consultation with employees by their incorporating statutes in the 1940s. In both cases a continuity of legal obligation and thus formal provision has not prevented clear fluctuation in interest in participation. In both cases, the need for further reform, or arguably for revival of flagging institutions, became apparent in the course of the 1960s after a prolonged period of little activity and participative atrophy.

A certain amount of ground is ceded in recent publications whose stance is evolutionary, yet which admit key features concordant with a cycles analysis. In his attempt to provide a sophisticated appreciation of patterns of national development in what he unequivocally calls an 'evolution of industrial democracy', Sorge (18) musters an observation which might be seen as ultimately destructive of his entire framework when reinterpreted:

> It will be shown that innovations of industrial democracy in Western Europe are clustered around the same points in time in every country, that is: the end of the First World War, the Second World War, its end and the years shortly after it, and the late 1960s and after (19).

Similar uniformity, though less historically insightful, is discerned by Roberts in his introduction to a recent comparative text. Within an unequivocally evolutionary and optimistic set of presumptions, Roberts notes:

> It is abundantly evident that in spite of significant differences in the patterns of industrial relations in the countries included in this study, they have all reacted to the same type of technological and economic forces in the same way (20).

For Roberts there is a convergence on a new, participative basis for mutual understanding in industry. In this expectation I cannot concur, and despite some attachment to the evolutionary view among most of the authors dealing with individual countries in the book, many of their discussions offer useful counterpoints to their editor's messianism. But clearly it is necessary to look beyond just the British experience to appreciate properly what does emerge as very much an international phenomenon. This last point marks my argument off from recent reviews seeking to clarify international *differences* (21). While these are not insignificant, they cannot conceal the far more emphatic similarities described below. I do not believe there is much incite in comparative analyses which conclude there is a primacy of 'cultural' variables over 'economic' ones, partly because it seems a weak inversion of the base/superstructure model, and also because the work which is praised for revealing this remains fixated on an evolutionary convergence account (22). But above all, if one looks for differences, then the very problematic seems destined to throw up such factors as distinctive, whilst obscuring and brushing under the carpet the shared contours of social relations and their movement which reek uncomfortably of capitalism at work.

In what follows, I shall look at a number of aspects of the current period of interest in participation; unfortunately space prevents other than passing reference to a longer sweep of history. I shall argue that the theoretical approach outlined earlier makes far more coherent sense of the pattern of events and responses than do competing accounts. I shall look at the timing and contingent factors associated with renewed interest in participation; at employer attitudes and the sorts of schemes they propose; at the unions' own proposals and their response to what they are offered; at the role of the State in initiating or encouraging (or ignoring) participation; at the outcomes of operating participation schemes, and at the current state of play, to assess whether an 'evolution' continues or whether recession has brought a downturn in the saliency of participation as an issue.

THE REVIVAL OF INTEREST IN PARTICIPATION

As Sorge has indicated, there is a simultaneity in the (re-)emergence of interest in participation in Europe and elsewhere during the 1960s. The cycles account sensitises the observer to seek the origins of this in terms of pressures on management to introduce participation schemes, where an evolutionary account might be more inclined to talk of the diffusion of 'progressive' management ideas of accountability and humanism or to look at other supposed transformations in the nature of the enterprise and its controllers (i.e. the 'managerial revolution').

The British experience was described in the original formulation of the cycles argument. The most recent wave of interest in participation came in the early 1960s when a persistent decline in the profit rate was accompanied by a progressive deterioration in international competitiveness. A number of British based companies, particularly in high technology sectors at first, sought to sign agreements with unions on improved employment levels and productivity. Amongst those at the forefront of this move were Esso, Shell and ICI. The strategy became popularised as 'productivity bargaining', and generally involved at least notional concern for 'involvement' of workers through joint productivity committees or like bodies. Available descriptions of such companies in Britain suggest that these and subsequent strategies (consultation, job enrichment, profit sharing) were fairly conscious efforts at incorporation of or at least at defusing rank and file or trade union 'interference' with management's aims (23). An impressionistic review of the adoption of such approaches more generally in British industry would suggest a far less coherent or cogent managerial response, however. It appears to have been a reaction not only to the piecemeal spread of productivity bargaining but also to the mounting challenges to management. In the British case these are well-documented, and seem to have been more gradual (to anticipate) than in other cases. The development of plant-level shop stewards in many industries, stemming from engineering, was the most visible publicly, and to management.

By the late 1960s a revival of consultation was underway even though a government commission had almost entirely dismissed it (24). Two studies showed about a third of firms had consultation committees (25), a considerable increase over the decade (26). Pressures grew after the defeat of the Conservative Party's effort to regulate the unions, the 1971 Industrial Relations Act, and the wave of factory occupations following that at Upper Clyde Shipbuilders (27), and by 1974 all the political parties officially favoured participation. A 1976 survey found 76% of firms reported some kind of consultative committee, a figure broadly confirmed by other investigations (28). The debate reached fever-pitch amidst the controversy over the report of the Committee of Enquiry on Industrial Democracy (The Bullock Report) early in 1977.

The British example, then seems paradigmatic. It is worth noting, too, that even within the 1970s there was some variation in the rate of innovation in the form of participation according to the circumstances management faced. There was at most slow growth down to the revival of the issue from about 1973; thereafter down to about 1978 at least, the challenge to management was experienced as fierce and disruptive on a wide front.

In evaluating experience elsewhere, it should first be observed that the rise in the incidence of strikes and the emergence of other forms of struggle were neither unique to nor even an innovation of British workers. The rise in indicators of industrial conflict was truly international, however parochial the reactions to it in each country, and this explains why Britain remains only mid-way up the strikes league despite the sharp increase there. The predominant source is also international – the crisis of world capitalism reflected in higher inflation rates and thus greater sensitivity to wage levels by workers. However, the nature of the demands and forms of struggle which emerged indicate that the impact on wages accompanied other lessons concerning the threat posed to employee well-being by the political economy of capital. Dubois (29) examines this for five illustrative cases (Belgium, Italy, France, West Germany and the UK) and identifies the emergence of new and uninstitutional-ised organisation at plant level, and of more radical and direct forms of action (such as occupations).

In fact the 'explosion' of militancy of which the 'May 1968' events in France and 1969 strikes in Italy are the most dramatic examples, was reflected during the period 1968-70 in most European countries far more markedly than in Britain. West Germany and Sweden, to cite two particularly prominent 'models' for discussions of worker participation, both experienced unofficial strike waves which, while not devastating in their effect on official recorded figures for stoppages, had a disproportionate impact on management (and official union) awareness, not least because they questioned non-militant traditions sharply in a period of vocal political protest. The unofficial strikes in 1969 in Germany, although they accounted for very few recorded days lost (the illegality of most such strikes in West Germany and Sweden makes the reported figures highly questionable, far more so than in the UK where the clamour about non-reportage is loud), had far greater effect than the official disputes of 1971 which lifted the figure more than tenfold.

Let us inspect the coincidence of pressures a little more closely for a few examples; the renewed interest in participation will be found to follow each closely. Some of the aspects of the wave of concern in each country will be further examined in subsequent sections.

For West Germany the historical pattern follows very closely the cyclical one identified for Britain, with waves of interest following periods of growing labour strength and protest (30) in the 1930s/40s, the 1880s/90s, the post-war period after 1918, and again after 1945. The last occasion was obviously a matter of special circumstances, following Hitler's crushing of the unions, and shaped by the Allied occupation and their strategies to control both employers who had backed fascism and the militant left who reappeared at factory level. In this light, works councils and co-determination can be seen as compromise strategies heading off radical demands for nationalisation and workers' control to which the hostility to fascism lent legitimacy. Works councils also had a further advantage; they kept the unions out of the workplace.

After the initial burst of legislation laying the foundations of the participation system up to 1952, the reconstruction and recovery of the rest of the 1950s and much of the 1960s brought an affluence which generated complacency on the part of unions, workforce and management. To associate the participative mechanisms with the industrial peace of this period in more than the sense of co-existence seems tenuous to say the least.

The impact of the wave of strikes in 1969 was to alert the unions to the need to justify their existence by being more aggressive in bargaining, and strengthen their presence in the company. Some union stewards or 'trustmen' began to emerge in response to the continuing challenges to the existing formal framework (31). The response of the State was to make some concessions extending the existing legal framework of participation, while employers resisted any radical moves and began to show some interest in 'work humanisation' and profit-sharing tactics.

In Sweden the strength of left-wing social democracy is often argued to change not just the *form* which a response to issues like industrial democracy takes, but the very *nature* of that response. If this were true, Sweden would not be amenable to the analysis advanced here. I shall suggest to the contrary that Sweden remains essentially capitalist, so that the processes to be examined are subject to the same broad 'rules' of the struggle between the political economies of capital and labour as in the other countries under discussion.

Previous to the late 1960s the arrangements for 'participation' in Sweden derived from the 1946 agreement between SAF and LO on works councils (which followed the war and the great 1945 engineering strike). These were, bluntly, ineffectual bodies having little impact on management or the workforce at large, consigned to a trivial role with a duty to 'maintain continuous collaboration between employer and employees' (32). Little was done by unions or management to repair this febrility until a minor restructuring of the councils in 1966, a response to the early stirrings of pressure. In the workplace, wages and conditions are officially determined by national negotiations between the industry's union and employers' association, but in at least some industries workplace bargaining plays a major role, particularly where piece-rate systems predominate (33). However, management long maintained as absolute the rights granted it in the infamous Article 32 of the 1938 Saltsjöbaden Agreement, giving them freedom to direct labour and hire and fire at their own discretion (34), and in consequence the scope of workplace bargaining had been severely constricted. This meant a growing number of unofficial strikes as labour rank and file began to challenge management prerogatives in the 1960s, many of which management preferred not to report to avoid the exacerbation of having to take legal action through the Labour Court, as the law forbade such strikes. In the late 1960s these strikes erupted in a wave, which persistently re-emerged throughout much of the 1970s (35). Gradually unions responded to this challenge to their representativeness by demanding changes in the law, above all to abolish the now suffocating constraint of Article 32. It is in these circumstances that participation schemes became a subject of close attention in Sweden, from worker directors and capital-sharing through to job enrichment, and from the late 1960s a number of innovations commenced.

In France a number of 'phases' of legislation, provoked by periodic political crises precipitated in turn by high mobilisation of the labour movement, can be identified (36). In 1945 the *Comites d'enterprise* were set up in the post-war crisis which arose partly from the collaboration by many employers with the now defeated Nazi forces during occupation. A more recent phase of interest in conciliating labour with offers of participation was inaugurated by the events of 1968. These led De Gaulle to cede the right for unions to organise branches at plant level in 1969, and to make proposals for profit-sharing. Subsequently the Sudreau Committee was established to look at the idea of 'co-supervision', reporting in 1975. All this, then, seems a clear response to the explosion of demands from the rank and file (often non-unionised), including many white collar, technical, unskilled and immigrant groups of employees previously not associated with active militancy (37). The French upsurge may have been far more violent and dramatic than most, but the impulse and the nature of the response to it fit firmly into the pattern exhibited by the UK, Sweden and Germany.

In the Netherlands a works council system was set up after World War II by a 1950 statute, but was trivial in consequence of its basis in an assumption of common interests between worker and employer (38). During the 1950s, stability reigned, but a tight labour market provoked aspirations and unrest from the mid-1960s onwards, culminating in a wave of unofficial strikes in 1970 and a series of further major disputes in the following years (39). This breakdown of the traditional order resulted in an attempt to revamp the works councils with a new Act in 1971, and later in the decade promises to further extend works council powers and to introduce profit-sharing were made by the government (40). Meantime, in the 1960s, management, latterly with government backing in the form of a Productivity Commission, had inaugurated a series of experiments in job redesign as their initial response to the shop floor challenge (41).

In Belgium works councils on a unitary basis had been set up in 1948 (42), and management resisted any extension of the powers of these bodies

(43). However, trade union growth, rising demands and the emergence of a workers' control movement, and the familiar burst of strikes from 1970 renewed concern (44).

In Italy the explosion of conflict in the 'hot autumn' of 1968/69 rivals that in France, but as elsewhere it climaxed a growth of discontent which existing arrangements could no longer contain, and it baptised a period of plant-level challenges to management (45). Before this period, the representative body for employees at plant level was the internal commission or works council, but the tasks of this council were specified in unitary terms as the advancement of production (46). After 1969 it was effectively displaced by the growth of factory councils, on a footing of conflict with the employer, and in 1970 these bodies were conceded backing in the Workers' Statute. If the conflictual basis has superceded the consensus orientation here, because of the extent of the shop floor initiative, this has not meant an absence of efforts by management to promote less power-oriented reforms. Rollier (47) associates the intensity of the confrontation from 1969 with the contradictions of the application of Taylorism in Italian factories in the post-war decades, and notes that after a period of retreat the response of employers was to encourage work re-design experiments from 1972 onwards. The initiative was led by Olivetti, reputedly far more prepared in its management philosophy for the challenges, and here changes were already being initiated in the 1960s which were extended in the 1970s (48).

In Europe the cycles analysis can be seen to offer a highly cogent account of events, despite the much-remarked differences between the societies concerned. To offer a convincingly international analysis, however, it is necessary to consider capitalist countries outside Europe. In particular, it is obvious this means showing that the United States and Japan fit the analysis, and this would seem to pose a particular challenge to the argument.

In the case of the United States however, it is quickly possible to find support for this approach. There is little difficulty fitting the wave of interest in profit-sharing and industrial welfare (or the two Government Commissions on industrial relations of 1898-1902 and 1913-15) in the early part of the twentieth century into the cyclical analysis. The decline of employer interest in the worker as a human being which accompanied the

defeat of the IWW and the decline of union
membership generally in the 1920s, was halted by the
upsurge in organisation and militancy of the late
1930s. This, too, marks the revival of interest in
profit-sharing. Hunnius has confirmed that the
cycles analysis is applicable to the United States
and Canada in that innovations were prompted not by
evolving humanism but by employer responses to
challenges to their authority (51).

The more recent decades of American industrial
relations history are commonly seen as contrasting
with those in Europe. Legislative or other State
intervention is resisted and the degree of even
supportive legislation protecting workers by laying
down minimum conditions is limited. The AFL-CIO
actively legitimates a pluralist (though not a
unitary managerial) conception of American
capitalism, and the traditional form of collective
bargaining is viewed as the touchstone of 'business
unionism' in action. Although negotiations can
notionally cover any issue, the core is the wage-
effort bargain, conceived economistically.

For many writers who take a pluralist,
evolutionary analysis of the United States as their
starting point, collective bargaining is the form of
industrial democracy which is evolving there,
spreading ever wider and dealing with ever more
extensive issues (52). This tends to squeeze out
the 'participative' solutions adopted in Europe,
shunned both by management (who see no need to
compromise their symbolic prerogatives) and unions
(who detest the unitary cast of joint consultation
and the like). But this account quickly collapses
when confronted with reality. Government
intervention on the side of employers has been
immense historically, acting to maintain the
conditions of *laissez-faire* for capital, and the
Taft-Hartly Act of 1947 sought precisely to restrain
union action threatening the 'freedom of exchange'
(53). The restrictions on labour imposed by the
State have arguably led to a narrowing of bargaining
to economistic issues, and to a restriction of the
right to strike (54). They have also contributed,
along with the cumbersome 'rights' granted unions
for forcing recognition from employers (contrasting
with the facility with which employers can call an
employee vote to reverse recognition), to a decline
in trade unionism and so effective bargaining in a
country where only a minority of employees have ever
experienced the trappings of pluralism's 'web of
rules' (55). It is thus even harder to accept the

view that the United States is seeing the emergence of a new ideology, heralded *inter alia* by the growth of interest in 'work humanisation', towards 'consensualism' and 'communitarianism' (56).

Neither the worker director issue nor European style works councils have ever gained much currency in the United States (57), but there have been innovations in labour-management productivity committees and on work reorganisation. It is not hard to show management motivations as control and productivity-oriented, and union reactions as generally suspicious, preferring bargaining-based changes. The question remains as to whether they can be fitted into a cyclical pattern of any sort. For Berg *et al.* the interest in work reorganisation is indeed cyclical, coinciding with managerial concern that collective bargaining is difficult to contain in a period of tight labour markets, but the cycles have been more rapid than those in Western Europe, provoked by the faster 'boom-bust' pattern of the US economy (58). Other sources indicate a broader pattern, however, coinciding with the progressive lagging of productivity rates in the United States by comparison with Japan and most of Europe. By the mid-1960s this was beginning to emerge as a threat to competitiveness. At the same time, where unions failed to step into the vacuum in work representation, individual responses of absenteeism, labour turnover, and widespread forms of shop floor resistance to change hampered management efforts to change matters.

The accounts now emerging of the resulting management initiatives suggest that motivation and protection against worker dissatisfaction intermingle. Either way, the response gathered momentum towards the end of the 1960s. A number of companies (such as IBM or Texas Instruments) adopted work 'humanisation' policies to motivate employees and keep out the unions. Meanwhile the State launched a series of Senate hearings in 1972 on 'worker alienation' leading to a report, *Work in America* (59). The timing and the contingent circumstances of the revived interest in participation thus match well with the approach advanced in this paper.

However, it remains difficult at first sight, to see how Japan can be accommodated to such an account. After all, the Japanese worker and manager are well known to exist in harmony under the successful unitary images of family and team, providing a perfect example of what Britain or the

271

US (and even Germany) is supposedly lacking. A combination of cultural values emphasising paternal obligation for the employer and loyal obedience for the employee, and the modern expression of this in the lifetime employment system with its guarantee of security and of seniority-based salary to seal the bond are seen as the source of this paragon. Thus Japan is depicted as a society of ant-like devotion to duty and master, characterised by harmony and willing determination to raise productivity.

This image has come under widespread attack in the academic literature in recent years (though not in journalistic accounts), chiefly from Japanese writers (60). Although many of these writers are employing no more than a pluralist perspective, and still see an evolving system different from the stereotype only in the recognition of real conflicts, they provide us with a counterweight that helps at least to suggest the possibility of a different picture altogether (61). It is from this that I shall draw a tentative contrasting account to the evolutionary ones of either media idealisation or academic pluralism.

It would be disingenuous to pretend that Japan could be treated as if it were of one piece with European capitalism. Unemployment has varied, but its recorded level remains at around 2% of the employed population whereabouts it has stood since the early 1950s (62). But this and the renowned lifetime employment, while they clearly do tie the worker to the company (economically as much as ideologically), disguise a system that is less stable than the usual account conveys, and one which does place certain pressures on management. The differing circumstances, at least partially mediating the impact of world capitalist developments, mean that the observed pattern may not replicate that elsewhere, yet might still be consistent with the basic 'cycles' arguments.

In the labour market the period after World War II was the first in which Japanese employers had not been able to make use of a large labour surplus to replace existing labour, though shortages of skilled workers had seen the emergence of the main features of lifetime employment in the interwar period. It was skilled labour above all which remained in short supply in the post-war years, and the shortage became an urgent one in the 1960s, thus coinciding with increased union power and other social changes causing an undermining of some of the foundations of management control (63).

The trade unions were never strong before World War II but in 1937 they were dismantled by the State. They reappeared after the war almost exclusively on an enterprise basis. In an explosive expansion, they recruited almost five million members by the end of 1946 (64) and built up to around 35% membership density by the early 1950s which they have since sustained. Unionisation remains very uneven in Japan's 'dual economy', being minimal in small companies and high in the large corporations. Although the average membership of Japanese unions is only about 380 (65), since 1955 their strategy for obtaining wage increases has been relatively co-ordinated within and between the main confederations via the *shunto* or 'Spring offensive' (66). This tactic yielded considerable advances in the initially very low level of wages in Japan, particularly after 1960 as the labour market offset by the successful productivity advances which preserved profits and prevented labour from making significant inroads into capital's share of generated revenue (67). None the less, this had to be 'achieved' by management rather than being granted, so pressure remained present. Afterwards unions were persuaded to modify their demands by the world crisis and its impact on Japan, which enabled the State and employers to pressurise them by fearmongering in the media and among employees.

Labour-management relations are commonly measured by strike figures, and on this basis Japan has a record over the decade 1969-78 of median or a little less than median strike activity depending on the measure employed (68). Employment security is far from an absolute as is often asserted (69), and has to be fought for at times, as during the recession of 1973-76 (70). This conflict is intensified by the existence of 'temporary' workers who enjoy none of the privileges of permanent employees (71). Hanami reports that in Japan the public image is of highly strained labour-management relations, once again in contrast to popularized Western accounts (72).

With this background, let us turn to management innovations in their relations with labour. The pre World War II period in Japan echoes experience elsewhere strikingly closely (73). Labour radicalism and unrest accompanied the economic boom engendered by World War I. Encouraged by the Government, employers in a number of enterprises introduced joint labour-management councils. The ensuing depression of the 1920s and early 1930s saw the rapid decline of these councils, but the recovery after 1932 led by rearmament also revived the interest in joint councils. These, too, were fatalities of the authoritarian direction adopted for the war however.

We have seen that the post-war period was one of a major resurgence of labour's presence. In such circumstances fresh innovations in the participation vein might be expected from experience elsewhere - and the expectation is not disappointed. Joint management councils appeared, though in Japan these frequently originated in union initiatives and often acted as a kind of pre-bargaining forum (74). Management and the State sought to channel these bodies into more acceptable courses. By June 1947 there were 11,823 local unions with such councils (75), and joint productivity councils at an industrial level were set up in some industries. However, in 1947 the Allies and the government took a more repressive view of labour's challenge, and by 1949 they argued for separate negotiations and advisory committees with employer support and union dissent (76). Employers took the offensive, and joint management councils either disappeared, became *de facto* weakened negotiation bodies, or lapsed into triviality (77).

In a number of firms, joint consultative committees were set up on an advisory basis, establishing participation on a model more appealing to management. But these appeared only slowly during the 1950s. It was the 1960s which saw such bodies set up on a wide scale (78) - the years when the labour shortage became a critical problem for management and when management organisation required restructuring. According to one survey, 52% of the joint consultative committees dealt with some matters of negotiation, or referred matters on for full negotiation in the event of disagreement (79). It was as technological change accelerated in the latter half of the 1960s that management responded further, introducing 'in a very short space of years' work group-based forms of participation and 'democratic' supervision for which there is so much publicity in the western press at the present time (80). In other words, Japanese management's interest in participation also seems to have been impelled by the kinds of forces identified for the US and Europe. Although the context and the timing are not identical, the parallels are highly suggestive, and it is significant that the dominance of evolutionary accounts, combined with images of

Japan as a model to follow, has obscured this pattern so completely. One implication is, of course, that the responses of Japanese management may change once more in fresh circumstances.

Finally, the Australian experience merits special consideration. Here again there seem to be problems since there is widespread agreement that the strength of the unions and of collective bargaining, backed by compulsory arbitration which has made government the focus of much negotiation and provided support for employers' prerogatives, has tended to squeeze out consultative or other participative responses (81). One well-known commentator concluded, in a comment widely quoted in Australia, that:

> The concept of workers' participation in management is less developed in Australia than in any other westernised country of my knowledge (82).

However, since 1970 interest in participation, at least on the part of management, seems to have blossomed. In familiar terms, this has been described as part of a 'tide of industrial democracy' (83). One explanation involves the enthusiasm of a new Labor Government in South Australia, another the return of a prominent job redesign consultant from Europe. Such factors may play a role, but they are not overly convincing in themselves - they do not explain labour enthusiasm nor employer receptivity and independent initiatives in major multinationals, for instance (84).

The timing of the rising Australian interest in fact synchronises quite closely with that in Europe, and the United States, it will be observed. Australia's high strike-proneness was sustained in the 1970s, but with a different edge as unemployment began to rise (from 1.5% in 1969 to 6.2% by 1979). This provoked intensifying worker resistance to management from the late 1960s (85).

In 1972 the South Australian government set up an enquiry on worker participation. The committee reported in favour of consultation, communication and human relations experiments - taking a unitary view of the firm and regarding management as an inviolate function (86). The resulting Unit for the Quality of Working Life set up in 1974 took this view on board also, in circumstances which are noteworthy:

275

During 1973 and the early months of 1974, work was plentiful and turnover and absenteeism rates were high. This caused problems for management ...stoppages and industrial strife increased and answers to such indiscipline were eagerly sought. Newspaper articles of the time give testimony to the sudden increase of interest in strategies that offered an alternative to increased wages.

Regardless of the Government's motives the message of job enrichment matched the disposition of management towards the idea of worker participation (87).

The pattern thus reappears. Worker resistance and a decline in management legitimacy, coinciding with problems of generating surplus value for capital, encouraged management and State to seek a solution in participation (88).

This examination of the onset of participation, therefore gives strong support to the cycles approach. It will be necessary, though, to examine the degree of consensus or conflict between the actors involved in the practice of participation, and the evidence on the operation of schemes, to see if this approach is further vindicated or whether a 'new era' alternative is to be preferred.

EMPLOYERS AND UNIONS

One central feature of the notion that participation is evolving and inevitable is that there is a sufficient consensus on the idea between capital and labour to form the basis of a new order in industrial relations. Since both employers and unions may be voicing a concern for workers' interests and rights in industry at the same time, and since terms like 'participation', 'industrial democracy', 'involvement' etc. are so vague and ambivalent (89), it may often seem that the two sides have shared objectives. In practice, as I have argued elsewhere (80), employers and unions have quite differing conceptions (and intentions) and these are in sharp opposition only a little below the surface of public rhetoric.

If this is to be validated, it will be found that employers favour schemes which are 'soft on power' (91), i.e. which have no purchase on their authority, and will find distasteful or even be outraged by those 'hard on power'. Employers will show a predilection for schemes defined in terms of common interest between themselves and employees, and which seek as their primary ('shared') goal the increase of efficiency, productivity and profitability, with a bonus of increased integration, satisfaction and motivation of the workforce. Specifically, employers will tend to lean towards strictly delimited and advisory consultative bodies, towards devices for 'communication' such as employee company reports, or for making the worker share in capital's interests such as profit-sharing, and towards job level reorganisation, which leave lines of authority untouched. They will show reluctance to approve of extensions of the rights of organised labour, or of any proposals for worker representation on the board (unless meticulously ensured to have management in full control of selection and contribution), or for extended bargaining rights affecting 'business' decisions. They will regard any legislation with suspicion, unless it leaves the initiative on introduction of the scheme and its precise form and powers firmly in their hands, not necessarily because they regard the State as hostile, but because they dislike being shackled in any way. They will regard with abhorrence any proposal ceding power to the union or to an effective plant-level organisation (they may prefer the union if the plant organisation is militant, but otherwise they will tend to prefer the latter to an outside body), and will condemn it as a danger to the social fabric via its effect on confidence and on profitability. Union-based worker directors will seem an abomination, capital-sharing a grotesque mutation.

Trade unions, to judge by British experience, can differ sharply on the desirability of various participation proposals. None the less, a common theme runs through their outlook - that participation is to be approved 'if it advances the interests and democratic rights of their members, and rejected if it ignores those rights and interests, or even endangers them (e.g. by inculcating worker representatives with management's outlook). If this perspective is confirmed internationally, the trade unions will make demands which contrast with managerial conceptions of participation and conform with their own outlook described above, and in consequence they will respond with suspicion or rejection to most management proposals. Their attitudes will lead to a preference for schemes 'harder' on power than those of employers, though how hard and how challenging to the *status quo* will vary from country to country, and between unions in each, as will their view of any State intervention. Fairly obviously, unions as organisations will feel threatened if participation is set up by management in an attempt to rival the union for members' allegiance. Whether they will want to keep their distance from any involvement will again vary with union outlook. Either way, they will challenge aims of capital, whether intentionally or not.

While one would expect to find significant differences between labour movements, then, affected by such factors as political outlook, the extent of rank and file militancy, political composition, the presence or absence of a labour-backed party in government, and employer outlook, none the less as before the common elements of union responses deserve far more emphasis than they have received in the literature. The dynamic of the interaction between management and union or worker interests may be found in consequence to constantly undermine the image of participation as jointly successful, co-operative harmony between the two sides of industry.

This conflict is easily confirmed in the British case. It was most visible in the storm of debate which broke over the Bullock Report, with its recommendation of statutory parity representation for union representatives on the boards of large private companies, in 1977. However, it may be expected that in other countries, which present an image of greater consensus and less industrial trouble, the conflict would be overcome. Certainly this is the picture painted by the British media, which constantly hold up the examples abroad to castigate workers (and, less audibly, managers) at home.

In fact, little is to be gained by trekking through all the countries mentioned in the previous section. France and Italy, for instance, are rarely seen as paragons in this respect, for obvious reasons. Instead I shall focus on those societies which are widely held up as exemplary.

The obvious starting point is West Germany. German employers are well-organised, with 80% of all private enterprise in the BDA (92) and a powerful collective voice. They 'see themselves as the guarantors of a free, efficient society' (93) and so as obligated to resist change which they feel might threaten efficiency. The illusion that they might view any change towards participation favourably is dispelled most visibly by their reaction to the 1976 reform of formal parity on the board for the workers' side, including union-nominated representatives; to them the new Act was an affront. They challenged it as an excuse to give the unions new powers of patronage, and reviled it in terms which find many echoes among British management reactions to the Bullock Report around the same time. It would bring delay and bargaining onto the board, it gave over-parity when considered along with new Works Council powers after 1972, threatened to make unions so powerful as to undermine free pluralistic society, endangered shareholders' interests, and most heinously it grossly infringed property rights (94). This last point was used as the basis for an appeal to the Karlsruhe Court in January 1977, with the accompanying claim that freedom to do business, also guaranteed in the Constitution, would be destroyed. In March 1979, the Court ruled the 1976 Act did not infringe constitutional rights, though further extension (still the unions' aim) would. Meantime in protest the DGB had withdrawn from the 'concerted action' meetings with the employers on economic and wages policy, and relations had cooled (in public at least) quite dramatically.

If the existence of worker directors and the 'responsible' attitudes of German unions seem hardly to have altered the attitudes and public fears of German employers on the extension of boardroom participation, then this is consistent with their approval of participation almost exclusively in terms of its contribution to profits. Management seems largely satisfied with the working of the works councils, but for the negative reason that it keeps worker organisations from 'interfering' and provides a channel for safely regulated concessions, or positively because the works council can be integrated into the management system, administering welfare services, selecting workers for redundancy, and supervising working conditions (95). As with co-determination, employers oppose any extension of works council powers for fear it would disturb the correct 'balance' (96).

The West German trade unions, meanwhile, follow very closely the rhetoric of democratic rights in the enterprise for which Jack Jones (ex-General Secretary of the T&GWU and member of the Bullock Committee) was the prototypical spokesman in Britain. Certainly the voice of more radical opposition to the political system and social structure is muted in Germany, but the DGB's spokesmen remain distinct from management in their stated goals. Thus Otto Brenner, whilst head of IG Metall, averred:

> .....political democracy by itself is not enough to overcome the absence of freedom and the relationship of dependence that exist at the workplace (97).

Others, such as Karl Hauenschild of IG Chemie, offer a moderated version of the same argument, and warn that if the concessions to democracy are not made, extremists will gain the ears of workers (98). The union line may legitimate capital extensively, it will be seen, yet still run counter to the essential goals and beliefs of management, however much 'moderation' and pragmatism may strive to achieve a working reconciliation. Thus it was that the DGB's line on the 1976 Co-determination Act led to confrontation with the employers. The DGB argued that co-determination had broken down authoritarian attitudes and improved awareness of employee opinions and interests on the board, but that whilst it remained hampered by the inequality of boardroom representation favouring shareholders democracy was obstructed. They felt the 1976 legislation fell seriously short of giving true parity by making provision for one of the 'worker' representatives to be a senior executive, and by giving the chairmanship and casting vote to the shareholders' side.

These conflicts manifest themselves in predictable forms in other areas of the participation debate. The unions have sought a collective wage-earners' fund for capital sharing (99), which companies have rejected, preferring to offer enterprise-based profit-sharing (100) which they hope would strengthen the workers' financial and loyalty ties with the firm. The unions see these as objectionable, seeking to delude workers, increase their risks, and undermine independent opposition. The dispute is reproduced on 'work humanisation'. German employers have shown little interest in this until fairly recent times (101), and where they have the unions feel it has been a diversionary tactic, hampering the development of bargaining which they feel to be the most effective way of improving labour conditions (102). The challenge to the autocratic control exerted by management over worker at the job level in West

German factories (103) remains feeble - rendering
the employers' public concern for 'individual
rights' in the factory (104) (an international
ideology for resisting labour collectivism) all the
more ironic.
     It should be noted that although German works
councils tend to be dominated by unionists, the
unions have no right to a presence on the councils
or in the plant. None the less, the unions
apparently have a reasonable regard for the councils
(105), in contrast to most European countries. This
may indicate a degree of incorporation of the German
unions which does indeed mark them apart from other
labour movements (106). However, the growing
tension which forced the unions and their employers
to take more note of the rank and file from the end
of the 1960s has led to a development of shop
steward-type representation (107), and may in the
long run force the unions to adopt a more militant
line to change works councils or augment them with
plant-level bargaining. Time will tell.
     Perhaps the story is different for Sweden with
its history of welfare socialism and its far more
powerful and officially legitimated labour
movement? As Nycander put it at a conference on
Swedish experiments with work organisation:

> The representatives of the Swedish trade unions
> and the Swedish employers will unconsciously
> give you the impression that progress in Swedish
> industrial relations is attained through
> agreements, and that agreements are made because
> people in Sweden are sensible and look to their
> common interest (108).

But this is a public image. It ignores the near-
vacuum outside the few famous studies. It gives no
clue to:

> ...the pressure that has been brought to bear on
> employers, centrally and locally, to attain even
> very moderate reforms (109).

It emerges from a closer look at attitudes to
existing schemes and proposed innovations that
Swedish unions and employers remain divided in their
essential conceptions of participation. On works
councils, for instance, while unions criticised
powerlessness and employer failure to give adequate
information or to take the councils seriously, the
employers themselves bemoaned the lack of worker

interest and the councils' failure to communicate information and management views to the workforce (110).

The unrest of 1969 provoked contrasting reactions from unions and employers. The LO, seeking to increase their relevance to the rank and file, felt compelled to demand a far more equal role for workers in decision-making if co-operation with employers was to continue. Experiments were to be tried which would 'toll the deathknell of the employers' sole right to manage' (111). Job satisfaction should take precedence over technology and organisation - a particularly meaningful conflict with employer conceptions of the purpose of work reorganisation (112). Above all, the task was to remove the shackles of Article 32, and pressure on the Social Democrats to this end led to the 1977 Co-determination At Work Act. A number of other legislative changes were sought and won by the unions in the 1970s in Sweden, including the right to two representatives (effectively observers) on the board, and a law on health and safety at work. These incurred varying degrees of employer displeasure, though the Meidner proposals adopted by the LO on capital sharing probably mark the sharpest ideological divergence. The attitude of LO has not become outrightly hostile to capital in any sense, but none the less one business journalist reports being told by a union official in the early 1970s 'we are going to be saying 'No' to any more of this "co-operation waltz"' (113), and this seems to be evocative of a general change in tone.

Employers, meantime, opposed the introduction of worker directors, and the 1977 Co-determination At Work Act which explicitly sought to dismantle the absolutism of the prerogatives from Article 32. They feared trade union education of worker directors as offering the 'wrong economics' and so threatening boardroom rationality. The SAF reacted so adversely to the LO proposals for capital-sharing that they threw themselves actively into the 1976 election campaign, helping to topple the Social Democrats. Their alternative to 10-20% of profits going into a Meidner-inspired union-administered fund was to propose 1% profit-sharing, which some companies introduced to try and forestall the LO's plans, arguing for the role of company-based schemes as superior at reducing conflict (114). Equally revealing are the work reorganisation proposals that have received such uncritical acclaim in Britain. Martin shows (115) that these have been essentially a management initiative, to try and resolve the discontent of the worker without ceding any power, and so to head off the union proposals for legislation. Unions have co-operated in some of them, but saw them optimistically as an adjunct to power-sharing (116). Eventually, as we shall see, this contradiction could not be held in check.

The Dutch experience introduces a divided union movement but little change in the now familiar pattern of attitudes and reactions on participation. The employers in the Netherlands have encouraged consultation and communication rather than the growth of the union's presence in the firm (117). In 1975 they argued against increasing works council co-decision rights (118) seeing it as a purely advisory body. Management should make all major business decisions unfettered. They have responded to union proposals for a collective fund derived from profits by saying it will harm Dutch industry when investors compare it with other countries, and will increase union power in the firm (119). They oppose any move beyond the 1973 law which provides for a shareholder-elected board to co-opt members, including possibly workers, in consultation with the works council. There is widespread rejection of any worker or union presence as of right on the board, let alone the parity system, and this is stated as a fear that left-wing unionists will create conflict and make the board unable to act in the interests of the company 'as a whole' (120).

The main employer 'concession' to worker democracy has been to initiate, with the co-operation of a group of management-oriented social scientists, a series of work reorganisation experiments. These were inspired at first by absenteeism and tight labour markets in the 1960s (121), but have been augmented by government support. The unions have remained hostile, thanks to the determination of management to ensure the experiments serve their purposes. Such experiments fail to acknowledge (but run foul of) conflicts over the wage-effort bargain, responsibility, job displacement and so on; they also fail to seek to change power relations, because of management refusals to countenance this (122).

Among the unions there has been a growing acceptance of the confrontation model, and one federation (the NVV) has called for workers' control in a planned economy as a long-term objective (123). Both this federation and the Catholic NKV

283

declared the law on boardroom representation far too weak (124). Though opposing parity on the grounds that they refused to join with management in accepting responsibility. In the late 1970s, the newly merged federation, the FNV, strongly attacked the existing system (125). Similarly the unions criticised works councils as ineffectual, and argued for them to become employee-only bodies with rights of co-determination on social policy and control of economic and financial policy (126). The common grounds with management seem small and growing smaller - hardly in line with the conventional wisdom on the evolution of participation.

Of the three non-European countries referred to in the previous section, two are easily dealt with. For Australia the illusion of consensus, and the fact of competing objectives, is clearly established in the literature, while the underlying preferences of the two sides match closely with those discussed above (127). For the United States commentary is more dominated by managerial writings which ignore such matters, but the attachment to participation experiments for strictly profit-oriented and authority-reinforcing goals is clear in management initiatives. The emphasis is on success as raising productivity and less openly on keeping out or weakening trade unionism (128). The counterpart of this has been union suspicion or indifference, with a continuing preference in all but exceptional cases for collective bargaining (129).

Documentation is weak on the Japanese case, but it does suggest a surprisingly similar picture from the few dispassionate accounts available. The determination by management to countenance only what will enhance their already powerful dominance is clearest. There is utter rejection of worker director proposals, and acceptance of joint consultation only as a sounding-board (130). Unions have been inclined to stress rights of workers, and the need for more effective ways to advance or defend these, though they have been ambivalent and split over the desirability of boardroom representatives for much the same reasons as British unions (131). There seems to be less hostility to the relatively new development of consultation from the unions, perhaps helped by the role of some such committees in the semi-official extension of bargaining (132). Unquestionably the ideological and coercive power of management and relative weakness of enterprise unions in Japan have entailed different attitudes to those observed elsewhere, but in degree rather than type.

THE STATE

The role of the State in the cyclical account is as the encourager and enabler of policies suitable to the maintenance of social order. That social order being a capitalist one, the interests served are ultimately those of the reproduction and accumulation of capital, and governments will be constrained to these ends, willingly or not, by the exigencies of their own survival and success. This leads to the expectation that the State will also tend to show an interest in participation when employer interest is aroused, and to do so largely from a managerial perspective, emphasising the potential field for co-operation and harmony rather than the genuine shifting of the distribution of power in the enterprise.

The State's view of worker participation may none the less be expected to diverge from that held by employers. To some extent this follows from the liberal-democratic system, which while it may readily be seen as an arrangement for the integration of the working class and the generation of consensus (133), also creates contradictory pressures to concede legitimacy to certain labour demands. Such pressures are undoubtedly greater for parties with Social Democratic pretensions, even if they are also able sometimes to extract more ready compliance from unions for capital-nourishing policies. More generally, though, the appearance of industrial relations requirements from the viewpoint of the State will be less concerned with local, detailed erosions of managerial prerogatives, and more concerned with preserving the overall conditions of accumulation. This is directly analogous to the different views of concessions to shop floor power at different levels of management, where managers lower down the hierarchy may experience a real loss of authority which is of little concern to their superiors (134). The State may be expected to encourage a uniform application of what is seen as 'best practice', in the interests of the legitimacy of the whole system, when many employers considering their own position may not accept the need for such changes (e.g. recognition of trade unions). It will also tend to stress the logic of integrative solutions which can be achieved with the aid of its intervention, and this employers may dislike if they feel it fetters their freedom of action. Of course, employers will probably be far more favourably inclined towards intervention by the State to control unions, just as unions will tend to approve of the imposition of obligations on the employer.

Because of the parochial business interests which the State may tread on when defending the general supremacy and prosperity of capital, and the pathological fear of legislative ties in particular, the State will not always have the consent of business. Apparent concessions to labour can infuriate employers and may represent at least symbolic tokens of the substance of the challenge from below. The reactions of employers to the Bullock Report in Britain, to the Co-determination Act of 1976 in West Germany, or to the Co-determination At Work Act of 1977 in Sweden are all vivid examples. It does not follow from this that the State's actions, or participation more generally, necessarily constitute an advance for labour.

The upsurge of State activity on the participation front did indeed follow the pressures identified in earlier sections. It can best be illustrated by summarising the legislative and related actions as I have sought to do in table 7.1. It should be stressed, though, that legislation is only a very rough index; it is obviously far from the only State activity relevant here. Encouragement of employer-union collaboration on participation, or setting up tripartite bodies to co-ordinate action, and widespread exhortation of improved management practice have also been of significance in most countries.

As indicated in table 7.1, the extent of State activity on the industrial relations front, in regulating collective bargaining and participation rights, is impressive across these European countries. A great deal of activity took place in many countries from the early 1970s (indicating a predictable delay in response from the shocks of the late 1960s) through to about 1977. If anything, Britain and Italy stand out by the lack of legislation on participation as such (though in Britain the legislative backing for safety representatives and the disclosure requirements of the Employment Protection Act modify this). Clearly then, whilst responding in differing specific ways (135), these capitalist countries conformed to the

TABLE 7.1: MAJOR LEGISLATION OF PARTICIPATION AND COLLECTIVE BARGAINING SINCE 1968 : SELECTED COUNTRIES *

	U.K.	WEST GERMANY	SWEDEN	FRANCE	ITALY	BELGIUM	NETHERLANDS	NORWAY	DENMARK
1968	Donovan Commission Report			Accords de Grenelle; sections syndicates legally backed; de Gaulle promises participation and profit-sharing				Eckhoff Committee on industrial democracy set up	
1969		Collective Agreement Act		Social security boards to be joint bodies by Ordonnance					
1970			Working Hours Act	Minimum Wage Machinery re-organised	Statute of Labour's Rights		Law on wages		
1971	Industrial Relations Act			Act on Collective Bargaining at Enterprise level		Centre National du travail - agreement on TUs presence in enterprises	Works Council Act; Company Structure Act (2-tier, co-optation of employees possible)		
1972		Works Constitution Act							
1973	Tax Relief to encourage share-option schemes		Boardroom Representation Act	Powers of Health and Safety committee reinforced		Royal decree on works council	Social and Economic Council asked to study works councils	Company Act sets up company assemblies and worker representatives on board	Company Act Amendment (workers on board); (LO proposal for capital sharing fails in Parliament)

TABLE 7.1 *(cont'd)*

Year								
1974	Trade Union and Labour Relations Act (replaces IR Act); Health and Safety at Work Act		Worker's Protection (on health and safety); Employment Security Protection Act Laws on labour conflicts and on workplace representatives	Sudreau Committee set up				Work Environment Act
1975	Employment Protection Act		(Meidner Report – broadly accepted by Social Democrats)	Sudreau recommends worker directors and profit-sharing	Royal decree extended to non-profit making organisations	Council report; proposal for capital growth sharing		
1976	Industrial Common Ownership Act (for worker co-ops) TULRA (Amendment) Act	Codetermination Act	Boardroom Representation Extended					
1977	Report of Bullock Committee on Industrial Democracy		Codetermination At Work Act				Working Environment Act	Committee on Economic Democracy set up
1978	Safety Representatives and Committees regulations in force; White Paper on industrial democracy; Profit-sharing tax concessions		Work Environment Act (replaces Workers' Protection Act)					
1979						Works Council Act		
1980	Profit-sharing – further tax concessions Employment Act				Safety Act			

* The reference to each Act gives only an indicative label or a descriptive note, not its formal title.

same broad pattern. In the United States, the government took a supportive stance and supported a research programme on 'quality of working life', though legislation as such was minor. In Australia the Federal Government rather belatedly set up a 'steering committee' to investigate and encourage the spread of participation (136). In Japan the State has played a major role in regulating industrial relations, passing heavy batches of legislation in the 1940s and further statutes on safety in 1973 and employment insurance in 1975 (137). Pluralist commentators have seen this activity as supportive of labour, but Halliday shows that they were reponses to pressure, and went unenforced until labour's strength became sufficiently threatening (138). Again benevolent encouragement rather than legislation marks this government's policy on managerial versions of participation.

The involvement of the State is promoting participation at this time does, however, have another possible explanation, and one that challenges that put forward here. According to this alternative view, the State has exhibited a qualitatively changed nature in recent times. It has become 'corporatist', playing an increasingly interventionist role in the accumulation of capital, and in the maintenance and regulation of labour power (through control of education, health and welfare). More specifically

> Although corporatism is an ill-defined concept it is clear that it implies a direct intervention by the state in relationships between wage labour and capital; it attempts to reduce the intensity of class struggle by the incorporation of subordinated classes (139).

It is agreed in quite divergent accounts on corporatism that one logical aspect of this is State encouragement of integrative participation schemes - by Crouch (140), for example, as by Panitch:

> Capitalist interest in workers' participation at the workplace level in the post-war period is in fact closely associated with the emergence within liberal democracy of neo-corporatist structures at the national level (141).

The debate on corporatism is relevant in this context, however, I shall observe only that it reexpresses debates between marxism and liberal-evolutionary accounts rather than concluding them. I have made my own views on the State clear elsewhere (142), and these pursue the argument that corporatism is simply an adaptive form of the capitalist State, not a displacement of it. This view is fully developed by Panitch (143), and I shall not pursue it far here myself. One point must be emphasised, though. On this account, corporatism, participation initiatives included, is not a permanent phenomenon. It is an attempt to cope with crisis, and one riddled with weaknesses and contradictions. Its problems will lead it to wax and wane, with changing circumstances and its own mottled success. This vulnerability is confirmed by Panitch (144), but also acknowledged by Crouch, a theorist more attached to the 'new system' view point. From a study of Britain, France, Italy, West Germany, Belgium and the Netherlands, Crouch concludes:

> ... the recent period has not been one of unambiguous increase in corporatism, but one in which governments have sought to initiate corporatist devices in a hostile environment ... the essential requirement of corporatism – sufficient ideological consensus to conceal the conflicts inherent in the class relationship – is lacking.
> ... Governments have been drawn towards corporatist policies, not as a result of grand design, or a carefully constructed plan for a new conservatism. Rather they have been driven to them in crises, *faute de mieux*, as they have sought to reinstitutionalise conflict following the breakdown of the late 1960s (145).

Moreover, Crouch finds that corporatism is by no means a successful adaptation. It prospers only when the conditions for integration are relatively ripe - as in West Germany, with a successful economy - and so the reasons for turning to it tend to be less urgent. More significantly still, the strategy was observed to recede as recession and unemployment spread in the late 1970s.

THE PRACTICE OF PARTICIPATION

In many cases the legislation and encouragement of the State give the appearance of ceding real portions of power to labour. In practice, though, it is hard to discover any major advances achieved by employees through participation, whether granted by the employer (as in Britain), negotiated between unions and employers (as in Sweden or Norway up to the 1970s), or enacted by the State (as in West Germany, and most of Europe in recent years).

First, the nature of the participation which has been granted is essentially unitaristic, presenting the enterprise as a sphere of fundamentally common interests in a way stressing above all the profit and efficiency preoccupations of capital. The bias of West German company law to such a conception is particularly strong (146), but the implicit leanings towards capital in the denial of proper legitimacy to labour's opposed interests is pervasive (147). The 'enterprise's' interests are almost invariably equated by the legal system with management's, for a strike is readily judged contrary to them while it is highly improbable that a refusal to concede labour's demands by management would be so regarded.

The 1972 Works Constitution Act in West Germany thus states (section 2) that 'the employer and the works council shall work together in the best interests of the employees and the works, and shall do so ... in a spirit of mutual trust'. In their judgement on the 1976 Co-determination Act the Karlsruhe judges commented that a certain loss of entrepreneurial freedom:

> ... is the price for supplementing the business mandate of the management of a large enterprise with a social mandate – a price for the co-operation and integration of all who work in the enterprise whose contribution of capital and labour is indispensable to its existence and efficiency (148).

In this manner the State's intent is reinforced and the employer's interests protected by the interpretations of the judiciary. The designated role of, for intance, works councils does not seem to be more conflict-oriented just because the body was set up by employer-union agreement. This seems to be a result partly of union suspicion of such bodies as potential rivals for their negotiating role unless they are official union institutions. Thus where works councils exist by local employer initiatives (as in Britain) or by national agreement (as in the Scandinavian countries) their role remains governed by the unitary conception applied in statutory constitutions also. In Sweden they are 'to maintain continuous collaboration between employer and employees' while in Norway they exist to create 'a feeling of unity' for the worker with the enterprise (149). In Belgium the goal is 'collaboration between the employees and employers', in France to 'promote co-operation' (150), and in the Netherlands to ensure the 'proper performance' of the undertaking (151). In the United States schemes are managerial initiatives, face union suspicion, and seek to 'catch flies with honey' (152). The Australian government's proposals remain emphatically consensus - oriented and powerless (153). And the Japanese experiments are emphatically not about reducing managerial control (154).

The aim of these models of participation is thus collaboration and integration; if democracy is agreed to entail increased worker power and the advance of labour's interests as against those of capital, then they are anti-democratic in intent. For some radical commentators in each country this is their main consequence. But if participation worked so well, it is hard to see why management would ever give it up.

The evidence on the operation of participation is presented by researchers who, for the most part, embrace an optimistic, evolutionary outlook on participation. None the less, although there is a dearth of good case study material and a consequent tendency to offer sweeping generalisations for all firms in a country, the available research points in other directions. No less a body than the OECD reported that:

> No matter how works councils have been conceived ... in Western European industry they have been a failure ... in most countries workers' reactions to the councils are overwhelmingly negative (155).

They explain the failure as due to 'the complete lack of decision-making power'.

The overwhelming impression is that works councils result in triviality, with petty matters or vague, powerless discussion dominating the business, each side expressing dissatisfaction with its operation. But this fails to resolve the problem common to many of these countries - namely the unrest exacerbated by the inadequacy of representation at enterprise level. Thus where the challenge is sustained, the existence of participation machinery is unlikely to prevent the emergence of a union (official or otherwise) presence in the plant. In the face of trivial results, neither side is likely to show any great attachment to the participative body, particularly if circumstances alter. Indeed, many emloyers, particularly in smaller companies, will ignore the requirements to set up a works council if they themselves feel no direct pressure to do so (156). The experience of the Scandinavian countries (157) is of triviality amidst extensive union membership, and their failure was probably a significant factor in the passing of Work Environment Acts in each country, extending areas of joint regulation on health and safety and other matters in a more negotiative framework. The Dutch and Belgian experience seems similarly dominated by triviality.

The West German case is one which arguably shows the need for caution in generalisation. Works councils are variously labelled devices for successful incorporation, trivial outcrops of a powerless labour movement, and *de facto* bargaining channels - all these on top of those accounts which see only glowing success. It seems plausible to suggest that there may be some foundation, in different contexts within German industrial relations, for different types of outcome. The problem is to assess the most important patterns. My own impression is that in those areas where rank and file militancy and union organisation is greatest, the works councils are most likely to shift over to being a surrogate negotiating body (158). In other circumstances,this adaption may meet resistance, and councils will become unstable, occasionally erupting with conflict they are ill-designed to contain, so becoming 'barometers of stability' (159).

In France too, there is evidence of instability, far more marked due to the intransigence of each side. Little may come of the *comites d'entreprise*, but their ineffectual nature feeds the illegitimacy of management in employee eyes (160) and may even aggravate matters (161). The French pattern is extreme, but it is none the less of a part with the others we have examined. the LKAB case in Sweden shows a strikingly similar instability (162).

We are told by one observer that with the revival of trade union growth in many countries, the change of works council status into effectively a bargaining body has spread across Europe (163). It should be noted that, if British experience is anything to go by, such a change, particularly if not recognised openly in law or written agreement, is speedily reversible in a time of receding strength and challenge from labour. Japanese councils likewise seem to perform pre-negotiating functions (164), but the same question marks hang over them. It would seem that the best that can be said of such a result of consultation committees is that it may marginally lubricate the bearings of industrial relations; this shift in status to bargaining in no way provides the heralded transformation of their entire substance.

Two other institutions deserve at least some attention in this section: worker directors and job enrichment. On the former, research evidence is thin, even that dealing with the most famous arrangements in West Germany. The general conclusion is that:

> ... the ability of management to manage has not been impaired nor have overall enterprise objectives been changed. A process seems to take place in which workers' representatives' orientations take on a managerialist colouring, and in which their activities become increasingly supportive of management strategies and goals (165).

This may seem to indicate a management victory, but if so then this success is unlikely to have much effect on labour-management relations. By their very defeat, and as part of it, worker directors distance themselves from the shop floor and become largely an irrelevance. A wider-ranging survey of European experience concluded:

> ... first, worker directors have generally had little effect on anything and, second and consequently, they have certainly had no catastrophic effect on anything or anybody (166).

Boardrooms are obviously concerned with major decisions, yet the role of the worker director becomes trivial because of her or his marginal contribution to the board, and minor impact on employee experience of the enterprise authority structure. As in the case of works councils, legislation in each country imposes a unitary conception of the board as a body serving the common interests of all in the enterprise, i.e. it echoes and reinforces management ideology on the subject.

Job reorganisation has already been noted as an employer proposition which leaves power structures untouched. If, however, it were a massive success, either in orthodox terms as a mutual enhancement of satisfaction for employees and productivity for management, or in more partial terms as a protection and extension of management's power, then the motivation to maintain and expand its operation would be considerable. A few examples show the reality to be otherwise, though.

In the Dutch experiments, the involvement of social scientists appears to have been part of a 'game' in which these individuals legitimised management (167) and the unions remained justifiably distanced and hostile. Little real power was ceded to workers who were often excluded even from the process of designing the experiments, and when groups demanded wider participation than just the organisation of their own tasks management sometimes curtailed the experiment altogether (168).

In the Swedish case, Nycander comments on the unreported resistance or indifference to change from many employers. He describes, too the adherence of employers to piecework, although this patently obstructs flexible work organisation, and the limitation of any experiments to strong unionised, troublesome locations and so, for example, to male not female labour (169). The Kalmar plant at Volvo, can be readily seen as a job control system revolving around computer progress monitoring and removing the informal job controls often exercised by work groups in manufacturing industry, rather than a major transformation of workplace democracy. This sort of reinterpretation may explain the complaints of American car workers brought across to Saab-Scania's plant at Sodertalje that while the conditions of work were better, the work became just as boring in the long run and the pressure of pace was higher (170). Similarly critical analysis of the reported findings in Norwegian experiments in work group autonomy confirm the need for scepticism (171).

In Britain, too, it is possible to find enthusiastic accounts of job enrichment, most notably at ICI (172). Yet a cooler appraisal of the evidence uncovers union scepticism concerning the salience of the changes (173), and no hard evidence of 'success' (in productivity terms) outside

white-collar areas where changes could be imposed
unilaterally as new working practices (174).
Moreover, the much vaunted 'Nylon Spinners'
experiment at Gloucester is conceded by its
researchers to have been severely constrained by
technological limits, resulting in 'the reduction of
boredom rather than any major increase in the
intrinsic interest in the job' (175).

Japanese efforts to establish 'quality control
circles' and other forms of work-level participation
should also be clearly recognised as pseudo-
democratic devices. Cole reports that studies of
schemes lead:

> ... many Japanese scholars to see QC circles as
> a device to break collective worker resistance
> and rebuild group solidarity on the basis of
> management goals (176).

He reports that public sector unions have
consequently blocked government efforts to apply
such techniques there (177). The reality may be
better described by Kamata's description of a 'car
factory of despair' (178). Reports on the Japanese
system imply that the techniques are reinforced by
paternalistic social and factory cultures and may
serve management better than in other countries, but
how far this relies on the dependent position of the
worker in lifetime employment, which may not survive
a deep recession, remains to be seen.

In the United States too, there is a
preponderance of celebration of job enrichment.
Again, though, the studies are suspect, and in
practice there is little to support either the claim
of a consistent positive effect on productivity and
labour relations, or the supposition of management
commitment to democracy at work (179).

WHICH WAY IN THE 1980S?

In the light of the findings so far, it remains to
inquire into the fate of the wave of interest in
participation. Comments here must be tentative,
based as they are on inevitably patchy information
about recent years. The question for the cycles
analysis must be: is the interest in participation
being sustained or is it declining once more?

In Britain a decline in the fervour about
participation is only too clear (180). Little
happened in the wake of the divisions in the labour
movement and the unanimous opposition of employers

which followed the publication of the Bullock Report. The victory of the Conservative Party in the 1979 elections removed all but occasional lip-service by the government. To business interests, the question had been 'swept under the carpet' (181). From 6% unemployment in 1978 the figures had risen past 14% of the working population even on official figures by the end of 1982, and the unions were left little energy to spare from desperate efforts to slow their retreat in the face of management power. Hard-won controls and defences were broken overnight, and employers have been able to exact massive concessions on working practices. If 'participation' retains a role for management, it tends to be in the administration of rundown. The facts of decline can be laid bare to the advantage of capital, so disclosure at least gains in popularity; it is prosperity that it is preferred to conceal, to evade the logic of sharing out its spoils. If factory deconstruction can be slow, 'involvement' can ease the process by offloading some of its contradictions onto those who might resist it; on the other hand, if it is ordained that it should be abrupt, resistance avails little and can usually be ignored.

It is harder to detect the trends in other countries, from where information filters through with a considerable time delay. There are none the less strong indications that interest in participation was in decline in other countries by the late 1970s. The decline in legislative activity after the burst in the early to mid-1970s is one sign of this. A growing dissillusionment with participation by unions and employers, partly occasioned by the outcomes reviewed in the last section above, was observed by at least one writer who had earlier celebrated a new era (182). He detects suspicion and growing rejection of work re-organisation in Sweden, Denmark, the Netherlands, France and elsewhere on the part of the unions, and also notes that very few companies have adopted participative management on any scale as an integral part of their corporate policy, for all the hullabaloo. The 'second wave of interest' in Co-determination in Germany he also admits to have produced no important results, and comments that interest in boardroom representation in Norway and Sweden is in decline.

Other developments reinforce this impression. In Sweden, the dissillusionment of the unions with job reorganisation experiments led to the disbanding of the joint management-union body monitoring the system (183). Moreover, the SAF also preferred those experiments over which they retained control to those involving independent researchers, nominally because the academics used 'outlandish' terminology (184) (but almost certainly more to do with functionality of design for productivity). In Norway, too, the rise in interest in work reorganisation experiments has reached a 'stagnation phase' without ever advancing the wider industrial democratic cause as it had been expected to (185). In the Netherlands the variability of company commitment to the grand principles which supposedly reform job enrichment was illustrated during the 1960s by the loss of interest during a recession period exhibited by Philips (186), and this fragility is reinforced by the increasingly hostile trade union view as the 1970s proceeded. In France one writer found, in 1974, an interest in work reform following a strike of bank employees, yet observed that by the late 1970s the issue had vanished from the agenda (187). The victory of the socialists in 1981 may reverse this trend somewhat, but this remains to be seen. In West Germany, works councils and traditional union compromise have been unable to cope with capital's strategies of rundown. As this provoked strikes and some factory occupations in the late 1970s, (188) the old system has come under severe strain with the new circumstances.

Meanwhile, three years after the passage of the Swedish Co-determination at Work Act not one basic agreement had been signed in the private sector (189), while the 1976 extension of worker director proposals was rendered ineffectual by the new non-socialist government's refusal to appoint new representatives (190). In the United States, the onset of the recession has revitalised the tradition of 'union-busting', and also produced the conditions for loss of management interest in participation (191). The story for the latter part of the 1970s is now familiar:

> ... if job enrichment and other new forms of work organization flowered in the expectation of 'chronically tight labour markets', these initiatives quickly wilted once the pressure was off (192).

In countries where the recession bites more slowly (such as Japan, and to some extent Australia where the labour movement has maintained its offensive on a 35-hour week), and perhaps where an electorate puts a government with vocal socialist commitments into office, the inclination of employers towards participative strategies may be more sustained than in Britain or the United States. The continuing susceptibility of interest in participation to changing circumstances none the less demonstrates convincingly the explanatory power of a cycles analysis, especially when compared with evolutionist alternatives.

CONCLUSIONS

The chief findings of the foregoing analysis may be summarised as follows:
1. In each case examined, participation coincides with a rise in the power and militancy of labour.
2. In most cases, it is a management and/or government initiative in response to this challenge, and seeks to contain it by some combination of concession and control.
3. In consequence, participation schemes remain ineffectual as means to advance industrial democracy. They tend to be dominated by unitary conceptions of their purpose which inevitably favour management's definition of the situation.
4. The demands of labour, and the reactions of unions to the participation schemes or proposals which emerge, conflict with those of management and (except where a social democratic party makes major concessions to labour) of the government, seeing them as either inadequate for or even threatening to industrial democracy.
5. A combination of this opposition, and the inability of participation to cope without becoming a negotiating channel entails widespread triviality and in some cases instability where this negotiation is not ceded. Thus participation fails to transform labour-management relations.
6. Where information was available, there were signs that the wave of interest in participation was receding with the changing circumstances attenuating the challenge of labour from the late 1970s in many countries.
These conclusions are inherently subversive of the evolutionary assumptions prevalent in the participation literature. Those who, like Daniel in his review of European experience, believe that 'the

tide appears irresistible' (193), should remember that tides are anything but irreversible. Participation would have to live up to its own mythology to maintain management interest when labour is in retreat and the need to be seen to compromise even symbolic prerogatives is past. This is the downfall of Sorge's analysis of evolution towards industrial democracy, along with the functionalist concern with integration which, despite his disclaimer, directs his approach (194).

Another 'new era' account, rather more carefully formulated, none the less faces some of the same problems. Brannen (195) argues that capital suffers new and permanent challenges due to the rise of the new working class and the degree of control these employees can exert in modern technology. The same displacement of scientific management and Fordism by new managerial controls based around job enrichment is also proposed by a number of marxist writers (196). Their fear is the apparent hope of their liberal counterparts - that the new methods may contain and incorporate labour. But it is tentatively suggested that it would make more sense, given the evidence reviewed here to view any reliance on participation as a transitional, not permanent, feature of the introduction of new technology.

Capitalist societies retain distinctive social and cultural patterns, and there is no convincing reason to believe that they will converge on uniformity. As such they have not been identical in the form, timing and outcome of the initiation of participation schemes. Differences have been indicated in the course of this chapter, though not examined closely or accounted for since this was not our purpose. The common pressures and features of capitalism in the 'advanced' world (197) have demonstrably produced a degree of similarity in reactions of greater significance than national peculiarities and their patterns for an understanding of the phenomenon of participation. In the process, evolutionary accounts of all hues have been found wanting. The outlook for participation in the 1980s may, then, be rather disappointing for some.

NOTES

1.   See H. Ramsay, 'Evolution or cycle?', in C. Crouch (ed.), First International Yearbook of Organisational Democracy, (Wiley, London, 1982);

also see the original article, H. Ramsay, 'Cycles of Control: worker participation in sociological and historical perspective', Sociology, vol. 11, no. 3 (1977) and in P. Boreham and G. Dow (eds.) Work and Inequality Vol. 2. (Macmillan, Melbourne, 1980).

2. Sir Frederick Catherwood 'Shop Floor Power', Bray Memorial Lecture, 16 March, 1976, reproduced in Production Engineer, June, 1978, p. 300.

3. A. Flanders, Collective Bargaining: Prescription for Change (Faber, London, 1967).

4. See H. Ramsay, 'Phantom participation: patterns of power and conflict'. Industrial Relations Journal 11(3), July/August, 1980.

5. H. Ramsay, 1980 'Cycles of Control'; and particularly in Ramsay, Participation For Whom? A Critical Study of Participation in Theory and Practice, Ph.D. Thesis, University of Durham, 1981: chs. 11, 14-16.

6. See J.E. Cronin, Industrial Conflict In Modern Britain, (Croom Helm, London, 1979). Cronin's cycles of strike conflict conform well and potentially add depth to the analysis of challenges to management offered here. See also his 'Stages, Cycles and Insurgencies: The Economics of Unrest in T.K. Hopkins and I. Wallerstein (eds.), Processes of the World System, (Sage, London, 1980).

7. See in particular Philip Corrigan, H. Ramsay, D. Sayer, Socialist Construction and Marxist Theory, (Macmillan, London, 1978); 'The State as a relation of production' in Philip Corrigan (ed.) Capitalism, State Formation and Marxist Theory, (Quartet, London, 1980).

8. The irony here is that M. Poole, who employs what amounts to a base/superstructure model in his Workers' Participation in Industry, (Routledge and Kegan Paul, London, 1975), has recently been critical of such causal models, and has emphasised the independent role of culture. In doing so, unfortunately, he merely inverts the causality of base/superstructure without going beyond its mechanical separations. Among a number of articles, see particularly M. Poole, 'Industrial democracy in comparative perspective' in R. Mansfield and M. Poole (eds.) International Perspectives on Management and Organisation, (Gower Press, London, 1981).

9. H. Ramsay, 'Evolution or Cycle' in C. Crouch (ed.), First International Yearbook of Organisational Democracy.

10. W.W. Daniel, 'Industrial democracy', in

D. Torrington (ed.) <u>Comparative Industrial Relations In Europe</u>, (Associated Business Programmes, London, 1978), p. 49.
   11. *Ibid.*
   12. It is, however, quite wrong to say Britain has *no* legislation. Nationalised industries and services had an obligation to consult placed on them in the statutes setting them up, mostly in the 1940s. Legislation for worker representatives and committees on health and safety has also been in effect since 1978.
   13. <u>European Industrial Relations</u> by the Industrial Democracy Europe International Research Team, (Oxford University Press, 1980) pp. 7-8; see also <u>Industrial Democracy in Europe</u>, (Oxford University Press, 1980) by the same authors.
   14. The Industrial Democracy Europe International Research Team, <u>European Industrial Relations</u>, p. 8.
   15. The Industrial Democracy Europe International Research Team, <u>Industrial Democracy in Europe</u>, p. 323: 'The time dimension, unfortunately, is still not well covered in our study'.
   16. See The Industrial Democracy Europe International Research Team, <u>Industrial Democracy in Europe</u>, p. 339. The method they use is to treat formal rights and institutions as the equivalent of actual power distribution - and to treat perceptions of power distribution likewise. Such a methodology, buried though it is beneath the conceptual apparatus and presentation of a 'systems'-type analysis, can hardly be regarded as convincing. Indeed numerous criticisms of such 'systems'-oriented approaches have demonstrated their inherent bias towards the *status quo* - for a succinct rendering, see R. Hyman and R. Fryer, 'Trade Unions - sociology and political economy' in J.B. McKinlay (ed.), <u>Processing People: Cases In Organisation Behaviour</u>, (Holt, Reinhart and Winston, London, 1975).
   17. Cronin, 'Stages, Cycles and Insurgencies'. Cronin's analysis seems to lean somewhat heavily on an implicit 'base/superstructure model (economic base moves, superstructure including protest follows) which is restrictively mechanical and insensitive, but remains highly thought-provoking in relation to the topic under discussion here.
   18. A. Sorge, 'The Evolution of Industrial Democracy in the Countries of the European Community', <u>British Journal of Industrial Relations</u>, vol. 14, no. 3 (1976).

19. *Ibid.*, p. 282.
20. B.C. Roberts   'Introduction'   to
B.C. Roberts (ed.), Towards Industrial Democracy
(Croom Helm, London, 1979), p. 19. The analysis is
strikingly mechanically determinist, ironically.
21. In particular, Sorge, 'The Evolution of
Industrial Democracy in the countries of the
European Community'; Poole, Workers Participation in
Industry.
22. This evolutionary fixation is evident in
Sorge 'The Evolution of Industrial Democracy in the
Countries of the European Community', the IDE
studies discussed earlier and in an article
associated with Poole's work, P. Blyton 'Cross-
national currents in joint consultation', in R.
Mansfield and M. Poole International Perspectives on
Management and Organisation and indeed in almost
every international survey in print in some degree
or another.
23. The observations in T. Nichols and
H. Beynon, of 'Chemco' in Living With Capitalism
(Routledge and Kegan Paul, London, 1977) are
particularly evocative, though perhaps describing a
rather more acquiescent workforce than found in
other contexts.
24. Report of the Royal Commission on Trade
Unions and Employers' Associations, 1965-1968,
(Donovan Commission), (HMSO, London, 1968).
25. R. Clarke *et. al.*, Workers' Participation
in Management in Britain (Heineman, London, 1972);
A. Marsh *et. al.*, Workplace Industrial Relations in
Engineering (Kogan Page, London, 1971). The former
showed a steep gradient in incidence of committees
by size of firm - 12% of those with under 199
employees up to 62% of those with 2000+.
26. Marsh and Coker's survey taken in 1961,
'Shop Steward Organisation in the Engineering
Industry', British Journal of Industrial Relations.
27. For information on this period of sit-ins
and work-ins see North East Trade Union Studies
Information Unit, Workers' Occupations and the North
East Experience, 1976 (Written by A.J. Mills); and
K. Coates, Work-Ins, Sit-Ins and Industrial
Democracy, (Spokesman, Nottingham, 1981).
28. I.B. Knight, Company Organisation and
Worker Participation (HMSO, London 1979), A recent
(1980) Scottish study found 67% of companies there
with such committees - see P. Cressey *et. al.*,
'Participation Prospects'.
29. P. Dubois, 'New Forms of Industrial
Conflict' in C. Crouch and A. Pizzorno (eds.), The

Resurgence of Class Conflict in Western Europe Since 1968: Vol. II Comparative Analyses (Macmillan, London, 1978).

30. See M. Poole, Workers' Participation In Industry (Routledge and Kegan Paul, London, 1978) for an analysis of German participation experience along these broad lines.

31. See e.g. D. Miller 'Trade Union Workplace Representation in the Federal Republic of Germany: an analysis of the post-war Vertrauensleute policy of the German Metal-workers union, 1952-77', British Journal of Industrial Relations, vol. 16, no. 3 (1978), pp. 335-354; also see the account in W. Muller-Jentsch and H.J. Sperling, 'Economic Development, Labour Conflicts and the Industrial Relations System in West Germany' in C. Crouch and A. Pizzorno (eds.), The Resurgence of Class Conflict in Western Europe: vol. 2: National Studies (Macmillan, London, 1978).

32. On the failure of works councils see R.B. Peterson, 'The Swedish experience of Industrial Democracy', British Journal of Industrial Relations, vol. 1, no. 2 (1968). The quotation is from the revised works councils agreement of 1966, quoted in C. Asplund, Some Aspects of Worker Participation (International Confederation of Free Trade Unions, Geneva, 1972), p. 16.

33. See the account in W. Korpi, 'Workplace Bargaining, the Law and Unofficial Strikes: the Case of Sweden', British Journal of Industrial Relations, vol. 16, no. 3 (1978).

34. See C. van Otter, 'Sweden: Labour Reformism Reshapes the System' in S. Barkin (ed.), Worker Militancy and Its Consequences 1965-76 (Praeger, London, 1975).

35. Ibid.; L. Hufford, Sweden: The Myth of Socialism (Fabian Society, London, 1973); K.O. Faxen 'Wage Policy and Attitudes of Industrial Relations parties in Sweden, Labour and Society, vol. 2, no. 1 (1977).

36. D. Marsden, Industrial Democracy and Industrial Control in West Germany, France and Great Britain (Research Paper no. 4, Department of Employment, 1978).

37. J.D. Reynaud, 'France' in Roberts (ed.), Industrial Democracy.

38. The Industrial Democracy Europe International Research Team, European Industrial Relations, pp. 151-2. See also Commission on Industrial Relations, Worker Participation and Collective Bargaining in Europe (HMSO, London,

1974), ch. 6; W. Albeda 'The Netherlands' in Roberts (ed.), Industrial Democracy.

39.   On the new disorder see T. Akkermans and P. Grootings, 'From Corporatism to Polarisation: Elements in the Development of Dutch Industrial Relations' in Crouch and Pizzorno, Class-Conflict vol. I; B. Peper, 'The Netherlands: from an Ordered Harmonic to a Bargaining Relationship', in Barkin (ed.) Worker Militancy.

40.   Albeda, 'The Netherlands', p. 126.

41.   J.L.J.H. van der Does de Gillebois, 'On the Quality of Working Life: some recent developments in industrial relations at company, factory, and shop floor level in the Netherlands, in W. Albeda (ed.), Participation in Management: Industrial Democracy in Three West European Countries (Rotterdam University Press, 1973).

42.   Commission on Industrial Relations, Worker Participation, ch. 7; The Industrial Democracy Europe International Research Team, European Relations, ch. 9.

43.   Commission for the European Communities, Employee Participation and Company Structure, Brussels, GEC, 1975 p. 50; M.H. Janne and F. Spitaels, 'Belgium: Collective Bargaining and Concentration Mold a New System', in Barkin (ed.), Worker Militancy.

44.   Janne and Spitaels, 'Belgium'; M. Molitor, 'Social Conflicts in Belgium', in Crouch and Pizzorno, Class Conflict, vol. 1. Molitor observes that factory occupations were only used rarely before 1967 in Belgium, but thereafter they became a part of systematic union strategy (p. 44).

45.   See I. Regalia et. al., 'Labour Conflicts and Industrial Relations in Italy' in Crouch and Pizzorno (eds.) Class Conflict, vol. I; P.M. Brandini 'Italy: Creating a New Industrial Relations System from the Bottom', in Barkin (ed.), Worker Militancy; T. Treu 'Italy' in Roberts (ed.), Industrial Democracy.

46.   For a description of this body and of the Italian Industrial relations setting in general see Commission on Industrial Relations, Worker Participation, ch. 8; Treau, 'Italy' Industrial Democracy Europe International Research Team; European Industrial Relations, ch. 11.

47.   M. Rollier 'Taylorism and the Italian Unions' in C.L. Cooper and E. Mumford (eds.), The Quality of Working Life in Western and Eastern Europe (Associated Business Press, London, 1979).

48.   Ibid., p. 221; F. Butera, 'Environmental

Factors in Job and Organisation Design: The Case of Olivetti', in L.E. Davis and A.B. Cherns (eds.), The Quality of Working Life: Volume 2: Cases and Commentary (Free Press, New York, 1975).

49. See A.F. Sturmthal, 'Workers participation in Management: a review of the United States experience', IILS Bulletin, 6th June, 1970, p. 181; R. Bendix, Work and Authority in Industry (Harper and Row, New York, 1956), ch. 5. See also R. Edwards, Contested Terrain (Heinemann, London, 1979), pp. 91-97.

50. Sturmthal, 'Workers' Participation', p. 181.

51. Hunnius, 'The Politics of Work Humanisation', pp. 507-508.

52. See M. Derber, The American Idea of Industrial Democracy 1865-1965 (University of Illinois Press, 1970); Sturmthal, 'Workers' Participation'.

53. M. Aglietta, A Theory of Capitalist Regulation (New Left Books, London, 1979), p. 191).

54. Ibid., p. 190 ff.

55. On the beleaguered state of United States unions, and their vulnerability to the employer onslaught, see e.g. R. Taylor 'Hard labour for US unions' Personnel Management, vol. 12, no. 1 (1980); C.Cooper 'Union Power switched into Reverse', Guardian, 22.11.1979. The 'web of rules' is a reference to the arch-pluralist formulations of J.T. Dunlop. Union membership density is below 25% and falling on most estimates.

56. For such a picture see G. Lodge and K. Henderson, 'United States of America' in Roberts (ed.), Towards Industrial Democracy.

57. The United Auto Workers' Union has recently moved towards favouring union representation on boards. The union president sits on Chrysler's board, and though Ford and General Motors reject the notion, American Motors has offered to concede a seat in return for a co-operative spirit and pay concessions by the union. The anti-trust authorities ruled, however, that it would be illegal for the union to be represented in more than one company. See Financial Times, 2nd March, 1981.

58. Berg, et. al., Managers and Work Reform, pp. 229, 255.

59. See S. Marglin 'Catching Flies with Honey: an inquiry into management initiatives to humanise work', and S. Deutsch, 'Capitalism, Crisis, and the Prospects for Worker Participation and Self-

management', both in Economic Analysis and Workers' Management', vol. 8, no. 4 (1979).   As T. Nichols notes 'Management, Ideology and Practice' in G. Esland and G. Salaman (eds.), The Politics of Work and Occupations (Open University, Bletchey, 1980), pp. 289-290, the use of the term 'alienation' seems quite startling in Europe, where Marx's useage remains influential.

    60.   For instance T. Shirai and H. Shimada, 'Japan', in Dunlop and Galenson (eds.), Labor in the Twentieth Century; J. Hanami, Labor Relations in Japan Today (John Martin, New York, 1980).

    61.   For a revealing marxist account of some of the aspects of Japanese labour-capital relations see J. Halliday, A Political History of Japanese Capitalism, (Monthly Review Press, London, 1975).

    62.   T. Shirai and H. Shimada, 'Japan', p. 298; Guardian, 29th May, 1981.   The figures disguise some unrecorded unemployment, particularly of women, as the agricultural sector declines.   Thus the labour force participation ratio had fallen from 71% to 63% between 1955 and 1975.   (Shirai and Shimada, 'Japan', p. 294).

    63.   Shirai and Shimada, 'Japan', pp. 296-298; Hanami, Labour Relations in Japan, p. 32.

    64.   Halliday, Japanese Capitalism, p. 207.

    65.   In 1974 there were 12.5 million unionists in 32,734 enterprise unions (Shirai and Shimada, 'Japan', p. 318).

    66.   See Shirai and Shimada, 'Japan', p. 311.

    67.   Halliday, Japanese Capitalism, shows labour's share fell markedly between 1953 and 1970.

    68.   When compared with 19 other capitalist OECD member states - see S. Creigh et. al., 'Stoppage Activity in OECD Countries', Employment Gazette, vol. 88, no. 11 (1980).

    69.   See Hanami, Labor Relations in Japan.

    70.   Shirai and Shimada,'Japan', p. 261.

    71.   A good example of the false image presented in the Western press appeared recently in the London Times, where a special feature on Toyota referred to the absence of divisions in the workforce (Times, 23rd March, 1981).   Halliday, Japanese Capitalism, p. 226 reports that Toyota, on the contrary, use a very large number of temporary workers, amounting to 52% of the workforce in 1961.   More recently, a book describing work in a Toyota factory called conditions there 'murderous' and described the suffering which the famous productivity record imposes on those regimented to produce it (S Kamata, Car Factory of Despair, as

described in Guardian 13th March, 1981).

72. Harani, Labour Relations in Japan, p. 236.

73. This account, but not the interpretation, is derived from T. Mitsufuji and T. Ishikawa, 'Workers' participation in management in Japan', Bulletin of IILS, no. 7 (1970).

74. Mitsufuji and Ishikawa, 'Workers' Participation', pp. 209-211; H. Okamoto, 'Japan', in Roberts (ed.), Towards Industrial Democracy, p. 197f.

75. Mitsufuji et. al., 'Workers' Participation', p. 213. A figure of 15,005 or 44.3% of unions are reported to have had such committees by the end of 1968 by Okamoto, 'Japan', p. 200.

76. Mitsufuji et. al., 'Workers' Participation', p. 216.

77. Below 7000 by 1950 - see Ibid., p. 201, Okamoto, 'Japan', p. 217.

78. Okamoto, 'Japan', p. 204.

79. Ibid., p. 203. The criteria for saying a committee dealt with bargaining issues, which may be crucial to an evaluation of their efficacy, are questionable since the respondents were 'firms not unions'. Fuller figures are given in Mitsufuji et. al., 'Workers' Participation', p. 240, though on these and other issues discussed here their figures often seem at least partly at odds with those cited by Okamoto.

80. Okamoto, 'Japan', p.206.

81. See H.A. Clegg, Trade Unionism Under Collective Bargaining (Blackwell, London, 1976).

82 M. Derber, 'Crosscurrents in Workers Participation', Industrial Relations, February 1970, p. 129. The quotation is reproduced in, for example, R. Lansbury, 'Industrial Democracy through Participation in Management: the Australian Experience' Industrial Relations Journal, vol. 9, no. 2 (1978), p. 79 and A. Crombie, 'Participative Design: an Educational Approach to Industrial Democracy', mimeo, (undated).

83. The phrase is used in the chronological appendix to R.L. Pritchard (ed.), Industrial Democracy in Australia (C.C.H., Sydney, 1976).

84. See R. Lansbury 'Industrial democracy through participation in management: the Australian experience', Industrial Relations Journal, vol. 9, no. 2, Summer 1978; and in very different vein, J. Collins, 'Work, Technology and Class', Intervention, 1978, no. 10/11.

85. See R. Catley and B. MacFarlane,

Australian Capitalism in Boom and Depression: Options for the 1980s, (APCOL, Sydney, 1981).

86. G. Anderson 'The South Australian initiative', in Pritchard, p. 158f.

87. *Ibid.*, p. 162–163.

88. The congruence between these events and the cyclical model is explicitly confirmed in these terms by P. Boreham in *The Political Economy of Labour: 2, the Labour Process, Management and Control* (University of Queensland, Division of External Studies, 1981), pp. 21–22.

89. See H. Ramsay, *Participation for Whom?*, which contains a more extended discussion.

90. *Ibid.*

91. This term is derived from C.W. Clegg *et. al.* 'Managers' attitudes towards industrial democracy', *Industrial Relations Journal*, vol. 9, no. 3, 1978. See similarly P. Brannen *et. al.*, *The Worker Directors: A Sociology of Participation*, (Hutchinson, London, 1978), ch. 3.

92. Muller-Jentsch and Sperling, *Economic Development*, p. 279.

93. H. Gunter and G. Leminsky, 'The Federal Republic of Germany' in J.T. Dunlop and W. Galenson (eds.), *Labor in the Twentieth Century* (Academic Press, London, 1978), p. 171.

94. See H.W. Hetzler and Schienstock, 'The Federal Republic of Germany' in Roberts (ed.), *Industrial Democracy*, p. 39–40; J. Schregle, 'Codetermination in the Federal Republic of Germany: a comparative view' *International Labour Review* vol. 177, no. 1 (1978), p. 84.

95. F. Furstenburg, *Workers' Participation in Management in the Federal Republic of Germany* (International Institute for Labour Studies, Geneva, 1978), pp. 15–16; Commission on Industrial Relations, *Worker Participation*, pp. 31–32.

96. Furstenburg, M. *Workers' Participation*, p. 31.

97. O. Brenner, 'Federal Republic of Germany', in C. Levinson (ed.) *Industry's Democratic Revolution*, (Allen and Unwin, London, 1974), p. 97.

98. K. Hauenschild, 'Federal Republic of Germany', in Levinson, *Industry's Democratic Revolution*.

99. Hetzler and Schienstock, 'The Federal Republic of Germany'.

100. *Ibid.*

101. Gunter and Leminsky, 'The Federal Republic of Germany', p. 193.

102. *Ibid.*

103. See the accounts of German factories in
G. Walraff The Undesirable Journalist, (Pluto Press,
London, 1977); M. Herzog From Hand to Mouth,
(Penguin, Harmondsworth, 1980).

104. Furstenburg, 1978, Workers Participation
in Management in the Federal Republic of Germany, p.
31.

105. Commission on Industrial Relations,
Worker Participation, p. 32; Gunter and Leminsky,
'The Federal Republic of Germany', p. 194.

106. See H. Schauer 'Critique of
Codetermination' in G. Hunnius et. al. (eds.)
Workers' Control, (Vintage, New York, 1973); T.
Kirkwood and H. Mewes, 'The limits of trade union
power in the capitalist order: the case of West
German labour's quest for codetermination', British
Journal of Industrial Relations, XIV(3), Nov. 1976.

107. See Muller-Jentsch and Sperling, Economic
Development, p. 291f; D. Miller, 'Trade Union
Workplace Representation in the Federal Republic of
Germany'.

108. S. Nycander, 'The importance of the
industrial relations setting in Sweden' in D.
Gregory (ed.) Work Organisation: Swedish Experience
and British Context, (SSRC, London, 1978), p. 19.

109. Ibid.

110. R.B. Peterson, 'The Swedish Experience of
Industrial Democracy', p. 194.

111. A. Geijer, 'Sweden', in Levinson,
Industry's Democratic Revolution, p. 274.

112. Ibid., p. 275.

113. D. Jenkins, Job Power, (Heinemann,
London, 1974), p. 263.

114. M. Elvander, 'Sweden', in Roberts,
Industrial Democracy, p. 157.

115. A. Martin, 'From joint consultation to
joint decision-making: the redistribution of
workplace power in Sweden' in J.A. Fry (ed.)
Industrial Democracy and Labour Market Policy in
Sweden, (Pergamon, London, 1979). See also
Elvander, 'Sweden', p. 150.

116. Ibid.

117. T. Akkermans and P. Grootings, From
Corporatism, p. 182. 98% of employers agree workers
should have a say via a works council. 95% reject
the union as a basis for joint decision-making. See
Commission on Industrial Relations, Worker
Participation, p. 76.

118. Industrial Democracy Europe International
Research Team, European Industrial Relations,
pp. 157-158.

119. Albeda, 'The Netherlands', p. 126.

120. Commission on Industrial Relations, Worker Participation, pp. 65-66.

121. Albeda 'The Netherlands', p. 122.

122. *Ibid*. My account is also based on two papers read to a seminar of the European Institute of Advanced Studies In Management, Brussels, May 1978, by Hubert de Man and M.R. van Fils, who expose the 'servants of power' role of the social scientists engaged in the project.

123. Albeda, 'The Netherlands', p. 121.

124. The different groups' views are summarised from Commission on Industrial Relations, Worker Participation, p. 65.

125. Albeda, 'The Netherlands', p. 121.

126. Industrial Democracy, Europe International Research Team, p. 158; Commission on Industrial Relations, Worker Participation, p. 75.

127. See particularly E. Vaughn, 'Industrial democracy:consensus and confusion', Industrial Relations Journal, vol. 11, no. 1, Mar/Apr. 1980: 50-56; and, despite their desperate efforts to find any evidence of agreement between managers and unionists, S. Goldstein *et al*., 'Managers' and union officials' perception of the Australian Commonwealth Government's policy on employee participation', Journal of Industrial Relations, Sept. 1979.

128. See Marglin, 1979, 'Catching Flies with Honey'; Deutsch, 'Capitalism, Crisis and the Prospects for Workers' Participation', J. Maher (ed.), New Perspectives in Job Enrichment, (van Norstrand Reinhold, The Hague, 1971), contains a number of explicit consultant statements to this effect. Most explicit is M.S. Meyers' book on job enrichment and other innovations, entitled Managing Without Unions, (Addison-Wesley, New York, 1976).

129. See Berg *et. al.*, Managers and Work Reform, especially ch. 14; Sturmthal, 'Workers' Participation in Management'.

130. See Mitsufuji and Ishikawa 'Workers' participation in management in Japan'; Okamoto, 'Japan'; R.E. Cole, Work, Mobility and Participation, (University of California Press, 1979); 217-18, 252.

131. Okamoto, 'Japan', p. 222; Cole, Work, Mobility and Participation, p. 217.

132. *Ibid*., and Mitsufuji and Ishikawa, 'Workers' participation in management in Japan', pp. 239; 241.

133. G. Causer, 'Private capital and the State in Western Europe' in S. Giner and M.S. Archer

(eds.) Contemporary Europe: Social Structures and Cultural Patterns, (Routledge and Kegan Paul, London, 1978), p. 41. Suggests that in these European countries with the most developed liberal-democratic systems, including West Germany, Sweden and Britain, there may be paradoxically greater, not less pressure to serve private capital than elsewhere. This arises from the need to sustain 'business confidence' and economic prosperity, without which votes are soon lost. This could readily be extended to the U.S. case.

134. See R. Elliott, A Case Study of Management and Worker Attitudes to Managerial Authority and Prerogatives, Ph.D. Thesis, University of London, 1975.

135. Sources of variation in State activity are explored in Causer, 'Private Capital'; R. Scase, in his Introduction to Scase (ed.) The State in Western Europe, (Croom Helm, London, 1980) and by C. Crouch 'The changing role of the state' in Crouch and Pizzorno (eds.) Class Conflict, vol. 2; analyses the common and differing features of industrial relations policy. Useful but narrower discussions of the roots of differing state methods and responses to them are to be found in A. Fox 'Corporatism and Industrial Democracy: the Social Origins of Present Forms and Methods in Britain and Germany' in Industrial Democracy: International Views, papers to SSRC conference (Cambridge 1977), SSRC, 1978. See also D. Marsden, Industrial Democracy; Sorge, 'Industrial Democracy'.

136. See Employee Participation: Ways and Means (1980) and Employee Participation: A Broad View (1979), both produced by the National Employee Participation Steering Committee and published by the Commonwealth of Australia.

137. T. Ariizumi 'The legal framework: past and present' in K. Okochi et. al. (eds.) Workers and Employers in Japan, (Princeton University Press, 1974).

138. Halliday, The Political Economy of Japanese Capitalism, p. 230.

139. Scase, The State in Western Europe, p. 18.

140. See C. Crouch, Class Conflict and the Industrial Relations Crisis, (Heinemann, London, 1979).

141. L. Panitch, 'The importance of workers' control for revolutionary change', Monthly Review, vol. 29, no. 10, March 1978, p. 39.

142. 'The State as a relation of production',

with Philip Corrigan and Derek Sayer, in Corrigan (ed.) <u>Capitalism, State Formation and Marxist Theory</u> (Quartet, London, 1980).

143. See L. Panitch, 'Recent theorisations of corporatism: reflections on a growth industry', <u>British Journal of Sociology</u> vol. XXXI, no. 2, June 1980; 'The development of corporatism in liberal democracies' in P.C. Schmitter and G. Lehmbruch (eds.) <u>Trends Towards Corporatist Intermediation,</u> (Sage, London, 1979); 'Trade unions and the capitalist state', <u>New Left Review,</u> no. 125, Jan/Feb. 1981.

144. See Panitch, 'Recent theorisations of corporatism', p. 145, which talks of 'cycles' of establishment and breakdown of corporatist solutions.

145. Crouch, <u>Class Conflict and the Industrial Relations Crisis.</u>

146. See especially T. Ramm 'Codetermination and the German Works Constitution Act of 1972', Industrial Law Journal, vol. 3, no. 1, March 1974.

147. An enlightening survey is provided by S. Simitis, 'Workers' Participation in the enterprise – transcending company law?', Modern Law Review, vol. 39, no.1, January 1975.

148. Quoted in <u>Financial Times,</u> 3rd May, 1979. Elsewhere the Court referred to the need for 'loyal co-operation' to make the Act acceptable – <u>FT</u> 2nd March 1979.

149. Both quoted from the negotiated agreements by C. Asplund, <u>Some Aspects of Worker Participation,</u> (International Confederation of Free Trade Unions, 1972), p. 16.

150. Both cited in R. Blanpain 'The influence of labour on management decision-making: a comparative legal survey', <u>Industrial Law Journal</u> vol. 3, no. 1, March 1974.

151. Commission on Industrial Relations, <u>Worker Participation,</u> pp. 66–67.

152. The last phrase is Marglin's, 'Catching flies with honey'; see also Berg *et. al.*, <u>Managers and Work Reform,</u> Deutsch, 'Capitalism, Crisis and the Prospects for Worker Participation'; R.J. Coleman, 'employee participation in the US enterprise', <u>British Journal of Industrial Relations,</u> vol. XVI, no. 2, July 1978, p. 191.

153. See P. Boreham, <u>The Political Economy of Labour: S, Class, Industrial Relations and the State</u> (University of Queensland, Division of External Studies, 1981), p. 27f; S. Clegg, 'Employee participation in Australia: the new legitimacy',

Social Alternatives, 1(4), 1979.
154. See Cole, Work Mobility and
Participation, p. 252.
155. Quoted by Asplund; Some Aspects of Worker
Participation from an OECD publication New
Perspectives in Collective Bargaining, 1969.
156. In West Germany, only 6% of enterprises
legally required to have works councils actually
possessed them in 1968 - and despite the 1972 Act,
the numbers of councils only rose from 25,000 to
34,000 by 1968-75. (Ramm, 'Codetermination',
pp. 22-23; European Industrial Relations Review,
no. 39 (1977), pp. 19-20). In France, only 9,000
committees of 24,000 required were actually set up
in the early 1970s. (Commission on Industrial
Relations, Worker Participation, p. 49).
157. See F. Emery and E. Thorsrud, 'Industrial
Democracy in Norway', Industrial Relations, vol. 9,
no. 1 (1970), p. 189; Peterson, 'The Swedish
Experience of Industrial Democracy'.
158. See e.g. Commission on Industrial
Relations, Worker Participation; European Industrial
Relations Review, no. 54 (1978), which reports two
brief case studies on this theme.
159. Furstenburg, Workers' Participation,
p. 17.
160. As shown in D. Gallie's case study in In
Search of the New Working Class (Cambridge
University Press, 1978).
161. L. Greyfie de Bellecombe 'Workers'
participation in management in France: the basic
problems', Bulletin of International Institute for
Labour Studies, no. 6 (1970), p. 88. T.C. Carnie,
'Industrial Law Society Conference on Worker
Participation: a comment', Industrial Law Journal,
vol. 3, no. 1 (1974), reports that more French works
councils may have become a form of institutionalised
union activity (p. 3).
162. See O. Hammarstrom, 'Joint Worker-
Management Consultation: the case of LKAB, Sweden',
in L.E. Davis and A.B. Cherns (eds.), The Quality of
Working Life, vol. 2.
163. J. Schregle, 'Labour relations in Western
Europe', International Labour Review, no. 109
(1974), p. 18. See also Carnie, 'Industrial Law
Society Conference'.
164. See Mitsufuji and Ishikawa, 'Workers'
participation in management in Japan, pp. 239-41;
Cole, Work, Mobility and Participation, p. 216.
165. P. Brannen et. al., The Worker Directors,
p. 218, summarising their own review of European

experience.

166. E. Batstone, 'Industrial democracy and worker representation at board level: a review of the European experience' in E. Batstone and P.L. Davies, Industrial Democracy: European Experience (HMSO, London, 1976), p. 35. These were reports prepared for the Bullock Committee.

167. Hubert de Man 'Social science in the game of Dutch labour relations: the case of the C.O.P. experiments in organisational democracy', paper to EIASM Conference on Power and Influence in Organisations, Brussels, May 1978.

168. Industrial Democracy Europe International Research Team, European Industrial Relations, pp. 152-153. A researcher on the Norwegian experiments indicated to me that management here were increasingly reluctant to continue if work group demands expanded. Albeda, 'The Netherlands', p. 122 reports this managerial response at Philips, one of the most famous examples of 'work humanisation' experiments.

169. Nycander, 'Industrial Relations in Sweden', pp. 24-25.

170. Financial Times, 28th January, 1975 and 30th July 1976. See also the comments in G. Hunnius, 'The Politics of Work Humanisation and Power Sharing', Economic Analysis and Workers' Management, vol. 13, no. 4 (1979), p. 512.

171. A. Carey, 'The Norwegian experiments in democracy at work: a critique and a contribution to reflexive sociology', Australian and New Zealand Journal of Sociology, vol. 15, no. 1, March 1979. Carey's article provoked a heated exchange with Emery in subsequent issues.

172. See e.g. W.J. Paul and K. Robertson, Job Enrichment and Employee Motivation (Gower Press, Farnbourough, 1970); J. Roeber, Social Change At Work (Duckworth, London, 1975); W.W. Daniel and N. McIntosh, The Right to Manage? (PEP, London, 1972).

173. C. Roberts and D. Wedderburn, ICI and the Unions: the Place of Job Enrichment in the Weekly Staff Agreement (Imperial College, London, 1974).

174. Paul and Robertson's study admits to being unable to operate openly on the shop floor level for fear of union anger at pre-emption of productivity agreements by the introduction of experimental changes in work practices.

175. S.Cotgrove et. al., The Nylon Spinners (Allen and Unwin, London, 1972), p. 134. This is the case repeatedly used by Daniel to back up his

arguments for job enrichment.
176. Cole, Work, Mobility and Participation.
177. *Ibid*.
178. See note 71 above.
179. See Berg *et. al.*, Managers and Work Reform, p. 161.
180. A fuller account of the wane of participation's star is given in H. Ramsay, 'Evolution or Cycle'.
181. A phrase used to me by a prominent business spokesman in Scotland when the topic of industrial democracy was raised, at a meeting in 1979.
182. D. Jenkins, who described its growth as 'inevitable' in 1971 in Job Power, in 'Forces and failures in European industrial democracy', Manchester Business School Review, vol. 3, no. 1, Autumn, 1978.
183. P. Brannen *et. al.*, The Worker Directors.
184. *Ibid*.
185. J.F. Bolweg, Job Design and Industrial Democracy (Martinus Nijhoff, The Hague, 1976), pp. 118-9. This contradicts the developmental model of Emery and Thorsrud, Form and Content in Industrial Democracy.
186. Daniel and McIntosh, The Right to Manage?, pp. 27-28.
187. Ivar Berg in Berg *et. al.*, Managers and Work Reform: A Limited Engagement (Free Press, New York, 1979), p. 299.
188. W. Muller-Jentsch, 'Strikes and strike trends in West Germany, 1950-78', IRJ, 12(4), July/August 1981.
189. Based on a letter dated 24th April, 1980 from Gerry Hunnius, in Sweden to investigate developments in industrial democracy, and confirmed verbally by other sources since.
190. Industrial Democracy, European International Research Team, European Industrial Relations, pp. 44-45.
191. See Berg *et. al.*, Managers and Work Reform, p. 255.
192. Marglin, 'Catching flies with honey', p. 478.
193. W.W. Daniel, 'Industrial democracy', in D. Torrington (ed.) Comparative Industrial Relations in Europe, (Associated Business Programmes, 1978), p. 49. Compare with the earlier quoted statement on Australia from Pritchard, referenced in note 83 above!
194. Sorge, 'Industrial Democracy'. Sorge

claims that he is concerned with system integration, not social integration (p. 282), but the latter subsequently becomes the focus for his attention (see p. 290).

195. See Postscript to P. Brannen *et. al.* The Worker Directors.

196. See M. Aglietta, A Theory of Capitalist Regulation, (New Left Books, London, 1979); E. Mandel, Late Capitalism, (New Left Books, London, 1975). See also A. Piccieri, 'Diffusion and crisis of scientific management in European industry', in S. Giner and M.S. Archer (eds.) Contemporary Europe: Social Structures and Cultural Patterns, (Routledge and Kegan Paul, London, 1978).

197. I have deliberately avoided examining 'third world' countries or socialist societies as these would introduce complications unmanageable in the confines of a single paper.

NOTES ON CONTRIBUTORS

Nixon Apple currently works at Sydney's Kuring-gai
College of Advanced Education. His research
interests, developed at Carleton University, where
he was a graduate student, are in comparative and
historical analyses of the OECD states, with a
particular interest in Sweden. He is currently
completing a book on *Class Mobilisation and Economic
Policy: The Struggle over Full Employment in Britain
and Sweden 1930-1980* with Winton Higgins and Mike
Wright.

Paul Boreham is a lecturer in the University of
Queensland's Division of External Studies. His
major teaching and research interests are in the
sociology of occupations, professions,
organisations, class and the state. He is the
editor of several volumes in these areas and is
currently collaborating with Stewart Clegg and Geoff
Dow on a volume on Class and Politics, as well as
preparing a manuscript on the 'new middle class'.

Stewart Clegg is the Reader in Sociology in the
School of Humanities at Griffity University in
Australia. His major research has been in the
sociology of power and organisations, to which he
has contributed several books and numerous shorter
studies. As well as his present collaboration with
Paul Boreham and Geoff Dow he is also the current
co-editor of the ANZJS (Austrlian and New Zealand
Journal of Sociology) and a founder member of APROS
(Australian and Pacific Researchers in Organisation
Studies).

Geoff Dow is also employed at Griffith Univerity, in
the School of Humanities. His major teaching and
research interests are in political economy and the

state. Together with Paul Boreham he is the editor of the recent two volume collection *Work and Inequality* and is currently researching the comparative relationship between ideology and economic policy in post-war Australia, Britain and Sweden.

Franco Ferraresi holds a professorial position in political science at the University of Turin. The author of a number of substantive studies, he has recently published a volume in Italy on the Italian State Bureaucracy, *Burocrazia e Politica in Italia*. Franco was a founder member of EGOS (European Group for Organisation Studies) and is active also in ECPR, the European Consortium for Political Research. His research interests stand at the intersection of political science's interest in the state and organisation sociology, with its interest in bureaucracy.

Claus Offe holds a professorial position at the University of Bilefeld. The author of some of the most important of recent work on the state, as well as the volume *Industry and Inequality*, he is currently engaged in empirical research on aspects of the West German Metalworkers trade union.

Harvie Ramsay currently works in Scotland at the University of Strathclyde. The author of a number of collaborative works with Philip Corrigan and Derek Sayer on Marxist and Maoist political theory and practice, he has also made important contributions to the comparative understanding of industrial relations.

Marino Regini is a leading Italian contributor to contemporary debates on the labour market, work organisation and trade unions. He holds a professorial position at the University of Milan where he teaches the sociology of work and economic sociology. Latterly his research has been on the state and industrial relations in Italy.

H.T. Wilson works in Canada, where he is a professor at York University, Toronto, in the Department of Administrative Studies. Tom Wilson is a prolific writer and contributor to a wide range of debates in sociology, organisation analysis, philosophy of the social sciences and jurispudence. Many of these interests came together to form his major study of *The American Ideology*.

NAME INDEX

Adenauer, Konrad 97
Amery, Julian 75
Apple, Nixon 20-24,
   30-34, 270

Balogh, Thomas 85
Barkley, Senator 89
Beaverbrook, Lord 75
Bell, Daniel 28, 35,
   158-159, 160, 182,
   194
Benn, Tony 38
Berg, Ivar 271
Beveridge, William 21,
   82-84, 114
Block, Fred 25, 78
Bolweg, J.F. 300
Booth, Albert 27
Brannen, Peter 300
Brenner, Otto 280
Brittan, Samuel 35
Burnham, James 157
Butler, R.A. 86

Cole, R.E. 296
Comte, Auguste 170, 186
Cooke, Morris 170-171
Coombs, H.C. 94
Cripps, Stafford 84
Cronin, J.E. 261
Crouch, C. 289-290
Crozier, Michel 197,
   207-211
Curtin, John 94

Dahl, Robert A. 17
Daniel, W.W. 260, 299
de Bonald, Louis 186,
   194
de Gasperi, P. 103
De Gaulle, Charles
   100-102, 268
de Maistre, J. 186, 194
de Tocqueville,
   Alexis 51
De Vittorio, Giuseppe
   103
Diesing, Paul 169, 183
Dodge, J. 99-100
Dreitzel, Hans P. 157
Dubois, Pierre 265
Durkheim, Emile 195,
   202-203, 207-209,
Einaudi, E. 103
Enfantin, C. 170, 186,
   194
Engels, Freidrich 191

Ferraresi, Franco 25,
   30, 34
Flanders, Alan 258
Fourier, Pierre 170,
   186, 194
Friedman, Georges 207

Galbraith, John Kenneth
   28, 157-158, 161,
   164, 175, 194-195
Gamble, Andrew 2
Gantt, Henry 170-171

Giddens, Anthony 34,
  157
Ginsburg, N. 11
Giolitti, F. 147
Goldthorpe, John 249
Gompers, Samuel 91
Gough, Ian 11
Gouldner, Alvin 28
Gramsci, Antonio 25,
  140

Habermas, Jürgen 184,
  196
Halevi, Joseph 104
Halliday, J. 289
Hanami, J. 273
Hauenschild, Karl 280
Higgins, Winton 34
Hirsch, Fred 69
Hirschman, Albert O. 54
Hitler, Adolf 266
Holland, Stuart 2
Hunnius, G. 270

Jessop, Bob 38
Jewkes, S. 84, 112
Jones, Jack 267, 279

Kalecki, Michal 1, 3,
  5-9, 20, 38, 72,
  87-88
Kamata, S. 296
Kautsky, Karl 53
Keynes, John Maynard 1,
  3, 63, 76-77, 80
Kleitz, William 88
Knight, Everett 191

Lane, Robert 158-160,
  194
Layton, Edwin 171-172
Lenin, V.I. 52
Leruez, Jacques 87
Lindblom, Charles E.
  173
Lipset, Seymour Martin
  17, 53
Lockwood, David 249
Luxemburg, Rosa 18, 55

Macmillan, Harold 86
Macpherson, C.B. 58
Mandel, Ernest 2, 12,
  282
Mann, Michael 34
Mannheim, Karl 158-161
  169, 178, 183,
  202-203, 205
Mao, Zedong 80
Marcuse, Herbert 17, 29
Marglin, Stephen 303
Martin, A. 283
Marx, Karl 51-52, 69,
  156, 191
Meidner, Rudolf 113,
  117
Merton, Robert K. 178
Meynaud, Jean 157, 197
Michels, Robert 18, 55
Mill, John Stuart 17,
  51-52, 69
Mills, C. Wright 183
Mosher, Ira 87
Murray, Senator 87-88
Mussolini, Benito 55,
  140
Myrdal, Gunnar 112

Nairn, Tom 19
Negri, Antonio 135
Neitzsche, Friedrich
  152
Neumann, Franz 239
Nycander, S. 281, 295

O'Connor, James 26,
  131-132
Offe, Claus 18-22, 26
  132-134, 239

Panitch, Leo 117,
  289-290
Pareto, V. 156
Parsons, Talcott
  201-206
Petain, Marshal 102
Popper, Karl 159-160,
  182-183, 191
Poulantzas, Nicos 26,
  131-132

Ramsay, Harvie 32-34
Reagan, Ronald 62
Regini, Marino 30-31, 34
Rehn, Gösta 113, 116
Roberts, B.C. 262
Robinson, Joan 5-6, 72
Rollier, M. 269
Roosevelt, Franklin D. 89

Schmitter, Phillipe C. 240
Schutz, Alfred 206
Sleeman, J.F. 11
Smith, Adam 54
Smyth, W.H. 170
Sorge, Andre 262-263, 300
Sraffa, Pierro 1
Stalin, Josef 100
Stephens, John D. 2, 25, 34
St. Simon,Comte Henri de 170, 186, 191-196

Taylor,Frederick W. 170-171
Thatcher, Margaret 62
Therborn, Göran 17-18
Thompson, Victor 165, 207, 209

Urry, John 2

Veblen, Thorstein 157, 170-172, 187, 192, 194-196, 210
von Hayek, Frederick 112

Wallerstein, Immanuel 2
Walton, Paul 2
Weber, Max 18-19, 27, 54-55, 153-155, 163-179, 185-186, 190-211
Whyte, William F. 164
Wilensky, Harold 164, 196
Williams, John 78

Wilson, Tom 27-29
Wittgenstein, Ludwig 192

SUBJECT INDEX

accumulation
    See capital
    accumulation
AFL-CIO 105, 270
Algeria 100
Alternative Economic
    Strategy (A.E.S.)
    34-41
American Federation of
    Labour (A.F.L.) 91,
    101, 105
apparatus (of the
    State)
    See State
arbitration 84, 275
associational unions
    242, 248, 249
Atlantic Charter 75
Australia 22, 37, 40,
    92-95, 105, 109,
    11-112, 275, 284,
    289, 292, 298
Australian Council of
    Trade Unions
    (A.C.T.U.) 105
Australian Labor Party
    (A.L.P.) 22, 93-95,
    275
Austria 30, 60

BDA 278
Belgium 104, 109, 265,
    268, 290, 292-293
Beveridge Report 84
Bizonal Economic
    Council 96

bourgeoisie 18, 54, 92,
    95, 102, 134, 199
Bretton Woods 21, 76-
    78, 110
Britain/British 19-24,
    37-40, 60, 74-79,
    82, 85, 93, 95, 105,
    109, 111-112, 117,
    257-265, 272,
    277-279, 283, 286,
    290-292, 295-297,
    299
Budget and Accounting
    Act 90
Bullock Committee 265,
    278, 279, 296
bureaucracy 13, 18, 27,
    29, 138, 141,
    144-147, 149,
    152-212
business confidence 22,
    25
business cycle 6, 8

Cambridge economics 1
Canada 22, 92-95, 108,
    270
capital accumulation 4,
    7-11, 14, 18, 37,
    40, 59, 61, 74, 81,
    131, 137-138, 149,
    252, 285, 289
capital formation 40

capital sharing 268, 280, 282
CCL 105
CDU 97
CGIL 102-103, 247, 251
CGT 101
China 98
Christian Democracy 23, 96-97, 103, 143
CIO 100
civil liberties 61, 18
civil society 18, 135, 138
class-oriented unions 31, 34, 239-245
class struggle 3-4, 8, 13, 53, 64, 72, 259, 289
Clearing Union Plan 76
clientelism 148-149
co-determination 266, 280, 284, 297
Co-determination Act 280, 286, 291
Codetermination at Work Act 34, 282, 286, 298
cold war 30, 89, 98, 105, 112, 143
collective bargaining 84, 115, 261, 270-271, 275, 284, 286
Comites d'enterprise 268, 293
communism 79, 91, 98, 100-103, 106
communist parties 23, 57, 101, 106, 134
See also PCI, PCF
compatibility of capitalism and democracy 18, 24, 52-54, 58-63, 69
Conservative Party 21, 83, 86-87, 107, 264, 297

consultation 14, 262-264, 270, 275, 283
corporatism 14, 19, 30-32, 59, 136, 155, 289
neo- 26, 32, 136, 138, 144, 148, 240, 254, 289
crisis 1, 7, 9, 12-16, 27, 34-36, 40, 52, 80, 131, 268, 273, 290
crisis of representation 31-32, 240-254
CSU 97
cycles of control 33, 257-262, 264-300
Czechoslovakia 80

deficit financing 10
deficit-spending 20, 66, 94
deflation 82, 95-96, 99, 104, 110
de-industrialisation 15
Democratic Socialism 261
democracy
See
economic democracy
parliamentary democracy
political democracy
social democracy
liberal democracy
industrial democracy
representative democracy
Denmark 109, 297
depression 81, 83, 90-91, 274
de-regulation 35
DGB 105, 279, 280
distribution of income 8, 12, 36-37, 84
division of labour 15, 163, 165, 168, 189, 207
dominant classes 12

East Germany 96
Ecole Polytechnique 170
economic allocation 191
economic democracy 2,
    9, 20, 24, 83
economic growth 13, 63,
    69, 252, 261
economic policy 6-13,
    24, 36-38, 90,
    95-96, 112-115, 284
empire 74-75, 78
Employment Protection
    Act 286
engineers 171-173,
    186-189, 192, 194,
    264, 267
enterprise unionism 99
    100, 261, 270, 273,
    285
Esso 264
Eurocommunism 34, 59,
    117
European Economic
    Community (E.E.C.)
    33, 98
evolution (of
    participation
    schemes) 257-260,
    262-263, 272, 275,
    284, 290, 292, 300
exceptionalism 34,
    204-119
export sector 100, 103,
    109, 111
export surplus 77-92,
    98

factory councils 30,
    241-243
fascism 20-23, 30, 51,
    55, 72, 79, 95-96,
    100-107, 147, 261,
    266, 268
feminism 19, 42, 59
FIOM CGIL 105
First World War 69, 83,
    140, 262, 273
FWV 284

France, French 22-23,
    95-109, 117, 253,
    261, 265, 268, 278,
    290, 292-293,
    297-298
free market 22, 87, 112
full employment 5-9,
    16, 21-22, 32, 34,
    37, 72-128
Full Employment Bill
    22, 87
full employment
    capitalism 20,
    72-73, 81-87, 104,
    108-110, 112, 116,
    118

Germany 22-23, 80, 91,
    95-106, 244
    See also
    West-, East-
gold standard 74, 78
Grand Alliance 100
Great Depression 4
Greece 79, 105
Greek Confederation of
    Labour 105

humanism 264, 267

IBM 271
ICI 264, 295
ideal type 153-155,
    162-163, 173, 176
ideology 6, 11, 17, 19,
    24, 152-153, 156,
    159, 162, 166, 257
IG Chemie 280
IG Metall 280
imperialism 74, 91
incomes policies 36,
    87, 85, 128, 113
industrial democracy
    10, 117, 257-300
    See also
    worker participation
    workers control
    participation

industrial relations
33, 35, 66, 92, 239,
245, 258, 260-261,
264, 269-271, 273,
276, 281, 285, 286,
289, 293-294
Industrial Relations
Act 264
inflation 1-4, 8, 10,
35-37, 100-103,
113-115, 137, 252,
265
intellectuals 28, 157,
161
interest groups 26, 27
International Bank of
Reconstruction and
Development 76
international liquidity
76-78, 80, 82, 110
International Monetary
Fund (I.M.F.) 21,
76-79, 89
international monetary
reconstruction (post
war) 73-77, 82, 92,
96, 104, 266
international monetary
system 73-74, 76,
80, 82, 91-92, 109,
118, 261
International Trade
Organisation 77
investment 4-9, 32, 37-
38, 68, 74-79, 85,
95, 100, 103, 109,
114-119, 251-253
Ireland 104, 109
Israel 261
Italy 22-34, 94-105,
108, 117, 129-150,
239-256, 265, 269,
278, 286, 290
I.W.W. 270

Japan 22, 23, 91,
94-105, 108, 110,
269, 271, 284, 289,
292, 294, 296, 298

job enrichment 264,
268, 276, 294-295,
298, 300
Joint Managment Council
274, 284

Kaleckian 6, 7, 10, 15
Karlsruhe Court 279,
291
Kennedy Administration
108
Keynesianism 3, 5, 9,
10, 15, 16, 20, 36,
63, 68-69, 82, 89,
90, 108, 239
post- 1, 6, 8
neo- 167
Korean War 80, 103

Labour Charter 102
labour market 21, 24,
33, 72, 81, 82, 91,
103, 107, 110, 66,
70, 140, 141, 113,
114, 115, 116, 268,
271, 273, 283, 298
labour movement 2, 8,
9, 18-19, 30, 37,
41, 72, 82, 86, 104,
107, 109, 111, 113,
115, 118, 136, 278,
281, 298
labour parties 7, 13,
32, 36, 38, 40, 109,
117
    See also
    British Labour Party
    Australian Labor
      Party
Labour Plan 103-194
labour process 7, 33,
258
Labour Relations
Adjustment Act 99
laissez-faire state
    See state
late capitalism 70,
155-156, 161
Leninism 52-53

liberal democracy 13,
  17, 22, 26, 51-52,
  97, 285, 289
LKAB 293
LO 24, 112-119, 267,
  282

Madagascar 100
Mafia 103
market economy 17,
  52-53, 94
Marshall Plan 21, 79,
  80, 89
Marxist/Marxian 1, 6-9,
  12, 17, 31, 52-53,
  156, 258, 290, 300
means of production 119
Meidner strategy 32,
  282
middle class 103, 210
Ministry of Labour 83
mixed economy 54
mode of production 31
monetarism 2, 6, 10,
  35, 69, 108, 111,
  117-118
Monopoly and
  Deconcentration Laws
  97
monopoly capitalism 5,
  12, 40, 74, 90, 130,
  132
multi-national
  corporations 16, 24,
  27, 110, 154
Mutual Aid Agreement 75
Mutual Defence
  Agreement 98

National Association of
  Manufacturers 87
National Institute for
  Social Security 241
nationalisation 266
  banks 22, 85, 95,
  100
  railways 147
  industry 10, 96, 100
nationalism 18-19, 109,
  261
NATO 24

neo-corporatism
  See corporatism
Netherlands 104, 105,
  268, 283, 292-293,
  295, 297
New Deal 89-090
new right 10, 20, 35,
  92
NKV 284
Norway 85, 291-292,
  295, 298
NVV 283

objective knowledge
  156-157, 160-163,
  172-175, 181, 189,
  191, 196, 210
OECD 20, 23-24, 33, 292
OEEC 77
OPEC 23, 67
overloaded governance
  26-27, 35, 136, 138,
  148, 245

parliamentary democracy
  14, 18, 52, 142-143,
  146
participation 14, 32
  See also
  worker participation
P.C.F. 23, 100-102
P.C.I. 23, 30, 100-103,
  135
peak organisations
  30-31
pension funds 10
petite bourgeoisie 22,
  93, 140
planning economy 83,
  284
planning agreements 38
political democracy 2,
  52, 55
political trade cycle
  6-7
post-industrialism 28,
  33
post Keynesianism
  See Keynesianism

post laissez-faire
   state
   See state
post war reconstruction
   5, 73, 83-84, 87,
   97, 103, 105, 111,
   118, 266
   See also
   international
   monetary
   reconstruction
Powers Referendum 94
price stability 82, 84
private enterprise 88,
   92-93, 95, 99, 114,
   278, 298
productivity bargaining
   264
Productivity Commission
   268
professions 13, 146,
   153, 161-162, 167,
   171-173, 177,
   181-184, 188, 196,
   204
professionalisation
   153, 162, 164
profitability 6-8, 279,
   291
profit margins 33, 109,
   115, 257
profit maximisation
   113-114, 157
profit-sharing 264,
   267-272, 277, 280,
   282
proletariat 51, 140,
   199
public enterprise 10
public sector 5, 12,
   24, 35, 39, 67,
   115-117, 132, 143,
   167, 196, 260, 262,
   296

rationality 12, 27-29,
   32, 152-212
rationalization 29, 155
recession 3-11, 34, 36,
   39, 80, 108, 110,
   116, 273, 290, 298

reconstruction
   See
   post-war
   reconstruction and
   international
   monetary
   reconstruction
reflation 38-39
Rehn-Meidner model 31,
   112-117
relative autonomy 26,
   138, 149
religion/religious
   parties 105, 109
representation 30-31,
   60-61, 134, 144,
   146, 239-246, 279,
   280, 294
   See also
   crisis of
   representation
representative
   democracy 11, 13,
   134, 199
research and
   development 154,
   169, 172, 174, 181,
   187, 200, 210
reserve army of labour
   87
resource allocation 62
RPF 101, 102
ruling class 14, 18,
   21-24, 41, 85, 90,
   92, 105, 112, 148,
   192, 252

SAF 111, 118, 267, 282,
   298
Saltsjobaden Agreement
   267
Sanbetsu 105
scalar cluster 154-155
Second International
   See
   Third and Second
   International
Second World War 54,
   62-63, 93, 134, 147,
   262, 268, 272
Shell 264

social contract 14, 21,
    30, 36, 148, 251
social democracy 12,
    24, 30, 57, 96, 106,
    109, 112, 115-116,
    267, 282, 285, 299
socialism 23-25, 34,
    84, 86-87, 96-111,
    115, 298
Socialist Party of
    Japan 99
social market economy
    97, 107
social movements 59,
    99, 261
social policy 13
social security 63-64,
    84, 92, 100, 147
socal welfare 11, 112,
    167
Sohyo 105
southern question 23,
    103, 140, 143
Soviet Union 52, 63,
    74, 79, 82, 98, 100
S.P.D. 96
specialization 153,
    165, 207
stagnation 90, 91, 108
state:
    apparatus 12-13, 26-
    27, 38, 61, 68, 90,
    96, 100, 107, 129,
    132, 134, 143, 148,
    203
    expenditure 10
    intervention 2, 6,
    9, 11, 25, 35-36,
    40, 63, 68, 90-91,
    115, 131-138, 147,
    270, 278
    laissez-faire 130,
    133, 139, 147
    post laissez-faire
    24, 129, 138-139,
    144
    power 13, 25-26, 37-
    40, 42, 59, 86
    regulation 5, 26,
    90, 155, 286, 289

state (contd)
    welfare state 3, 10,
    12, 14, 18, 53-54,
    62-70, 76, 83, 85-
    86, 147
steering capacity 26
strikes 85, 91-92, 96,
    99, 101, 103, 114,
    265-266, 269-270,
    298
Sudreau Committee 268
surplus value 13, 276
Sweden 20, 24, 30, 31,
    34, 60, 85, 104-119,
    261, 265-270,
    281-282, 286,
    291-298, 291, 297
Switzerland 80

Taft-Hartly Act 91, 270
T.C.O. 115
Taylorism 269
technical rationality
    169-170
technocratic elite 28,
    155, 156, 162, 170,
    181, 193
technocratic ideology
    28, 160, 161, 188,
    193, 194
technocrats 153, 156,
    168, 170, 181, 184,
    210
technocracy 13, 29,
    152-212
technostructure 155,
    156, 158, 194, 196
Texas Instruments 271
T & GWU 279
Third and Second
    Internationals 53,
    54, 63
TLC (Canada) 105
Tories
    See Conservative
    Party
trade cycle 7, 109, 259
Trade Union Council
    (TUC) 83, 105, 118

trade unions
See
associational unions
enterprise unionism
class-oriented
unions
ACTU (Australia)
AFL (USA)
AFL-CIO (USA)
CCL (Canada)
CFDT (France)
CGIL (Italy)
CIO (USA)
DGB (West Germany)
FNV (Holland)
IG (Metal) (West
Germany)
LO (Sweden)
NKV (Holland)
NVV (Holland)
TCO (Sweden)
TGWU (UK)
Treaty of Rome 110
Trilaterial Commission
137
Truman Doctrine 21, 79,
89
Turkey 79

UCS 264
unemployment 1-5, 9,
20, 25, 33, 63, 66,
77, 80-88, 90-92,
95-96, 99, 102-109,
111, 119, 167, 272,
275, 290, 297
uneven development 27,
102-103
union-incorporation
239, 242, 258, 277,
279, 281, 285-286,
289, 293, 300
United Kingdom (U.K.)
See Britain
United Nations (U.N.)
77-79, 85, 93
United Nations Economic
and Social Committee
79

United States of
America (USA) 21-24,
74-105, 158, 161,
191-192, 261, 269-
271, 274-276, 289,
295-296, 299
Unit for the Quality of
Working Life 275,
289
USSR
See Soviet Union

valorisation 11-14, 33
Vietnam 100

wage restraint (or
modification) 7, 8,
21, 84-85, 87,
114-117, 239-246
Weberian 153, 162
welfare state
See state
West Germany 30, 60,
91, 105, 260,
265-264, 268, 272,
278-281, 286,
290-294, 298
White Papers 83, 92-94
worker participation
33, 257-300
workers' control 260,
266, 269
workers' councils 96,
260, 279
worker directors 260,
268, 271, 277, 279,
282, 284, 294
Workers Statute 241,
247
working class 14, 17,
23-24, 52, 72-73,
81-84, 87, 93,
95-96, 102, 114,
239-251
militancy 23, 98-99,
104, 107-108
mobilisation 14, 16,
22, 83, 95-96,
99-102, 116-143,
241, 248

Working Environment
    Committee 293
works councils 266-268,
    271, 279, 281,
    283-284, 291, 293
World Bank 77
world economy 1-2, 11,
    15, 22-23, 78, 99,
    109, 154, 265
world trade 77, 79
Works Constitution Act
    291

Zaibatsu System 97, 98
Zionism 261

DATE DUE